THE JUDAEO-CHRISTIAN MYTH

THE JUDAEO-CHRISTIAN MYTH

By

Tina Rae Collins, PhD

M. F. Sohn Publications
New York, New York
2015

ISBN-13: 978-1505902693

ISBN-10: 150590269X

All Scripture references are from Theophilos Bible Software, with the following versions being used:

Bible in Basic English (BBE)
Darby's Version (DBY)
Douay-Rheims (DR)
English Standard Version (ESV)
Geneva Bible (GEN)
King James Version (KJV)
New American Standard Bible (NASB)
New International Version (NIV)
New Jerusalem Bible (NJB)
New Revised Standard Version (NRSV)
World English Bible (WEB)
Young's Literal Translation (YLT)

Except as noted, the KJV is used.

Any emphasis in the biblical texts or the words of others, unless noted otherwise, is as follows: bold and/or underlined, me; italicized, the author of the quote.

Disclaimer: Any quotations from others contained herein should not necessarily be construed as support of my beliefs. I may have interpreted wrongly, applied the authors' ideas in a manner they did not intend, or added my own thoughts.

M. F. Sohn Publications
444 W 19th St, Apt 1102
New York, NY 10011

TABLE OF CONTENTS

ACKNOWLEDGMENTS . . . vii
DEDICATION . . . viii
INTRODUCTION . . . ix
DISCLAIMER . . . xi

1. GODS AND GODDESSES . . . 1
Our Mother, the First Deity . . . 2
From the Womb and Back Again . . . 3
Where Babies Come From . . . 5
Life in the Blood . . . 5
Sacred Blood . . . 6
A Savior . . . 7
Tammuz and Ishtar . . . 7
Gods Harsher Than Goddesses . . . 9
The Death . . . 9
Breath of Life . . . 11

2. JEWISH HENOTHEISM/POLYTHEISM . . . 13
The Elohim . . . 13
Other Scriptures Referring to Multiple Gods . . . 15
Yahweh's Jealousy . . . 17

3. DARK SAYINGS OF OLD . . . 22
Dating of the Old Testament . . . 23
Author of the Old Testament . . . 24
Creation . . . 25
Old Testament God-Men . . . 28
No Archaeological Records . . . 38
No Hebrew History . . . 40

4. MAKING NEW SAYINGS . . . 42
Unknown Authors . . . 42
The Canon . . . 47
Unknown Jesus . . . 50
No Risen Savior . . . 53
Eusebius, Constantine, and the Making of the New Testament . . . 55
No Reason to Believe . . . 63
Same Girl, Different Dress . . . 65

5. SAVIORS, CHRISTS, AND OTHER GODS . . . 67
Aten/Aton . . . 67
Baal . . . 68
Attis . . . 72
Dionysus/Bacchus . . . 74
Osiris . . . 78
Osiris/Horus . . . 79
Hercules/Heracles/Herakles . . . 82
Mercury and the Logos . . . 85
Zoroaster/Zarathustra . . . 85
Mithra(s) . . . 86
Krishna/Chrishna/Christna/Chrisna/Kreeshna . . . 87
Confucius . . . 89
Buddha . . . 90
Yahweh and Jesus . . . 91

Yaldabaoth (Father of Yahweh and Elohim) . . . 97
Serapis Christ . . . 99
Alexander the Great, Plato, Pythagoras, Caesar, and Socrates . . . 101
Caves, Crosses, and Sacrificial Deaths . . . 103
Think Think Think . . . 105

6. RECYCLED MYTHS . . . 108
Double Fulfillment and *Haggadah* . . . 109
Same Sayings . . . 111
Jesus Story Better Developed . . . 113
Stories from Secular Literature . . . 114
More Hebrew Syncretism . . . 115
Church Fathers Defend Their Faith . . . 117

7. SOURCE OF ALL DEITY MYTHS . . . 122
Sun Gods . . . 123
Precession of the Equinoxes . . . 126
Dying and Rising Gods . . . 128
Sex and Regeneration . . . 130
Nursery Tales . . . 132
The Zodiac and the Numbers Twelve and Seventy . . . 134
More Magic Numbers . . . 138
The Zodiac and Ezekiel's Wheel . . . 138
Identity Theft . . . 139
Ritual Baptism . . . 140
The Amazing Sun . . . 143

8. GNOSTIC CHRIST . . . 145
Jesus the Sky God . . . 146
Crossified Man . . . 147
Passover . . . 148
Early Christian Writings . . . 149
Pagan Easter . . . 154
Historical Jesus . . . 154

9. GNOSTIC NEW TESTAMENT . . . 160
The Apostle Paul . . . 160
Paul's Gnostic Resurrection . . . 164
Place of the Skull . . . 167
Heinous Human Sacrifice . . . 171
The Book of Hebrews . . . 173
The Allegory . . . 174
Closing of the Breach . . . 176
Destruction of Evidence . . . 179
Summary . . . 180

10. OUR LEGACY . . . 183
That Old-Time Religion . . . 184
Hats Off to the Israelites . . . 187
The Facts of Life . . . 188
We Are Free . . . 190
The Clock's Running . . . 192

BIBLIOGRAPHY . . . 195
ABOUT THE AUTHOR . . . 210

ACKNOWLEDGMENTS

I am grateful for all of my teachers, both those who agree with me and those who don't. I believe I learn from all people, and most of those I gain insight from probably wouldn't want their names mentioned here. But I hope they know I appreciate what they have taught me.

I offer my sincere thanks to my dear friend and publisher, Dr. Mark F. Sohn, who has supported me throughout most of my adult life and helped me achieve goals I never could have attained without his encouragement and friendship. Words truly can't express my gratitude for his presence in my life.

I must give my son Seth great credit for challenging me on my thoughts and insisting that I consider scientific, historical, archaeological, and anthropological truths. Had he not sat up with me until 4 a.m. one morning and 3:30 a.m. another, challenging my views and integrity, as well as nine hours one day questioning my thinking, I could never have reached the conclusions I have. Thanks also, Seth, for the beautiful cover photo and design. You always do a perfect job, and this one is no exception.

I thank my daughter Rebecca for her heartfelt insights on the development of Christianity and its impact on our lives. Thanks for sharing your wisdom and understanding, Rebecca. Our recent discussion has been a comfort to me and helped me to appreciate your spiritual journey.

I must also thank my daughter Rachel for listening to my incessant chatter about my thoughts, ideas, and beliefs. You have been a great sounding board, Rachel, and I appreciate being able to ramble on and on without interruption or condemnation. Talking to you helped me think, and your interest, your own thoughts, and your questions encouraged me and helped me keep searching.

Finally, a huge and heartfelt appreciation goes to my children, Seth Collins, Rebecca Harmon, and Rachel Johnson, just for being my greatest blessings; to my sons-in-law, Robert Harmon and Michael Johnson; and to my grandchildren: Jonathan, Matthew, and Nicholas Harmon; and Elijah, Abigail, and Elizabeth Johnson. You are all my love and my life, and you give me reason to get up in the morning.

DEDICATION

I dedicate this book to my late son, Aaron Joseph Collins (1982-2012), whose generous heart prompted a national movement that NBC's Kerry Sanders called "The Inspirational Power of Sharing (TIPS)" (aaroncollins.org). Aaron taught me to be brave and to be real. I am unsure as to whether I will ever see him again, but I know that "I will go down into the grave to my son mourning" (Gen. 37:35).

Not long after Aaron passed from this life he spoke to me. I'm not saying I heard a sound, but words came to me that I believed to be from him. He said, "I am always with you, Mom."

I replied (in my head), "Yes, I know, Aaron. You are, and always will be, in my heart."

He said, "No. God is with you, right?"

I responded, "Yes."

Aaron said, "Well, *I* am . . ."

At that point I censored my son. I knew what I heard, but I couldn't accept the concept he was presenting to me; so I forced him to say, "Well, *I* am with *God*." I thought that made sense—if God was with me and Aaron was with God, then Aaron was also with me.

But that's not what Aaron said. He said something that was so foreign to my thinking that I shut it out at the time. The suggestion he provided would never have occurred to me, and I wasn't ready to accept such a strange idea. What Aaron actually said was, "Well, *I* am *God*."

Aaron's words kept playing in my mind, and I determined to search through the Bible to see whether such an idea might be presented there. Does a person come from (being) God (whoever or whatever that might be) and return to (being) God? If the dust (body) goes back to (returns to, or becomes) dust once more, does the spirit return to or become God (once more) as well (Eccles. 12:7)?

I had no notion that Aaron's words would send me on a search that would help me not only resolve questions I already had but also provide answers I didn't know I had been seeking. What I discovered was not merely that we return to our source but that here, in this life, we are a part of that source (again, whatever it might be). The energy that is "out there" is the energy that is "in here." We are all one—one with one another and with the entire universe. Thank you, my sweet Aaron, for helping me satisfy my curiosity and find understanding and peace, knowing I am united to the whole world and especially to you.

When I am down, please don't kick me,
Talk about me, hate me, stick me;
Because someday, my friend, you'll see
That I was you and you are me.

Robert Rutherford

INTRODUCTION

My goal herein is to present evidence to support the thesis that Judaeo-Christianity is a religion based on myth. A myth is a parable, allegory, or unproven story; and the biblical tale certainly qualifies. We don't know who wrote the Bible or when, and, I believe, it is a parable explaining the reuniting of the god to the goddess (which includes the reconciliation of the man to the woman and the god to humanity).

I don't want to mock anyone's faith, whether that faith is in the god Tammuz or the god Jesus. Until recently I believed in the deity of Yahweh and Jesus from the time I can remember, and my faith has always been extremely important to me. I love my fellow seekers no matter where they may be on their spiritual path. Sometimes my words may sound mocking, but my purpose is only to motivate a desire to reevaluate inherited beliefs. We are all searching, and none of us has all the answers to life's questions. It is my sincere desire not to appear arrogant or condemning, but I also don't want to pussyfoot around and not make myself clear. If something I say is upsetting, I ask the reader to pretend I'm saying it about Bacchus, Hercules, or Zeus. If it wouldn't seem horrible for me to speak what I'm saying about those gods, then I trust the reader to understand that, from my perspective, that's exactly what I'm doing when I talk about Yahweh or Jesus. I'm not judging those who believe in Jesus and Yahweh. **My heart is to share my own thinking about Judaeo-Christianity, not to condemn others.**

Finally, I want to say that my new beliefs regarding the gods of the Bible came about due to great love for them and deep search for truth. And my de-conversion from Judaeo-Christianity proceeded more from studying the Bible than by examining other literature. While the writings of scholars have helped to open my eyes, **it is the words in the biblical scriptures themselves that have convinced me that they are not the word of a god**. As I worked on my doctoral project, *We Are Emmanuel: How Man Became God*, many questions arose from the pages of the Bible that provoked a great desire to seek answers; and each new solution I found served to prompt more questions. Preparing my dissertation was the most difficult mental and spiritual undertaking of my life. I've heard of others who went to seminary and lost their faith in the biblical gods. I'm not sure what the varied reasons are, but for me it wasn't what the school itself taught me but what I discovered in my studies while searching for resolutions to my own questions so I could present an honest paper. As answers came, I found myself torn between explaining the metaphorical meaning of the biblical texts and declaring that the whole Bible is a myth. In the end, I cut about fifty pages from my dissertation and saved it for this book, leaving in the dissertation only my interpretation of the biblical texts, without my thoughts concerning their veracity or inspiration. I believe my dissertation makes a good companion book (to be read first) for this one, as I think it prepares one for moving beyond fairy tales and fantasies to the reality we all need to grasp: if there *is* a god, it is not Yahweh; his story is simply another myth like that of other gods.

Having come to this conclusion, I am compelled to put my thoughts on paper. This book is a brief introduction to a great volume of information that is available to any who wish to pursue these ideas further. Again, I hope my thoughts will be received with an open mind and that my words won't be a source of pain, anger, or disillusionment. We all flow together in this great big ocean we call life, and we need one another. Therefore, whether we agree or disagree, we should exhibit love toward one another and grant free will to all to make personal choices without fear of persecution or loss of affection, friendship, or association. My readers are, of course, free to criticize my thinking or take it and toss it out the window just as they are free to do with the Bible or any other piece of literature. I hope, of course, that all who read this book will seriously consider the evidence I present and, if they disagree, provide absolute confirmation for their own beliefs before proclaiming me to be a godless heathen. Without absolute proof, my readers (no matter how many agree among themselves) must admit the possibility that they could be wrong. And if they could be wrong, I could be right. So, if they can't *substantiate* their own beliefs to be *100 percent accurate*, then I pray that they do the right thing and not judge or condemn me; and, whether we agree or not, I pray that we remain loving family, devoted friends, congenial acquaintances, or kind and considerate strangers.

With deep love for one and all,

Tina Rae Collins

DISCLAIMER

When I speak of Yahweh I'm not talking about an unfathomable creative force or all-encompassing spirit or energy. I'm referring rather to Israel's tribal god, who inherited the house of Jacob from the Canaanite high god Elyon (Deut. 32:8-9). I'm discussing the main god of the Old Testament, who is the protagonist/antagonist in the Israelite scriptures and whose rivals are the likes of Baal, Molech, and Ashtoreth.

There's a reason we don't wake up in the morning to find a story on Facebook about Prince William and Prince Charming playing cricket together. Will is real, but the disarming Charming is a figment of our imagination. The Duchess of Cambridge doesn't sit down to tea with Cinderella; at least, she hasn't since she's been a grown woman and given up fairy tales. As with princes and princesses, so with gods and goddesses. A true god doesn't do battle with fake gods. If Molech and Baal (gods whom Yahweh fought) aren't real, we ought to assume the same about Yahweh.

So, we can't confuse the make-believe Yahweh with any consciousness that might pervade the world. Obviously, we and our universe are good; therefore the force, energy, or entity that developed us must be good (and I have no quarrel with him/her/it). Whether that power is sentient or concerned with us or our planet is not the subject of this book. Here we are dealing only with the Judaeo-Christian myth.

CHAPTER ONE
GODS AND GODDESSES

These infantile stories of the creation of man and the remarkable revelations made by God, are conflicting and bear upon their face the evidence of exaggeration and credulity. The evolution theory has swept from us the myth of Adam and Eve and the eating of the forbidden fruit in the Garden of Eden, which does away with the necessity of a redeemer and the vicarious atonement and original sin. It has opened our eyes to the knowledge that there is no one standing between us and our Creator; that every one must work out his own salvation and be his own savior, answering for his sins according to the law of compensation; that the laws of nature are unchangeable; that the same force that shapes a dewdrop will round a world; that suns and stars float in space, and are held in their place by the same law that guides the earth in its course around the sun; that spring comes to gladden the earth and make it green; that winter's frost robes it in a white winding sheet of snow; but the vegetable world is not dead, it is only asleep to blossom again.[1]

James Palatine Dameron

It is often not truth that we seek, but comfort. Comfort me. Tell me something that makes me feel wanted, needed, cared for, loved, safe, protected, absolved, acquitted, guaranteed, accepted, valued, and even noticed, even if it's not the entire truth . . . These are the instinctive characteristics of a child's yearnings toward . . . mother.[2]

Ken Dahl

Gods and goddesses, whether they be real or imagined, and whatever we call them—Hercules, Jesus, Adonai, Cupid, Santa Claus, El Shaddai, Mother Mary, Superman, Superfly, or even Crowley the King of Hell[3]—they intrigue us and give us someone to revere and adore as well as someone to lean upon in times of trouble or seek out when we need a favor. But from where did we obtain our concepts of the gods and goddesses?

In the beginning was the goddess.[4] Even if she has been "obscured after fifteen centuries of assiduous cover-ups," the **Mother Goddess "preceded male gods in every mythology in the world."**[5] As agriculture developed in the Paleolithic period, "the cult of the Mother Goddess expressed a sense that the fertility which was transforming human life was actually sacred."[6] The Spirit that moved on the waters (Gen. 1:2) was the mother of Jesus. He stated: "Even now did <u>my Mother the Holy Spirit</u> take me by one of my hairs, and carried me away to the great mountain Tabor" (*Gospel According to the Hebrews* 4:1).[7] Although not included in the canon, this Gospel may have been written as

---

[1] James Palatine Dameron, *Spiritism; The Origin of All Religion* (San Francisco, self-published, 1885), 2.

[2] Ken Dahl, *What Is God and How Does It Work? A Call For Honesty About Reality and Religion* (2014), 84.

[3] *Supernatural*, created by Eric Kripke, 2005-present, TV show.

[4] Wilhelm Schmidt, in *The Origin of the Idea of God* (1912), theorized that originally the primitives believed in one god, known as the Sky God. Karen Armstrong, *A History of God: The 4,000-Year Quest of Judaism, Christianity and Islam* (New York: Ballantine Books, 1993), 3.

[5] Barbara G. Walker, *Man Made God* (Seattle, WA: Stellar House Publishing, 2010), 14, 268.

[6] Armstrong, 5.

[7] *B'sorah HaEv'rim: The Goodnews according to the Hebrews*, reconstructed by James Scott Trimm, 4:1:34, pdf.

early as the first century CE and is the only one the early church fathers mentioned by name (Jerome, *Commentary on Ephesians 3*, and other frequent mentions during the first five centuries of the common era).[8] [9]

While Mother is warm and loving, Father has power; and religion is not only about a soft place to lay our heads and rest; we also want a powerful god who can defeat our enemies and do away with the one aspect of life that brings us the most fear: death. Barbara G. Walker, who has spent thirty years studying more than 400 reference books as well as ancient texts in order to find the sources for religious concepts, wrote:

> In all cultures around the world, supreme deities are always parent figures: a mother at first, then later on, a father. People apparently desire the parent figure to provide for them, nurture, love and help them, get them out of trouble, tell them what to do, punish them when they disobey, and be available for appeals. These are all the functions of God; these are the reasons for God's existence in the human mind.[10]

Our Mother, the First Deity

Our love for our mother is natural. She feeds us, cuddles us, and kisses our booboos. She provides everything we need, and we love her because she first loved us (1 Jn. 4:19). She went into the valley of the shadow of death for us, destroyed her body for us, gave of her own sustenance to bring us into being, and then sustained us, again, from her own body through breastfeeding. Mother is "food, warmth, comfort, reassurance. She is the only help of the helpless."[11] She is life, for without her we wouldn't exist and then, as soon as we were born, we would die. We "eat and drink" her so that we might have life (Jn. 6:54). In summary, our mother gave us her blood wherein is life (Lev. 17:11), she provided for us the breath of life (Gen. 2:7), she birthed us through "water and blood" (1 Jn. 5:6), and we partake of her body as we nurse from her sweet "manna" (Ex. 16:1).

We now know that the connection between a mother and her children is even greater than we once realized, as we have discovered that a fetus leaves DNA in his or her mother, which travels to her brain and "many organs of the body including the lung, thyroid muscle, liver, heart, kidney and skin," remaining with her throughout her life and even being passed to other children.[12] Walker wrote that the "supreme deity . . . before fatherhood was understood, was a Great Mother, the creatress of the universe." We have generally called her "Ma, or Mah, or Maa, or Ma-Ma, which linguists say refer to 'mother's breasts' in nearly all languages."[13] As Walker noted, when we pray we lift up our arms like a baby reaching for his mother.[14]

---

[8] "Gospel of the Hebrews," wikipedia.org, 18 Jan. 2015, web, 24 Jan. 2015.

[9] Steve Rudd, "Rejected Books," bible.ca, n.d. web, 24 Jan. 2015.

[10] Walker, *Man Made God*, 38.

[11] Walker, *Man Made God*, 23.

[12] Robert Martone, "Scientists Discover Children's Cells Living in Mothers' Brains: the connection between mother and child is ever deeper than thought," scientificamerican.com, 12 Dec. 2012, web, 16 Nov. 2014.

[13] Walker, *Man Made God*, 57. See also: Peter Farb, *Word Play* (New York: Alfred A. Knopf, 1974), 317.

[14] Walker, *Man Made God*, 58.

Because women create and sustain life, the natural inclination of the ancients was to imagine a goddess as the supreme being, as any god *had* to be related to the birth process. Joshua J. Mark wrote regarding the ancient goddess Inanna:

Inanna is the ancient Sumerian goddess of love, procreation, and of war who later became identified with the Akkadian goddess Ishtar, and further with the Phoenician Astarte and the Greek Aphrodite, among others. She was also seen as the bright star of the morning and evening, Venus. Through the work of the Akkadian poet and high priestess, Enheduanna (2285-2250 BCE) daughter of Sargon of Akkad (who conquered Mesopotamia and built the great Akkadian Empire) Inanna was carefully identified with Ishtar and rose in prominence from a local vegetative deity of the Sumerian people to the Queen of Heaven and the most popular goddess in all of Mesopotamia. . .

In the Mesopotamian pantheon Inanna is the daughter of the sky-god An, but also is depicted as the daughter of the moon-goddess Ningal and her consort Nanna. Alternately, she is the daughter of the god of wisdom Enki and sister to Ereshkigal (goddess of the underworld) and Utu the sun god. Her husband Dumuzi transforms in time (as Inanna does into Ishtar) into the dying-and-reviving god Tammuz and, annually at the autumn equinox, the people would celebrate the sacred marriage rites of Inanna and Dumuzi as he returned from the underworld to mate again with Inanna, thus bringing the land to life. Her temples throughout Mesopotamia were numerous, and sacred prostitutes of both genders were employed to ensure the fertility of the earth and the continued prosperity of the communities.[15]

Regarding Inanna, historian Gwendolyn Leick wrote:

Inanna was the foremost Sumerian goddess, patron deity of Uruk. Her name was written with a sign that represents a reed stalk tied into a loop at the top. This appears in the very earliest written texts from the mid-fourth millennium B.C. She is also mentioned in all the early god lists among the four main deities, along with Anu, Enki, and Enlil. In the royal inscriptions of the early Dynastic Period, Inanna is often invoked as the special protectress of kings. Sargon of Akkad claimed her support in battle and politics. It appears that it was during the third millennium that the goddess acquired martial aspects that may derive from a syncretism with the Semitic deity Ishtar.[16]

From the Womb and Back Again

The Egyptians traced their lineage through their mothers;[17] and in the Bible we see the same practice, as men of the Old Testament didn't relate to their sisters by another mother in the same way they did to sisters through their own mother. The story of

---

[15] Joshua J. Mark, "Inanna," *Ancient History Encyclopedia*, ancient.eu, 15 Oct. 2010, web, 23 Apr. 2015.
[16] Gwendolyn Leick, *The A to Z of Mesopotamia* (Scarecrow Press, 2010), 89.
[17] Walker, *Man Made God*, 63. See also: G. Maspero, *Popular Myths of Ancient Egypt* (New York: University Books, 1967), 3.

Absalom and Tamar proves this point about maternal relationships. According to 2 Samuel 13:1: "<u>Absalom the son of David had a fair sister</u>, whose name was Tamar; and <u>Amnon the son of David loved her</u>." Tamar is not even said here to be the sister of Amnon, although he was her brother through King David. As the story goes, Amnon used Tamar to satisfy his lust and then discarded her, incurring the wrath of her "real" brother, Absalom. Verse 22 says that Absalom hated Amnon for what he had done, and verse 32 relates the sad end to this story: "Amnon only is dead: for by the appointment of Absalom this hath been determined from the day that he forced his sister Tamar." Deuteronomy 13:6 speaks of "thy brother, the son of thy mother." Thus, in Israel as in Egypt, the only "real" brothers and sisters were those belonging to one's mother.[18]

Women truly were and are amazing life givers. Even today we call our planet Mother Earth. We come from her and we go back to her, as Job declared when he said, "Naked came I forth from the <u>womb of my mother</u>, and naked I <u>turn back thither</u>" (Job 1:21 YLT; see also: Gen. 3:19). Job expected to go back to his mother's womb. This was an ancient concept, and found in the oldest of mythologies. Walker wrote: "A hymn attributed to the Hindu god Vishnu described her thus: 'Material cause of all change, manifestation and destruction... the whole Universe rests upon Her, rises out of Her and melts away into Her... <u>She is both mother and grave</u>."[19] This makes sense particularly when we understand that the "primal Mother Goddess was the Earth, who took the seed of the dying vegetation-god and savior back into the tomb-womb of her body, to give him a new birth with the next season, mythologized as his springtime resurrection."[20]

This is a comforting thought, and one the Bible presents in its "return to dust" concept (Gen. 3:19, Ps. 104:29, Eccles. 12:7). Who wouldn't want to go back to the paradise of his/her mother's womb—comforted, secure, nourished, and loved unconditionally? (After all, we left a part of ourselves there.) As Walker noted, we are cast abruptly from our mother's body, from a "primal utopia where life was infinitely pleasurable and easy."[21] Like Dorothy Gayle from Kansas, we are whisked away into a world of "thorns and thistles," where we moan "I wanna go home."[22] Finally, our wish comes true. But who helps us make that journey? Not the magnificent "man behind the curtain." We can "pay no attention" to him. It is the beautiful, soft-spoken Glinda, good witch of the North.[23] (Yes, *The Wizard of Oz* is a gospel story, a story of salvation.)

As innocent children, we still have our mother's love, of course, but a separation has occurred even when we are born; and as we grow, and face the slings and arrows of the world, that separation becomes even greater. We want to experience that perfect existence again; we long to go back into our mother's warm and comforting womb, back into her garden of bliss where all our needs were provided before we could even ask (Is. 65:24). Our subconscious mind remembers that glorious "Eden," our land of "milk and honey" (Ex. 3:8).

---

[18] Walker, *Man Made God*, 69.

[19] Walker, *Man Made God*, 93. See also: Philip Rawson, *Erotic Art of the East* (New York: G. P. Putnam's Sons, 1968), 159.

[20] Walker, *Man Made God*, 191.

[21] Walker, *Man Made God*, 24.

[22] Frank Baum, *The Wizard of Oz*, dir. Victor Fleming, Metro-Goldwyn-Mayer, 1939, film.

[23] Baum, *The Wizard of Oz*.

Where Babies Come From

Until about "five or six thousand years ago,"[24] people were unaware that males had anything to do with the *making* of life. All they knew was that women gave birth and men didn't. Naturally, they pondered this, and came up with some strange ideas.

The ancients—including the Polynesian Maori, the South American Indians, the Romans, the Europeans, the Mesopotamians, and the Jews—**thought babies were made out of women's menstrual blood**[25] ("Adam" means "bloody clay"[26]). The Koran states that man was created from "an extract of clay. Then We made him as a drop in a place of settlement, firmly fixed. Then We made the drop into an alaqah (leech, suspended thing, and **blood clot**), then We made the alaqah into a mudghah (chewed-like substance)" (*Noble Quran* 23:12-14).[27] The Chinese term for this blood clot was "red yin juice."[28] "Aristotle (*De gener. animal.* 1.19, 727b) stated that every human life is made of a 'coagulum' of menstrual blood,"[29] and **Pliny the Elder (23-79 CE) wrote that a baby is made from a "curd" of his or her mother's menstrual blood.**[30] According to John M. Allegro, the "best time for conceiving was thought to be at the beginning or end of a menstrual period, which is why in the story of David and Bathsheba in the Old Testament it is said specifically that the lovers had their illicit intercourse just after Bathsheba had menstruated (II Sam 11:4)."[31] It's understandable that these people thought this way. The blood ("flowers," Lev. 15:24) stopped for nine months and a baby popped out covered in blood. Then the blood flowed again each month until the woman made a new baby.

Life in the Blood

Because it was thought that blood made babies, blood was considered to be sacred, and a biblical author wrote that the "life of the flesh is in the blood" (Lev. 17:11). Again, nothing could be as critical as making or continuing life (which is one reason people thought blood must be shed to obtain eternal life). But this all-important job was done by the weaker sex! Men no doubt felt left out. The most important event of all—the survival of the species—and they had no part in it.

According to Walker, the "long list of 'begats'" in the Bible "**show how important it seemed to credit the fathers, although these lists probably were plagiarized from earlier mother-lists, since many of the names are actually female** and the word translated 'begat' in English originally meant 'gave birth to.'" Indeed, the **word "beget"**

---

[24] Walker, *Man Made God*, 23.

[25] Walker, *Man Made God*, 77.

[26] Walker, *Man Made God*, 77. See also: S. H. Hooke, *Middle Eastern Mythology* (Harmondsworth: Penguin Books Ltd., 1963), 110.

[27] "Quran on Human Embryonic Development," scienceislam.com, n.d. web, 15 Nov. 2014.

[28] Walker, *Man Made God*, 77. See also: Philip Rawson, *The Art of Tantra* (Greenwich, CT: New York Graphic Society, 1973), 149, 234.

[29] Walker, *Man Made God*, 77. See also: Aristotle, *De Partibus Animalium I and De Generatione Animalium I*, tr. C. M. Balme (Oxford: Oxford University Press, 1992), 47ff.

[30] Walker, *Man Made God*, 77. See also Robert Briffault, *The Mothers II* (New York: Macmillan, 1927), 444.

[31] John M. Allegro, *The Sacred Mushroom and the Cross: A study of the nature and origins of Christianity within the fertility cults of the ancient Near East* (Garden City, NY: Doubleday & Company, Inc., 1970), 63.

means to bear, to bring forth, or to travail.[32] Therefore, once men had the idea that blood made babies, they created male gods and began to finagle a way for them to produce life from their blood. According to Egyptian myth, Ra needed genital blood to make the first people, so he was castrated for that purpose.[33] The Hindu Mahadeva underwent the same operation, and the Mexican Quetzalcoatl cut his penis to extract life-giving blood while the Babylonian Bel did the same, mixing his blood with clay.[34]

Sacred Blood

Because blood was necessary to life, the ancients believed the gods needed it to survive. **Even bloody circumcision, which the Jews copied from the Egyptians, was assumed to appease the gods**.[35] Walker wrote that the ancients thought blood was "the divine substance of life, responsible for making babies in the womb, and the **gods themselves needed blood to keep their incorporeal selves alive**. Blood was therefore poured out on their altars to **feed them and keep them happy**."[36]

Naturally, if tribes wanted their gods to be virulent, they poured out more blood to them; thus, they killed innocent animals, and even humans, in an attempt to appease an angry god. Walker noted that, in Greece and Rome, people literally bathed in the blood of sacrificial animals in order to be born again and have their sins removed.[37] Yahweh, god of Israel, demanded every firstborn animal and human child as a sacrifice (Ex. 13:2, Lev. 27:28-29, Ezek. 20:24-26). According to Karen Armstrong, ancient people thought every firstborn child was "the offspring of a god," and that in "begetting the child, the god's energy had been depleted"; so, to correct this, the "firstborn was returned to its divine parent."[38] Valerie Tarico wrote:

> When our ancient ancestors slit the throats on humans and animals or cut out their hearts or sent the smoke of sacrifices heavenward, many believed that they were literally feeding supernatural beings. In time, in most religions, the rationale changed—the gods didn't need feeding so much as they needed signs of devotion and penance. The residual child sacrifice in the Hebrew Bible (yes it is there) typically has this function. Christianity's persistent focus on blood atonement—the notion of Jesus as the be-all-end-all lamb without blemish, the final "propitiation" for human sin—is hopefully the last iteration of humanity's long fascination with blood sacrifice.[39]

---

[32] "Yalad," Strong's H3205, blueletterbible.org, 2015, web, 8 Nov. 2014.
[33] Walker, *Man Made God*, 77.
[34] Walker, *Man Made God*, 77. See also: E. A. Wallis Budge, *Gods of the Egyptians, II* (New York: Dover, 1969), 61, 257, 364.
[35] Walker, *Man Made God*, 78.
[36] Walker, *Man Made God,* 4, 6.
[37] Walker, *Man Made God*, 78-79. See also: S. Angus, *The Mystery-Religions* (New York: Dover, 1975), 94.
[38] Armstrong, 18.
[39] Valerie Tarico, "These are the 12 worst ideas religion has unleashed on the world," rawstory.com, 24 Jan. 2015, web, 31 Jan. 2015.

A Savior

The idea of appeasing the gods with blood eventually, as noted, included the death of the god's own son, which was purported to do exactly what the ancients thought blood accomplished—give those who partook of it the characteristics of the one being sacrificed. This was a handy way to deal with evil in the world. Not only was the god appeased, but someone took the blame for humans' bad deeds! People "hid" in the blood of the savior-god, and Daddy punished his son, or the sinner's older brother.[40] Even a satan (the evil twin) was invented to take the blame for the sinful act. If the good god brought the harvest, who brought the drought and famine? Only two ideas made sense: the good god was angry or there was a bad god, and the ancients accepted both concepts.

The Egyptian Sata, the serpent, was the "dark underground twin of the sun god Ra."[41] The good sun god Horus did battle every day with the evil god Set/Seth, with Horus winning during the day and Set overcoming him and bringing darkness at evening.[42] This was the story of Yahweh and Satan as well. The battle had to have an eventual winner, and the winner was the savior of humanity. With someone to blame "sin" on and someone to take the fall for it, mankind was off the hook and had found a way to return to paradise and circumvent death. But we find another reason for a savior—an earthly, this-world reason; and we can see it in the story of Ishtar and her beloved Tammuz.

Tammuz and Ishtar

Previously I spoke about Tammuz and Ishtar (also called Inanna, Hathor, Astarte, and *possibly* even Asherah/Ashtoreth of the biblical texts since the Israelites worshiped both Asherah and Tammuz). This story shines light on the beginnings of religious ideas.

Donald A. MacKensie wrote: "Among the gods of Babylonia none achieved wider and more enduring fame than Tammuz, who was loved by Ishtar, the amorous Queen of Heaven—the beautiful youth who died and was mourned for and came to life again.[43] In Ezekiel 8 the prophet condemns the Israelites for worshiping everything under the sun (v. 10), and the sun itself (v. 16). He stated: "Then he brought me to the door of the gate of the LORD'S house which was toward the north; and, behold, there sat women weeping for Tammuz" (Ezek. 8:14). This weeping was associated with agricultural rituals.

> The holy one of Ishtar, in the middle of the year the fields languish . . . The shepherd . . . the man of sorrows, why have they slain . . . In his temple, in his inhabited domain, The child, lord of knowledge, abides no more . . . In the meadows, verily, verily, the soul of life perishes.[44]

---

[40] Walker, *Man Made God*, 27.

[41] Walker, *Man Made God*, 218.

[42] *The Century*, XXXVIII (London: T. Fisher Unwin, 1889), 728. See also: D. M. Murdock, *Christ in Egypt: The Horus-Jesus Connection* (Seattle: Stellar House Publishing, 2009) 44, 425.

[43] Donald A. MacKensie, *Myths of Babylonia and Assyria* (1915), "Myths of Tammuz and Ishtar," Ch. V, sacred-texts.com, n.d., web, 15 Nov. 2014 <http://www.sacred-texts.com/ane/mba/mba11.htm>.

[44] MacKensie, "Myths of Tammuz and Ishtar."

"Corn deities were weeping deities, they shed fertilizing tears; and the sowers simulated the sorrow of divine mourners when they cast seed in the soil 'to die', so that it might spring up as corn."[45] As MacKensie noted, we see biblical references to this, as Psalm 126:5 speaks of sowing in tears and reaping in joy. Also, the apostle Paul spoke of sowing seed that dies and is raised as something new (1 Cor. 15:36-37). (Jesus, of course, would end all the mourning. He would be the final "man of sorrows," the ultimate god-man sacrifice made "once for all" to end all tears as well as all hunger [Is. 53:4, Jn. 6:35, Heb. 10:10, Rev.21:4)].)

MacKensie continued:

> It was believed to be essential that **human beings should share the universal sorrow caused by the death of a god**. If they remained unsympathetic, the deities would punish them as enemies. Worshippers of nature gods, therefore, **based their ceremonial practices on natural phenomena**.[46]

Tammuz wasn't the only god whose death and resurrection were necessary to human life. The "blood of Tammuz, Osiris, and Adonis reddened the swollen rivers which fertilized the soil. Various animals were associated with the harvest god, who appears to have been manifested from time to time in different forms, for his spirit pervaded all nature."[47]

Ishtar mourned for Tammuz, calling him her brother although he was also her lover and spouse. But Tammuz, and other slain gods, came back from Hades and brought life once again to all of nature.[48] We see this too in the Bible, as Yahweh, after the resurrection of Jesus, rules over everybody, acts through everybody, and dwells in everybody and everything. He fills the universe, being in "everything in heaven and on earth and under the earth and in the sea, and of all things which are in them" (Rev. 5:13 BBE; see also: Ps. 139:7-10; Jn. 14:20, 17:22-23; Acts 17:28; Eph. 1:9-10, 20, 2:5-6, 3:19, 4:6, 10; Col. 1:20 and 27, 2:10, 3:11). According to *The Gospel of Thomas*, Jesus said, "Split a piece of wood; I am there. Lift up the stone, and you will find me there."[49]

The point here, which Christians in particular need to consider, is: (1) the notion of a god's giving his life or shedding his blood for humanity didn't begin with Jesus; (2) in religious rites humans have always been required to participate in the "death and resurrection" of the gods, and (3) the concept of religion is based on nature and a need to sustain human life (for the provision of food and circumvention of death).

One final thought must be presented regarding Ishtar. She seems to have come to the people's defense, providing for them and never letting them down. When the prophet Jeremiah condemned his people for worshiping the "queen of heaven," they replied:

[45] MacKensie, "Myths of Tammuz and Ishtar."
[46] MacKensie, "Myths of Tammuz and Ishtar."
[47] MacKensie, "Myths of Tammuz and Ishtar."
[48] MacKensie, "Myths of Tammuz and Ishtar."
[49] Robert J. Miller, ed., *The Gospel of Thomas*, tr. Stephen Patterson and Marvin Meyer, *The Complete Gospels: Annotated Scholars Version* (Polebridge Press, 1992, 1994), 77.

Jeremiah 44 (BBE): 17 <u>But we will certainly do every word which has gone out of our mouths, burning perfumes to the queen of heaven</u> and draining out drink offerings to her as we did, we and our fathers and our kings and our rulers, in the towns of Judah and in the streets of Jerusalem: <u>for then we had food enough and did well and saw no evil.</u> 18 <u>But from the time when we gave up burning perfumes to the queen of heaven and draining out drink offerings to her, we have been in need of all things, and have been wasted by the sword and by need of food.</u>

I point this out to say: **Although we may believe our god/goddess helped us maintain our sanity in times of trouble, provided a job for us when we were down and out, healed a toenail fungus, or found our lost keys, it may all be our imagination.**

Gods Harsher Than Goddesses

The goddess, of course, would never have needed the shedding of blood in order to provide for her children, forgive them, or take them back into herself. She was much more tolerant, as most mothers are, than the male gods. Walker noted:

Father gods tended to be more demanding, more warlike, more given to unpredictable fits of wrath and more severe in their punishments than the Mother Goddesses. Goddess religions never had a hell, never defined sexuality as sinful, never ordered genocidal slaughters of biblical magnitude and never imposed so heavy a burden of guilt on their children as did the father gods. In general, the Goddess was a more tolerant parent than the Heavenly Father.[50]

Walker continued: "The Mother never made a hell for her children; and unlike the children of the Father, they did not make for each other a hell on earth."[51] This, Walker surmised, is why Mary the mother of Jesus has been put on a pedestal. She is the "goddess" of Christianity, and receives "more praise and prayers" than the Father does.[52]

The Death

The gods were envious not only of the goddesses' ability to create life, but also of human sexuality.[53] In the biblical account (Gen. 1:27, 5:2), the "gods" created the first man and woman (yes, the word "god" in Genesis 1:1 is plural, as it is in Job 1:6 and 2:1), but only as one being (with "both male and female in one body," enjoying "perpetual sexual bliss"[54]). The Gnostics believed that not only Adam and Eve were once one being but that Yahweh had a female counterpart, "whom the cabalistic Jews called Shekinah

---

[50] Walker, *Man Made God*, 23.
[51] Walker, *Man Made God*, 41.
[52] Walker, *Man Made God*, 41-42.
[53] Walker, *Man Made God*, 26.
[54] Walker, *Man Made God*, 26.

and Christians called Sophia."[55] Some Jews believed that "this mating of the male and female elements within God symbolizes the restored order." It was a salvation that "did not depend upon historical events like the coming of the Messiah but was a process that God himself must undergo."[56] According to some of the Gnostics:

> Sophia (Wisdom), the last of the emanations, fell from grace because she aspired to a forbidden knowledge of the inaccessible Godhead. Because of her overweening presumption, she had fallen from the Pleroma and her grief and distress had formed the world of matter. Exiled and lost, Sophia had wandered through the cosmos, yearning to return to her divine Source.[57]

The Jewish *Zohar* links the loss of the Shekinah with Adam's Fall, as Adam chose to worship only the Shekinah, or "female aspect of God."[58] In Jewish mythology Yahweh put the combined Adam to sleep and separated them. *The Gospel of Philip* regards this separation as death, or it at least created death; and this death was to end when the man and woman were reunited: "<u>When Eve was still with Adam, death did not exist</u>. When she was separated from him, death came into being. <u>If he enters again and attains his former self, death will be no more</u>."[59] *The Gospel of Thomas* has Jesus saying: "When you make the two into one . . . and when you make male and female into a single one, so that the male will not be male nor the female be female . . . then you will enter [the kingdom]."[60] This, of course, explains the biblical concept that Christ's union with his ecclesia is the end of the death curse and that within his kingdom there is neither male nor female but the two have, once again, become one (Gal. 3:10-13, 28; Rev. 21:4, 22:3).

In Greek mythology, Zeus ripped the first couple apart. Because he was in a hurry, he left a small piece of the woman stuck to the man, leaving a hole in the woman. Naturally, this small piece always wants to return to its home.[61] Again, we have a longing for home, for unity, for our first bliss. And, again, the concept of a god is natural, earthy, and sensual; that is, it has to do with life and its continuation.

An old myth that the Hebrews probably knew (since it was older than their own creation myth) was that children's *flesh* was made from the mother's intrauterine blood and their *bones* from the mother's ribs. The Sumerian name for the goddess who oversaw childbirth was Nin-Ti, which means "Lady of the Rib" or "Lady of Life."[62] In the Mesopotamian myth, *man* (Adamu) was made from *woman's* rib while in the Jewish patriarchal story, *woman* was made from *man's* rib.[63] Gnostic literature has Eve making

---

[55] Walker, *Man Made God*, 26. See also Carol Ochs, *Behind the Sex of God* (Boston: Beacon Press, 1977), 121.

[56] Armstrong, 269.

[57] Armstrong, 95.

[58] Armstrong, 249.

[59] James M. Robinson, ed., *The Gospel of Philip,* tr. Wesley W. Isenberg, *The Gnostic Society Library* (San Francisco: HarperCollins, 1990) <http://gnosis.org/naghamm/gop.html>.

[60] James M. Robinson, ed., *The Gospel of Philip,* tr. Thomas O. Lamdin, *The Gnostic Society Library* (San Francisco: HarperCollins, 1990) <http://gnosis.org/naghamm/gthlamb.html>.

[61] Walker, *Man Made God*, 26.

[62] Walker, *Man Made God*, 99. See also: Hooke, *Middle Eastern Mythology*, 115.

[63] Walker, *Man Made God*, 99.

both Adam and Yahweh.[64] No matter which, if any, story we might believe, we can see that the problem was one of separation.

Because of the Dark Ages (c. 500-1000 CE), and the burning of any document that went against the prevailing religious thinking of the time, we have very little information about the rule of the goddess. Eventually patriarchy took over, causing men to push aside the goddess for the more testosterone-laden gods. As Walker explained it, the goddess was then either declared to be a demon (becoming a witch, hag, or crone), humanized or turned into fairy tale creatures (Pandora), or absorbed into a patriarchal myth (as Hera was absorbed by the cult of Zeus and Mary/Mari was absorbed by Yahweh).[65] At that point, not only were the goddesses subjugated, but so were women. Armstrong wrote that the Israelites continued to honor women like Esther and Judith, but "after Yahweh had successfully vanquished the other gods and goddesses of Canaan and the Middle East and become the *only* God, his religion would be managed almost entirely by men. The cult of the goddesses would be superseded."[66] Thus we have heaven (god/man) and earth (goddess/woman) separated and in a struggle for supremacy until they could be reunited, ending the death.

Breath of Life

Another concept men imagined was that life began with a breath, as Yahweh breathed life into Adam. Yahweh's breath (through words) could create anything—even light, and morning and evening, before there was a sun. As Walker noted, the ancients thought light came from a source other than the sun because when the sun set they could still see until it became too dark. So it made perfect sense to them that the gods could make light on the first day of creation although no sun existed until the fourth day.[67]

The idea of "breath creation" came from India. The great goddess grunted the word "OM" to create the universe. The word "omega" (the beginning and end), literally means "Great Om."[68] This was picked up by Judaism and Christianity. The god Marduk's words could "reanimate the dead,"[69] and Ezekiel 37:5 pictures Yahweh doing the same. Just as he brought Adam forth by breathing into him, he promised to raise the Israelites by causing his breath to come upon them. It would seem then, at least at some point, that while the goddess may have made the body (and takes it back into herself, as she *is* the body), the god made (and *was*) the spirit (wind or breath, which returns to him), as "breath of life" came to be regarded as the spiritual aspect of man (Eccles. 12:7).

There is more to the breath, and the Word, than meets the eye. According to John M. Allegro:

---

[64] Walker, *Man Made God*, 99. See also: Elaine Pagels, *The Gnostic Gospels* (New York: Random House, 1979), 30.
[65] Walker, *Man Made God*, 71.
[66] Armstrong, 50.
[67] Walker, *Man Made God*, 46.
[68] Walker, *Man Made God*, 46. See also: Barbara G. Walker, *The Woman's Encyclopedia of Myths and Secrets* (HarperSanFrancisco, 1983), 546.
[69] Walker, *Man Made God*, 47. See also: Eric Fromm, *The Anatomy of Human Destructiveness* (New York: Holt, Rinehart & Winston, 1973), 164.

Quite simply, the reasoning of the early theologians seems to have been as follows: since rain makes the crops grow it must contain within it the seed of life. In human beings this is spermatozoa that is ejected from the penis at orgasm. Therefore it followed that <u>rain is simply heavenly semen</u>, the all-powerful creator, God. The most forceful spurting of this "seed" is accompanied by <u>thunder and the shrieking wind. This is the "voice" of God</u>. Somewhere above the sky a mighty penis reaches an orgasm that shakes the heavens. The "lips" of the penis-tip, the glans, open, and the divine seed shoots forth and is borne by the wind to earth. As saliva can be seen mixed with breath during forceful human speech, so the "speaking" of the divine penis. This "spittle" is the visible "speech" of God; <u>it is his "Son" in New Testament terms, the "Word"</u> . . . "By the word of the Lord the heavens were made, and all their host by the breath of his mouth" (Ps 33:6); or, "when you send forth your breath they are created, and the face of the earth is restored" (Ps. 104:30). This idea of the creative Word of God came to have a profound philosophical and religious importance . . . the subject of much metaphysical debate. But originally it was not an abstract notion; <u>you could see the "Word of God", feel it as rain on your face, see it seeping into the furrows of mother earth, the "labia" of the womb of creation</u>. Within burns an eternal fire which every now and then demonstrates its presence dramatically, by bursting to the surface in a volcano, or by heating spring water to boiling point where the earth's crust is thinnest. It was this uterine heat which made generation possible, and which later theologians identified with the place and means of eternal punishment. Since common observation showed that dead and decaying matter melted back into the earth, it was thought that the imperishable part of man, his "soul" or <u>spirit, the creative breath that gave him life in the womb, must either float off into the ether or return through the terrestrial vagina into the generative furnace</u>.[70]

Since rain/semen brought life to Mother Earth, the Father had to be in heaven ejaculating. Genesis 1:20 says: "Let the waters bring forth abundantly." "Waters" can mean "<u>figuratively, juice; by euphemism, urine, semen</u>."[71] In time, perhaps the spirit/breath formed by this "semen" was seen as separate from the physical being and became the more important aspect. Earthly life is fraught with thorns and thistles. This world is full of sin. The devil has power over the natural realm. The woman (flesh, mother, sinner, goddess, earth, matter) is inferior, and the man (spirit, heaven, god) must rule over her (Gen. 3:16, 4:7)—because she is incapable of guiding her own steps (Jer. 10:23). The whole earth is feminine, as heaven is the male ruler. This hierarchy of the gods' ruling mankind had to be enacted upon the earth, with men ruling over women (Lk. 11:2).

Thus, the god, providing the *water* (rain, breath, spirit), became preeminent while the goddess, providing the *blood* (clay, physical body), fell out of favor with humanity. But, deep down our love is still for the goddess, and our heart's desire is to return to her bosom. Likewise, the heart of both man and woman has always been to be put back together, to become one again, to end the separation or death.

---

[70] Allegro, 20-22.
[71] "Greek/Hebrew Definitions: Strong's #4325: *mayim*," bibletools.org, 1992-2015, web, 28 Jan. 2015.

CHAPTER TWO
JEWISH HENOTHEISM/POLYTHEISM

Jewish priests, *in making a history for their race*, have given us but a shadow of truth here and there; it is almost wholly mythical.[72]

T. W. Doane

In all ages of the world revelations of various kinds . . . have been given to mankind, through the inspiration of prophets, sages, philosophers, seers and mediums. It all comes from the same source; it all bears the same earmarks, and it all tells us to be good and virtuous, if we wish to be happy. . . Nor was it confined to the Jews alone, but was taught to the Hindoos, Persians, and Chinese, by Brahma, Zoroaster and Confucius, long before the Jews were a nation. The writings and teachings of these men to the whole Eastern world was that sin would ultimately be abolished, that everlasting righteousness would be brought in, and that then the good deity, Ormuzd, would rejoice with joy unspeakable forever and ever, for having triumphed over his evil brother, Ahnman (the devil).[73]

James Palatine Dameron

While most Christians think the Bible presents only one god, who is known as Yahweh, this is simply not so. **The ancient Jews were not monotheistic; they just thought their god was best, and they tried to prove it over and over.**

The Elohim

Even the first sentence in the book of Genesis says that, in the beginning, "gods" (the word is plural) created the heavens and earth (Gen. 1:1). Christians gloss over this or say it refers to Yahweh, Jesus, and the Holy Spirit (still not *one* god), a view that is a later interpretation according to Dr. Tony Nugent, a scholar of world religions.[74] This passage is one of many teaching polytheism, and it and other such scriptures can't be ignored.

Job 1:6 (BBE) And there was a day when the <u>sons of the gods</u> came together before the Lord [Jehovah], and the Satan came with them.

The Bible in Basic English is the only translation I found that boldly uses the *proper* plural word ("gods") in the above verse. We also read:

Genesis 1:26 And God [Gods, *Elohim*] said, Let <u>us</u> make man in <u>our</u> image, like <u>us</u>:

---

[72] Thomas W. Doane, *Bible Myths and Their Parallels in Other Religions* (The Truth Seeker, 1882), Ch. VI.

[73] Dameron, 49.

[74] Tony Nugent, PhD, "'Many of These Gods Come From Stars': The Fascinating True Story of Angels, Virgin Birth and Jesus: A religious scholar shares his thoughts on the mythologies of Christmas," interview with Valerie Tarico, alternet.org, 10 Dec. 2014, web, 26 June 2015.

Genesis 3:22 And the Lord [*Jehovah*] God [Gods, *Elohim*] said, Now the man has become like one of <u>us</u>,

Genesis 11:6 And the LORD [*Jehovah*] said . . . 7 Go to, let <u>us</u> go down, and there confound their language, that they may not understand one another's speech.

Exodus 15:11 Who is like unto thee, O LORD [*Jehovah*], <u>among the gods</u> [*El*, mighty <u>one</u>]?

Psalm 82:1 God [Gods, *Elohim*] standeth in the congregation of the mighty [*El*]; he judgeth <u>among the gods</u> [*Elohim*]. [**This, as noted, literally says the gods stand in the congregation of the mighty one (the supreme god *El*), who judges among the gods.**]

Psalm 82:6 I have said, <u>Ye are gods</u>; and all of you are <u>children of the most High</u> [*Elyon*]. 7 But ye shall die like men, and fall like one of the princes. 8 Arise, O God [*Elohim*, gods], judge the earth: for thou shalt inherit all nations.

Psalm 86:8 <u>Among the gods</u> [*Elohim*] there is none like unto thee, O Lord [*Adonay*];

"Gods" in Psalm 82:1 is the same as "gods" in Psalm 86:8. We can't say the "God" (gods, *Elohim*) who stands in the congregation of the mighty, El (82:1), is real but the "gods" (*Elohim*) who aren't like Adonay (86:8) *aren't* real but are imagined by the pagan mind. These gods don't become fake whenever we like. Psalm 86:8 says that among the *Elohim* (the *gods* who *created the world* in Genesis 1:1) there is none like Adonay. Psalm 82:1 states that the gods (*Elohim*) stand in the congregation of El (the mighty one) and he judges among them. According to Henry Binkley Stein, "Jehovah is a singular name, the Elohim are plural. Jehovah Elohim should connote a person of a family or one of a priesthood."[75] By the way, the first creation account in Genesis speaks of Elohim, but the second, beginning in Genesis 2:4, changes the creator to Yahweh or Jehovah.

Some will probably declare that *Elohim* can be singular or plural. True or not, that wouldn't fix the problem within the verses above. Clearly, more than one being was involved as El was judging among the Elohim, and the pronoun used in other passages is plural. No doubt some will say Yahweh was using the "royal" *we*. But, again, the context doesn't support this claim, nor does the rest of the Bible or other literature.

By the way, *El* (used many times in the Bible to refer to the supreme god) was the Canaanite/Ugaritic father of man and the other gods.[76] He was also the "principal Phenician deity"; and, John Parkhurst (1728-1797) wrote in his Hebrew Lexicon that **<u>El</u> <u>"was the very name the heathens gave to their god Sol</u>, their Lord or Ruler of the**

---

[75] Henry Binkley Stein, *The Axe Was God* (Health Research Books, 1996), 17.
[76] N. S. Gill, "The God El," ancienthistory.about.com, 2014, web, 11 Nov. 2014.

Hosts of Heaven."[77] The Jews only gradually accepted Yahweh as the one true god, and he is sometimes identified with El. Lloyd M. Graham noted:

> The later [Jews] deleted many of their gods and devils yet their literature as a whole is replete with them. There were, for instance, seven evil spirits of which Satan, or Beelzebub, was the prince; Vessels of Iniquity, whose chief was Belial; Deluders whose chief, Nahash, deluded Eve; Tempters, whose chief was Mammon; the Turbulents (Turbulentos), chief, Meriram. There were also Lying Spirits, Furies, Revengers, and Inquisitors. Against these were the seven opponents: Cherubim, Seraphim, Virtues, Thrones, Dominions, Powers and Principalities. There were also the seven archangels: Michael, Gabriel, Raphael, Kamiel, Kadriel, Uriel and Zophkiel.
>
> In Tobias, an Apocryphal book, it is related that the archangel Raphael seized Asmodeu, prince of the fourth order of evil spirits . . . and bound him in the wilderness of Upper Egypt (earth). This is the angel Saint John said he saw binding Satan, billions of years after the event. A parallel myth is that of Apollyon, Prince of Darkness . . . This is he whom the Bible calls "the prince of this world." In the myth, his kingdom was over those "wandering stars for whom is laid up the blackness of darkness for ages and ages." . . . This is all part of the wisdom-knowledge of Creation of which the Bible is but a plagiarized and religionized relic.
>
> [The Bible's deities], including its God, are just as mythic as Zeus and Apollo, Prometheus and Epimetheus, yet to any praise of the Greeks and their art the Christian priest makes haste to reply, "Oh, they were only myth-makers." Yes, and the difference between the two is that the myth-makers did not believe in their myths literally, and we do, in ours.[78]

Other Scriptures Referring to Multiple Gods

Here are some other passages expressing the Jews' belief in many gods.

Exodus 18:11 Now I know that the LORD is greater than all gods: for in the thing wherein they dealt proudly he was above them.

Exodus 20:3 Thou shalt have no other gods before me.

Exodus 23:13 And in all things that I have said unto you be circumspect: and make no mention of the name of other gods, neither let it be heard out of thy mouth.

Deuteronomy 8:19 And it shall be, if thou do at all forget the LORD thy God, and walk after other gods, and serve them, and worship them, I testify against you this day that ye shall surely perish.

---

[77] Doane, XXXIX (484:3).

[78] Lloyd M. Graham, *Deceptions and Myths of the Bible* (New York: Bell Publishing Company, 1979), 108.

Deuteronomy 13:6 If thy brother . . . entice thee secretly, saying, Let us go and serve other gods, which thou hast not known, thou, nor thy fathers; 7 Namely, of the gods of the people which are round about you, nigh unto thee, or far off from thee, from the one end of the earth even unto the other end of the earth; Deuteronomy 29:26 For they went and served other gods, and worshipped them, gods whom they knew not, and whom he had not given unto them:

Psalm 89:6 For who **in the skies** can be compared to Yahweh? Who among the **sons of the heavenly beings** is like Yahweh, 7 A very awesome God in the **council of the holy ones**, To be feared above all those who are around him?

Psalm 97:5-7 (WEB) The mountains melt like wax at the presence of Yahweh . . . Worship him, all you gods!

We can say these weren't *really* gods while Yahweh was/is, but that would be wishful thinking on our part. The *Jewish god believed in other gods*. The Old Testament declares Yahweh to be the god of *Israel* more times than I want to count, and he is also called this in Matthew 15:31 and Luke 1:68. That's who he was: the tribal god of Israel, the people given to him by Elyon. As Karen Armstrong wrote:

> The Israelites did not believe that Yahweh, the God of Sinai, was the *only* God but promised, in their covenant, that they would ignore all the other deities and worship him alone. It is very difficult to find a single monotheistic statement in the whole of the Pentateuch.[79]

While the Egyptian king Akhenaton began to worship only the sun god, this seemed foolhardy to the Israelites. Yahweh had proven himself in war, but he wasn't much of a fertility god; hence, the Jews kept worshiping Asherah and Baal.[80] This is why Elijah became so excited that he chased after King Ahab in jubilation when Yahweh brought rain from the sky after Baal couldn't accomplish the feat. "In ecstasy, Elijah tucked up his cloak and ran alongside Ahab's chariot. By sending rain, Yahweh had usurped the function of Baal, the Storm God, proving that he was just as effective in fertility as in war"[81] (1 Kings 18:46). Finally Yahweh was developing his agricultural skills! And, according to Armstrong, he became the one and only God during the exile of the Jews in Babylon, which was also the time when the Jews showed interest in Yahweh as the creator of the universe.[82] Armstrong wrote that the "story of Elijah contains the last mythical account of the past in the Jewish scriptures. Change was in the air throughout the Oikumene. The period 800-200 BCE has been termed the Axial Age. . . Power was shifting to the marketplace." This "new Yahweh of the Axial Age . . . was no longer a mere god of war. Nor was he simply a tribal deity, who was passionately biased in favor

[79] Armstrong, 23.
[80] Armstrong, 23.
[81] Armstrong, 26.
[82] Armstrong, 393, 395.

of Israel: his glory was no longer confined to the Promised Land but filled the whole earth."[83]

Yahweh's Jealousy

If the Jews didn't believe in multiple gods, why was Yahweh angry when they worshiped another god? Of what was he jealous, that the Israelites believed in a figment of their imagination or that they called him by the wrong name? No god should be upset because his people have an imaginary friend or can't get his name right. Is Yahweh jealous of Santa Claus or the Easter Bunny? (I know some would say yes.)

If we read a story about General Zod doing battle with Superman and we know General Zod isn't real, shouldn't we realize that Superman also isn't real? As I noted in my disclaimer, if we read about Baal's doing battle with a god named Yahweh (1 Kings 18), and we know that Baal doesn't really exist, shouldn't we understand that Yahweh is just part of a fake story too? In 2 Kings 10:19 Jehu called all of the prophets, priests, and servants of Baal together so he could destroy all Baal worshipers. Jehu believed in Baal. And Yahweh instilled and fostered that belief.

Regarding the name of the Israelite god, it was impossible for the Jews to know what to call Yahweh since he refused to give them a name, claiming to be I Am That/What I Am. Later he offered the name Jehovah/Yahweh/YHWH and said he had not been known to Abraham, Isaac, and Jacob by that name (as they knew him only as El Shaddai, Ex. 6:3), although the name Yahweh is used in the first few chapters of Genesis (2:4, 5, 7, 8, 9, etc.; 3:1, 8, 9, 13, 14, etc.; 4:1, 3, 4, 6, 9, etc.), and it continues to be used all the way up to Exodus 6 where Yahweh says it is a new name they have not heard. Abraham, in fact, called Yahweh by the name of Jehovah (YHWH/Yahweh) in Genesis 14:22. It seems that, in the beginning "Yahweh was unknown to the patriarchs . . . they are depicted as worshipers of El."[84] Later, of course, the Jews tried to make it look like El and Yahweh, as well as El Shaddai, were the same god.

The truth most likely is that the high Canaanite god, El, was considered by the Jews to be the main god, then at some point Yahweh became the Israelite god, and then, eventually, Yahweh merged with El as the Israelites became monotheistic. Karen Armstrong explained this by saying that two different people wrote Genesis and Exodus, with one author (J from Judah) calling God Yahweh and the other (E from Israel) calling him El or Elohim.[85] She noted:

The Israelites called Yahweh "the God of our fathers" yet it seems that he may have been quite a different deity from El, the Canaanite High God worshiped by the patriarchs. He may have been the god of other people before he became the God of Israel. In all his early appearances to Moses, Yahweh insists repeatedly and at some length that he is indeed the God of Abraham, even though he had

---

[83] Armstrong, 27, 41.

[84] *Pagan Origins of the Christ Myth*, pocm.info, n.d., web, 16 Jan. 2015 <http://pocm.info/pagan_ideas_god.html>.

[85] Armstrong, 12-14.

originally been called El Shaddai. This insistence may preserve the distant echoes of a very early debate about the identity of the God of Moses. It has been suggested that Yahweh was originally a warrior god, a god of volcanoes, a god worshipped in Midian, in what is now Jordan. We shall never know where the Israelites discovered Yahweh, if indeed he really was a completely new deity. . . In pagan antiquity, gods were often merged and amalgamated, or the gods of one locality accepted as identical with the god of another people. All we can be sure of is that, whatever his provenance, the events of the Exodus made Yahweh the definitive God of Israel and that Moses was able to convince the Israelites that he really was one and the same as El, the God beloved by Abraham, Isaac and Jacob.[86]

Armstrong continued to say that "The so-called 'Midianite Theory'—that Yahweh was originally a god of the people of Midian—is usually discredited today, but it was in Midian that Moses had his first vision of Yahweh."[87]

In the New Testament Yahweh doesn't seem to care that his people believe in other gods. His name, if he really has one, is of little significance. The apostle Paul told the Athenians he was going to declare to them the "unknown god" they were worshiping (Acts 17:22-23). He existed in their minds the same as Baal or Molech, the same as I Am That I Am. As someone wrote, "Paul's God and the Greeks' God were both Gods. Everyone knew what 'God' meant. . . The Athenians liked theirs better. Paul liked his better. Go figure."[88] The Athenians had no idea who the unknown god was, so he wasn't Yahweh. Yet Paul said he *was* Yahweh. Why? Because he didn't exist, so he could be Yahweh as easily as he could be any other god. Why didn't this work in the Old Testament if, at that time, the Jews were monotheistic? Yahweh was the god of a thousand names anyway, so what difference did it make if one or two more names (Baal or Molech) were thrown into the mix? Was Yahweh seriously angry that they got his name wrong? Was it better to call him No Name (unknown)? If the Athenians called him No Name and he was Yahweh, why wasn't he Yahweh when the Hebrews called him Molech? In 1 Corinthians 8:4-13, Paul states that not all of the Christians of his day understood that other gods didn't exist. (Of course they didn't! The Jews believed in multiple gods, which is why the Old Testament presents these gods as real!) He didn't reprimand these Christians or tell them they were going to hell; he said nothing at all to them, as his admonition was to those who would judge the polytheists. He told the monotheists to accept the polytheists. Paul said the fathers of the Corinthians all went down into the Red Sea (1 Cor. 10:1), so perhaps these were *Jews* still believing in other gods; however, some say the Corinthians were Gentiles rather than Jews and therefore didn't realize only one god existed. Either way, if "it was good for Paul and Silas,"[89] why

---

[86] Armstrong, 20-21. See also: L. E. Bihu, "Midianite Elements in Hebrew Religion," *Jewish Theological Studies*, 31; and Salo Wittmeyer Baron, *A Social and Religious History of the Jews*, 10 vols., 2nd ed. (New York, 1952-1967), I, 46.

[87] Armstrong, 21.

[88] *Pagan Origins of the Christ Myth, Ibid.*

[89] "(Give Me That) Old-Time Religion," traditional gospel song, 1873, written down by Charles Davis Tillman, 1889, wikipedia.org, 20 Jan. 2015, web, 23 Jan. 2015.

not Abraham, Isaac, and Jacob? If Yahweh was lenient in Paul's day, why rant and rail against the early Israelites for being polytheistic?

Some say that Yahweh was angry not because his name was wrong or the people believed in other gods, but because of the evil the Jews were practicing in the name of other gods; however, they were, for instance, only offering their seed to Molech, which Yahweh enjoyed when the children were burnt for him (more will be said about this later). Yahweh's jealousy makes no sense unless the Jews believed, and they did, that other gods existed. And because they believed this, so did their god. And so did their scribes and "prophets."

Regarding the first of the Ten Commandments ("Thou shalt have no other gods before me," Ex. 20:3), Bob Seidensticker wrote:

> Have you ever thought much about the wording of this commandment? Why doesn't it say that Jehovah is the only god? It's because this section of the Bible was written in the early days of the Israelite religion (roughly 10th century BCE) when it was still polytheistic. The next commandment notes, "I, Jehovah, your God, am a jealous God"—jealous because there were indeed other viable options, and Jehovah insisted on a commitment. . .

> Let's use the proper term for this, henotheism. Polytheists acknowledge many gods and worship many gods; henotheists acknowledge many gods but worship only one. In this view, different gods ruled different territories just as kings did, and tribes owed allegiance to whichever god protected them.[90]

Again, the Jews were not always monotheistic. Their literature expresses this fact. Ze'ev Herzog wrote:

> How many gods, exactly, did Israel have? . . . The question about the date at which monotheism was adopted by the kingdoms of Israel and Judea arose with the discovery of inscriptions in ancient Hebrew that mention a pair of gods . . . At two sites, Kuntiliet Ajrud in the southwestern part of the Negev hill region, and at Khirbet el-Kom in the Judea piedmont, Hebrew inscriptions have been found that mention "Jehovah and his Asherah," "Jehovah Shomron and his Asherah," "Jehovah Teman and his Asherah." The authors were familiar with a pair of gods, Jehovah and his consort Asherah, and send blessings in the couple's name. These inscriptions, from the 8th century BCE, raise the possibility that monotheism, as a state religion, is actually an innovation of the period of the Kingdom of Judea, following the destruction of the Kingdom of Israel.[91]

Armstrong also called Asherah God's wife and confirmed that archaeologists have unearthed inscriptions dedicated to "YHWH and his Asherah."[92] Because El and Asherah were together and "bore" seventy children, we see, once again, that Yahweh and El were

[90] Bob Seidensticker, "Polytheism in the Bible," patheos.com, 13 Feb. 2013, web, 8 Feb. 2015.
[91] Ze'ev Herzog, "Deconstructing the walls of Jericho," haaretz.com, 29 Oct. 1999, web, 1 June 2014.
[92] Armstrong, 47.

eventually merged.[93] According to Thom Stark, the progression went like this: "(1) Yahweh as up-and-coming junior deity in the pantheon of El Elyon; (2) Yahweh as enthroned over the nations, yet still distinct from the high god El; (3) Yahweh and El Elyon conflated; (4) monotheism."[94] Robert Wright concurred, writing: "Nothing in the Deuteronomistic texts, and nothing said by any prophets up to Josiah's time, expresses the clear belief that Yahweh *alone* exists—that the gods of other peoples are mere figment of their imagination."[95] Wright wrote that "monotheism didn't prevail in Israel until after the Babylonian exile of the sixth century BCE."[96] Stark continued:

> Indeed, El is called "father of mankind," as well as "father of the children of El" (i.e., "father of the gods"). But this is not at all how Yahweh is described in Deut 32:6. Yahweh is described solely as the father of Israel. This is not an insignificant distinction. The second quote from the Baal cycle identifies El as the father of Baal, and states that El sets up Baal as king (this takes place directly after Baal defeats Yamm). Obviously, as the high god, El is identified as the father of humankind and as father of the gods. But this is not how Yahweh is identified in Deuteronomy 32. Nowhere is Yahweh said to be the father of any deity; nowhere is Yahweh said to be the father of humankind in general. Yahweh is only identified as the father of his people Israel. This was not uncommon. In Num 21:29, the Moabite deity Chemosh is pictured as the father of the Moabite people (they are his sons and daughters). This does not mean that an El characteristic is being applied to Chemosh. It just speaks to the special relationship between Chemosh and his own people; that's why we call national deities "patron" deities. The same goes for Yahweh in Deut 32:6. . .
>
> Once again, the distinction is obvious. El is identified as the creator of the earth, and the creator of the gods, but Yahweh is identified here only as the creator of Israel. El is also described as the creator of humankind. But not so Yahweh here. The word for "create," *qanah*, can mean "buy," "get," "acquire," "possess," as well as "create." So it may or may not need to be translated "create" here. That it stands in parallel to 'asah ("to make, fashion") may indicate that it should be translated "create." But the key point here is that *qanah* does not feature here as an epithet; it is a verb describing Yahweh's action. Moreover, understand that the notion of "creation" in the ancient Near East has nothing to do with *creation ex nihilo*. The concept refers to shaping, fashioning, or building, out of raw materials. Thus, Yahweh fashioned Israel from Abraham up. He literally created them from Sarah's barren womb. This has nothing to do with the concept of the creation of the earth or of humankind or of the pantheon of gods, as with the Ugaritic El epithets.[97] [98]

---

[93] Murdock, *Did Moses Exist? The Myth of the Israelite Lawgiver* (Seattle: Stellar House Publishing, 2014), 406. Theologian Dr. Robert M. Price wrote in his Amazon review of this book: "This would make a fine dissertation, and you can tell anyone I said so! I wish I could award you a doctorate! You deserve one, my friend."

[94] Thom Stark, "The Most Heiser: Yahweh and Elyon in Psalm 82 and Deuteronomy 32," *Religion at the Margins: Postcards and Postscripts from the Periphery of Faith*, religionatthemargins.com, 16 July 2011, web, 12 May 2015.

[95] Robert Wright, *The Evolution of God* (New York: Little, Brown and Company, 2009), 164.

[96] Wright, 431.

[97] Stark, "The Most Heiser: Yahweh and Elyon in Psalm 82 and Deuteronomy 32."

Laurence Gardner wrote:

Originally, these four consonants [in YHWH] represented the four members of the Heavenly Family: Y represented El the Father; H was Asherah the Mother; W corresponded to He the Son; and H was the Daughter Anath. In accordance with the royal traditions of the time and region, God's mysterious bride, the **Matronit, was also reckoned to be his sister. In the Jewish cult of the Cabbala God's dual male-female image was perpetuated. Meanwhile other sects perceived the Shekinah or Matronit as the female presence of God on Earth. The divine marital chamber was the sanctuary of the Jerusalem Temple, but from the moment the Temple was destroyed, the Matronit was destined to roam the Earth while the male aspect of Jehovah was left to rule the heavens alone.**[99]

Garner obviously sees Yahweh and El as the same being. While I believe they were eventually presented that way, in the beginning it was not so. And no matter how we view this matter, the biblical record reveals that the **most high god judged among the lesser gods**; thus, henotheism/polytheism reigned in Israel. Also, as we can see, again, the separation of male and female (even among the gods) is the problem the Bible addresses. Unity, or restored unity, is the goal of the Old and New Testaments. The male and female had to be put back together to end the separation, or death.

[98] Note: Stark's view is that Yahweh is the one standing (as Father El would be sitting) in the congregation of the gods, accusing the other gods before El. But the word for the one(s) standing is *Elohim*, which I would interpret as being the lesser gods who have come to stand before El, the judge, as per Job 1:6: "Now there was a day when the sons of God came to present themselves before the LORD, and Satan came also among them." This seems to make more sense because in verse 8 is an admonition to *Elohim* to arise and judge righteously. If *Elohim* in verse 1 is Yahweh, then he is urging himself in verse 8 to judge righteously.
[99] Laurence Gardner, *Bloodline of the Holy Grail: The Hidden Lineage of Jesus Revealed* (Rockport, MA: Element Books Ltd., 1997), 18.

CHAPTER THREE
DARK SAYINGS OF OLD

For every street, every marketplace is full of Zeus. Even the sea and the harbor are full of this deity. Everywhere everyone is indebted to Zeus, For we are indeed his offspring[100] (Greek Poet Aratus [c. 310-240 BCE], *Phaenomena* 1-5). For in him we live, and move, and have our being; as certain also of your own poets have said, For we are also his offspring (Apostle Paul, Acts 17:28). He fills the universe, being in "everything in heaven and on earth and under the earth and in the sea, and of all things which are in them" (Rev. 5:13 BBE).

When you understand why you dismiss all the other possible gods, you will understand why I dismiss yours.[101]

Stephen F. Roberts

In the meantime, be wary of those who won't buy a car until they've visited a dozen car lots, test driven 20 vehicles, checked the accident history, insurance, payments, safety record, gas mileage and resale value, but they'll accept the bible as Absolute Truth without even knowing who wrote the book of Genesis.

Seth Andrews, "Free Will," *The Thinking Atheist Blog*

With eyes lifted heavenward, we can't see the intricate beauty beneath our feet. Devout believers put their spiritual energy into preparing for a world to come rather than cherishing and stewarding the one wild and precious world we have been given.[102]

Valerie Tarico

When a well-packaged web of lies has been sold gradually to the masses over generations, the truth will seem utterly preposterous and its speaker a raving lunatic.

Dresden James

One of the saddest lessons of history is this: If we've been bamboozled long enough, we tend to reject any evidence of the bamboozle. We're no longer interested in finding out the truth. The bamboozle has captured us. It's simply too painful to acknowledge, even to ourselves, that we've been taken. Once you give a charlatan power over you, you almost never get it back.

Carl Sagan, *The Demon-Haunted World: Science as a Candle in the Dark*

When the Church Mythologists established their system, they collected all the writings they could find, and managed them as they pleased. It is a matter altogether of uncertainty to us whether such of the writings as now appear under the name of the Old

---

[100] E. Christopher Reyes, *In His Name* (Bloomington, IN: Trafford Publishing, 2014), Vol. 4, 260.
[101] Carl S., "Everyone Is Lacking In Faith," exchristian.net, 24 Jan. 2015, web, 24 Jan. 2015.
[102] Tarico, "These are the 12 worst ideas religion has unleashed on the world."

and New Testament are in the same state in which those collectors say they found them, or whether they added, altered, abridged, or dressed them up.[103]

Thomas Paine

We may define "faith" as a firm belief in something for which there is no evidence. Where there is evidence, no one speaks of "faith." We do not speak of faith that two and two are four or that the earth is round. We only speak of faith when we wish to substitute emotion for evidence. The substitution of emotion for evidence is apt to lead to strife, since different groups substitute different emotions."

Bertrand Russell ("Human Society in Ethics and Politics," 1954)

Many Christians profess that their sacred texts came from Yahweh, being "God breathed" and inerrant. They also believe in superheroes and magical events. In this chapter we'll reflect on the source of some of the legends in the Old Testament, and consider whether these stories were given by inspiration or lifted from, or culturally shared with, other nations. We'll look at when the texts were written and compare them to other literature, study the lives of some "men of God" and relate the events of their lives to those in the lives of other mythical characters, and then look at historical and archaeological records to see whether they corroborate the biblical story.

Dating of the Old Testament

The *Tanakh* (Old Testament) was not necessarily written in the time period in which the stories are purported to have happened. Even the *Pentateuch* (first five books) may not have existed before the third century BCE.[104] According to Russell Gmirkin, the **Pentateuch was written "in its entirety" by Jewish scholars around 273-272 BCE in Alexandria.**[105] The *Catholic Encyclopedia* states: "It is true that the Pentateuch, so long attributed to Moses, is now held by the vast majority of non-Catholic, and by an increasing number of Catholic, scholars to be a <u>combination of four independent sources put together in final shape soon after the Captivity</u>."[106] Max I. Dimont wrote:

Biblical scholars have conjectured that the Old Testament is composed essentially of four major narratives, the "J," "E," "JE," and "P" documents woven together into one. <u>The "J" documents are so named because in them God is always referred to as "Jehovah."</u> They are the oldest, written around the ninth century BC, in the southern kingdom of Judah. <u>The "E" documents, so called because in them God is referred to as "Elohim,"</u> were written about a hundred years after the "J" documents in the eighth century in the northern kingdom of Israel. <u>Scholars assume the "P" or "Priestly" documents were composed some two-hundred years or so after the "E," about 600 BC.</u> In the fifth century, Jewish

[103] Thomas Paine, *Age of Reason,* Part 1, Section 4.
[104] Murdock, *Did Moses Exist?* 25.
[105] Russell E. Gmirkin, *Gerossus and Genesis, Manetho and Exodus: Hellenistic Histories and the Date of the Pentateuch* (New York/London: T & T Clark International, 2006), 1.
[106] *Catholic Encyclopedia*, Vol. 1, 622; as quoted by E. Christopher Reyes, *In His Name*, Vol. 3, 16.

priests combined portions of the "J" and "E" documents, adding a little handiwork of their own (known as pious fraud), which are referred to as "JE" documents, since God in these passages is referred to as "Jehovah-Elohim" (translated as "Lord God").[107]

The Law of Moses is so similar to Plato's Laws that Russell Gmirkin "theorizes that the creators of the Mosaic law had before them a copy of Plato's Laws, at Alexandria during the third century BCE, when they drafted the Pentateuch as we know it."[108] Whether this is true or not, the **Old Testament was not canonized until the tenth century CE**, thus nearly a millennia after the supposed birth of Jesus Christ. Many changes, corrections, additions, and deletions could have been made to it during all those centuries. Armstrong noted that the "reformers rewrote Israelite history" and that the "historical books of Joshua, Judges, Samuel and Kings were revised according to the new ideology." She said the lost Book of the Law found by Hilkiah "was the core of the text that we now know as Deuteronomy" and that it was a "timely discovery" by the reforming party. She further noted that in the rewriting of this history, "the myth of the Exodus is clad in imagery that reminds us of the victory of Marduk over Tiamat, the primal sea."[109] Certainly, as with the New Testament, the stories in the Old Testament *were*, through the years, "edited, interpolated, mutilated and forged."[110] Even the *Catholic Encyclopedia* **admits that "forgery and interpolation as well as ignorance . . . wrought mischief on a grand scale."**[111] Dr. Isaac M. Wise noted regarding the ancient Hebrews: "They adopted forms, terms, ideas and myths of all nations with whom they came in contact, and, like the Greeks, in their way, *cast them all in a peculiar Jewish religious mode*."[112] The *Talmud* states, for instance, that the names for angels (Gabriel, Michael, etc.) came from Babylon.[113] Ernst von Bunsen wrote: "There is no trace of the doctrine of Angels in the Hebrew Scriptures composed or written before the exile."[114]

Author of the Old Testament

Many mistakenly believe that the authors of the books in the Bible are those whose names appear at the top of each book. Since most of the stories we will consider here are in the *Pentateuch*, the author of it is our main concern. It's generally accepted that Moses wrote the *Pentateuch*, but this claim doesn't hold up under scrutiny.

---

[107] Max I. Dimont, *Jews, God, and History*, 2nd ed., ed. and rev. Ethel Dimont (New York: Signet Classics, 1990), ebook.

[108] Murdock, *Did Moses Exist?* 269.

[109] Armstrong, 52, 54, 60.

[110] Murdock, *Did Moses Exist?* 25, 269.

[111] Graham, 445.

[112] Doane, *Bible Myths and Their Parallels in Other Religions* (The Truth Seeker, 1882), Ch. XI. See also: Thomas W. Doane, *Bible Myths and Their Parallels in Other Religions Being a Comparison of the Old and New Testament Myths and Miracles with Those of Heathen Nations of Antiquity Considering Also Their Origin and Meaning* (USA: public domain, 1882, 1910), Kindle ed.

[113] Ignaz Goldziher, *Muslim Studies*, ed. S. M. Stern, tr. C. R. Barber and S. M. Stern (Chicago: Aldine Publishing Company, 1966), 319. See also: Doane, XI.

[114] Ernst von Bunsen, *The Angel-Messiah of Buddhists, Essenes, and Christians* (London: Longmans, Green, and Company, 1880), 285. See also: Doane, XI.

Deuteronomy 34:6 states that "no man knoweth of his [Moses'] sepulchre unto this day," from which we can surmise that (1) Moses didn't write this about himself, and (2) many, many days, months, and years had passed since Moses' death when Deuteronomy was written. We don't say "to this day" unless much time has passed. Moses was supposed to be the meekest man on the earth, but a meek man wouldn't say that he himself was the meekest of all (Num. 12:3). And Moses took credit for what his father-in-law did regarding judging the people, so he wasn't meek (Ex. 18:12-27, Deut. 1:9-19). Genesis speaks of kings in Israel before any kings reigned (Gen. 36:31), so the book was obviously written at some point after kings began to rule in Israel.

DeRobingne Mortimer Bennett enumerated seventeen reasons why Moses couldn't have been the author of the Pentateuch.[115] And, according to Porphyry, a Greco-Phoenician philosopher (234-c. 305 CE), **the writings that supposedly belonged to Moses were burnt when the temple was destroyed and "afterwards were composed inaccurately one thousand one hundred and eighty years after Moses' death by Ezra and his followers."**[116] This would have been somewhere in the vicinity of 480-440 BCE. According to D. M. Murdock, the language used in the *Tanakh* "flourished mainly during the sixth century" BCE. This was about the time of the exile of the Jews in Babylon,[117] when Ezra worked under the authority of the kings of Persia (Ezra 1:1-2, 7:11-14).

While we can't know the exact date of the writing of the Old Testament scriptures or who wrote them, the view of modern scholars is that the Bible is not as old as we have assumed. We really can't be sure who wrote the initial documents or when they were written. More than that, the **Bible's stories and legends are not original or unique**.

Creation

The Old Testament book of Genesis presents an account of creation that has been passed down within the Hebrew nation as a communication of their source and establishment. But from where did the tale originate?

Several hundred years before the Hebrew creation account was penned, the Babylonians promulgated their own creation record known as *Enuma Elish* (*When on High*). Eric H. Cline noted that this story is "sometimes referred to as the Babylonian Genesis because of the obvious parallels to the account in the Hebrew Bible."[118] Cline wrote that Mesopotamia greatly impacted biblical Israel, giving us, for example, Hammurabi's Law Code with its "eye for an eye, tooth for a tooth" long before the Hebrew Bible was written. Cline surmised:

One of the best ways to explain both the similarities and the differences between the details in this myth and the biblical story found in Genesis is to suggest that

---

[115] DeRobingne Mortimer Bennett, *The Gods and Religions of Ancient and Modern Times . . .* (1880), 617-622.
[116] M. Stern, ed. and tr., *Greek and Latin Authors on Jesus and Judaism*, 3 vols. (Jerusalem, 1974-1984), II: 480. See also: Bennett, 652.
[117] Murdock, *Did Moses Exist?* 53. See also: Bennett, 647.
[118] Eric H. Cline, "The Garden of Eden," bibleinterp.com, Oct. 2009, web, 21 Feb. 2014; reprinted with permission of the National Geographic Society from the book *From Eden to Exile: Unraveling Mysteries of the Bible*, 2007.

the original Mesopotamian story (or the concepts contained within it) may have been passed down from the Sumerians . . . to the Babylonians, Assyrians, and the peoples of Ugarit and Canaan . . . and then to the Israelites, eventually making its way into the Hebrew Bible.[119]

Most of the nations that existed in the area where the early Hebrews lived have a chronicle of origins that resembles the Hebrew and Babylonian stories. The Egyptian *Papyrus Insinger*, for instance, notes that God "created light and darkness in which is every creature."[120] And, as the primordial sea is an adversary in the Hebrew Bible, it is "personified by Nammu in Sumer and by Nun in Egypt," and is "perceived in an adversarial role" (Gen. 6:17, Is. 60:5).[121]

The Zoroastrians of Persia, in their ancient scriptures, called *Zend Avesta*,[122] tell a creation story of Ormuzd, who, like the gods of Genesis, created the whole world and two people in six days and afterwards rested on the seventh day. E. Christopher Reyes wrote that Ormuzd created as follows: first day, heavens; second, water; third, earth; fourth, plants; fifth, animals; and sixth, man.[123] (This actually makes more sense—since the heavens would include the sun, moon, and stars—than the biblical story, which has plants being created on the third day and the sun's not being created until the fourth day.) The names of the two people were Adama and Evah. We have copies of these texts dating back to the tenth century BCE (thus, they are older than the Hebrew texts).[124]

According to Graham,

Adam Adami is found in Chaldean scriptures much older than those of the Hebrews; it was also known to the Babylonians. Among their clay tablets George Smith found an account of Creation identical with that of the Bible, and in this the first man is Adamu. And in a Hindu book two thousand years older than the Bible, *The Prophecies*, by Ramutsariar, the Hebrew story is given almost word for word, and there the first man is Adama and the first woman Heva.[125]

Greek mythology also portrays the world's being created in seven days, and the Hindu Brahma likewise supposedly accomplished the job in seven days, the names of these days being found in Hindu manuscripts that date to 5000 BCE.[126] In the Babylonian creation myth, Aruru (a female creator) makes the first man by first washing her hands and then pinching clay and spitting on it to make her human being.[127]

---

[119] Cline, "The Garden of Eden."

[120] John H. Walton, PhD, *The Lost World of Genesis One: Ancient Cosmology and the Origins Debate* (Downers Grove, IL: InterVarsity Press, 2010), Kindle ed., 31-32.

[121] Walton, 51.

[122] Melloson Allen, "10 Ways the Bible Was Influenced by Other Religions," listverse.com, 30 June 2013, web, 5 Apr. 2014.

[123] Reyes, Vol. 4, 10.

[124] A. Moore, "8 Biblical Concepts and Stories That Originated Outside of The Bible," atlantablackstar.com, 3 Feb. 2014, web, 13 Aug. 2014.

[125] Graham, 52.

[126] Graham, 41.

[127] Graham, 46.

Graham wrote that the "Hebrew word *Eden* comes from an old Babylonian name for Mesopotamia, *Gan-Eden*, the garden of the Middle East."[128] The Fall of mankind in this garden is "yet another pre-Hebraic Mesopotamian myth, represented in the Akkadian tradition as humanity's seduction" by a dragon.[129] The tree of life that grew within the garden likewise didn't originate with the Hebrews, as "every ancient race had its 'tree of life.'"[130] The Greek tree was called Gogard, and came with a serpent called Ladon. The Tibetan tree of life was Zampun, and the Persian tree was called Homa. (The Chinese even had a "tree of knowledge," called Sung-Ming-Shu.) The Norse tree of life was Yggdrasil, at the foot of which dwelt the serpent Nidhogg.[131] Odin in fact hanged himself from this tree, declaring, "I know that I hung on a windy tree, nine long nights, <u>wounded with a spear</u>, dedicated to Odin, <u>myself to myself</u>."[132] (He refused to receive even a drop of water while he was there; see Matthew 27:34.) His sacrifice was accepted, and he became wise; so this act, like that of Jesus' sacrifice, was not just about death but also life, as we see an "imagery of rebirth and fecundity in the following verses that speak of [Odin's] being 'fertilized,' and, like a seedling, 'growing,' and 'thriving.'"[133]

The four rivers of the book of Genesis are also the rivers of other ancient myths. In the older story of Brahma, four rivers emerged from Mount Mery. For the Buddhists four rivers flowed from Tawrutisa, where the god of life, Sikia, lived. The Tien-Chan of the Chinese "was watered by four perennial fountains of Tychin, or immortality."[134] The Scandinavian Asgard also boasted four rivers.[135] Historian Flavius Josephus recognized these rivers as being symbolic when he wrote that the "garden was watered by one river, which ran round about the whole earth, and was parted into four parts."[136] No river can run around the earth, of course; but the constant appearance of movement of the sun, moon, and stars around the earth looked like a river. (We will discuss the significance of the number four later.)

As Dennis Bratcher observed:

there are simply too many similarities to deny any relationship between the [creation] accounts. . . there is little doubt that the Sumerian versions of the story predate the biblical account by several hundred years. . . it is best to see the Genesis narratives as freely using the metaphors and symbolism drawn from a common cultural pool to assert their own theology about God.[137]

[128] Graham, 43.
[129] A. Smythe Palmer, *Babylonian Influence on the Bible and Popular Beliefs* (London: David Nutt, 1897), 30. See also Murdock, *Did Moses Exist?* 225.
[130] Graham, 48.
[131] Graham, 48.
[132] "Hávamál," wikipedia.org, 4 Mar. 2015, web, 15 Apr. 2015; see also: Carolyne Larrington, tr., *The Poetic Edda* (Oxford World's Classics, 1999), 34.
[133] *Hávamál*, an Old Norse poem that comprises part of the *Poetic Edda*, stanzas 137-163; see also: "Odin's Discovery of the Runes," *Norse Mythology for Smart People*, norse-mythology.org, 2012-2015, web, 15 Apr. 2015.
[134] Graham, 50.
[135] Graham, 50.
[136] Flavius Josephus, *Antiquities of the Jews*, 1, 1, 3.
[137] Dennis Bratcher, "Enuma Elish: 'When on High . . . ' The Mesopotamian/Babylonian Creation Myth," *Christian Resource Institute: The Voice: Biblical and Theological Resources for Growing Christians*, cresourcei.org, 2013, web, 16 Feb. 2014.

John Calvin considered the Genesis creation account as "baby talk," presenting a complex process in a language that "simple people" could understand and thus have faith in God.[138] And Karen Armstrong noted that "cosmology was not a scientific description of the origins of the world but was originally a symbolic expression of a spiritual and psychological truth."[139]

Old Testament God-Men

Many similarities exist between the characters in the Bible and persons we read about in other, often older, scriptures. The reason is that the biblical characters are gods, and the same story is told over and over. Throughout the biblical record various "gods" (as characters in the story) appear, retelling the same story. T. W. Doane wrote:

> Immaculate conceptions and celestial descents were so currently received among the ancients, that whoever had greatly distinguished himself in the affairs of men was thought to be of supernatural lineage. Gods descended from heaven and were made incarnate in men, and men ascended from earth, and took their seat among the gods, so that these incarnations and apotheosises were fast filling Olympus with divinities.[140]

Christians like to call these individuals "types" of Christ. They are in fact deities in their own little stories. We see them repeatedly in and out of the Bible, and will talk later about why this is so. For now, let's look at some of these god-men from the Old Testament.

Job

The story of Job is no doubt a fable, although he is mentioned in the New Testament (Jas. 5:11). Job was a lot like Christ. St. Zeno (who was named Bishop of Verona in 362 CE and died in 371) wrote that Job was tempted three times (as was Christ), was "ulcerated and disfigured" (like Christ on the cross), was insulted by his neighbors (as Christ was rejected), and was restored to his former place (like Christ).[141] Although Satan supposedly brought these miseries upon Job, in the end Job was comforted for "all the evil that Yahweh had brought on him" (Job 42:11 WEB). Job's story is no doubt the Hebrew version of an "allegory common to all antiquity" (as the Talmud explains) since the Babylonians produced a poem about a "virtuous man named Tabu-utul-Bel who was sorely afflicted for some inscrutable reasons." Like Job, he ends his story with "an apology by ignorance and a recantation by fear."[142] Job also reminds us of Aesop's "The North Wind and the Sun," as he, like Aesop's wayfaring man, was used in a power play between two divine beings.[143]

---

138 Armstrong, 289.
139 Armstrong, 395.
140 Doane, XII.
141 "Job was a type of Christ," *Catholic Radio Dramas*, catholicradiodramas.com, 2014, web, 16 Mar. 2014.
142 Graham, 269-271.
143 Aesop, "The North Wind and the Sun," aesopfables.com, n.d., web, 26 May 2015.

Noah

Noah, like many other biblical characters, is another Adam (and another savior); thus Yahweh told Noah, as he did Adam (and Christians), to "be fruitful and replenish the earth" (Gen. 1:28, 9:1; Jn. 15:8).

Noah was based on the Chaldean Nuah, who belonged to the Chaldean Trinity and was the third sign of the Chaldean zodiac.[144] Noah named his sons from other legends.

In Maurice's history of Hindustan we find this: "It is related in Padmapooraun that Satyavrata, whose miraculous preservation from a general deluge is told at large in the Matsya, had three sons, the eldest of whom was named Jyapeti, or Lord of the Earth; the others were Charma and Sharma, which last words are in the vulgar dialects usually pronounced Cham and Sham." In *The City of God*, St. Augustine uses these same forms, also Chanaan for Canaan.[145] [146] [Noah's sons were Shem, Ham, and Japheth (Gen. 5:32).]

The *Book of Enoch* says: "Noah was transfigured at birth, the light of his body illuminating the whole house—the planetary entity."[147] Thus, Noah, like Jesus, was a "light shining in darkness" (Jn. 1:5). Immediately after this occurrence, and as a baby, Noah rose and spoke with Yahweh. Noah's father, Lamech, rushed to his own father, Methuselah, to find out what was transpiring, and Methuselah ran to his father, Enoch, who said Noah was a "wonder child" who "would become the Savior of the race during a subsequent Deluge," coming because sons of the gods had mated with humans (Yahweh thought only he, not his brothers, should do that) and created giants (Gen. 6:2-4). These giants were "the same as the Titans, the Cyclops, the 'mighty men' of mythology."[148]

As Jesus was savior to those in the path of death in Jerusalem in 70 CE, Noah was the savior of those who died in the Flood. Both were "god" figures preaching salvation.

Noah's Flood

Doane noted that the Egyptian holy book, which is the "most ancient of all holy books," doesn't mention the Flood.[149] However, flood stories abound in ancient myths and legends. Christians and Jews, naturally, claim that their story was plagiarized. However, **"the Hindu, Chaldean, Babylonian and Egyptian accounts antedate the Hebrew version by many centuries. Who did the copying then is obvious."**[150]

Noah's raven and dove that he sent out to check for dry land are copies of the dove, swallow, and raven of the Babylonian Utnapishtim's flood story. The Babylonian ark came to rest on Mount Nisir, the "Hindu ark [built by Vaivasvata[151]] on Mount Himalaya,

---

[144] Graham, 87.
[145] Graham, 94.
[146] Bible Hub also lists Cham as the name of Ham. "Cham," biblehub.com, n.d., web, 15 Dec. 2014 <http://biblehub.com/hebrew/2526.htm>.
[147] Graham, 85.
[148] Graham, 85-86.
[149] Doane, II.
[150] Graham, 100.
[151] Graham, 100.

and the Greek ark on Mount Parnassus."[152] The Greek god Zeus permitted Pyrrha and Deucalion, who "found grace" in his eyes, to live through the flood, as Yahweh did for Noah and his unnamed wife (Gen. 6:8).[153] After the Babylonian flood, Utnapishtim built an altar and made a sacrifice to his god just as Noah did, and this god also "smelled a sweet savor" while Ishtar "hung out her multicolored necklace" (rainbow)[154] (Gen. 8:18-21, 9:12-17). Among the Incas, Viracocha also produced a rainbow with the promise never to bring another drowning flood, and the god Bochica (of the Chibehas of Bogota) ended his flood while he sat on a rainbow.[155] In Mexico, Tangaloa, who was god of the Tepanecans, brought a flood; and Sing Bonga, god of the Mundari in Central India, destroyed humanity with both water and fire.[156]

Melloson Allen listed ten ways in which the Bible was influenced by other religions, and one striking story is the tale of a flood that predated Noah's. The *Epic of Gilgamesh* (2600 BCE) gives an account of a man, Enkidu, who was formed out of the earth by a god. Enkidu lived with the animals in a paradise until a woman named Shamhat tempted him. He ate food she gave him and then was forced to leave his home after realizing that he was naked. Later in the story, he met a snake that robbed him of his "plant of immortality."[157] Enkidu also battled Gilgamesh for forty days and forty nights.[158] His story most likely came to the attention of the Jews around the time of the Babylonian exile (sixth century BCE).[159] Barbara Walker wrote:

> The biblical flood story, the "deluge," was a late offshoot of a cycle of flood myths known everywhere in the ancient world. Thousands of years before the Bible was written, an ark was built by the Sumerian Ziusudra. In Akkad, the flood hero's name was Atrakhasis. In Babylon he was Uta-Napishtim, the only mortal to become immortal. In Greece he was Deucalion, who repopulated the earth after the waters subsided [and after the ark landed on Mt. Parnassos]. In Armenia, the hero was Xisuthros—a corruption of Sumerian Ziusudra—whose ark landed on Mount Ararat.
>
> According to the original Chaldean account, the flood hero was told by his god, "Build a vessel and finish it. By a deluge I will destroy substance and life. Cause thou to go up into the vessel the substance of all that has life."[160]

Some Christians claim that if a great flood occurred, the Bible must be true. However, **other flood stories preceded Noah's; and one of them, as Walker noted, has the ark landing on Mount Ararat.** Even if it could be proven that the Jewish story

---

[152] Graham, 92.
[153] Graham, 98.
[154] Graham, 93.
[155] Graham, 93.
[156] Graham, 100.
[157] Melloson Allen, "10 Ways the Bible Was Influenced by Other Religions."
[158] Murdock, *Did Moses Exist?* 240.
[159] Moore, "8 Biblical Concepts and Stories That Originated Outside of The Bible."
[160] Barbara G. Walker, *The Woman's Encyclopedia of Myths and Secrets*, 315. See also: Peter Joseph and D. M. Murdock, *The Zeitgeist Sourcebook, Part 1: The Greatest Story Ever Told: Zeitgeist the Movie*, 2010, 80.

was the first to be conceived or written, this would suggest only that a flood probably occurred and all cultures concocted far-fetched stories about it. It makes no sense to assume the Jews told the truth while others lied.

Abraham

Terah's son Abraham was a friend to Yahweh and father of the Jews (Gen. 17:5, Lk. 1:73, Jas. 2:23). He was the reigning patriarch to whom Yahweh made a promise to bless Israel, and possibly the whole world (Gen. 22:18, 26:4). Abraham was another god-man.

Abraham and his sister/wife Sarah are the Hebrew version of the Indian god Brahma and his beautiful sister/wife Saraiswati (Gen. 12:11, 20:1-12). (Again, the gods like to marry their siblings.) Brahman, universal spirit, manifested himself as Lord Brahma, who split himself to make Saraiswati.[161] Brahma was therefore the first created being in the Hindu religion, as Abraham was the father of the Jews. According to D. M. Murdock, Abram (Abraham) may be "an anthropomorphization of the Indian god Brahm or Brahma, thus subordinated under Melchizedek and El Elohim."[162]

Brahma's son (or grandson), Daksha, was killed at a sacrifice to the gods and resurrected with a ram's head, while Abraham was willing to offer his son Isaac to Yahweh but was given a ram to sacrifice instead (Gen. 22). (The Indian Siva/Shiva also was prepared to kill his son as a sacrifice, but his god provided to him a rhinoceros to sacrifice. Saturn was willing to sacrifice his "only begotten son" to Uranus, his father.[163])

Just as Abraham's grandsons, Jacob and Esau, struggled in the womb for preeminence, in Greek mythology "the twins Proetus and Acrisius struggled with each other in the womb of Queen Algaia."[164] As Jacob tricked his father-in-law, Laban, by "marking" his cows to change their color (Gen. 30:31-43), the Greek god Hermes gave Autolycus the "power to metamorphose the cattle he stole from Sisyphus."[165] (Even today some believe a baby can be "marked" by what his/her mother sees while pregnant.) Graham wrote:

> Jacob becomes Israel at exactly the same point in the Hebrew myth that Uranus became Cronos in the Greek . . . [Jacob's twelve sons] appear in this myth at exactly the same time and place in the creative process as the twelve Titans in the Greek myth. These titanic twelve create the world and man, and the **Hebrew twelve create the human race, or so says Israel**. . . So now begins the history of Jacob's sons. All of them were born in or near Beth-el, the house of God, later changed to Beth-el-hem and finally to Bethlehem, where another "son of God" was born. The word means *house of bread*, but not earthly bread, cosmic bread,

---

[161] "Brahma and Saraiswati," *Leventy Leven: A Trip Around the World*, leventyleven.com, 14 Sept. 2013, web, 26 June 2014.

[162] Murdock, *Did Moses Exist?* 374.

[163] Graham, 125.

[164] Graham, 127.

[165] Graham, 133.

the substance of the earth.[166] [Bethlehem was thus in heaven as the virgin, or Virgo.[167]]

While today's Jewish scholars admit that "Adam, Cain and Noah belong in the realm of mythology," they teach that, beginning with Abraham, this mythological story becomes historical.[168] However, Abraham's birth story, according to Jewish legend, is reminiscent of that of Jesus. The star of Abraham ran across the sky and ate up four other stars, prompting Terah's friends to proclaim that the baby would be great.[169] And, quoting Graham again:

As with all the patriarchs, tales were told of Abraham so fantastic they could not apply to a mortal man. According to one, **King Nimrod, like Herod, learning from the stars that a child would be born that would dethrone him, commanded all male children to be killed as soon as born. So when Abram was born his father Terah substituted a slave woman's child for his own and thus saved Abram.** Another says that his mother Amitlai bore him in a cave, and that the light of his face lit up the whole interior. There she left him for ten days in which the angel Gabriel fed him milk from his little finger. On returning his mother found no infant but a grown man. She did not recognize him, but he recognized her. Now Nimrod on hearing of this wonder child sent soldiers to kidnap him but God blinded them with a cloud of darkness. This so frightened Nimrod he fled to the land of Babel.[170]

All the stories about Abraham didn't make it into the Bible (although chapter 8 of the *Book of Jasher*, referred to in Joshua 10:13 and 2 Samuel 1:18, relates the tale about his being hidden from the king and having a servant's child offered to the king in his place[171]). Around 400 BCE someone gathered together excerpts from all the writings available and "inserted them as he saw fit, sometimes a whole chapter, sometimes but a single verse."[172]

Moses the Man

Moses, the great biblical lawgiver, is one of the most prominent men in the Bible. But was he real or was his story taken from other legends?

When Moses was born, the Egyptian Pharaoh was killing Hebrew boys in an attempt to thin out the Israelites (Ex. 1). We have no Egyptian record of either this slaughter or the later deaths of the firstborn of Egypt (Ex. 11:5-12). The meaning of the tale of the Jews' sojourn in Egypt is that when humans go down into the earth (Egypt), they come back up, or return to their source—their land of Canaan or first home.[173] Nevertheless, as

---

[166] Graham, 135.
[167] "Real Proof that Jesus was NOT real," maythetruthbeknown, youtube.com, 28 May 2008, web, 10 Mar. 2015.
[168] Graham, 110.
[169] Doane, XIII.
[170] Graham, 110.
[171] *The Book of Jasher*, tr. from Hebrew to English, 1840 (Salt Lake City: J. H. Parry & Company, 1887), Ch. 8.
[172] Graham, 111.
[173] Graham, 144.

the story goes, Moses' mother hid him from Pharaoh by placing him in a basket and setting him adrift on the river. Pharaoh's daughter found Moses and raised him as her own (Ex. 2:1-10).

This is a sweet story, but is it original? No, it is not. **Some aspects of Moses' story were taken from the myth of the Akkadian king Sargon the Great, who reigned in Mesopotamia from 2334 to 2279 BCE. Sargon was supposedly set adrift in a basket on the Euphrates, as Moses was on the Nile**, and, again as with Moses, the reason was in order to avoid infanticide.[174] Dr. George Smith, British Assyriologist, wrote:

> In the palace of Sennacherib at Kouyunjik I found another fragment of the curious history of Sargon... This text relates, that Sargon, an early Babylonian monarch, was born of royal parents, but concealed by his mother, who placed him on the Euphrates in an ark of rushes, coated with bitumen, like that in which the mother of Moses hid her child, see Exodus ii. Sargon was discovered by a man named Akki, a water-carrier, who adopted him as his son, and he afterwards became king of Babylonia.... The date of Sargon, who may be termed the Babylonian Moses, was in the sixteenth century B.C. or perhaps earlier.[175]

Barbara Walker added:

> The Moses tale was originally that of an Egyptian hero, Ra-Harakhti, the reborn sun god of Canopus, whose life story was copied by biblical scholars. The same story was told of the sun hero fathered by Apollo on the virgin Creusa; of Sargon, king of Akkad in 2242 BC; and of the mythological twin founders of Rome, among many other baby heroes set adrift in rush baskets. It was a common theme.[176]

The same story is told of Osiris of Egypt. He was put in a coffin and placed in the Nile, and his own mother rescued him. Perseus, Greek god, was also placed in a chest and put into the sea, and found and taken care of by Dictys. A similar story is written of the Persian Mithra and the Greek Alexander.[177] As Walker noted, this same fable was reported regarding Romulus and Remus (the twins who founded Rome), and infant killings appear in the stories of Oedipus, Perseus, and Zeus,[178] as well as Nimrod, Jason, Krishna and Mordred.[179] The Indian virgin-born hero Karna was said to have been laid by his mother in a "reed boat on a river, to be discovered by others."[180] In Egypt Herut attempted to kill the god Horus; in Greece, Python tried to kill Apollo, but his mother

---

[174] Joshua J. Mark, "Sargon of Akkad," *Ancient History Encyclopedia*, ancient.eu.com, 2 Sept. 2009, web, 6 June 2014.

[175] George Smith, *Site of Nineveh* (New York: Scribner, Armstrong & Co., 1876), 224-225. See also Joseph and Murdock, 81.

[176] Barbara G. Walker, *The Woman's Dictionary of Symbols and Sacred Objects* (San Francisco: HarperOne, 1988), 441. See also Joseph and Murdock, 82.

[177] Graham, 148.

[178] Murdock, *Did Moses Exist?* 196.

[179] Walker, *The Woman's Encyclopedia of Myths and Secrets*, 435. See also Murdock, *Did Moses Exist?* 196.

[180] Murdock, *Did Moses Exist?* 254. See also: George Smith, *Assyrian Discoveries: An Account of Explorations and Discoveries on the Site of Nineveh, During 1873 and 1874* (London: Sampson Low, Marston, Low and Searle, 1875), 224-225.

Dioné "fled into the wilderness" (Rev. 12:6); in India Kansa tried to kill Krishna, but a "heavenly voice" warned Krishna's earthly father to fly the child across the River Jumna, which he did while Kansa sent out a message to kill all the infants in the area;[181] and when Cronus endeavored to kill Jupiter, he "was saved by being wrapped up in rags . . . and cared for by Amalthea in the hills, wilderness."[182] Many myths involve tales about the slaughter of infants, as occurred at the birth of not only Moses but also of Jesus (Heb. 11:23, Mt. 2:13). According to Murdock, "infants" represented stars that the evil night, or "prince of darkness," attempted to destroy when he fought the great sun god."[183] Graham, however, wrote that this represented an attempt to devour "the young in the egg."[184] Whatever the symbolism may be, as Doane noted, "When a marvellous occurrence is said to have happened *everywhere*, we may feel sure that it never happened anywhere."[185]

Moses has been compared to other gods as well, specifically the Greek god Dionysus/Bacchus in that Moses was, like Dionysus, "Taught by the twofold tablet of God's law."[186] Dionysus has been pictured holding two stone tables engraved with law.[187] Both Voltaire and Dutch theologian Gerhard Johann Voss/Vossius (1577-1649) compared Moses to Dionysus, and so did Pierre Daniel Huet, Bishop of Avranches (1630-1721). Murdock wrote:

> Another commentator was French novelist Charles-Antoine-Guillaume Pigault-Lebrun or "Le Brun" (1753-1835), who in his *Doubts of Infidels* remarked: The history of Moses is copied from the history of Bacchus, who was called Mises by the Egyptians, instead of Moses. Bacchus was born in Egypt; so was Moses... Bacchus passed through the Red Sea on dry ground; so did Moses.
>
> Bacchus was a lawgiver; so was Moses. Bacchus was picked up in a box that floated on the water; so was Moses.... Bacchus by striking a rock made wine gush forth... Bacchus was worshipped...in Egypt, Phenicia, Syria, Arabia, Asia and Greece, before Abraham's day.[188]

While some would claim that Dionysus was copied from Moses, the truth is that **Dionysus appeared in history centuries before Moses appeared**.[189]

Moses the God

Moses, like Abraham, may have actually *been* a god before he became a man. Dr. Robert Taylor wrote in *The Diegesis*:

---

[181] Joguth Gunder Changooly, *Life and Religion of the Hindoos with a Sketch of My Life and Experience* (Boston: Crosby, Nichols, Lee and Company, 1860), 134. See also: Doane, XVIII; and Bennett, 100.

[182] Graham, 310, 377.

[183] Murdock, *Did Moses Exist?* 196.

[184] Graham, 310.

[185] Doane, XVIII.

[186] Eusebius, *Praeparatio Evangelica* (*Preparation for the Gospel*), Vol. 15, tr. E. H. Gifford (Oxonii: Typographeo Academico/H. Frowde, 2003), 15.720. See also Murdock, *Did Moses Exist?* 288.

[187] Graham, 178.

[188] D. M. Murdock, *The Gospel According to Acharya S.* (Seattle: Stellar House Publishing, 2009), 72. See also Joseph and Murdock, 83.

[189] Murdock, *Did Moses Exist?* 356.

In the ancient Orphic verses sung in the orgies of Bacchus, as celebrated through Egypt, Phoenicia, Syria, Arabia, Asia Minor, Greece, and ultimately in Italy, it was related that God, who had been born in Arabia, was picked up in a box that floated on the water, and took his name Mises, in signification of his having been "saved from the water," and Bimater, from his having had two mothers; that is, one by nature, and another who had adopted him [Jesus had two *fathers*]. He had a <u>rod with which he performed miracles, and which he could change into a serpent at pleasure</u>. He passed the Red Sea dry-shod, at the head of his army. He <u>divided the waters</u> of the rivers Orontes and Hydraspus, by the touch of his rod, and passed through them dry-shod. By the same mighty wand, he <u>drew water from the rock</u>, and wherever he marched, the <u>land flowed with wine, milk, and honey</u>.[190]

Like Moses, Krishna and Poseidon smote a rock to bring forth water,[191] while Dionysus struck the ground for water.[192] From Voltaire we find this regarding Bacchus/Dionysus:

The ancient poets have placed the birth of Bacchus in Egypt; he is exposed on the Nile and it is from that event that he is named Mises by the first Orpheus, which, in Egyptian, signifies "saved from the waters"... He is brought up near a mountain of Arabia called Nisa, which is believed to be Mount Sinai. <u>It is pretended that a goddess ordered him to go and destroy a barbarous nation and that he passed through the Red Sea on foot, with a multitude of men, women, and children</u>. Another time the river Orontes suspended its waters right and left to let him pass, and the Hydaspes did the same. He <u>commanded the sun to stand still</u> [like Joshua, Josh. 10:12]; two luminous rays proceeded from his head. He made a fountain of wine spout up by striking the ground with his thyrsus, and <u>engraved his laws on two tables of marble</u>. He wanted only to have afflicted Egypt with ten plagues, to be the perfect copy of Moses.[193]

Interestingly, the numerical number for the name Moses is 345 while that of Jehovah is 543; therefore, Moses is simply the reverse of God. Also, "Jehovah reversed is Satan, say the Kabbalists. And to carry it further: 543 plus 345, or **888**, is the Gnostic number of Jesus Christ, who, with name and title, is both."[194] This would be why the sin was placed on Jesus. The soul that sins, dies (Ezek. 18:4, 20). Jesus was simply the Adam (sinner) of Genesis, finally dying for the sin. Of course, as the Christ, he rose a victor, and the story had a happy ending. (See my book *We Are Emmanuel: How Man Became God*.)

---

[190] Robert Taylor, PhD, *The Diegesus; Being a Discovery of the Origin, Evidences, and Early History of Christianity, Never Yet Before or Elsewhere So Fully and Faithfully Set Forth* (London: W. Dugdale, 1845), 190-191. See also: Dameron, 93; and Doane, VI.

[191] Murdock, *Did Moses Exist?* 239. See also James Tod, *Annals and Antiquities of Rajasthan, or The Central and Western Rajput States of India*, Vol. 2, 1204-1205; and *Herodotus*, tr. A. D. Godley (Cambridge, MA: Harvard University Press, 1920), Vol. 8, 55.

[192] Pausanias, *Description of Greece*, tr. W. H. S. Jones, et al. (New York: G. P. Putnam's Sons, 1926), 4.36.7. See also Murdock, *Did Moses Exist?* 306.

[193] Murdock, *The Gospel According to Acharya S.*, 71-72.

[194] Graham, 154.

Moses the Lawgiver

Moses was not, as has been shown, the only, or even first, lawgiver in mythological history. According to Acharya S (D. M. Murdock), the Indian lawgiver was Manou, the Syrian Mises (who, again, was taken from a floating basket, whose law was written on two stone slabs, who performed miracles using a rod,[195] and who had horns like Moses[196]), and the Cretan was Minos (who received his law on Mount Dicta[197]).[198] Also in Egypt was Mneves, who was given law by Hermes; and Zoroaster said the Good Spirit gave him the law,[199] called *Zend Avesta* (*Book of the Law,* or *Living Word*[200]), on a mountain, with accompanying thunder and lightning.[201] Diodorus, who lived in the first century BCE,[202] wrote:

> After the establishment of settled life in Egypt in early times. . . the first, they say, to persuade the multitudes to use written laws was Mneves, a man not only great of soul but also in his life the most public spirited of all lawgivers whose names are recorded. According to the tradition he claimed that Hermes had given the laws to him, with the assurance that they would be the cause of great blessings, just as among the Greeks, they say, Minos did in Crete and Lycurgus among the Lacedaemonians, the former saying that he received his laws from Zeus and the latter his from Apollo. Also among several other peoples tradition says that this kind of a device was used and was the cause of much good to such as believed it. Thus it is recorded that among the Arians Zathraustes claimed that the Good Spirit Ahura Mazda gave him his laws, among the people known as the Getae who represent themselves to be immortal Zalmoxis asserted the same of their common goddess Hestia, and among the Jews Moyses referred his laws to the god **who is invoked as Iao.** translator's note: This pronunciation seems to reflect a Hebrew form Yahu; cp. Psalms 68. 4 "His name is Jah."[203]

Another among Allen's list of similarities between Judaeo-Christianity and previous religions is the giving of the Ten Commandments.[204] This was thought to have taken place around 1490 BCE, but Spell 125 of the Egyptian *Book of the Dead* (written around 2600 BCE[205]) proves that the Ten Commandments were not original to Moses.

Book of the Dead: I have not oppressed the members of my family.
Exodus 20:12: Honor thy father and thy mother.

---

[195] Acharya S, *The Christ Conspiracy: The Greatest Story Ever Sold* (Kempton, IL: Adventures Unlimited, 1999), 241.
[196] Graham, 147.
[197] Graham, 178.
[198] Acharya S, *The Christ Conspiracy: The Greatest Story Ever Sold*, 241.
[199] Diodorus Siculus, *The Antiquities of Egypt* (New Brunswick, NJ: Transaction Publishers, Rutgers, 1990), 1.94. See also: Murdock, *Did Moses Exist?* 253.
[200] Doane, VII.
[201] Graham, 178.
[202] "Diodorus Siculus," britannica.com, 2015, web, 16 Jan. 2015.
[203] Diodorus Siculus, *Library of History*, 1.94 (1st century BC), C. H. Oldfather, *Diodorus of Sicily, The Library of History*, Books I - ii. 34 (Loeb Classical Library #279, 1933, 1998), 319-321. See also: *Pagan Origins of the Christ Myth, Ibid.*
[204] Melloson Allen, "10 Ways the Bible Was Influenced by Other Religions."
[205] Some date this book to be closer to 1600 BCE. See Murdock, *Christ in Egypt,* 6.

Book of the Dead: I have not scorned any god.
Exodus 20:7: Thou shalt not take the name of the Lord thy God in vain.

Book of the Dead: I did not rise in the morning and expect more than was due me [for wages]. I have not encroached on the land of others.
Exodus 20:17: Thou shalt not covet.

Book of the Dead: I have not killed.
Exodus 20:13: Thou shalt not kill.

Book of the Dead: I have not fornicated. I have not polluted myself.
Exodus 20:14: Thou shalt not commit adultery.

Book of the Dead: I have not stolen.
Exodus 20:15: Thou shalt not steal.

Book of the Dead: I have committed no evil upon men. I have not brought evil in the place of right and truth.
Exodus 20:16: Thou shalt not bear false witness against thy neighbor.[206]

Those who claim we can't possibly know right from wrong without the help of a god have to accept that a god wrote the *Book of the Dead* or we *can* know right from wrong on our own. By the way, these words from the *Book of the Dead* were said upon death, or on Judgment Day; so, long before Jesus, and even before Abraham, we find people expecting to be judged for their behavior on Earth.[207]

Moses was not only not the first lawgiver but his laws, as we have shown, were not original. The Ebla texts present a "complex legal code and scapegoat rituals, preceding not only the Hebrew but also the Canaanite/Ugaritic cultural equivalents."[208] The idea of scapegoating, as the Israelites practiced (Lev. 16:6-11), through which one animal (or person) died for the good of all, was common before Moses and certainly "common centuries before Jesus's purported advent, exemplified also in the stories of Prometheus and Persephone."[209] In fact, the first King of Vermaland, a Swedish province, was burned in sacrifice to the god Odin in an attempt to end a dearth. And Aun, who was once King of Sweden, gave to Odin the blood of his nine sons in an attempt to lengthen his own life. According to Eusebius of Caesarea (260/265–339/340 CE), who is known as the "Father of Church History,"[210] the Phoenicians yearly sacrificed their children to Saturn. And, of course, we know that the Israelites offered their offspring to Molech (Lev. 20:2-5). As Doane wrote, the ancients "considered the gods as being like themselves. They loved and they hated; they were proud and revengeful; they were, in fact, savages like themselves."[211] Therefore, the offering up of a child to a deity seemed like a good idea.

---

[206] *The Coming Into Day* (*Book of the Dead*), "Chapter 125: The Judgement of the Dead," richard-hooker.com, 1997, web, 31 Dec. 2014 <http://richard-hooker.com/sites/worldcultures/EGYPT/BOD125.HTM>.
[207] Wright, 318.
[208] Murdock, *Did Moses Exist?* 264.
[209] Murdock, *Did Moses Exist?* 282.
[210] "Eusebius," wikipedia.org, 12 Jan. 2015, web, 25 Jan. 2015.
[211] Doane, IV.

(And a *god* who would offer his own son would seem to be the greatest god of all.) Regarding the idea of a scapegoat, Murdock wrote the following:

> These biblical beasts were sacrificed during the "feast of the lamb" or Passover (Exod 12) on the 14th day of the first month, equivalent to the vernal equinox. . . in astrology, the ram is equivalent to Aries, representing the precessional age of the era as well as the month in which spring transitions from winter.[212]

Walker stated that the "stone tablets of law supposedly given to Moses were copied from the Canaanite god Baael-Berith [Jdg 8:33], 'God of the Covenant.'"[213] And Murdock noted: "There is little reason to suppose that the Israelite law truly was handed down supernaturally by Yahweh to a historical Moses, rather than representing a continuation of the very old code."[214]

No Archaeological Records

Ze'ev Herzog wrote:

> Following 70 years of intensive excavations in the Land of Israel, archaeologists have found out: The patriarchs' acts are legendary, the Israelites did not sojourn in Egypt or make an exodus, they did not conquer the land. Neither is there any mention of the empire of David and Solomon, nor of the source of belief in the God of Israel. These facts have been known for years. . .

> This is what archaeologists have learned from their excavations in the Land of Israel: the Israelites were never in Egypt, did not wander in the desert, did not conquer the land in a military campaign and did not pass it on to the 12 tribes of Israel. Perhaps even harder to swallow is the fact that the united monarchy of David and Solomon . . . was at most a small tribal kingdom. And it will come as an unpleasant shock to many that the God of Israel, Jehovah, had a female consort and that the early Israelite religion adopted monotheism only in the waning period of the monarchy and not at Mount Sinai. Most of those who are engaged in scientific work in the interlocking spheres of the Bible, archaeology and the history of the Jewish people - and who once went into the field looking for proof to corroborate the Bible story - now agree that the historic events relating to the stages of the Jewish people's emergence are radically different from what that story tells. . .

> The many Egyptian documents that we have make no mention of the Israelites' presence in Egypt and are also silent about the events of the exodus. . . Most historians today agree that at best, the stay in Egypt and the exodous occurred in a few families and that their private story was expanded and "nationalized" to fit the needs of theological ideology. . .

---

[212] Murdock, *Did Moses Exist?* 347. See also: Charles François Dupuis, *The Origin of All Religious Worship* (New Orleans, 1872), 174.

[213] Walker, *The Woman's Encyclopedia of Myths and Secrets*, 677. See also: Murdock, *Did Moses Exist?* 264.

[214] Murdock, *Did Moses Exist?* 264.

Biblical scholars suggested a quarter of a century ago that the conquest stories be viewed as etiological legends and no more. But as more and more sites were uncovered and it emerged that the places in question died out or were simply abandoned at different times, the conclusion was bolstered that there is no factual basis for the biblical story about the conquest by Israelite tribes in a military campaign led by Joshua. . .

The archaeological findings blatantly contradict the biblical picture: the Canaanite cities . . . were not fortified and did not have "sky-high walls." The heroism of the conquerors, the few versus the many and the assistance of the God who fought for his people are a theological reconstruction lacking any factual basis. . .

The archaeological findings dovetail well with the conclusions of the critical school of biblical scholarship. David and Solomon were the rulers of tribal kingdoms that controlled small areas: the former in Hebron and the latter in Jerusalem. Concurrently, a separate kingdom began to form in the Samaria hills, which finds expression in the stories about Saul's kingdom. Israel and Judea were from the outset two separate, independent kingdoms, and at times were in an adversarial relationship. Thus, the great united monarchy is an imaginary historiosophic creation, which was composed during the period of the Kingdom of Judea at the earliest. Perhaps the most decisive proof of this is the fact that we do not know the name of this kingdom.[215]

Jewish writer Josh Mintz agrees. He wrote:

The reality is that there is no evidence whatsoever that the Jews were ever enslaved in Egypt. Yes, there's the story contained within the bible itself, but that's not a remotely historically admissible source. I'm talking about real proof; archeological evidence, state records and primary sources. Of these, nothing exists. . .

So, as we come to Passover . . . let us enjoy our Seder and read the story by all means, but also remind those . . . who may forget that it is just a metaphor.[216]

Certainly some scholars disagree with regard to archaeological findings. But as Tremper Longman III and Raymond B. Dillard, in their book *An Introduction to the Old Testament*, said, "it is much too simplistic to expect from archaeology either an independent verification of biblical claims or a certain scientific refutation of them."[217] In other words, as much as Longman and Dillard would like it to be so, archaeology has not proven Judaism (or Christianity) to be true.

---

[215] Ze'ev Herzog, "Deconstructing the walls of Jericho."
[216] Josh Mintz, "Were Jews ever really slaves in Egypt, or is Passover a myth?" *Jewish World Blogger*, 26 Mar. 2012, web, 23 Mar. 2015; reprinted on haaretz.com, 24 March 2015 (Nisan 4, 5775).
[217] Tremper Longman III and Raymond B. Dillard, *An Introduction to the Old Testament*, 2nd ed. (Grand Rapids, MI: Zondervan, 2006), 24.

No Hebrew History

We have no real Hebrew history from the time period relative to our religious heritage. And what we do have can't be trusted. Regarding Jewish history, Graham wrote:

Their political history began with the Maccabees, and their system was a commonwealth. One objective clue to the political antiquity of any race is its coins, and there are no Jewish coins prior to the Maccabean period, and even those they had are of Greek imprint. The first of these are of the year 138 B.C., the time of Simon the Maccabee. Another political and national clue is the calendar, and the Jews had none; they used the Babylonian. Their present calendar 5,700 plus has no basis in fact. It is based on the absurd date of creation 3760 B.C. . .

The Maccabean period is Jewish history the rest is mythology historized. Save for its peculiarly Jewish theology and exaggeration, the Book of the Maccabees is historical, and this the compilers of the canon threw out as "uninspired." And what was the inspiration of the inspired? The unlimited license of mythology. This our saints mistook for the divinely revealed truth and rejected the factual and historical; they weren't sufficiently incredible for a supernatural religion. Only the tall tales of mythology can supply this foundation. . .

The world was not created by this God in six days or a million. There was no Garden of Eden or talking snake. There was no first man, Adam, or woman, Eve. They did not commit a moral sin and so we are not under condemnation for it. They did not fall from grace and so there is no need of redemption. Cain and Abel were not their sons. There was no Deluge and no Noah. There was no racial Father, Abraham, nor was he promised Palestine. The Jews never were in bondage in Egypt, nor did Moses lead them out. They did not walk through the Red Sea, nor did they conquer Canaan. There was no David or Solomon or even a wondrous temple.[218]

Israel Finkelstein and Neil Asher Silberman also claimed that no mass exodus from Egypt occurred.[219] In speaking of this, Robert Wright noted that

some biblical historians now doubt that Moses even existed, and virtually none now believe that the biblical accounts of Moses are reliable. These stories were written down centuries after the events they describe, and were edited later still, sometimes by monotheists who presumably wanted to suffuse their theology with august authority.[220]

This really shouldn't surprise us as even the Bible leaves us doubting that its stories are true. The best we can hope for is that the book might be a metaphor, which, of course,

---

[218] Graham, 234-235.

[219] Israel Finkelstein and Neil Asher Silberman, *The Bible Unearthed* (Simon and Schuster/Touchstone, 2002). See also: Wright, 108-109.

[220] Wright, 109.

I believe to be the truth. The book of Psalms indicates that nearly all of the stories handed down from old are mere parables. Psalm 78:2-3 (WEB) states: "I will open my mouth in a **parable**. I will utter **dark sayings of old**, Which <u>we have heard and known</u>, And our <u>fathers have told us</u>." This psalm goes on to describe what should be considered as a "parable" or "dark sayings": "wondrous works," a "testimony in Jacob," and a "law in Israel" (v. 5); "<u>marvelous things in the sight of their fathers, In the land of Egypt</u>" (v. 12); Yahweh "<u>split the sea</u>, and caused them to pass through; He <u>made the waters stand as a heap</u>" (v. 13); "In the daytime he also <u>led them with a cloud</u>, And <u>all night with a light of fire</u>" (v. 14); he "<u>split rocks</u>," "<u>gave them drink</u>," and "<u>brought streams also out of the rock</u>" (vv. 15-16); he "<u>rained down manna on them to eat</u>" (v. 24); when angry he "struck down the young men of Israel" (v. 31); he "<u>Turned their rivers into blood</u>" (v. 44); he sent "swarms of flies" and frogs (v. 45); he "destroyed their vines with hail" (v. 47); he sent a "band of angels of evil" (v. 49); he "<u>struck all the firstborn in Egypt</u>" (v. 51); he <u>led the Israelites safely</u> while the sea "<u>overwhelmed their enemies</u>" (v. 53); he "<u>brought them to the border of his sanctuary, To this mountain</u>" (v. 54); he "<u>drove out the nations before them</u>" and "<u>Allotted them for an inheritance</u>" (v. 55); he "gave his people over to the sword" and was angry with them (v. 62); "Fire devoured their young men; Their virgins had no wedding song" (v. 63); the "priests fell by the sword" (v. 64); he "<u>chose the tribe of Judah, Mount Zion which he loved</u>" (v. 68); "He built his sanctuary like the heights, Like the earth which he has established forever" (v. 69); he "<u>chose David his servant</u>, And took him from the sheepfolds" (v. 70); he brought David "<u>to be the shepherd of Jacob, his people, And Israel, his inheritance</u>" (v. 71).

All of the above is a parable, or "dark sayings of old." The writer didn't attempt to proclaim the truthfulness of the stories. He understood, as should we, that Israel's stories are simply that—Israel's stories. According to the New Testament, the entire Old Testament is a mere type or shadow (Col. 1:27, 2:17; Heb. 8:5, 10:1). If the Old Testament is not literal, and if no fall of man actually occurred, then any literal plan in the New Testament to reverse the fall is unnecessary. If the Hebrew history is not believable, then the whole biblical story falls apart. And when we look at how the New Testament came to be, the knowledge we acquire will not inspire us to believe.

CHAPTER FOUR
MAKING NEW SAYINGS

When it comes to Mohammed flying on a winged horse to visit the heavenly realms, or the golden plates that Joseph Smith supposedly translated into the Book of Mormon, or Scientologists' claim that an intergalactic emperor named Xenu placed people in a volcano and blew them up, do you require sufficient evidence in order to believe them? Why are your superstitious claims exempt from this same requirement?

John W. Loftus

"The t'ings dat yo' li'ble/To read in de Bible/It ain't necessarily so."[221]

Many people are under the mistaken impression that the Old Testament was written and closed at the writing of Malachi and then Jesus came along and fulfilled it all, at which point his story was written within a few years and all prophecy ceased to be written or considered. That's not the case, however, as the Old Testament canon was not closed, as stated earlier, until the tenth century CE, long after Jesus lived on the earth. This means that it could be added to, altered, rearranged, made up, or, perhaps, even if the *Pentateuch* was not based on Plato's Laws as suggested previously, it might have been changed drastically to reflect Plato's thinking.[222] The New Testament likewise was not canonized early on but only at the Council of Rome in 382 CE (if even then). This was accomplished by the authority of the Catholic Church, meaning that the document came to us through and by the **Catholic Church. It is they who determined truth for the Christian world.** And, again, this document could be added to up to that point (or even longer if the Church chose to do so); therefore, any prophecies Jesus needed to fulfill regarding Israel could be added afterwards.[223] How then did the New Testament, with its miracles and fantastic story of a god who died for the world, come to us?

Unknown Authors

The Church admits that the authors of the Gospels are unknown. The first few centuries of the common era produced tons of fables and myths, and, in order to put together a somewhat coherent and consistent religious document, the various manuscripts had to be perused and a determination made as to whether they were worthy of inclusion in the holy book. Walter Cassels wrote:

No period in the history of the world ever produced so many spurious works as the first two or three centuries of our era. The name of every Apostle, or Christian teacher, not excepting that of the great Master himself, was freely

---

[221] George and Ira Gershwin, "It Ain't Necessarily So," 1935; performed by Louis Armstrong and Ella Fitzgerald in the opera "Porgy & Bess" (Polygram Records, 1957).
[222] Murdock, *Did Moses Exist?* 269.
[223] Alan Watts, MA, "Jesus: His Religion or the Religion About Him?" lecture transcribed by Scott Lahteine, 2004, *Phenomenology . . . with Thinkyhead*, thinkyhead.blogspot.com, 16 Aug. 2012, web, 3 Sept. 2014.

attached to every description of religious forgery. False gospels, epistles, acts, martyrologies, were unscrupulously circulated.[224]

Tony Bushby noted that the **"Church maintains that 'the titles of our Gospels were not intended to indicate authorship', adding that 'the headings . . . were affixed to them.'"**[225] As Jerome Neyrey noted: "The bottom line is we really don't know for sure who wrote the Gospels."[226]

Dr. Craig Lyons wrote:

Justin Martyr, writing in the middle of the second century in Rome, never mentions *Matthew, Mark, Luke* or *John* in his entire extant works and yet just a generation later in the same part of the world Irenaeus states that there are only four gospels and the canon is closed. Celsus, writing c. 170 CE, knows nothing about *Matthew, Mark, Luke* or *John*.[227]

The fact that the first mention and quote by a Christian writer from either the Gospel of Mark, Matthew, Luke, or John cannot be found before 180 C.E. should speak loud to us about the late date for the Four Canonical Gospels that are touted by Roman tradition today to have been written "early."[228]

The Gospels under the names of these men seem to have magically appeared sometime near the end of the second century. As for the Epistles, The *Encyclopedia Biblica* states:

With respect to the Canonical Pauline Epistles, none of them are by Paul. They are all, without distinction, pseudographia (false writings). The group (ten epistles) bears obvious marks of a certain unity, of having originated in one circle, at one time, in one environment, but not of unity of authorship.[229]

Many early Christian writers—Clement of Rome, Hermas, Polycarp (108 CE), Ignatius (107 CE), and Barnabas—don't mention the Gospel writers.[230] The *Shepherd of Hermas* cites nothing from the Gospels; and the *Epistle of Barnabas* (c. 130 CE) says nothing about either the four writers of the Gospels or the Gospels themselves.[231] (The

---

[224] Walter Richard Cassels, *Supernatural Religion: Introduction. Miracles. The Synoptic gospels* (Longmans, Green and Company, 1875), 460. See also: Acharya S, *Suns of God: Krishna, Buddha and Christ Unveiled* (Kempton, IL: Adventures Unlimited Press, 2004), 375.

[225] Tony Bushby, "The Forged Origins of the New Testament," March 2007, extracted from *Nexus Magazine*, Vol. 14, No. 4 (June-July 2007), nexusmagazine.com, web, 22 June 2014. See also: *Catholic Encyclopedia*, Farley ed., Vol. 1, 117; Vol. VI, 655-656.

[226] Jim Walker, "Did a historical Jesus exist? nobeliefs.com, 12 June 1997, ed. 22 Apr. 2011, web, 2 Mar. 2015. See also: Jerome Neyrey, Weston School of Theology, Cambridge, Massachusetts, "The Four Gospels," *U.S. News & World Report*, Dec. 10, 1990.

[227] Craig M. Lyons, MsD, DD, MDiv, "The Evolution of the Jesus Myth," *Bet Emet Ministries*, firstnewtestament.com, n.d., web, 4 June 2014.

[228] Craig M. Lyons, MsD, DD, MDiv, "Marcion and the Marcionites," *Bet Emet Ministries*, firstnewtestament.com, n.d., web, 4 June 2014, 5 June 2014.

[229] *Encyclopedia Biblica* III, 3625-26. See also: "Father Eusebius - Forger," Christianity-Revealed.com, jdstone.org, 2003, web, 12 Nov. 2014.

[230] Acharya S, *Suns of God*, 412.

[231] Acharya S, *Suns of God*, 412.

Sinaiticus contains three Gospels not included in modern-day Bibles: *Shepherd of Hermas*, *Missive of Barnabas*, and *Odes of Solomon*.[232]) Bronson Keeler stated that the Gospel of John "was not heard of till about the year 180 A.D."[233] In fact, the first mention of this Gospel is by Irenaeus (177-202 CE), who, based on the evidence available, was most likely its author.[234]

The Catholic Encyclopedia acknowledges that "documentary sources of knowledge about [Christianity's] earliest development are chiefly the New Testament Scriptures, the authenticity of which we must, to a great extent, take for granted."[235] The *Encyclopedia* admits, as has been stated, that "the earliest of the extant manuscripts" of the New Testament date back no further than the "middle of the fourth century AD."[236] It also confirms that the book of Luke couldn't have been written until about 200 years after the time of Jesus. This is because Luke addressed Theophilus, who was bishop of Antioch from 169 to 177 CE. The *Encyclopedia* notes that Pope Clement I (around 97 CE) didn't quote from any of the Gospels or mention the authors. No Gospel was referred to until about 185 CE, being first mentioned by Irenaeus in his Book II, Chapter XVI. This explains why **Justin Martyr, who lived around 140 CE, never quoted anything from the Gospels, apparently never hearing of them.**[237]

If these books didn't appear until after all of the apostles were dead, then the apostles didn't write them. The New Testament is completely anonymous. And, again, the oldest complete copy of the New Testament dates to the fourth century CE.[238] Samuel Butler noted: "There is . . . a reason why there were no New Testaments until the fourth century: they were not written until then."[239] That's not to say that nothing existed; however, although much had been written, there was nothing resembling any kind of canon, and people were still writing. Piero Scaruffi wrote:

> In 170 Tatian admits he was working on a new gospel that would summarize all the other ones, thereby implying that Christians were still writing and rewriting gospels based on their own assumptions and preferences, not on historical facts. Also in the second century, Clement of Alexandria admits that two versions of Mark's gospel existed but one was being suppressed because it contained two passages that should not be viewed by average Christians (both passages could be interpreted as Lazarus being Jesus' lover and his "resurrection" as being an "initiation" to some kind of sexual rite, the way most pagan "mysteries" implied a death and a rebirth). Thus, the texts were being chosen, edited and purged for the first two centuries of the Christian era.[240]

---

[232] Bushby, "The Forged Origins of the New Testament."

[233] Bronson Keeler, *A Short History of the Bible* (California: Health Research, 1965), 15. See also: Acharya S, *Suns of God*, 417.

[234] Doane, XXIII.

[235] John M. Farley, ed., *The Catholic Encyclopedia* (New York: Encyclopedia Press, Inc., 1913), Vol. III, 712.

[236] Farley (1913), Vol. VI, 656-57.

[237] Graham, 284.

[238] "Codex Sanaiticus: Experience the oldest Bible," codexsinaiticus.org, n.d., web, 9 Mar. 2014.

[239] Samuel Butler, "How Christianity Was Invented: The Truth!" beyondallreligion.net, 21 Jan. 2012, web, 13 Aug. 2014.

[240] Piero Scaruffi, "Jesus and Christianity," scaruffi.com, 2010, web, 3 Jan. 2015.

According to Gerald Massey, Origen wrote that there were several "different versions of Matthew's gospel in circulation" in the third century and that Origen attributed this "partly to the forgers of gospels."[241] Jerome, at the end of the fourth century, asserted the same thing; and of the Latin versions he said there were as many different texts as manuscripts. The copies we have access to were made by fallible men claiming no inspiration, and uninspired men determined which books to include. (Protestants removed several books that were in the Septuagint Version of the Old Testament.)[242] When the present canon appeared, it was not presented "as a novelty, but as an ancient tradition."[243] And it was presented as having been written by those who walked and talked with Jesus.

It's commonly agreed that Mark (or whoever wrote Mark) was the first to write a Gospel that is included in the New Testament. Burton L. Mack wrote:

> Before Mark there was no such story of the life of Jesus. Neither the earlier Jesus movements nor the congregations of the Christ had imagined such a portrayal of Jesus' life. It was Mark's composition that gathered together earlier traditions, used the recent history of Jerusalem to set the stage for Jesus' time, crafted the plot, spelled out the motivations, and so created the story of Jesus that was to become the gospel truth for Christianity. All the other narrative gospels would start with Mark. None would change his basic plot. And the plot would become the standard account of Christian origins for the traditional Christian imagination. . . . Mark took the many little sayings and stories of Jesus that were available to him from earlier traditions and used them to create a new image of Jesus. Then he arranged these stories to develop some themes, such as that of Jesus' power or the plot to have him killed, and he brought the story to focus on a conflict that Jesus and God had with the Jerusalem establishment.[244]

Mack went on to explain how the New Testament was pieced together.

> When the rabbis turned their backs on the Jewish scriptures in Greek translation, they left behind a large body of Jewish literature produced during the Hellenistic period. A Greek translation of the five books of Moses had been made as early as the third century B.C.E. in Alexandria. The prophets were translated into Greek sometime during the second century, and many other writings . . . continued to be written in Hebrew or Aramaic and translated into Greek during the first centuries B.C.E.-C.E. Other books . . . were composed in Greek and still considered Jewish scriptures. These are only some examples from the large body of Jewish literature thought to be unhelpful or dangerous by the early rabbis. This literature survived because Christians continued to read it. Some of these writings eventually took their places on lists that Christians made of Jewish scriptures considered helpful for public reading in the churches. When, toward the end of the fourth century

[241] Gerald Massey, *Gerald Massey's Lectures* (New York: A&B Books), No. 6.
[242] "Catholic and Protestant Bibles," cathtruth.com, n.d., web, 6 Apr. 2014.
[243] Brooke Foss Westcott, MA, *The General Survey of the History of the Canon of the New Testament During the First Four Centuries* (Cambridge: MacMillan & Co., 1855), 537. See also: Doane, XXXVIII.
[244] Burton L. Mack, *Who Wrote the New Testament? The Making of the Christian Myth* (San Francisco: HarperOne, 1996), 151-152.

C.E., manuscripts began to be produced on the order of these lists, the Christian "Old Testament" finally can be recognized. Even then, however, other Jewish scriptures continued to be read and used. The Psalms of Solomon, for instance, were still being listed with the books of the Old Testament in the ninth century Stichometry of Nicephorus, and 4 Ezra was not finally excluded from the Christian Bible until the Council of Trent in 1546. Christians thought of all these writings as their scriptures. The rabbis wanted to consign this literature to oblivion. By rejecting it, they bequeathed the legacy of Hellenistic Judaism to the Christians.

Consulting Jewish scripture had always been occasioned by some circumstance that had arisen in the course of early Christian history. If that circumstance called for a Christian revision of the epic, that is what Christians did. If it called for arguments against the Pharisees from the books of Moses, they could be found. If it called for a little help from the prophets, citations could be garnered. If it called for a Christian meditation on the Psalms, Christ hymns could be written. And if some citations from Jewish literature, such as the Testament of the Twelve Patriarchs, the Wisdom of Solomon, or the Maccabean histories, might help to make a point, these references also counted. A quick count of the references to non-canonical Jewish literature in the writings of the New Testament adds up to about 400 entries (McDonald 1989, 172-77). This means that early Christians were not dealing in sacred literature. They were involved in a new religious movement that had to construct its mythology with borrowed ingredients. They combed through the Jewish scriptures this way and that, not because they thought these texts contained the word of God, but because they were the literature of a parent culture.[245]

. . . they needed texts. And so the writing of texts in the name of some disciple or apostle became standard practice. It is for this reason as well that previously written anonymous literature, such as the New Testament gospels, were now attributed either to a disciple, as in the cases of Matthew and John, or to an associate of a disciple, such as Mark, or to an associate of Paul, as in the case of Luke. A cursory glance at the large collection of early Christian writings traditionally known as the apocryphal New Testament (Elliott 1993) and at the corpus now known as the gnostic scriptures (Layton 1987; Robinson 1988) reveals many texts purportedly written by a disciple as well as many stories about the disciples' acts, missions, and preachments. . .

This literature, most of which was written during the second, third, and fourth centuries, documents the success of the shift in early Christian mythmaking that took place at the turn of the second century. The shift produced the notion of an apostolic period, a notion that eventually made it possible for the Christian church to imagine the first chapter of early Christian "history" as the assured foundation for its institutions and offices. It also had the effect of turning the disciples into heroes and creating a model for writing subsequent Christian

---

[245] Mack, 282-283.

history as a series of exemplars of the faith. And it had the effect of concentrating authority in texts.[246]

Books written by anonymous writers at an anonymous time in history—that's what Christians base their lives on, use to judge and condemn others, build temples and statues to honor, and are willing to die for. Furthermore, they know this to be the case. It's impossible to determine who wrote the books in the Bible and when they were written, and resolving when the canon was decided upon is also a thorny issue. "Even theologians know that the Bible didn't fall from heaven, of course, and that the history of its production spans more than one thousand years."[247]

The Canon

We can't be sure exactly when the present canon was settled after all the writing was done. In fact, we don't even know when the writing stopped.

Doane wrote:

> We know when [the canon] was *not* settled. We know it was not settled in the time of the Emperor Justinian, nor in the time of Cassiodorus; that is, *not any time before the middle of the sixth century*, by any authority that was decisive and universally acknowledged; but Christian people were at liberty to judge for themselves concerning the genuineness of writings proposed to them as apostolical.[248]

According to Bushby, in 1562, "the Vatican established a special censoring office called Index Expurgatorius. Its purpose was to prohibit publication of 'erroneous passages of the early Church Fathers' that carried statements opposing modern-day doctrine."[249] Professor Edmond S. Bordeaux, in *How the Great Pan Died*, said:

> The Church ante-dated all her late works, some newly made, some revised and some counterfeited, which contained the final expression of her history . . . her technique was to make it appear that much later works written by Church writers were composed a long time earlier, so that they might become evidence of the first, second or third centuries.[250]

---

[246] Mack, 202-203.

[247] Mack, 276.

[248] Doane, XXXVIII.

[249] Bushby, "The Forged Origins of the New Testament." See also: *Index Expurgatorius Vaticanus*, R. Gibbings, ed. (Dublin, 1837); Joseph Mendham and J. Duncan, *The Literary Policy of the Church of Rome*, 2nd ed. (London, 1830, 1840); and Peter Elmsley, *The Vatican Censors*, Oxford, n.d., 328.

[250] Bushby, "The Forged Origins of the New Testament." See also: Edmond S. Bordeaux, "The Whole of Church History is Nothing but a Retroactive Fabrication," *How The Great Pan Died* [Vatican archivist] (USA: Mille Meditations, MCMLXVIII), 46.

Edwin Johnson wrote that the fourth century, in particular, was "the great age of literary forgery, the extent of which has yet to be exposed."[251] *The Catholic Encyclopedia* admits that even the "genuine Epistles were greatly interpolated to lend weight to the personal views of their authors."[252] Jerome (340-420) declared the book of Acts to be "falsely written."[253] And Loftus wrote: "No reasonable person today should believe 2nd 3rd 4th handed testimony coming from a lone part of the ancient world as we find in 4th century manuscripts written by pre-scientific superstitious people who doctored up and forged many of these texts."[254] As an example of a fabrication, Jesus told any without sin to cast the first stone at an adulteress; but it was 1,000 years before anyone commented on the story. As Michael Runyon wrote, "It appears that it was added by a scribe as a means to further define the characteristics of a fictionalized Jesus."[255]

The entire Bible was handed down through oral tradition, and the earliest documents weren't written until at least 1400 BCE.[256] It seems odd that a god would disclose his truths to prophets so they could write down every idea he wanted revealed, and yet he didn't have the foresight, power, or desire to make sure one original, perfect manuscript survived for even a few hundred years. The apostles' writings (if there were any apostles with writings) didn't manage to last long enough for many to even read them. **Not one document—not a word or even a jot or tittle—written by an inspired apostle survived**. The most important inspiration of all time, if it really ever existed, vanished immediately. Yet Christians are supposed to trust that Yahweh can take care of them and has a plan for their lives that he's watching over meticulously. I have to say, the **loss of the Christian scriptures doesn't inspire great confidence in this god's ability to watch over anyone or anything**. Surely an intelligent divine being would not present his truths in such a slipshod manner and then not even bother to protect them for future generations. (And let's not even talk about how we can't get two Christians in the same room who can agree on what the Bible actually says about much of anything.)

Protestant Christians in particular should consider the fact that the manuscripts they prize dearly and claim to be inerrant were handed down to them by the hands of Jews and Catholics, neither of whose religious beliefs they hold in high regard and both of whom feel free to add or subtract to the "writings." Those in the know among Jews and Catholics, of course, are aware of where their texts originated; since they wrote them in the first place, they naturally feel perfectly comfortable adding to them. St. Hilary (c. 300-c. 368) admitted: **"The error of others compels us to err in daring to embody in human terms truths which ought to be hidden in the silent veneration of the heart."**[257] Jim Walker noted:

[251] Edwin Johnson, *Antiqua Mater: A Study of Christian Origins* (London: Trubner & Co., Ludgate Hill; Edinburgh and London: Ballantine Press, 1887), 251.

[252] *Catholic Encyclopedia*, Farley ed., Vol. VII, 645.

[253] "The Letters of Jerome," *Library of the Fathers*, Oxford Movement, 1833-45, Vol. 5, 445.

[254] John W. Loftus, "Why I Am An Atheist," *Debunking Christianity*, debunkingchristianity.blogspot.com, 5 June 2013, web, 16 June 2014.

[255] Michael Runyon, "How I Figured Out Christianity Is Not Real," exchristian.net, 11 Nov. 2013, web, 29 Dec. 2014.

[256] "When was the Bible written?" *Biblica: Transforming lives through God's Word*, biblica.com, 26 Dec. 2013, web, 6 Apr. 2014.

[257] St. Hilary of Poitiers, *De Trinitate*, Book 2, Paragraph 2, Line 6.

In the 5th century, John Chrysostom in his "Treatise on the Priesthood, Book 1," wrote, "And <u>often it is necessary to deceive, and to do the greatest benefits by means of this device</u>, whereas he who has gone by a straight course has done great mischief to the person whom he has not deceived." . . .

Martin Luther opined: "<u>What harm would it do, if a man told a good strong lie for the sake of the good and for the Christian church</u> … a lie out of necessity, a useful lie, a helpful lie, such lies would not be against God, he would accept them." [The apostle Paul agreed: Romans 3:7 <u>For if the truth of God hath more abounded through my lie unto his glory; why yet am I also judged as a sinner?</u>]

With such admission to accepting lies, the burning of heretical texts, Bible errors and alterations, how could any honest scholar take any book from the New Testament as absolute, much less using extraneous texts that support a Church's intransigent and biased position, as reliable evidence?[258]

According to *The Catholic Encyclopedia*,

The idea of a complete and clear-cut canon of the New Testament existing from the beginning, that is from Apostolic times, has no foundation in history. The Canon of the New Testament, like that of the Old, is the result of a development, of a process at once stimulated by disputes with doubters, both within and without the Church, and retarded by certain obscurities and natural hesitations, and which did not reach its final term until the dogmatic definition of the Tridentine Council.[259]

The Tridentine Council took place at Trent between 1545 and 1563.[260] This was the sixteenth century and Christians were still trying to determine God's word. What if we still don't have it all? What if there really is a 3 Corinthians or a letter to the Laodiceans, and what if they contain information necessary to our salvation (Col. 4:16)? Actually, there *is* a 3 Corinthians, and the Syriac Orthodox Church accepts it as canonical.[261] We also have, as noted earlier, the *Book of Jasher* (Josh. 10:13, 2 Sam.1:18), but we ignore it because it didn't make it into the Catholic or Protestant canon.[262]

With all the writings available at the time, and even today, it would be impossible for uninspired men to know which documents to include in the "true" New Testament and which to cast aside. (People still argue about which books are genuine.) While Christians may say "God guided the men who chose the books of the Bible," that's just a feeble wish. **If Yahweh didn't watch over the original documents' preservation, why in the world would he guide these men to choose the correct copies?** It can be proven, and I have given some evidence regarding this previously, that stories and concepts in the Bible have been copied from earlier writings. After "validating the fabricated nature of the New

---

[258] Jim Walker, "Did a historical Jesus exist?"
[259] "Canon of the New Testament," *Catholic Encyclopedia* (New York: Robert Appleton Company, 1913).
[260] "Council of Trent," wikipedia.org, 25 Dec. 2014, web, 10 Jan. 2015.
[261] "Third Epistle to the Corinthians," wikipedia.org., 16 Sept. 2013, web, 20 Nov. 2014.
[262] "Book of Jasher (Pseudo-Jasher)," wikipedia.org, 11 Oct. 2014, web, 22 Jan. 2015.

Testament,"[263] Dr. Constantin von Tischendorf (1815-1874), a German Bible scholar and professor of theology, wrote that "it seems that the personage of Jesus Christ was made narrator for many religions."[264] Bushby wrote:

> This explains how narratives from the ancient Indian epic, the Mahabharata, appear verbatim in the Gospels today (e.g., Matt. 1:25, 2:11, 8:1-4, 9:1-8, 9:18-26), and why passages from the Phenomena of the Greek statesman Aratus of Sicyon (271-213 BC) are in the New Testament.
>
> Extracts from the Hymn to Zeus, written by Greek philosopher Cleanthes (c. 331-232 BC), are also found in the Gospels, as are 207 words from the Thais of Menander (c. 343-291), one of the "seven wise men" of Greece. Quotes from the semi-legendary Greek poet Epimenides (7th or 6th century BC) are applied to the lips of Jesus Christ, and seven passages from the curious Ode of Jupiter (c. 150 BC; author unknown) are reprinted in the New Testament.[265]

When determining the canon, the first council voted the books of Acts and Revelation out, the next (363 CE [Council of Laodicea]) voted them in, and yet another (406 CE) voted them, along with some others, out again.[266] **While these books were out, nobody knew Acts and Revelation were inspired by God.** They were looked at the way Christians today look at *The Gospel According to Mary Magdalene.*

During twenty-four different councils several books at a time were voted out, whole chapters were omitted, and insertions were made "till it may now be assumed to be thoroughly changed... altered and amended by fifty translations and a hundred and fifty thousand alterations... and is still believed by millions to be the same old book."[267] However, according to Kurt Eichenwald,

> the beliefs that became part of Christian orthodoxy were pushed into it by the Holy Roman Empire. By the fifth century, the political and theological councils voted on which of the many Gospels in circulation were to make up the New Testament. With the power of Rome behind them, the practitioners of this proclaimed orthodoxy wiped out other sects and tried to destroy every copy of their Gospels and other writings.[268]

Unknown Jesus

We don't know who wrote the New Testament or when, and we also don't know for sure that its main character ever actually lived. D. M. Murdock wrote that nobody outside the New Testament writings seems to have known Jesus. This is odd for a man who was supposedly a legend in his own time (Mt. 9:31).

---

[263] Bushby, "The Forged Origins of the New Testament."

[264] Bushby, "The Forged Origins of the New Testament."

[265] Bushby, "The Forged Origins of the New Testament."

[266] Walker, *Man Made God*, 108. See also: Kersey Graves, *Bible of Bibles* (Kila, MT: Kessinger Publishing), 361-362, 398.

[267] Walker, *Man Made God*, 108. See also: Graves, *Bible of Bibles*, 361-362, 398.

[268] Kurt Eichenwald, "The Bible: So Misunderstood, It's a Sin," newsweek.com, 23 Dec. 2014, web, 10 Jan. 2015.

Philo of Alexandria (20 BCE-50 CE), Jewish historian and philosopher, lived in or near Jerusalem when Jesus' miraculous birth and the massacre of little children occurred, yet he never mentioned Jesus.[269] Plutarch (c. 46 to c. 120 CE) also never said anything about Jesus, nor did Jesus' contemporary Pliny the Elder (22 to 79 CE) speak of him. Pliny the Younger (62-110 CE) mentioned Christians (Chrestians), but the only Christ he knew was as the object of Christian worship. The historian Tacitus wrote when the New Testament was supposedly written; and, like Pliny the Younger, had "nothing but contempt" for the Christians he mentioned. Tacitus (64 CE) presumably wrote:

> Nero looked around for a scapegoat, and inflicted the most fiendish tortures on a group of persons already hated for their crimes. This was the sect known as Christians. Their founder, one Chrestus, had been put to death by the procurator, Pontius Pilate in the reign of Tiberius. This checked the abominable superstition for a while, but it broke out again and spread, not merely through Judea, where it originated, but even to Rome itself, the great reservoir and collecting ground for every kind of depravity and filth. Those who confessed to being Christians were at once arrested, but on their testimony a great crowd of people were convicted, not so much on the charge of arson, but of hatred of the entire human race.[270]

This passage from Tacitus, however, is suspect. John G. Jackson wrote: "Eusebius made a list of Jewish and Pagan references to Christianity, but Tacitus is not mentioned by him. In fact, the passage in question was not quoted by any Christian writer before the fifteenth century."[271] First-century Justus of Tiberius, who hailed from Galilee, authored a history of the time in which Jesus lived; and Christian scholar Photius, writing in the ninth century ("Biblioteca," 33), was amazed that it didn't contain "the least mention of the appearance of the Christ."[272]

John E. Remsburg listed forty-two authors living during the time of Christ and then noted:

> Enough of the writings of the authors named in the foregoing list remains to form a library. Yet in this mass of Jewish and Pagan literature, aside from two forged passages in the works of a Jewish author, and two disputed passages in the works of Roman writers, there is to be found no mention of Jesus Christ.[273]

Many look to Josephus, who was born after the Christ events occurred, and claim he talked about Jesus; but the main citation has been proven to be false. The passage is out of context with the surrounding text, and it wasn't present in the earliest copies of Josephus' works. Even Origen, in the second century, didn't know of it. This mention of

---

[269] John E. Remsburg, "Silence of Contemporary Writers," *The Christ*, positiveatheism.org, 2000, web, 27 Aug. 2014 <http://www.positiveatheism.org/hist/rmsbrg02.htm>.

[270] Publius Tacitus, *Annals*, Book XV, Sec. 44, c. 109 CE. See also: "Evidence for the historical existence of Jesus Christ," rationalwiki.org, n.d., web, 19 Dec. 2014.

[271] John G. Jackson, *Pagan Origins of the Christ Myth* (Cranford, NJ: American Atheist Press, 1989), 8.

[272] Walker, *Man Made God*, 146. See also: Dan Barker, *Losing Faith in Faith: From Preacher to Atheist* (Madison, WI: FFRF, Inc., 1992), 361.

[273] Remsburg, "Silence of Contemporary Writers."

Jesus was first spoken of at the beginning of the fourth century, and Eusebius, a known liar, may have been the one who wrote it.[274] If it were possible to get away with it, people today would most likely be making up stories, characters, and "historical" evidence and cramming them into the biblical texts.

Frederic Farrar (1831-1903), of Trinity College in Cambridge, wrote:

It is amazing that history has not embalmed for us even one certain or definite saying or circumstance in the life of the Saviour of mankind . . . there is no statement in all history that says anyone saw Jesus or talked with him. Nothing in history is more astonishing than the silence of contemporary writers about events relayed in the four Gospels.[275]

Sometime in the nineteenth century, the renowned scholar Rabbi Wise "searched the records of Pilate's court, still extant, for evidence" of the trial of Jesus and found nothing.[276] **The truth is, no one who lived during that time spoke of Jesus.** All we have is a bunch of stories from a century or two later. We *know* this! We have *always* known it. **Until Justin Martyr (141 CE), we find nothing of a Christ on the earth**.[277]

Scaruffi summed up the evidence we have regarding a historical Jesus as follows:

The Romans kept accurate records of every political and judicial event. There is no record of Pontius Pilate trying and executing a man named Jesus. Only two Roman writers of Jesus' time mention Christians (Pliny and Svetonius [Suetonius]) but they don't mention Jesus. The first Roman to mention Jesus is Tacitus, but almost a century after the death of Jesus. The Jewish historian Josephus certainly mentions Christians, but his words about Jesus are generally considered a later forgery (the Christian historian Origen of the third century wrote that Josephus never mentioned Jesus). The Jewish philosopher Philo, who lived in Egypt at the time of Jesus, does not seem to know anything about Jesus or Christians (he died in the year 40).[278]

And not only was Jesus not mentioned but, as Scaruffi pointed out, events that supposedly happened during the lifetime of Jesus have not been recorded in history either. Jim Walker wrote:

Then we have a particular astronomical event that would have attracted the attention of anyone interested in the "heavens." According to Luke 23:44-45, there occurred "about the sixth hour, and there was darkness over all the earth until the ninth hour, and the sun was darkened, and the veil of the temple was rent in the midst." Yet not a single mention of such a three hour ecliptic event got recorded by anyone, including the astronomers and astrologers, anywhere in the world, including Pliny the Elder and Seneca who both recorded eclipses from

[274] Walker, *Man Made God*, 145-146. See also: Bennett, 666.
[275] Bushby, "The Forged Origins of the New Testament." See also: Frederic W. Farrar, *The Life of Christ* (London: Cassell, 1874).
[276] Graham, 343.
[277] Graham, 290-291.
[278] Scaruffi, "Jesus and Christianity."

other dates. Note also that, for obvious reasons, solar eclipses can't occur during a full moon (passovers always occur during full moons). Nor does a single contemporary person write about the earthquake described in Matthew 27:51-54 where the earth shook, rocks ripped apart (rent), and graves opened.[279]

No Risen Savior

Whether Jesus lived or not, we cannot prove from the earliest biblical sources that he was born of a virgin or resurrected as a Messiah. These ideas were added to the manuscripts by later editors.

On February 4, 1859, an ancient document was found at St. Catherine's monastery containing "346 leaves of an ancient codex."[280] Dr. Tischendorf named the document the Sinaiticus, or Sinai Bible (*Codex Sanaiticus*). It's our oldest complete copy of the Bible. Bushby wrote:

> A shudder of apprehension echoed through Christendom in the last quarter of the 19th century when English-language versions of the Sinai Bible were published. Recorded within these pages is information that disputes Christianity's claim of historicity. Christians were provided with irrefutable evidence of willful falsifications in all modern New Testaments. So different was the Sinai Bible's New Testament from versions then being published that the Church angrily tried to annul the dramatic new evidence that challenged its very existence. . .

> When the New Testament in the Sinai Bible is compared with a modern-day New Testament, a staggering 14,800 editorial alterations can be identified. . . Serious study of Christian origins must emanate from the Sinai Bible's version of the New Testament, not modern editions.[281]

Yes, this was a problem. According to Lucy Mangan,

> Between them [the Old and New Testaments in the Sinai Bible] **they had 35,000 edits and corrections made by three or four different scribes**, including one to the words spoken by Jesus on the cross – marked as doubtful by one of the writers, and reinstated later by another. Imagine finding a big question mark beside "Forgive them, Father. They know not what they do." You'd have to take a moment, wouldn't you?[282]

As Bushby noted, today's Bibles contain many errors, but this document suggests that Jesus was not even born miraculously. Bushby stated that the Catholic Church admitted

[279] Jim Walker, "Did a historical Jesus exist?"
[280] Bushby, "The Forged Origins of the New Testament."
[281] Bushby, "The Forged Origins of the New Testament."
[282] Lucy Mangan, "Bible Hunters: the Search for Bible Truth; The Good Wife - TV Review," 14 Feb. 2014, web, 22 Nov. 2014 <http://www.theguardian.com/tv-and-radio/2014/feb/14/bible-hunters-the-good-wife-tv-review>.

that "like Paul, even the earliest Gospels knew nothing of the miraculous birth of our Saviour."[283] Armstrong agreed, writing:

> Mark's Gospel, which as the earliest is usually regarded as the most reliable, presents Jesus as a perfectly normal man, with a family that included brothers and sisters. No angels announced his birth or sang over his crib. He had not been marked out during his infancy or adolescence as remarkable in any way.[284]

As Joseph Wheless wrote, the virgin birth is the concept that "the whole forged fabric of Christianity is based on."[285] Yet even Bishop John Shelby Spong wrote:

> It is clear the first gospel writer, Mark, had never heard of the virgin birth. When Mark was written, over 40 years had passed since the crucifixion, and some 70 years had passed since the birth of Jesus. Mythological traditions build slowly. The story of the virgin birth of Jesus is one of these mythological traditions.[286]

Bushby continued to say that

> when Eusebius assembled scribes to write the New Testimonies, he first produced a single document that provided an exemplar or master version. Today it is called the Gospel of Mark, and the Church admits that it was "the first Gospel written" . . . The scribes of the Gospels of Matthew and Luke were dependent upon the Mark writing as the source and framework for the compilation of their works. The Gospel of John is independent of those writings, and the late-15th-century theory that it was written later to support the earlier writings is the truth.[287]

Furthermore, Bushby noted that "No supernatural appearance of a resurrected Jesus Christ is recorded in any ancient Gospels of Mark, but a description of over 500 words now appears in modern Bibles (Mark 16:9-20)."[288] But there is more. Bushby also wrote:

> Not only are those narratives missing in the Sinai Bible, but they are absent in the Alexandrian Bible, the Vatican Bible, the Bezae Bible and an ancient Latin manuscript of Mark, code-named "K" by analysts. They are also lacking in the oldest Armenian version of the New Testament, in sixth-century manuscripts of the Ethiopic version and ninth-century Anglo-Saxon Bibles.[289]

Mangan confirmed this when she wrote: "The greatest body blow for literalists, however, was the fact that the Gospel of Mark [in the Sinai Bible] lacked its rather crucial final 12

---

[283] Bushby, "The Forged Origins of the New Testament." See also: *Encyclopaedia Biblica* (London: Adam & Charles Black, 1899), Vol. III, 3344.
[284] Armstrong, 80.
[285] Joseph Wheless, *Forgery in Christianity: A Documented Record of the Foundations of the Christian Religion* (1930), 74.
[286] John Shelby Spong, Bishop, *The Birth of Jesus* (progressivechristianity.org, 2014), 18.
[287] Bushby, "The Forged Origins of the New Testament." See also: *Catholic Encyclopedia*, Farley ed., Vol. VI, 657, and Tony Bushby, *The Crucifixion of Truth* (Buddina Queensland, Australia: Joshua Books, 2004), 33-40.
[288] Bushby, "The Forged Origins of the New Testament."
[289] Bushby, "The Forged Origins of the New Testament."

verses, in which Jesus is resurrected and his divinity thus proved."[290] According to Armstrong, the idea of the "crucifixion as an atonement" for sin "did not emerge until the fourth century and was only important in the West."[291] She continued to say that the "doctrine that Jesus had been God in human form was not finalized until the fourth century. The development of Christian belief in the Incarnation was a gradual, complex process."[292] Jared Bailey wrote: "The resurrection verses in today's Gospels of Mark are universally acknowledged as forgeries, and the Church agrees, saying, 'The conclusion of Mark is admittedly not genuine . . . almost the entire section is a later compilation.'"[293] We know that, right? We've known it for years.

After the Sinai Bible was discovered, many flocked to Egypt in search of old Bibles, and Scottish twin sisters Agnes and Margaret Smith found one (*Codex Syriac*) that rivaled the Sinai Bible in age. It too lacked the important last verses of Mark. Someone finally came upon a copy with the resurrection verses attached, but not until the end of the nineteenth century. Charles Lang Freer uncovered one dating from the fifth century that contained not only the final twelve verses of Mark but also some extra verses that had Jesus saying Satan was dead.[294] Those who claim that the original stories of other mythical gods don't show them as being resurrected or born on December 25, or whatever the claim might be, need to think about the fact that the original stories of Jesus didn't show him as being born on December 25 either; and, more importantly, they didn't show him as being resurrected from the dead.

Most people freely accept that the conclusion to Mark isn't genuine.[295] And what this means is that **Christians may be left without a risen Savior**. Some might want to deny the evidence, but surely we believe what the Catholic Church says when its words harm its cause. If not, it is nonsensical to entertain the idea that the books of the New Testament have any merit at all, since they also came to us from this organization. Besides, we know for a fact that the **earliest manuscripts didn't contain any information about a virgin birth or resurrection of Jesus from the dead**.

Eusebius, Constantine, and the Making of the New Testament

Eusebius wrote "Historia Ecclesiastica," or the "History of the Church." He was friends with Emperor Constantine the Great and helped Constantine win the crown. Because of this friendship, the Edict of Milan (313 CE), removing penalties for professing to be a Christian, was enacted. Mack wrote: "The Bible was created when Christianity became the religion of the Roman Empire. . . with Constantine converted, the age-old model of the temple-state could start to work again, and the history of

---

[290] Mangan, "Bible Hunters: the Search for Bible Truth."
[291] Armstrong, 87.
[292] Armstrong, 81.
[293] Jared Bailey, *Crimes of Humanity*, lulu.com, 2014. See also: *Encyclopaedia Biblica*, II, 1880; III, 1767, 1781; and *Catholic Encyclopedia*, III, "The Evidence of Its Spuriousness," and *Catholic Encyclopedia*, Farley ed., III, 274-279, "Canons."
[294] Mangan, "Bible Hunters: the Search for Bible Truth."
[295] Bushby, "The Forged Origins of the New Testament." See also: *Encyclopaedia Biblica*, Vol. II, 1880, Vol. III, 1767 and 1781; *Catholic Encyclopedia*, Vol. III, under the heading "The Evidence of its Spuriousness"; *Catholic Encyclopedia*, Farley ed., Vol. III, 274-279, under heading "Canons."

Christendom began."[296] Until then, there was no New Testament, but only writings by *unknown authors*.[297]

Constantine, with Eusebius by his side, presided over the Council of Nicaea in 325 CE. Eusebius' *Life of Constantine* states that bishops came from all over the world. Two hundred fifty men (both young and old) came together from "all quarters" and "all nations,"[298] Eusebius listed the following areas from which these men traveled:

> In effect, the most distinguished of God's ministers from all the churches which abounded in Europe, Lybia, and Asia were here assembled. And a single house of prayer, as though divinely enlarged, sufficed to contain at once Syrians and Cilicians, Phœnicians and Arabians, delegates from Palestine, and others from Egypt; Thebans and Libyans, with those who came from the region of Mesopotamia. A Persian bishop too was present at this conference, nor was even a Scythian found wanting to the number. Pontus, Galatia, and Pamphylia, Cappadocia, Asia, and Phrygia, furnished their most distinguished prelates; while those who dwelt in the remotest districts of Thrace and Macedonia, of Achaia and Epirus, were notwithstanding in attendance. Even from Spain itself, one whose fame was widely spread took his seat as an individual in the great assembly.[299]

Constantine urged that they sit down and discuss their differences and come to unity.[300] When all the delegates were seated, Constantine urged them to get a handle on their doctrine and be "united in a common harmony of sentiment."[301] He "gave permission to those who presided in the council to deliver their opinions."[302] Eusebius wrote that

> the emperor gave patient audience to all alike, and <u>received every proposition with steadfast attention, and by occasionally assisting the argument of each party in turn, he gradually disposed even the most vehement disputants to a reconciliation.</u> At the same time, by the affability of his address to all, and his use of the Greek language, with which he was not altogether unacquainted, he appeared in a truly attractive and amiable light, <u>persuading some, convincing others by his reasonings</u>, praising those who spoke well, and urging all to unity of sentiment, <u>until at last he succeeded in bringing them to one mind and judgment respecting every disputed question.</u>[303]

[296] Mack, 293.
[297] "Father Eusebius - Forger," 30 Oct. 2014.
[298] Eusebius, *Life of Constantine*, III, Chs. 6, 7, and 9; tr. Ernest Cushing Richardson; from *Nicene and Post-Nicene Fathers*, Second Series, Vol. 1; ed. Philip Schaff and Henry Wace (Buffalo, NY: Christian Literature Publishing Co., 1890); rev. and ed. for New Advent by Kevin Knight; newadvent.org, 2009, web, 9 Apr., 2015.
[299] Eusebius, *Life of Constantine*, III, Ch. 7.
[300] Eusebius, *Life of Constantine*, III, Ch. 12.
[301] Eusebius, *Life of Constantine*, III, Ch. 12.
[302] Eusebius, *Life of Constantine*, III, Ch. 13.
[303] Eusebius, *Life of Constantine*, III, Ch. 13.

When all was said and done, all were "united as concerning the faith."[304] Then, **"Those points also which were sanctioned by the resolution of the whole body were committed to writing, and received the signature of each several member."**[305]

In his book *Crimes of Humanity*, Jared Bailey noted that tales were taken from all over the world, "using the standard god-myths from the presbyters' manuscripts."[306] Constantine's hope, Bailey wrote, was that by including facets of all the myths, East and West would be united in a uniform religion.[307] We have no record of what the book contained, but Mack wrote that other "lists would be produced from the fourth to the ninth century, showing that total agreement was never reached."[308] Mack continued: "When the Jewish scriptures and the apostolic writings were combined in a single book, the church finally had its story straight. The Bible could be used to claim antiquity for the Christian religion and serve as the Christian epic."[309]

According to Eusebius, he was told to make fifty copies of the scriptures,[310] and later Constantine wrote a letter to the churches as follows:

> Having had full proof, in the general prosperity of the empire, how great the favor of God has been towards us, I have judged that it ought to be the first object of my endeavors, that unity of faith, sincerity of love, and community of feeling in regard to the worship of Almighty God, might be preserved among the highly favored multitude who compose the Catholic Church. And, inasmuch as this object could not be effectually and certainly secured, unless all, or at least the greater number of the bishops were to meet together, and a **discussion of all particulars relating to our most holy religion to take place**; for this reason as numerous an assembly as possible has been convened, at which I myself was present, as one among yourselves (and far be it from me to deny that which is my greatest joy, that I am your fellow-servant), and <u>every question received due and full examination, until that judgment which God, who sees all things, could approve, and which tended to unity and concord, was brought to light, so that **no room was left for further discussion or controversy in relation to the faith**</u>.[311]

I couldn't tell whether the following was written by Constantine or Eusebius: "Receive, then, with all willingness **this truly Divine injunction, and regard it as in truth the gift of God. For whatever is determined in the holy assemblies of the bishops is to be regarded as indicative of the Divine will**."[312] Because "It was by the Will of God that Constantine became possessed of the Empire,"[313] naturally it was perceived that God guided him in leading these men to truth.

---

[304] Eusebius, *Life of Constantine*, III, Ch. 14.
[305] Eusebius, *Life of Constantine*, III, Ch. 14.
[306] Bailey, *Crimes of Humanity*.
[307] Bailey, *Crimes of Humanity*.
[308] Mack, 288-289.
[309] Mack, 290.
[310] Eusebius, *Life of Constantine*, IV, Ch. 36.
[311] Eusebius, *Life of Constantine*, III, Ch. 17.
[312] Eusebius, *Life of Constantine*, III, Ch. 20.
[313] Eusebius, *Life of Constantine*, I, Ch. 24.

And why shouldn't Constantine know the truth? After all, he was inspired (according to Eusebius). On a day previous to the convening of this council, God had sent Constantine a vision of a "Cross of Light" and

> about noon, when the day was already beginning to decline, he saw with his own eyes the trophy of a cross of light in the heavens, above the sun, and bearing the inscription, CONQUER BY THIS. At this sight he himself was struck with amazement, and his whole army also, which followed him on this expedition, and witnessed the miracle.[314]

Then, to ensure that Constantine understood, God appeared to him in the form of Christ.

> He said, moreover, that he doubted within himself what the import of this apparition could be. And while he continued to ponder and reason on its meaning, night suddenly came on; then in his sleep the Christ of God appeared to him with the same sign which he had seen in the heavens, and commanded him to make a likeness of that sign which he had seen in the heavens, and to use it as a safeguard in all engagements with his enemies.[315]

This sounds a lot like the story the apostle Paul told about his own vision, which also appeared "about noon" and in the presence of his companions (Acts 22:6-9). Many Christians believe Paul's story while disbelieving Constantine's; then they turn around and trust Constantine to give them their holy book with its holy words from God (including the story about Paul). I don't think they can have it both ways.

After this miracle Constantine "sent for those who were acquainted with the mysteries of His doctrines, and enquired who that God was, and what was intended by the sign of the vision he had seen. They affirmed that He was God, the only begotten Son of the one and only God"[316] (whatever that means). At that point Constantine began to worship the gods Yahweh and Jesus.

Constantine was enthralled by the writings of Eusebius, and wrote to him, saying:

> I am, notwithstanding, filled with admiration of your learning and zeal, and have not only myself read your work with pleasure, but have given directions, according to your own desire, that it be communicated to many sincere followers of our holy religion. Seeing, then, with what pleasure we receive favors of this kind from your Sagacity, be pleased to gladden us more frequently with those compositions.[317]

Constantine himself was a speaker, author, philosopher, and prophet. Eusebius wrote of him:

---

[314] Eusebius, *Life of Constantine*, I, Ch. 28.
[315] Eusebius, *Life of Constantine*, I, Ch. 29.
[316] Eusebius, *Life of Constantine*, I, Ch. 32.
[317] Eusebius, *Life of Constantine*, IV, Ch. 35.

For himself, he sometimes passed sleepless nights in furnishing his mind with Divine knowledge: and much of his time was spent in composing discourses, many of which he delivered in public; for he conceived it to be incumbent on him to govern his subjects by appealing to their reason, and to secure in all respects a **rational obedience to his authority**. Hence he would sometimes himself evoke an assembly, on which occasions vast multitudes attended, in the hope of hearing an emperor sustain the part of a philosopher. And if in the course of his speech any occasion offered of touching on sacred topics, he immediately stood erect, and with a grave aspect and subdued tone of voice seemed reverently to be initiating his auditors in the mysteries of the Divine doctrine . . . And he himself both felt and uttered these sentiments in the genuine confidence of faith.[318]

Perhaps both these men had a hand in writing these New Testament scriptures. Whoever did the work of piecing together information from far and wide (whether Eusebius, Constantine, or the 250 bishops), at some point a new merged manuscript was turned into a document that would through the years, and other councils, grow into what we have sitting on our coffee tables today. As Robert Wright noted, "politics and economics gave us the one true god of the Abrahamic faiths."[319]

"Having by these means banished dissension, and reduced the Church of God to a state of uniform harmony,"[320] Constantine turned his attention to the false prophets and heretics, addressing them as follows: "Understand now, by this present statute, you Novatians, Valentinians, Marcionites, Paulians, you who are called Cataphrygians, and all you who devise and support heresies by means of your private assemblies."[321] He informed these people that "from this day forward none of your unlawful assemblies may presume to appear in any public or private place."[322] Eusebius wrote:

Thus were the lurking-places of the heretics broken up by the emperor's command, and the savage beasts they harbored (I mean the chief authors of their impious doctrines) driven to flight. . . Thus the members of the entire body became united, and compacted in one harmonious whole; and the one catholic Church, at unity with itself, shone with full luster, while no heretical or schismatic body anywhere continued to exist. And the **credit of having achieved this mighty work our Heaven-protected emperor alone, of all who had gone before him, was able to attribute to himself**.[323]

Thus the emperor in all his actions honored God, the Controller of all things, and exercised an unwearied oversight over His churches. And God requited him, by subduing all barbarous nations under his feet, so that he was able everywhere to raise trophies over his enemies: and He proclaimed him as conqueror to all mankind, and made him a terror to his adversaries: not indeed that this was his

[318] Eusebius, *Life of Constantine*, IV, Ch. 29.
[319] Wright, 134.
[320] Eusebius, *Life of Constantine*, III, Ch. 63.
[321] Eusebius, *Life of Constantine*, III, Ch. 64.
[322] Eusebius, *Life of Constantine*, III, Ch. 65.
[323] Eusebius, *Life of Constantine*, III, Ch. 66.

natural character, since he was rather the meekest, and gentlest, and most benevolent of men.[324]

After that, God revealed traitorous plots to Constantine in visions so that he was able to dispose of threats against him. In fact,

> God frequently vouchsafed to him manifestations of himself, the Divine presence appearing to him in a most marvelous manner, and according to him **manifold intimations of future events**. Indeed, it is impossible to express in words the indescribable wonders of Divine grace which God was pleased to vouchsafe to His servant.[325]

Eusebius believed Constantine's flights of fancy. I do not. However, I believe the stories he told of his visions as much as I believe the stories he (Eusebius, or whoever) told of Paul's visions. Paul also was supposedly given exceeding or abundant revelations (2 Cor. 12:7).

Now, what are the chances that a non-Christian emperor of Rome (he wasn't baptized until right before he died[326]) and his bishops were able to decide which of all the contradictory writings that existed were the true word of God? We can boldly proclaim that "God watched over the process and made sure only the inspired material was put in the book these men made," but that is the epitome of naiveté, particularly when Yahweh wasn't even able to preserve any original writings.

Edward Gibbon wrote:

> The gravest of the ecclesiastical historians, Eusebius himself, indirectly confesses that he has related what might rebound to the glory, and that he has suppressed all that could tend to the disgrace, of religion. Such an acknowledgment will naturally excite a suspicion that a writer who has so openly violated one of the fundamental laws of history has not paid a very strict regard to the observance of the other; and the suspicion will derive additional credit from the character of Eusebius, which was less tinctured with credulity, and more practiced in the arts of courts, than that of almost any of his contemporaries.[327]

Gibbon further noted:

> It must be confessed that the ministers of the Catholic Church imitated the profane model which they were impatient to destroy. The most respectable bishops had persuaded themselves that the ignorant rustics would more cheerfully renounce the superstitions of Paganism if they found some resemblance, some compensation, in the bosom of Christianity. The religion of Constantine achieved

---

[324] Eusebius, *Life of Constantine*, I, Ch. 46.
[325] Eusebius, *Life of Constantine*, I, Ch. 47.
[326] Eusebius, *Life of Constantine*, IV, Ch. 62.
[327] Edward Gibbon, *Rome*, Vol. II (Philadelphia, 1876), as noted at "Father Eusebius - Forger," 12 Nov. 2014.

in less than a century the final conquest of the Roman empire; but the victors themselves were insensibly subdued by the arts of their vanquished rivals.[328]

Dr. Robert L. Wilken, the "first Protestant scholar to be admitted to the staff of Fordham University," wrote: "Eusebius wrote a history of Christianity in which there is no real history. Eusebius was the first thoroughly dishonest and unfair historian in ancient times."[329] Joseph Wheless wrote that Eusebius was "one of the most prolific forgers and liars of his age in the church."[330] Paul L. Meier noted: "They cannot deny their crime: the copies are in their own handwriting, they did not receive the Scriptures in this condition from their teachers, and they cannot produce originals from which they made their copies."[331]

These books Eusebius put together were, according to Bushby and Bailey, called the "New Testimonies." Bushby wrote that "this is the first mention (c. 331) of the New Testament in the historical record."[332] After the book was presented Constantine ordered all other writings that had been brought to the meeting to be burnt; and, according to Bushby, "presbyterial writings previous to the Council of Nicaea no longer exist, except for some fragments that have survived."[333] As Mack noted:

The writings in the New Testament were not written by eyewitnesses of an overpowering divine appearance in the midst of human history. That is the impression created by the final formation of the New Testament. Dismantled and given back to the people who produced them, the writings of the New Testament are the record of three hundred years of intellectual labor in the interest of a thoroughly human construction. . . It is charged with the intellectual battles and resolutions of untold numbers of persons who invested in a grand project three centuries in the making. . . To be quite frank about it, the Bible is the product of very energetic and successful mythmaking on the part of those early Christians.[334]

It should come as no surprise to us that we have been fooled. According to my research,

The original encyclopedias produced under the name of Britannica probably provided the first and last opportunity for unaffiliated biblical specialists outside Vatican control to release factual information about the development of the Christian religion. In the 1895 version alone, 344 Christian experts contributed to articles associated with biblical sections in the 8th, 9th, 10th and 11th Editions. The knowledge they provided was subsequently published, and the priesthood

[328] Gibbon, *Rome*, Vol. III, 163, as noted at "Father Eusebius - Forger," 12 Nov. 2014.
[329] Robert Louis Wilken, *The Myth of Christian Beginnings, History's Impact on Belief, Chapter III: The Bishop's Maiden: History Without History* (Garden City, NY: Doubleday & Company, Inc., 1971), 73, 57. See also: "Father Eusebius - Forger," 12 Nov. 2014.
[330] Wheless, *Forgery in Christianity*; quoted in Gibbon, *History*, Ch. 37; Lardner, IV, 91. These citations were retrieved from: "Father Eusebius - Forger," 12 Nov. 2014. See also: Taylor, *Diegesis*, 272.
[331] Eusebius, *The Church History*, Book 5, Section 28; retrieved from: "Father Eusebius - Forger," 12 Nov. 2014.
[332] Bushby, "The Forged Origins of the New Testament."
[333] Bushby, "The Forged Origins of the New Testament."
[334] Mack, 308.

had endowed the Encyclopaedists with disclosures that shocked the Christian hierarchy. Pope Leo XIII (1878-1903), in particular, was horrified by the revelations, and realizing something had to be done, circuitously arranged for a group of Catholic businessmen to purchase Encyclopedia Britannica.[335]

Apparently by the eleventh edition (1898), the new ownership was in place and earlier versions were destroyed. The Roman Catholic University in Chicago[336] took over the encyclopedia's dissemination, and church missionaries began selling the new version door to door.[337] Vati Leaks said researchers today need to check at their local libraries for information in Britannica's Ninth Edition, Volume 10. The author noted:

> Christians with access to libraries holding older pre-edited copies of Encyclopedia Britannica, particularly the Ninth Edition, Volume 10, will be shocked to read page 783 onwards under the heading of "Gospels". It confirms what church leaders knew about the crooked nature of early Christian bishops, the **Fourth Century compilation of the Gospels**, later inclusion of forged narratives into now-canonical New Testament texts, the papal suppression of 1200 years of church history (Encyclopedia Biblica, Adam & Charles Black, London, 1899), contradictions between Gospels, the **retrospective fabrication of the Christian story**, and the anonymous nature of Gospels now official to Christianity. With the discovery of the Dead Sea Scrolls, the Secret Vatican Scrolls and the Nag Hammadi Scrolls, that earlier knowledge was reinforced and reveals that the Vatican hierarchy know that the origin and authenticity of its Gospels is falsely presented. Persons in a position to compare earlier editions with "under Vatican management" editions should do so for personal confirmation that a new and fictitious Christian history was written and published, omitting previously available detrimental information.[338]

After suppressing the evidence, the Vatican was able to create its own false history.[339] From there the bogus information began to spread.

Protestants speak about the Catholic Church in derogatory terms (some even calling her the whore of Babylon) while they gobble up every poison niblet she has poured into their bowl. Valerie Tarico wrote that the printing press "brought the written word to the masses," fueling the Protestant Reformation; and in time the "authority of the papacy and Catholic hierarchy were replaced by the authority of the Bible, the Reformation's 'sola scriptura.'" The irony here is that it "was the Catholic hierarchy itself that had assembled the collection of texts and declared them, on papal authority, to be God's best and most complete revelation to humankind."[340]

---

[335] D. H. Gordon and N. L. Torrey, *History in the Encyclopedia* (New York, 1947); and Norman Segal, *The Good News of the Kingdoms* (Australia, 1995). See also: Vati Leaks, "Why the Vatican purchased Encyclopedia Britannica," vatileaks.com, 6 July 2011, web, 11 Apr. 2015.

[336] *Encyclopedias: Their History Throughout the Ages*, 1966. See also: Vati Leaks.

[337] Vati Leaks.

[338] Vati Leaks.

[339] Cardinal Caesar Baronius, *Annales Ecclesiastici*, tome vii, Fol. Antwerp, 1597.

[340] Valerie Tarico, "In Defense of Cherry Picking the Bible," exchristian.net, 9 July 2015, web, 10 July 2015.

No Reason to Believe

Dr. Tischendorf, in considering the information revealed by the Sinai Bible, concluded: **"We must frankly admit that we have no source of information with respect to the life of Jesus Christ other than ecclesiastic writings assembled during the fourth century."**[341] In 506 CE the Bishop of Tunis said that the Gospels had been written by "idiot evangelists" and that they were later "censored and corrected."[342]

Physicist Victor Stenger wrote: "Many former evangelical preachers have written eloquently about how they lost their faith once they learned the truth about how the Bible came to be written."[343] Certainly this is understandable. We have no reason to believe that the Bible is the inspired word of God. **No Roman census ever required families to return to their native cities in order to register. Herod never slaughtered infants under the age of two. In fact, Herod died in 4 BCE, and the census that was even spoken of took place in 6 CE. Therefore, Herod was dead ten years before the Roman census.**[344] Dr. Richard Carrier wrote regarding the birth of Jesus that "experts have long known the Gospel of Matthew sets the date around 6 B.C. (or no later than 4 B.C.), while Luke sets the date at 6 A.D."[345] Thus, these two authors (Matthew and Luke) contradict each other. Even if no fakery had been involved, the biblical books were handpicked by mortal men. The Gospel of Luke barely made it into the canon, "winning by only one vote at the Council of Nicea."[346] Again, **the four Gospels were only a few of the many that were written, and even they were accepted as part of the canon only in the fourth century**. Barbara Walker wrote:

Early Christians liberally practiced pseudepigraphy, which means an anonymous writer signing his work by another's name. Scholars have pretty conclusively proved that all the gospels were created by this kind of forgery, excepting only a few of Paul's epistles out of the rest of the New Testament.[347]

Walker continued:

The canonical gospels used today have been extensively worked over, mistranslated, re-translated, added to, subtracted from, reworded and produced in so many different versions that it seems absurd for anyone to claim any particular set as "the inerrant word of God," as some of the more naive worshippers do. Yet even in their early days, the canonical gospels were neither unique nor rare.

---

[341] Bushby, "The Forged Origins of the New Testament." See also: *Codex Sinaiticus*, Dr Constantin von Tischendorf, British Library, London.

[342] Walker, *Man Made God*, 114. See also: Miles R. Abelard, *Physicians of No Value* (Winter Park, FL: Reality Publications, 1979), 43.

[343] Victor Stenger, PhD, "How to Debate a Christian Apologist," huffingtonpost.com, 28 Feb. 2014, updated 30 Apr. 2014, web, 18 Mar. 2015.

[344] Walker, *Man Made God*, 154.

[345] Richard Carrier, PhD, *Hitler Homer Bible Christ: The Historical Papers of Richard Carrier 1995-2013* (Richmond, CA: Philosophy Press, 2004), 165.

[346] Walker, *Man Made God*, 131.

[347] Walker, *Man Made God*, 153.

Christian bishops of the fourth and fifth centuries spoke of hundreds of different gospels still in circulation. Copies of a few of these—the so-called Gnostic Gospels—were rediscovered during the 1950s; others were absorbed into the Apocrypha. Most were destroyed, in conformity with the dictates of the early Church. But there is plenty of evidence that the miracle tales and the biography of a sacrificed savior-god were common elements of popular literature in the Greco-Roman world and throughout the Middle East.[348]

Today's more informed Bible scholars and theologians know perfectly well that Jesus was never an identifiable single person, but rather a composite figure drawn from numerous savior-god traditions. They know that there never was a single coherent philosophy that could be called Christian, dating from the early years of our era. But today's theologians seldom dare to make this knowledge clear to the general public. Why not?[349]

If only Christians would question the motives and actions of the ancient Roman and Jewish leaders as they cast doubt upon the motives and actions of the religious and political leaders of today, they would recognize that the scriptures they prize came to them via smoke and mirrors! But we are told that we shouldn't probe into these genuine and grave problems with the inspiration of the "word of God." We are encouraged to "take it on faith" and not allow the devil to "put doubts in our heads." Just *believe*, we are told. Hang onto *faith*. We are urged to think that blind faith in fables, in the midst of a million screaming facts to the contrary, is somehow noble. The truth is, even if everything written in the book called the Bible had been penned by good and honest men who thought their words came straight from the creator, **one man's revelation is another man's hearsay**. As Thomas Paine wrote:

> It is a contradiction in terms and ideas, to call anything a revelation that comes to us at second-hand, either verbally or in writing. Revelation is necessarily limited to the first communication — after this, it is only an account of something which that person says was a revelation made to him; and though he may find himself obliged to believe it, it cannot be incumbent on me to believe it in the same manner; for it was not a revelation made to me, and I have only his word for it that it was made to him.[350]

Why should we believe Saul of Tarsus and anonymous Gospel writers who couldn't get their stories straight, yet not believe Joseph Smith, Constantine, or any other man or woman who wishes to present a divine vision or a God-put-it-on-my-heart story? After all, the old prophet of Bethel deceived the younger prophet into believing a lie (1 Kings 13:11-32). Perhaps we should consider not listening to old prophets and try rather to think with our own minds and hearts. And, seriously, if the "inspired prophet" Constantine *didn't* write the New Testament, or at least some of it, why in the world not?

---

[348] Walker, *Man Made God*, 157.
[349] Walker, *Man Made God*, 158.
[350] Thomas Paine, *Age of Reason* (1796), from *The Writings of Thomas Paine*, Vol. IV, ed. Moncure Daniel Conway, Part I, Chapter II, "Of Missions and Revelations."

Same Girl, Different Dress

If the incredible stories found in the Bible had come from China and were called *The Adventures of Super God*, Christians would immediately declare them false. But for some reason, because they are said to be inspired by a Jewish god, these Christians believe the strange fables although they know that the stories can't be true, as they themselves have never known the laws of nature to be overruled.

Craig Duckett wrote:

In the Bible animals can talk, wizards and witches summon spirits, demons possess pigs, sticks turn into snakes, food falls from the sky, people walk on water or through walls or remain lost for forty years in an area roughly the size of West Virginia. In the Bible the dead can come back to life, enough rain falls in seven weeks to cover the entire planet, all sorts of magical things happen that have no basis in the way we know the "real world" works. If you know the world doesn't work this way, if all the evidence shows it impossible for the world to work this way, then what are your reasons for believing the Bible when it claims otherwise? You'd consider yourself crazy if you believed Greek and Roman myths that claimed the same types of things, or fairy tales, or old European fables, simply because you know how the world works and it doesn't work that way! And yet, <u>when the Bible makes claims contrary to the way you know the world works, not only do you believe and defend it, but consider all those who don't as the ones who are living in error.</u> Is this an honest assessment? Shouldn't what we believe somehow coincide with what we actually know?[351]

Graham stated:

The Bible is not the "word of God," but stolen from pagan sources. Its Eden, Adam and Eve were taken from the Babylonian accounts; its Flood and Deluge is but an epitome of some four hundred flood accounts; its Ark and Ararat have their equivalents in a score of Deluge myths; even the names of Noah's sons are copies, so also Isaac's sacrifice, Solomon's judgment, and Samson's pillar acts; its Moses is fashioned after the Syrian Mises; its laws after Hammurabi's code. Its Messiah is derived from the Egyptian Mahdi, Savior, certain verses are verbatim copies of Egyptian scriptures. Between Jesus and the Egyptian Horus, Gerald Massey found 137 similarities, and those between Christ and Krishna run into the hundreds. How then can the Bible be a revelation to the Jews?[352]

English Unitarian Bill Darlison stated: "I don't think there's any history in the Bible whatsoever. I don't think any of it is history." He continued to say that those who wrote the biblical books were geniuses who knew the stories were myths, and then said, "*We are the dodos who have been trying to make it into history.*"[353]

---

[351] Craig Lee Duckett, "The World Simply Does Not Behave the Way Described in the Bible," *25 Reasons Why I Am No Longer a Christian*, 2007-2012, web, 28 Aug. 2014.
[352] Graham, 5.
[353] Bill Darlison, "The New Age," UKUnitarians, youtube.com, 26 Apr. 2014, web, 24 Apr. 2015.

Mack noted:

> Christians in particular have never thought to be critical of Christianity. Christians know about being critical, of course. They render critique on society all the time, but always from the vantage point of the Christian vision, a protected sphere of ideals held to be inviolate, never to be questioned.[354]

This inability of Christians to critique the Bible is a problem. Their holy book, as stated, is an anonymous book that is presented as a history of real people. However, **its authors, the date of its writing, and its main character are unknown, and we have no original copy of the documents it contains**. Furthermore, the book boasts innumerable depictions of events that we know can't happen as well as events we know *didn't* happen. Evidence is mounting up against the veracity of the biblical texts. With no eyewitnesses to testify to its inspiration, and no knowledge of who even wrote the book, the entire Bible must be declared a work of men and its superheroes no more real than the mythical characters we will now consider.

---

[354] Mack, 307.

CHAPTER FIVE
SAVIORS, CHRISTS, AND OTHER GODS

The day will come when the mystical generation of Jesus by the supreme being as his father in the womb of a virgin will be classed with the fable of the generation of Minerva in the brain of Jupiter.[355]

Thomas Jefferson, President of the United States

The Christian religion contains nothing but what Christians hold in common with heathens; nothing new, or truly great.[356]

Celsus, Epicurean philosopher

We know Yahweh was a mythological deity just like the many other deities that were believed to exist in the ancient world. And they too had wives (or, goddesses) and were part of their own pantheon of gods. We know this! Come on now, after all, we read in the Bible that Yahweh had sons. If he had sons then he had a wife. She was just edited out of the OT, but we know she existed in the minds of the Hebrews.[357]

John W. Loftus

Various savior-gods have appeared in the world, many having mothers with similar names. Mary (Myrrha/ Maria[358]) was the mother of Jesus, Maia was Buddha's mother and also the mother of Hermes and Mercury, Maya was Agni's mom, Myrrha was the mother of Adonis and Bacchus, Maya Maria was the mother of Sommona Cadom,[359] and Krishna's mom (Devaki) wore the title Mariama.[360] All of these women whose names begin with Ma are "the planetary Mother."[361] In this chapter we'll look, in no particular order, at some of the sons of these blessed mothers/goddesses.

Aten/Aton

This first god needs to be mentioned because of his antiquity and the fact that he was the earliest god we know of to be presented as the one true god, thus expressing monotheism in the land of Egypt. Also, the god Aten helps us to see where gods originated and gives us a glimpse into what a good god might look like.

Aten, or Aton, was the sun disk; and he was first referred to in *The Story of Sinuhe* (from the 12th Egyptian dynasty), an account of a <u>dead king's rising to heaven</u> to unite

---

[355] Thomas Jefferson, letter to John Adams, 11 Apr. 1823. See also: Jim Walker, "Thomas Jefferson on Christianity & Religion," nobeliefs.com, n.d., web, 7 July 2015; Graham, 304; and D. M. Murdock/Acharya S, "Were George Washington and Thomas Jefferson Jesus Mythicists?" truthbeknown.com, 2015, web, 4 July 2015.
[356] Doane, XXXVI; from Origen, *Contra Celsus*.
[357] John W. Loftus, "Asherah, the Israelite Goddess," *Debunking Christianity*, debunkingchristianity.blogspot.com, 6 Aug. 2013, web, 31 Dec. 2014.
[358] Godfrey Higgins, *Anacalypsis: An Attempt to Draw Aside the Veil, or The Saitic Esis*, I (London: J. Burns, 1878), 304; See also: Doane, XXXII Notes.
[359] Graham, 300-301.
[360] Douglas L. Laubach, *The Parallax from Hell: Satan's Critique of Organized Religion & Other Essays* (Bloomington, IN: iUniverse, 2012), 98.
[361] Graham, 300-301.

with the sun disk,[362] the "divine body merging with its maker."[363] When Amenhotep IV (18th dynasty[364]) and Nefertiti came into power, they made Aten the single Egyptian god; Amenhotep changed his own name to Akhenaten to be linked to Aten.[365] "All creation was thought to emanate from the god and to exist within the god. In particular, the god was not depicted in anthropomorphic (human) form, but as rays of light extending from the sun's disk."[366] He was the "light of the world," and in him was "no darkness at all" (Jn. 8:12, 1 Jn.1:5).[367] In him all things existed (1 Jn. 1:5; Col. 1:16, 20), and his worshipers were not allowed to make graven images to him, as this was viewed as idolatry.[368] His priests offered him limited cakes, flowers, and fruits.[369] Aten was formless; he was simply the "life-giving intangible essence," the "power that produced and sustained the sun," the "creator that held all things in hand," and the "presence of the divine within matter and in human form." He dwelt in the trees and the flowers, and was the "energetic force that acted through the sun," the "original causation and continuous presence."[370]

Amenhotep's goal was to create a world religion with a universal god. He was the first king to "reject lavish wealth" and extravagant temple rituals. Aten was like a compassionate mother or father. He was totally benevolent and possessed no evil qualities, such as jealousy or wrath. Unlike Yahweh, he was a good god; he was "lord of love" and threatened no divine judgment or hell fire.[371] The Egyptian "Great Hymn to the Aten," in which Akhenaten praised Aten as the "creator and giver of life,"[372] and Psalm 104 are quite similar, although some Christians deny the similarities.[373]

Baal

Baal (the warring son of the most high god, El) performed somewhat like another hero, that is, Jesus Christ (Baal's brother, nephew, or son). Moses' Song of the Sea (Ex. 15:1-8, Ps. 29) mimics the Ugaritic Baal story in his battle with Yam/Yamm (the sea god)."[374] [375]

Alan G. Hefner wrote regarding Baal (also known as Beelzebub, Lk. 11:15):

[362] Richard H. Wilkinson, *The Complete Gods and Goddesses of Ancient Egypt* (London/New York: Thames & Hudson, 2003), 236–240.
[363] Miriam Lichtheim, *Ancient Egyptian Literature: Volume I: The Old and Middle Kingdoms* (1980), 223. See also: "Aten," wikipedia.org, 28 Jan. 2015, web, 31 Jan. 2015.
[364] "Akhenaten," wikipedia.org, 30 Jan. 2015, web, 31 Jan. 2015.
[365] Wilkinson, 236-240.
[366] "Aten," wikipedia.org.
[367] Wim van den Dungen, "Great Hymn to the Aten," maat.sofiatopia.org, 2005-2015, web, 31 Jan. 2015.
[368] "Aten, god of Egypt," Siteseen Ltd., June 2014, web, 31 Jan. 2015. See also: "Aten," wikipedia.org.
[369] "History embalmed: Aten," Siteseen Ltd., July 2014, web, 31 Jan. 2015. See also: "Aten," wikipedia.org.
[370] Ted Nottingham, "The Mystery of the Essenes," youtube.com, 15 Nov. 2010, web, 30 Jan. 2015.
[371] Nottingham, "The Mystery of the Essenes."
[372] "Aten," wikipedia.org.
[373] Nottingham, "The Mystery of the Essenes."
[374] William M. Schniedewind and Joel H. Hunt, *A Primer on Ugaritic: Language, Culture and Literature* (Cambridge: Cambridge University Press, 2007), 30. See also Murdock, *Did Moses Exist?* 129.
[375] Brian D. Russell, *The Song of the Sea: The Date of Composition and Influence of Exodus 15:1-21* (New York: Peter Lang, 2007), 39. See also Murdock, *Did Moses Exist?* 130, 133.

> In ancient religions the name [Baal] denoted sun, lord or god. Baal was a common name of small Syrian and Persian deities. Baal is still principally thought of as a Canaanite fertility deity. The Great Baal was of Canaan. He was the son of El, the high god of Canaan. The cult of Baal celebrated annually his death and resurrection as a part of the Canaanite fertility rituals.[376]

Notice the word "lord." Now look at this: "And it hath come to pass, in that day, An affirmation of Jehovah, Thou dost call Me -- My husband, And dost not call Me any more -- My lord" (Hos. 2:16 YLT). Baal's name denotes "lord," so this translation is correct, but the KJV translates this: "thou shalt call me Ishi; and shalt call me no more Baali." Now I know the passage is saying the Jews wouldn't call Yahweh master (*Baali*) but would call him husband (*Ishi*), but the meaning of the word "Baali" is "1. my lord; A. a deity in the northern kingdom, variation of the name 'Baal.'"[377] In fact, the ESV translates Hosea 2:16-17: "And in that day, declares the LORD, you will call me 'My Husband,' and **no longer will you call me 'My Baal.'** For I will remove the names of the Baals from her mouth, and they shall be remembered by name no more." Karen Armstrong wrote:

> In the Old Canaanite religion, Baal had married the soil and the people had celebrated this with ritual orgies, but Hosea insisted that since the covenant, Yahweh had taken the place of Baal and had wedded the people of Israel [Israel was the land, or the earth; see my book *We Are Emmanuel*]. They had to understand that it was Yahweh, not Baal, who would bring fertility to the soil.[378]

Yahweh was therefore Baal or Baalim. And *Bali* ("my Baal") is symbolic for Yah, who is Yahweh.[379] Jesus did, after all, tell the Jews they were descended from the devil (Jn. 8:44). If they descended from Beelzebub or Baal, then Yahweh was that devil.

According to Mark S. Smith,

> The Ugaritic mythical texts largely feature the deities El, the aged and kindly patriarch of the pantheon; his consort and queen mother of the divine family; the young storm-god and divine warrior, Baal; his sister, Anat [or Anath], likewise a martial deity; and finally, the solar deity.[380]

As we saw in Psalm 82:1, the **Bible calls the supreme god by the name of El**. In the Bible El may morph into Yahweh; various Jewish writings and other documents also equate El and Yahweh. If Yahweh *was* El, then he was Baal's father, not his brother and not Baal. But we read:

---

[376] Alan G. Hefner, "Baal," *Encyclopedia Mythica*, pantheon.org, 3 Mar. 1997, rev. 11 Jan. 2004, web, 31 Dec. 2014.

[377] "Baali," Strong's H1180, blueletterbible.org, 2015, web, 22 Jan. 2015.

[378] Armstrong, 47.

[379] "Bali," Strong's 1180, biblehub.com, 2015, web, 11 Apr. 2015.

[380] Mark S. Smith, *The Early History of God: Yahweh and the Other Deities in Ancient Israel (Biblical Resource Series)*, 2nd ed. (Grand Rapids, MI/Cambridge, U.K.: William B. Eerdmans Publishing Company, 2002), 2.

Jewish ritual and mythology developed directly from Canaanite ritual and mythology. **Yahweh was originally the son of the Canaanite God El and brother of the Canaanite God Baal.** . . In 1927 they dug up a Canaanite clay tablet library buried at Ugarit, an ancient city along the northern coast of Syria. Hundreds of ancient texts. Same myths. Same rituals. Same Gods. Only centuries earlier than Judaism.[381]

John W. Loftus wrote: "Yahweh was sired by the god El (short for Elyon) and later superseded him in the evolutionary development of the Israelite religion." Loftus pointed out several names in the Old Testament that were taken from El's name: "Ab-el, Emmanu-el, Ishma-el, Samu-el, El-isha, El-ijah, Jo-el, Zerubbab-el (who was supposed to be the long awaited Messiah). They were named after a different god than Yahweh, El." Loftus further noted that <u>Israel, Michael and Gabriel were also named for El</u>. He pointed out that Yahweh himself was called: "El Shaddai: 'El Almighty.' (Gen. 17:1; 28:3; 35:11; Ex. 6:1; Ps. 91:1, 2). El Elyon: 'El the Most High.' (Gen. 14:19; Ps. 9:2; Dan. 7:18, 22, 25). El Olam: 'The Everlasting El.' (Gen. 16:13)." Smith wrote that "the tradition in ancient Israel favors Bethel originally as an old cult-site of the god El (secondarily overlaid--if not identified--with the cult of Yahweh), perhaps as the place-name Bethel (literally, "house of El") would suggest (Genesis 28:10-22)."[382] We saw earlier that Jacob's sons were born in Bethel, so this makes sense. (And, as noted previously, Jesus was born in Beth-el-hem or Bethlehem.)

Baal wanted supremacy, but Father El gave it to Yam, an evil sea god. The other gods cried to Mother Asherah, who petitioned Yam to be more lenient. When he refused "Kindly Asherah, who loves Her children, offered Herself to the God of the Sea. . . Asherah returned to the Source of the Two Rivers. She went home to the court of El."[383]

When Baal learned of this he was furious, and he set out to do battle with his brother Yam. When Yam heard of Baal's plot against him, he sent messengers to Father El, saying:

Do not prostrate Yourselves before the Convocation of the Assembly, But declare Your information!
And say to **The Bull, My father, El**,
Declare to the Convocation of the Assembly:
"The message of Yam, Your Lord,
Of Your master Judge River:
Give up, O Gods,
Him whom You harbor, Him whom the multitude harbor!
Give up Baal and His partisans,
Dagon's Son, so that I may inherit His gold!"[384]

---

[381] *Pagan Origins of the Christ Myth, Ibid.*
[382] Mark S. Smith, *The Origins of Biblical Monotheism: Israel's Polytheistic Background and the Ugaritic Texts* (New York: Oxford University Press, 2001), 32.
[383] "Canaanite Myth: The Baal Epic," theologywebsite.com, 1997-2009, web, 26 Nov. 2014.
[384] "Canaanite Myth: The Baal Epic."

Father El heard Yam's petition and declared that Baal would bow to Yam. This infuriated Baal, who tried to kill the messengers; but Astarte and Anath grabbed his hands.

After that, Baal built a palace of cedar, brick, and gold. It took six days to prepare the silver and gold, and the brick was laid on the **seventh day**, at which point there was a big party with slaughtered animals. This is reminiscent of the building of the Jewish temple with its cedars and gold, but Solomon's temple took **seven years**, not seven days, to build (1 Kings 6). (It had to be bigger and better than Baal's temple, I suppose.)

Baal apparently got the big head and refused to give tribute to Mavet (Mot, Mut, Moth, Maweth[385]), the god of death and the underworld. Mavet killed Baal, and Father El was heartbroken. Ashtar the Terrible took over in Baal's place, declaring that he couldn't rule in the "heights of Saphon," and he went down to "rule over all the grand earth."[386]

By the way, the Hebrew word for "death" is *maveth*,[387] and the Hebrew word for "sea" is *yam*.[388] So when we see a Hebrew god (Yahweh/Jesus) conquering death or ruling over the sea, he is actually ruling over the gods Mavet and Yam, just as Baal was. The Hebrew scriptures have simply been cleaned up to help us forget that the Bible presents many gods. Both Baal and Yahweh conquered Mavet (as did Jesus, 1 Cor. 15:26; and we see a prediction of the deaths of gods in Psalm 82 and the prophecy that Mavet would eventually be swallowed up forever, Is. 25:8). Wright wrote regarding Psalm 74:13-14:

> That same chapter of Psalms credits Yahweh with subduing the sea. Or, perhaps, Sea: some translators capitalize the word, because underlying it is *yam*, the ancient Hebrew word for the sea god that Baal smote. The Bible also promises, in the book of Isaiah, that Yahweh will "swallow up death forever"—and underlying "death" is the Hebrew word for Mot, the god of death with whom Baal struggled dramatically.[389]

But back to Baal's story. The virgin Anath, after **sacrificing seventy of various animals** for poor dead Baal, set out to face Mavet and **demand Baal out of Sheol**. She seized Mavet, ripped his clothes, and said, "Come, Mavet, yield My brother!" Mavet said **he had been roaming to and fro on the earth** looking for a lost soul, but he had run into Baal and eaten, or devoured, him (Job 2:2, 1 Pet. 5:8). (Mot swallowed Baal, but Yahweh would prove he was more powerful than Mot or Baal when he swallowed Mot up forever, Is. 25:8.) Anath chopped Mavet to pieces. Then we read:

The Virgin Anath departs.
Then She sets face toward the Torch of the Gods, Shapash.
She lifts Her voice
And shouts:

---

[385] "Mot (Semitic god)," wikipedia.org, 20 Jan. 2015, web, 6 Mar. 2015.
[386] "Canaanite Myth: The Baal Epic."
[387] "Maveth," Strong's H4194, blueletterbible.org, 2015, web, 12 May 2015.
[388] "Yam," Strong's H3220, blueletterbible.org, 2015, web, 12 May 2015.
[389] Wright, 120.

"The message of **Bull-El, Thy father**,
The word of the God of Mercy, Thy begetter:
'Over the furrows of the fields, O Shapash,
Over the furrows of the fields let El set Thee!
As for the Lord of the Furrows of His plowing,
Where is Aliyan **Baal**?
Where is the Prince, **Lord of Earth**?'"

And the Torch of the Gods, Shapash, replies:
"I shall seek Aliyan Baal!"

And the Virgin Anath answers:
"As for Me, tis not I, O Shapash!
As for Me, tis not I, but El summons Thee!
May the Gods guard Thee in Sheol!"

Shapash then trekked down into the underworld to rescue Baal from Sheol. **When she returned she was carrying him with her, and Baal ascended back to the heights of Saphon (returning to reign with his father).** He then set out to destroy Mavet, who was somehow still alive after being hacked up by Anath. **Baal vanquished Mavet, the death angel and god of the underworld.**

And here, written on "tablets that date to the fourteenth century BCE,"[390] we have a god (son of El) who loses a fight with the sea monster and tastes of death. **But the "Torch of the Gods" goes down to Sheol and brings him back up again, at which point he vanquishes death and the god of the underworld and ascends back to his throne.** Yes, it is a familiar story, a tale of a resurrected god who vanquishes death and returns to reign again from the lofty heights. It's an old theme—far, far older than the Christian myth. As Armstrong noted, "The death of a god, the quest of the goddess and the triumphant return to the divine sphere were constant religious themes in many cultures and would recur in the very different religion of the One God worshipped by Jews, Christians and Muslims."[391]

Attis

Dr. Andrew T. Fear is a professor of Classics and Ancient History at the University of Manchester in England. He stated that Attis "after his murder was <u>miraculously brought to life again three days after his demise</u>. . . Attis therefore represented a promise of reborn life and . . . we find representations of the so-called mourning Attis as a common tomb motif in the ancient world."[392] This savior-god Attis "died on a tree at the spring equinox on Black Friday, or the Day of Blood."[393] Another source says he died in

---

[390] Armstrong, 10.
[391] Armstrong, 11.
[392] Eugene N. Lane, *Cybele, Attis and Related Cults* (Leiden, Netherlands: E. J. Brill, 1996), 39.
[393] Walker, *Man Made God*, 162. See also: James G. Frazer, *The Golden Bough* (London: Penguin Classics, 1996), 422; Gerald Berry, *Religions of the World* (New York: Barnes & Noble, 1955), 20; and Guilia Sfameni Gasparo, *Soteriology and Mystic Aspects in the Cult of Cybele and Attis* (Leiden: E. J. Brill, 1985), 40, 84.

the winter and rose again in the spring. Either way he was a "dying and rising" sun and vegetation god, and he began to be worshiped in Greece around 1250 BCE.[394] The people wailed and lamented his passing, and he rose on the third day. He was considered the Most High God who brought salvation, and bread was eaten to commemorate his body. Regarding Attis' timing, Dr. Tryggve Mettinger, retired professor of the Hebrew Bible at Lund University, wrote: "Attis worship is centuries older than Jesus worship and was popular in some parts of the Roman Empire before and well into the 'Christian era.'"[395] The "temple dedicated to him and the Mother Goddess Cybele stood on Vatican Hill in Rome for six centuries, up to the fourth century AD/CE."[396] This, of course, was when Christianity became popular. **Attis is evidence that a savior-god died and rose for the salvation of man at least a century or two before Jesus was born.**

Dr. David Adams Leeming wrote: "Attis is the son of Cybele in her form as the virgin, Nana, who is impregnated by the divine force in the form of a pomegranate."[397] And Professor Merlin Stone noted that "Roman reports of the rituals of Cybele record that the son . . . was first tied to a tree and then buried. Three days later a light was said to appear in the burial tomb, whereupon Attis rose from the dead, bringing salvation with him in his rebirth."[398]

Upon his death, Attis' blood dripped down to the ground, making the ground fertile and productive.[399] Therefore, his dying blood redeemed the earth, bringing life. (When I was in Jerusalem in 2014, I saw the piece of ground that Jesus' blood supposedly dripped onto and soaked down into the earth to redeem Adam.) Remember, babies were thought to be made of menstrual blood, so the ancients thought blood produced life. (That's why the blood of Jesus offered life and was redemptive. It was all about the seed that was buried, died, and was resurrected—1 Corinthians 15. Jesus too was a sun and vegetation god.) Leeming wrote that the **resurrection of Attis "was held by his disciples as a promise that they too would issue triumphant from the corruption of the grave."**[400]

The apostle Paul was aware of Attis, which affected his teaching; and not merely with regard to the resurrection, and triumph over the corruption of the grave, which, again, we can see in 1 Corinthians 15. The *Sierra Reference Encyclopedia* states:

Paul's originality lies in his conception of the death of Jesus as saving mankind from sin. Instead of seeing Jesus as a messiah of the Jewish type human saviour from political bondage he saw him as a salvation-deity whose atoning death by violence was necessary to release his devotees for immortal life. This view of Jesus' death seems to have come to Paul in his Damascus vision. Its roots lie not in Judaism, but in mystery-religion, with which Paul was acquainted in Tarsus.

---

[394] "Attis," wikipedia.org, 9 Jan. 2015, web, 25 Jan. 2015.

[395] Tryggve N. D. Mettinger, *The Riddle of Resurrection: "Dying and Rising Gods" in the Ancient Near East* (Philadelphia: Coronet Books, 2001), 159.

[396] Walker, *Man Made God*, 162. See also: Edward Clodd, *Magic in Names and Other Things* (London: Chapman & Hall, Ltd., 1920), 408.

[397] David Adams Leeming, *Mythology: The Voyage of the Hero* (New York: Oxford University Press, 1998), 25.

[398] Merlin Stone, *When God was a Woman* (New York: Dorset Press, 1990), 146.

[399] Rebecca Zorach, *Blood, Milk, Ink, God: Abundance and Excess in the French Renaissance* (Chicago: University of Chicago Press, 2005), 72.

[400] Leeming, 231.

The violent deaths of Osiris, Attis, Adonis, and Dionysus brought divinization to their initiates. <u>Paul, as founder of the new Christian mystery, initiated the Eucharist, echoing the communion meal of the mystery religions</u>. The awkward insertion of eucharistic material based on I Corinthians 11:23-26 into the Last Supper accounts in the Gospels cannot disguise this, especially as the evidence is that the Jerusalem Church did not practise the Eucharist.[401]

Simcha Jacobovici noted:

"Paul of Tarsus" came from Tarsus, an area of modern-day Turkey. What people don't know is that in the Tarsus of Paul's day they worshipped a god named Attis. Perhaps not coincidentally, Attis was a dying and resurrecting god. . . and his earliest depictions show him with a sheep across his shoulders. All these images were later incorporated into the iconography of Paul's version of Christianity. Put simply, <u>Paul's Jesus looks a lot like Attis</u>.[402]

As a sacrificial act, Attis castrated himself on his wedding night when he married Cybele (yes, **Cybele was his mother and his wife just as the heavenly Jerusalem was both the mother and wife of Jesus and the earthly Jerusalem was both the wife and daughter of Yahweh**—Jer. 3:8, Lam. 2:13, Gal. 4:26, Rev. 21:2). Thus celibacy was an important part of Attis' worship. Some of his worshipers castrated themselves, as church father Origen (184/185–253/254[403]) did in worship to Jesus (Mt. 19:12).[404] Paul approved of celibacy, saying that it was "good for a man not to touch a woman" and he wished all people were like he was—capable of being celibate (1 Cor. 7:1, 7).

Yes, Jesus looked a lot like Attis. So, <u>can we believe that Attis, who died and was resurrected centuries before Jesus in order to bring salvation, was just a myth while the story of Jesus, *almost exactly like that of Attis*, was the gospel truth?</u>

Dionysus/Bacchus

Of Greek origin, Dionysus/Bacchus was the son of Zeus.[405] We have seen already that Moses has been compared to this god; now we find that, like the apostle Paul, Dionysus was "freed from prison by an earthquake"[406] (Acts 16:26-28). Whereas Jesus was a lamb, Dionysus was a "Kid or baby goat,"[407] and he "became the universal savior-god of the ancient world."[408]

Meghan Sullivan noted:

[401] "Paul, St.," *The Sierra Reference Encyclopedia*, P. F. Collier, L. P., 1996; see also: "The Apostle Paul Founder of Christianity," justgivemethetruth.com, n.d., web, 26 May 2015.

[402] Simcha Jacobovici, "Jesus' Marriage to Mary the Magdalene Is Fact, Not Fiction," *The Blog*, huffingtonpost.com, 26 Nov. 2014, web, 27 Nov. 2014.

[403] "Origen," wikipedia.org, 21 Feb. 2015, web, 4 Mar. 2015.

[404] Jacobovici, "Jesus' Marriage to Mary the Magdalene Is Fact, Not Fiction." See also: Armstrong, 101.

[405] Joseph and Murdock, 42.

[406] Robert M. Price, "New Testament Narrative as Old Testament Midrash," *Theological Publications*, robertmprice.mindvendor.com, 2004, web, 25 June 2014.

[407] Murdock, Did *Moses Exist?* 275.

[408] Martin A. Larson, *The Story of Christian Origins* (Washington: Village, 1977), 82. See also: Joseph and Murdock, 42.

Many people are aware that Dionysus (also Bacchus) was the Greek god of wine. But I think fewer people are familiar with the many similarities between the mythic figure Dionysus and the historical figure Jesus Christ. Like Jesus, Dionysus was born of a god (Zeus, the king of the Greek gods) and a virgin (Semele, the princess of Thebes). Just as the infant Jesus narrowly escaped death at the hands of King Herod, Dionysus narrowly survived Hera's attempt to murder him as an infant. Both Jesus and Dionysus performed to illustrate their divinity. Both figures endured rejection by friends and family in their hometowns. Both suffered grotesque deaths – Dionysus died at the hands of the Titans, who cut up his body and ate it. And both Jesus and Dionysus ascended into heaven where they joined their Fathers.[409]

Sir Arthur Weigall confirmed that Dionysus was the son of God, and his mother was a mortal (Semele). Weigall wrote that Dionysus

not only taught mankind the use of the vine but had also been a law-giver . . . preaching happiness, and encouraging peace. He, <u>like Jesus, had suffered a violent death, and had descended into hell, but his resurrection and ascension had followed</u>; and these were commemorated in his sacred rites.[410]

Swedish author Roger Viklund penned a book called *The Jesus That Never Was* (*Den Jesus Som sldrig Funnits*). He wrote:

Dionysus was believed to have <u>risen after his death</u>. On the island of Thasos, in north-eastern Greece, an old inscription speaks of <u>Dionysus as a god who each year renews himself and returns rejuvenated</u>. After doing this <u>he was thought to have ascended to heaven</u>. The <u>Christian apologist Justin Martyr confirms about 150 CE the existence of these ideas</u>, but at the same time, he denies that the events described actually had occurred and he claims that the devil had forged the writings of the Greeks:

For when they tell that Bacchus, son of Jupiter, was begotten by [Jupiter's, that is Zeus'] intercourse with Semele, and that he was the discoverer of the vine; and when they relate, that being torn in pieces, and having died, he rose again, and ascended to heaven; and when they introduce wine into his mysteries, do I not perceive that [the devil] has imitated the prophecy announced by the patriarch Jacob, and recorded by Moses? (Justin Martyr, Dialogue with Trypho the Jew, 69) . . .

<u>Justin Martyr knew of several pagan sons of god</u> (for example the sons of Zeus) <u>whose respective death each was filled with agony and suffering and in his opinion was in that respect similar to the death of Jesus</u>. He asserts, however, that the sons of god died in various ways and that the pagans did not imitate the crucifixion, since they considered it symbolic. Whether they are symbols or not,

---

[409] Meghan Sullivan, "Dionysus—Just the God of Wine?" winetrailtraveler.com, 2006-2014, web, 11 July 2014.
[410] Arthur Weigall, *The Paganism in Our Christianity* (London: Hutchinson & Co., 1928), 220; (New York: G. P. Putnam's, 1928, and The Book Tree, 2008), 241. See also: Joseph and Murdock, 46-47.

Dionysus the Vine is depicted on a tree and the wine is said to be hung on the cross. As a consequence, the legend of Jesus' crucifixion may be seen as a development of the legend of Dionysus' crucifixion.[411]

Godfrey Higgins wrote that "the myth of the crucifix was common to all nations, before the time of Jesus of Nazareth, from Thule to China."[412] (One thing we might remember here, besides the obvious similarities of Jesus and Dionysus, is that Martyr made mention that the pagans considered the cross symbolic. We will talk more about this later on.)

The crucifix is not the only common theme among the gods. Another, which we see in the myth of Dionysus, is the eating of the flesh of a god and drinking his blood. Before we move on, we'll consider this universal practice here since we are studying the god of wine.

Bacchus/Dionysus was called the "vine" just as Christ was.[413] According to *The Book Your Church Doesn't Want You to Read*, Dionysus "at his annual festival in his temple of Elis filled three empty kettles with wine—no water needed! And on the fifth of January wine instead of water gushed from his temple at Andros. If we believe Jesus' miracle, why should we not believe Dionysus's?"[414] [Pliny (2.103) wrote that a temple of Bacchus "had a fountain where the water tasted like wine during the Nones of January (5th)."[415]] According to Dr. Craig M. Lyons, "red wine was drunk at the bacchanals by the devotees of the god Dionysus in a symbolic ritual of his blood," just as Christians drink wine to represent the blood of Jesus (Mt. 26:28, 1 Cor. 11:25).[416] Sullivan affirmed that the "ancient Greeks who consumed Dionysus' blood in the form of wine received a blessing from their gods. In some instances, consumption even enabled the Greeks to take on Dionysus' immortal nature." Sullivan further noted that this "parallels Jesus' words in John's Gospel: "Those who eat my flesh and drink my blood have eternal life, and I will raise them up on the last day" (Jn. 6:54 NRSV).[417] Centuries before Jesus was born, Euripides, an Athenian playwright (c. 485-406 BCE), wrote regarding Dionysus:

His blood, the blood of the grape, lightens the burden of our mortal misery. When, after their daily toils, men drink their fill, sleep comes to them, bringing release from all their troubles. There is no other cure for sorrow. Though himself a God, it is his blood we pour out to offer thanks to the Gods. And through him, we are blessed.[418]

---

[411] Roger Viklund, "The Jesus Parallels," from *The Jesus That Never Was*, 2007, web, 10 Nov. 2014 <http://www.jesusgranskad.se/jesus_parallels.htm>.

[412] Godfrey Higgins, *Anacalypsis: An Attempt to Draw Aside the Veil*, or *The Saitic Esis, II* (London: J. Burns, 1878), 129.

[413] Murdock, *Did Moses Exist?* 364.

[414] Tim Leedom, ed., *The Book Your Church Doesn't Want You to Read* (Dubuque, IA: Kendall/Hunt, 1993), 125. See also: Joseph and Murdock, 45.

[415] Murdock, *Did Moses Exist?* 338.

[416] Craig M. Lyons, MsD, DD, MDiv, "Jesus Turned Water into Wine at the Wedding Feast at Cana: Truth or Sun-Myth Retold? *Bet Emet Ministries*, christianityasamysteryreligion.com, n.d. web, 31 May 2014.

[417] Sullivan, "Dionysus—Just the God of Wine?"

[418] Stephen L. Harris, *The New Testament*, 6th ed. (Boston: McGraw Hill, 2009), 76. [Euripides' play tr. by Michael Cacoyannis.]

The eating and drinking of blood "in the hope of gaining some Christlike virtue," is, according to Graham, "a relic of the savage rite of omophagia—the eating and drinking of another person's or animal's flesh and blood to acquire his or its qualities, strength, courage, and so on." Christians, and others, have gone further and "eat a god instead of a man, and so the savage's anthropophagy is now theanthropophagy."[419] The worshipers of Osiris ritually ate bread and drank wine, believing they were "flesh and blood" of Osiris.[420] Doane wrote:

> The *Eucharist* **was instituted many hundreds of years before the time assigned for Christ Jesus. Cicero**, the greatest orator of Rome, and one of the most illustrious of her statesmen, **born in the year 106 B.C., mentions it in his works, and wonders at the strangeness of the rite**. "How can a man be so stupid," says he, "as to imagine that which he eats to be a God?" There had been an esoteric meaning attached to it from the first establishment of the *mysteries* among the Pagans, and the **Eucharista is one of the oldest rites of antiquity**.[421]

Doane noted that the ancient Egyptians celebrated the resurrection of Osiris and partook of a cake, or wafer, which became "mystically the body of Isis or Osiris."[422] More than that, the "cakes of Isis" given by the priests were taken to the homes of those who were unable to attend the worship service, a practice of some churches even today.[423] Pythagoras (c. 570 BCE) also performed and partook of this ritual,[424] and Tertullian (193-220 CE) wrote that the worshipers of Mithra partook of the eucharist.[425] The following was written regarding the Mithraic eucharist: "He who will not eat of my body and drink of my blood so that he will be made one with me and I with him, the same shall not know salvation."[426] Wine and bread were used as well in the worship of Adonis.[427] And, as Graham noted, "every race of antiquity had its Judeo-Christian equivalents."[428] Doane confirmed this with the following words: "In fact, the communion of bread and wine was used in the worship of nearly every important deity."[429]

One final comparison between Jesus and Dionysus must be made. Murdock wrote:

> Since antiquity, grape juice and wine have been perceived as the "blood" of both the fruit itself and of the vine and wine deity. After it was pressed, the grape juice would flow into underground pots, depicted as the god "cultivated in the underworld." Out of this tomb, Dionysus was said to reemerge during the festival of Anthesteria, in February, when "the urns were opened, and the god's spirit was

[419] Graham, 335.
[420] Murdock, *Did Moses Exist?* 362, 375. See also: Iain Gately, *Drink: A Cultural History of Alcohol* (New York: Gotham Books, 2008).
[421] Doane, XXX. See also: Bennett, 594.
[422] James Bonwick, *Egyptian Belief and Modern Thought* (London: C. Kegan Paul & Co., 1878), 417. See also: Doane, XXX.
[423] Bonwick, 418.
[424] Higgins, *Anacalypsis*, II (1878), 60. Doane, XXX.
[425] Doane, XXX.
[426] Walker, *Man Made God*, 136.
[427] Doane, XXX.
[428] Graham, 336.
[429] Doane, XXX.

reborn as an infant." The "graves of the dead released their spirits as well at this time, and for the three days of the festival, ghosts roamed abroad in Athens."[430]

In Matthew 27:52-53 we read that the "graves were opened; and many bodies of the saints which slept arose, And came out of the graves after [Jesus'] resurrection, and went into the holy city, and appeared unto many." As did Dionysus, Jesus woke the dead.

Of course, the Christian explanation as to why worshipers performed "Christian" practices before there was a Christ, was that the sly devil made the pagans practice this ritual in order to deceive the people when the true savior arrived.[431] One would think Yahweh could, and would, have kept that from happening; after all, it doesn't promote faith to allow other, older gods to be exactly like Yahweh's own son. How is anyone to tell the difference?

Osiris

He is born! He is born! O come and adore him! Women and men, O come and adore him, Child who was born in the night. People of earth, O come and adore him, bow down before him, kneel down before him, King who was born in the night. Worship the Child of God's own begetting. Heaven and Earth, O come and adore him! God who was born in the night.[432]

The words above are taken from an Egyptian hymn worshiping the newborn Osiris. **One of the oldest gods for whom we have records, the name of Osiris was discovered on the "Palermo Stone of around 2500 BC.** He was widely worshiped until the suppression of the Egyptian religion during the Christian era."[433] According to "The Osiris Legend,"

The story of Osiris is one of Egypt's most ancient myths. So old, it's [sic] origins have been lost in time. It was an important story to the Egyptians because of Osiris' role as the king of Egypt who is resurrected as the "King of the dead". A king that every Egyptian, from the mightiest pharaoh to the lowliest peasant, hoped to join in the afterlife.[434]

Osiris is another Christ figure, who, of course, predated Jesus. Nut, the sky goddess, spoke from heaven (in the *Pyramid Texts*) regarding Osiris, calling him **her son**, **her firstborn**, and her beloved **with whom she was satisfied**.[435] (See Matthew 3:17.) Osiris, again, was also worshiped with the use of bread and wine. John Yarker wrote: "Over a

---

[430] Murdock, *Did Moses Exist?* 365.

[431] Edward King, *Antiquities of Mexico* (London: 1830 31, 1848), Vol. VI, 221. See also: Doane, XXX.

[432] Walker, *Man Made God*, 135. See also: Timothy Freke and Peter Gandy, *The Jesus Mysteries* (New York: Harmony Books, 1999), 32.

[433] "Osiris & Horus," ambrosiasociety.org, 2009, web, 7 Nov. 2014.

[434] Deurer, "The Osiris Legend," egyptartsite.com, 1996-2010, web, 22 Jan. 2015.

[435] Samuel Mercer, *The Pyramid Texts* (London: Longmans, Green & Co., 1952), 20. See also: Murdock, *Christ in Egypt*, 31.

cup or chalice these words appear in Greek: 'This is not wine, this is the blood of Osiris,' and over a piece of bread: 'This is not bread, this is the very body of Osiris.'"[436]

Osiris also turned water to wine, just as Jesus did. The Feast of Epiphany of January 6, commemorating this event in Christ's life, "is also the anniversary of the water-wine transformation performed by Osiris."[437] Furthermore, **the dead in Egyptian mythology always became Osiris upon death.**[438] This is, of course, true as well with Jesus (1 Cor.15:42-49). (See my book *We Are Emmanuel* for more detail.)

Nut, mother of Osiris, was considered the mother of the sun. The sun was "thought to gestate at night within her womb and to be born at dawn from between her thighs."[439] Today we call Nut by the name of Virgo.[440] Thus, the virgin gave birth. Regarding the virgin birth,

> It is . . . Philo who first formulated the idea of the Word or ideal ordering principle of the Cosmos being born of an ever-virgin soul, which conceives, because God the Father sows into her his intelligible rays and Divine seed, so begetting His only well-loved Son the Cosmos.[441]

Osiris/Horus

Osiris and then Horus (circa 3000 BCE) were "crucified in the heavens,"[442] as was Jesus Christ (which will be shown in a later chapter and can be found in my book *We Are Emmanuel*). **A Passion Play regarding the death and resurrection of Osiris was actually performed for Osiris "ages before the common era."[443]** Epiphanius (c. 310-403), who was an early church father, wrote that Aion (identified as Osiris in the *Suda*, a Greek encyclopedic lexicon[444]) was produced from a manger every year.[445] Church father Hippolytus (c. 236), in *Refutation of All Heresies* (8.45), alleged that Aion's mother was "the virgin who is with child and conceives and bears a son, who is not psychic, not bodily, but a blessed Aion of Aions."[446]

Murdock told the story of the god Si-Osiris as follows:

---

[436] John Yarker, *The Arcane Schools* (Triad Press, 2006), 75. See also: Murdock, *Christ in Egypt*, 292.
[437] Erich Neumann, *The Origins and History of Consciousness* (London: Routledge, 1999), 239. See also: Murdock, *Christ in Egypt*, 292-293. According to Murdock, Neumann quoted Hugo Gressman in his *Tod und Auferstehung des Osiris*.
[438] James G. Frazer, *Adonis, Attis, Osiris: Studies in the History of Oriental* Religion (London: MacMillan and Co., 1906), 217. See also: Murdock, *Christ in Egypt*, 36.
[439] James P. Allen, *The Ancient Egyptian Pyramid Texts* (Atlanta: Society of Biblical Literature, 2005), 9. See also: Murdock, *Christ in Egypt*, 143.
[440] Orlando P. Schmidt, *A Self-verifying Chronological History of Ancient Egypt* (Ohio: George C. Shaw, 1900), 52-53. See also: Murdock, *Christ in Egypt*, 143.
[441] Frederick C. Conybeare, *Philo about the Contemplative Life* (Oxford: Clarendon Press, 1895), 302-303. See also: Murdock, *Christ in Egypt*, 469.
[442] Doane, 484. See also: Murdock, *Christ in Egypt*, 335.
[443] Murdock, *Christ in Egypt*, 382.
[444] *Pseudo-Callisthenes*, I.30–33, as cited by Jarl Fossum, "The Myth of the Eternal Rebirth: Critical Notes on G. W. Bowersock, Hellenism in Late Antiquity," *Vigiliae Christianae* 53.3 (1999), 309, Note 15.
[445] Joseph and Murdock, 17.
[446] Marvin W. Meyer, *The Ancient Mysteries: A Sourcebook of Sacred Texts* (Philadelphia: University of Pennsylvania Press, 1987), 152. See also: Joseph and Murdock, 17.

When Si-Osiris was twelve years old he was wiser than the wisest of the scribes. This story includes fantastical elements—such as a visit to the underworld—that indicate it is not historical but may well revolve around Horus, son of Osiris. Thus, in Egypt we find a similar tale as in the gospel about the "son of God" who is 12 years old and is precocious in intelligence and knowledge, besting the elders and scribes.[447]

Horus possessed many attributes that Jesus also bore. The mother of Horus was a virgin named Isis-Mery/Meri. She said of herself, "I am the great virgin,"[448] and she was referred to as the Virgin Mother by her worshipers.[449] A star in the East announced Horus' birth, which three wise men attended. He began teaching at the age of twelve and was baptized at the age of thirty. His baptizer, Anpu (Anubis, Inpu) was beheaded. Horus walked on water and was crucified between two thieves, and then was resurrected after three days. He was called "Son of Man," "Good Shepherd, "Lamb of God," and "Word made flesh." He did battle with the evil god Set/Seth and was to reign on the earth for 1,000 years.[450] Horus, in fact, was the incarnation of his father, Osiris.[451] His mother was refused lodging and fled into Egypt to escape Set.[452] Horus was born around the time of the winter solstice,[453] and his birth was signaled by a star in the East and the "Three Kings" (the Magi) or three stars in the belt of Orion.[454] (These "three kings," or stars, line up on December 24 and point to the rising sun on December 25.) Horus was "mediator between heaven and earth, and between creation and destruction."[455] He also "goes to visit the spirits in prison or in their cells and sepulchres,"[456] The evil Set was chained, and Horus "took possession of the house once more on a lease of a thousand years to establish his reign of peace, plenty and good luck in the domain of time and law, justice and right by the inauguration of another millennium."[457] [458]

Horus, like Jesus, was lost when he was twelve years old, and was "later found in the Temple of the Sun teaching the priests."[459] Horus died in order to remove sins,[460] and he ascended into heaven.[461] Osiris, father of Horus, also ascended to heaven and was said to

---

[447] Murdock, *Christ in Egypt*, 213. See also: Joseph and Murdock, 21.

[448] G. Johannes Botterweck, *Theological Dictionary of the Old Testament*, 2:338. See also: Bennett, 147.

[449] Bennett, 147.

[450] *The Century*, 728. See also: Murdock, *Christ in Egypt*, 44, 425.

[451] Murdock, *Christ in Egypt*, 62.

[452] Murdock, *Christ in Egypt*, 164.

[453] Plutarch, *Isis & Osiris*, 65:387C. See also: Plutarch, *Moralia*, tr. Frank Cole Babbitt (Cambridge, MA: Harvard University Press, and London: William Heinemann Ltd., 1936), 5.

[454] Murdock, *Christ in Egypt*, 199-200.

[455] Bennett, 150.

[456] Gerald Massey, *Ancient Egypt: Light of the World*, II (Whitefish, MT: Kessinger, 2002), 772. See also: Murdock, *Christ in Egypt*, 386.

[457] Massey, *Ancient Egypt: Light of the World*, II, 733. See also: Murdock, *Christ in Egypt*, 425.

[458] For more evidence for claims regarding Horus, see: "Tat Tvam Asi's 'Evidence' - Page 1," kingdavid8.com, 2012, web, 2 Jan. 2015 <http://www.kingdavid8.com/_full_article.php?id=63746a72-ca29-11e1-a119-842b2b162e97>.

[459] Graham, 311.

[460] Murdock, *Christ in Egypt*, 277.

[461] Raymond O. Faulkner, *The Ancient Egyptian Pyramid Texts* (Oxford: Clarendon Press, 1969), 92; Mercer, *The Pyramid Texts*, 102 <www.sacred-texts.com/egy/pyt/index.htm>; James P. Allen, *The Ancient Egyptian Pyramid Texts*, 57. See also: Murdock, *Christ in Egypt*, 399.

sit at God's right hand in Paradise "as judge of the dead."[462] **The "Last Judgment" of the *Book of the Dead* sounds very much like Matthew 25.** The person speaking in the *Book of the Dead* Spell 125 says that "he has given food to the hungry, drink to the thirsty, clothes to the naked, and a boat to the shipwrecked." People who have "done these things on earth are held to have done them to Horus, the Lord; and they are invited to come to him as the blessed ones of his father Osiris."[463]

The parable of the rich man and Lazarus (Lk. 16) was apparently taken from an Egyptian folktale about a journey made by Si-Osiris (Horus the Elder) into the underworld. The story concludes: "He who has been good on earth, will be blessed in the kingdom of the dead, and he who has been evil on earth, will suffer in the kingdom of the dead."[464]

Horus and his exploits are the source of the story of the raising of Lazarus in the Bible. While Jesus went to Bethany to raise Lazarus, the brother of Mary and Martha, Horus "went to Bethanu to raise his father. What is more, the names Mary, Martha and Lazarus all came from Egypt. There the two sisters are Meri and Merti, and their brother . . . El-Azar-us."[465]

Gerald Massey wrote regarding Osiris:

> The scene in the Mount of Transfiguration is obviously derived from the ascent of Osiris (or Horus), and his transfiguration in the Mount of the Moon. The sixth day was celebrated as that of the change and transfiguration of the solar god in the lunar orb, which he re-entered as the regenerator of its light. With this we may compare the statement made by Matthew that "After six days Jesus" went "up into a high mountain apart, and he was transfigured." "And his face did shine as the sun" (of course!), "and his garments became white as the light."[466] . . . As before said, the scene on the mount of transfiguration reproduces the ascent of Buddha into Mount Pandava or Yellow-White, and of Osiris into the Moon![467]

> The Egyptian "*Book of the Dead* promised resurrection to all mankind, as a reward for righteous living, long before Judaism and Christianity embraced that concept."[468]

> Through the sufferings and death of Osiris, the Egyptian hoped that his body might rise again in a transformed, glorified, and incorruptible shape, and the devotee appealed in prayer for eternal life to him who had conquered death and had become the king of the underworld through his victory and prayer.[469]

---

[462] Robert M. Price, "Jonathan Z. Smith: Drudgery Divine. On the Comparison of Early Christianities and the Religions of Late Antiquity," *Journal for Higher Criticism*, Institute of Higher Critical Studies, Spring 1996, web, 22 Mar. 2015 <depts.drew.edu/jhc/jzsmith.html>. See also: Murdock, *Christ in Egypt*, 406.

[463] Massey, *Gerald Massey's Lectures*, 59. See also: Murdock, *Christ in Egypt*, 489.

[464] Joachim Jeremias, *The Parables of Jesus*, rev. ed. (London: SCM Press, 1972), 183.

[465] Graham, 338.

[466] Massey, *Gerald Massey's Lectures*, No. 23.

[467] Massey, *Gerald Massey's Lectures*, No. 26.

[468] D. Ogden Goelet, *The Egyptian Book of the Dead: The Book of Going Forth by Day - The Complete Papyrus of Ani Featuring Integrated Text and Full-Color Images* (San Francisco: Chronical Books, 2008), 18.

[469] E. A. Wallis Budge, *A Guide to the First and Second Egyptian Rooms*, British Museum, 1904, 4-5. See also: Murdock, *Christ in Egypt*, 409.

This really should not surprise us, as the Egyptians invested much time and expense in their mummification process. The following Egyptian beliefs should also remind us of the promises made in the Bible for the followers of Jesus.

In heaven the beatified eat bread which never grows stale, and drink wine which grows not musty; they wear white apparel, and sit upon thrones among the gods who cluster round the tree of life near the lake in the Field of Peace; they wear the crowns which the gods give unto them, and no evil being or thing has any power to harm them in their new abode, where they will live with Ra for ever.[470]

For more on Osiris' resurrection, note the following quotes from the Egyptian *Pyramid Texts* (possibly the oldest of all religious texts[471]) and the *Book of the Dead*:

O Osiris the King, you have gone, but you will return, you have slept, (but you will awake), you have died, but you will live. (PT 670:1975a-b/N 348)

I am…the Lord of Resurrections, who cometh forth from the dusk and whose birth from the House of Death. (BD 64) [See John 11:25.]

The tomb is open for thee; the double doors of the coffin are undone for thee. (PT 676:2009a/N 411)

Flesh of (the Osiris), rot not, decay not, let not thy smell be bad. (PT 412:722a-b/T 228) [See Psalm 16:10; Acts 2:27, 13:35.]

Let them who are in their graves, arise; let them undo their bandages. (PT 662:1878a/N 388)[472] [See John 5:28-29.]

Hercules/Heracles/Herakles

Hercules and Jesus bear many resemblances. Hercules was born, long before Jesus, to the virgin Alcmene and Zeus. A Roman coin, dated around 215-15 BCE, showing the goddess Juno on the front, depicts Hercules on the back fighting a centaur.[473] Hercules was the "only begotten" of Zeus and was called savior, good shepherd, and Prince of Peace. He died, went to the underworld, and "ascended to heaven from Mount Orca."[474]

Viklund wrote that from the "very beginning, Hercules was seen as the reconciler of humanity and the Son of God" and that at the "beginning of our Common Era, the faith of Heracles was spread in large parts of the Mediterranean area, such as Greece, Syria and Rome."[475] Hercules lived hundreds of years before Christ, so any copying from one myth

---

[470] Higgins, *Anacalypsis*, II (1878), 102. See also: Murdock, *Christ in Egypt*, 419.
[471] Wilkinson, 6.
[472] Murdock, *Christ in Egypt*, 306-307.
[473] "Hercules," wikipedia. org, 20 Oct. 2014, web, 12 Nov. 2014.
[474] Graham, 287.
[475] Viklund, "The Jesus Parallels."

to the other should be seen as Christians' copying from the Herculean myth. Viklund, in writing of Hercules, cited well his sources (which can be found on the web site below).

There are points of close similarity between the life of Jesus and the life of Heracles. Heracles' mother, a woman named Alcmene, becomes pregnant through a union with the god Zeus, and she gives birth to Heracles. Heracles is consequently a Son of God. Just like Jesus, Heracles has a mortal stepfather named Amphitryon. But like Joseph (Matthew 2:4ff), Amphitryon does not have sexual intercourse with his wife until the divine conception has taken place and she still is a virgin. Heracles' mortal parents make a trip from their hometown Mycenae to Thebes where Zeus makes Alcmene pregnant and she gives birth to Heracles. It was commonly held that virgin sons were born during flights or travels, and that was the case when Isis gave birth to Horus. While Jesus, according to the Gospels, was born in Bethlehem, he was still known as Jesus of Nazareth. Also Heracles was known to hail from his father's hometown, despite the fact that he was born in Thebes.

When Heracles is born, the goddess Hera, Zeus' wife, is told that a king of her tribe is born. Knowing that Zeus is the father, and enraged by jealousy and fear of losing her power to the new king, she attempts to kill Heracles. Jesus' parents fled with Jesus to Egypt in order to escape Herod's persecution, and after Herod's death, they returned to Palestine. Heracles' mother Alcmene leaves Heracles in the woods to escape Hera's wrath and persecution. Athena rescues Heracles and eventually she brings him back to Alcmene.

Before Heracles begins his public mission, he spends – just like Jesus – a long time by himself. During this period, he is tempted, and like Jesus, he overcomes the temptations. The god Hermes shows Heracles the realms of the king and the tyrant from a high mountain. Jesus also meets this fate, when the Devil shows him the glory of the kingdoms of the earth from a high mountain, and promises that he can rule them all (Matthew 4:8). . .

Heracles is called The Saviour. Like Jesus, he walks on water, and he raises Alcestis from the dead, but his true feat is to overcome death, and his death leads to eternal life. Heracles' second wife Deianira causes his death by accident, and like Judas Iscariot she is overcome by horror and remorse, and hangs herself. . .

When Heracles is dying, both his mother and a beloved disciple are present. According to John 19:25f, the conditions were the same when Jesus died. Before Heracles dies, he invokes his heavenly Father:

I pray you admit this spirit of mine to the stars – – – See, my father is summoning me now and opening heaven. I come, father!

… spiritum admitte hunc, precor, in astra – – – vocat ecce iam me genitor et pandit polos; venio, pater (Seneca, *Hercules Oetaeus*, 1703–4, 1724–6, Loeb)

According to Luke 23:46 (NASB), Jesus cries out: "Father, into your hands I commit my spirit." As both Sons of God are dying, they say: "it is completed" or

"It is finished". **When Heracles as well as Jesus dies, both an earthquake and a solar eclipse occur.** After his death, Heracles still can communicate with this world (he is resurrected?) and calls out: "<u>Mother, now cease your wailing ... I must go up now into the heavenly climes</u>", which he is also said to have done. The resurrected Jesus says to his Mary Magdalene: "Woman, why are you weeping? ... I ascend to my Father and your Father" (John 20:15–17 NASB). <u>Even the information that the most beloved disciple cared for the Saviour's mother is found in the legend of Heracles.</u>

The author of the Gospel of John in particular seems to have borrowed a lot from the cult of Heracles. The concept of "Logos", which is so important in the Prologue to the Gospel of John, is borrowed from the Stoics, and was also part of the religion of Heracles. Compare John 3:17: "For God did not send his Son into the world to condemn the world, but to save the world through him", to Cornutus, who in the first century wrote: "For the Logos [the word] is not there to harm or to punish, but to save".[476]

Comparing Hercules to Jesus, Jim Walker wrote:

Likewise the "evidence" of Hercules closely parallels that of Jesus. We have historical people like Hesiod and Plato who mention Hercules in their writings. Similar to the way the gospels tell a narrative story of Jesus, so do we have the epic stories of Homer who depict the life of Hercules. Aesop tells stories and quotes the words of Hercules. Just as we have a <u>brief mention of Jesus by Josephus in his Antiquities, Josephus also mentions Hercules (more times than Jesus), in the very same work</u> (see: 1.15; 8.5.3; 10.11.1). Just <u>as Tacitus mentions a Christus, so does he also mention Hercules many times</u> in his Annals. And most importantly, <u>just as we have no artifacts, writings or eyewitnesses about Hercules, we also have nothing about Jesus. All information about Hercules and Jesus comes from stories, beliefs, and hearsay. Should we then believe in a historical Hercules, simply because ancient historians mention him and that we have stories and beliefs about him? Of course not, and the same must apply to Jesus if we wish to hold any consistency to historicity.</u>[477]

Resembling the story of Jonah, in the "older Greek myth the demigod Herakles was swallowed by a whale, and he too had departed from Joppa!"[478] (Jon. 1:3, Mt. 12:40). Also like Jonah, Hercules remained in the whale's belly for three days. The Persian Jamshyd was swallowed by a "sea monster" and vomited onto the land. We saw earlier that Baal was devoured by the sea god, Yam; and in the Samadeva Bhatt the Indian Saktadeva was ingested by a fish and, when it was opened, came out unharmed. Vishnu is pictured coming out of a fish's mouth.[479] (We'll discuss these "fish" stories later.)

[476] Viklund, "The Jesus Parallels."
[477] Jim Walker, "Did a historical Jesus exist?"
[478] C. M. Houck, "Jonah and the Whale Myth," *Time Frames and Taboo Data Blog*, timeframesandtaboodata.com, 2011, web, 18 June 2014. See also: Doane, IX.
[479] Graham, 264.

Mercury and the Logos

Like Hercules, Mercury was called the Logos. Pagan philosopher Amelius spoke of this, as did Justin Martyr (100-165 CE) in his apology to Emperor Antoninus Pius. Martyr's apology was that Christians shouldn't be criticized for believing the Logos was with God in the beginning, was God himself, and should be worshiped as God because the worshipers of Mercury believed the same. Martyr wrote: "you have your Mercury in worship, under the title of the word and messenger of God."[480] Dameron noted that "Christ" and "Logos" were terms that "existed ages before Christianity."[481] Barbara Walker wrote: "Logos doctrine descended from very primitive ideas through Neolithic magic, Oriental mysticism, pagan philosophy and Gnostic beliefs into an uneasy resting place in Christianity."[482]

Zoroaster/Zarathustra

Zoroaster was a descendant of kings. When his mother was pregnant she saw a vision wherein she was told that she was "favored among women by bearing a son to whom Ormuzd (good — god) would make known his laws and who should spread them through all the East." Her child would face many trials but would triumph and "ascend to the side of Ormuzd [Ahura Mazda[483]] in the highest heaven," while his foe would sink into hell.[484]

King Darius attempted to kill Zoroaster as a child. As Darius tried to saw the boy into pieces, the king's "arm was grasped by some unseen power and was withered to the shoulder, which so frightened the king that he dropped the sword and fled in terror." Zoroaster was then stolen and thrown into the fire, but he just lay there unharmed and was returned to his mother. He was poisoned and put in the way of wild animals but always escaped injury.[485]

At the age of thirty, Zoroaster began his work, leaving home to go to Iran. However, he was "warned in a vision" to turn aside to the mountains of Albordi, where he was given many revelations and was "lifted up into the highest heaven, where he beheld Ormuzd in all his glory encircled by a host of angels." There he was provided sweet food like honey and saw all that was happening in heaven and on the earth. He learned the "inmost secrets of nature" and the "terrible condition of the sinful." He went down to hell and faced the evil one, and always "put his enemies to flight" by "repeating a few verses of his divine gospel."[486]

Believers of Zoroastrianism were thought by some to be the first people to believe in angels, Satan, and the unending battle between good and evil. Zoroastrian art pictures the

[480] Richard Carlile, ed. *The Republican* (London: R. Carlile, 1824), Vol. X, 217. See also: Doane, XXXV.
[481] Dameron, 87.
[482] Walker, *Man Made God*, 45.
[483] Bennett, 124.
[484] Dameron, 57-58.
[485] Dameron, 57-58.
[486] Dameron, 57-58.

prophet as surrounded by the same halo of light that encircles Jesus and Mary.[487] Jim Walker wrote:

> the religion of Zoroaster, founded circa 628-551 B.C.E. in ancient Persia, roused mankind in the need for hating a devil, the belief of a paradise, last judgment and resurrection of the dead. Mithraism, an offshoot of Zoroastrianism, probably influenced early Christianity. The Magi described in the New Testament appears [sic] as Zoroastrian priests. Note the word "paradise" came from the Persian *pairidaeza*.[488]

Zoroastrianism thus had a huge impact on future religious thinking.

Mithra(s)

Dr. Tischendorf wrote that the "allegory of Jesus Christ derived from the fable of Mithra/Mithras, the divine son of God (Ahura Mazda) and messiah of the first kings of the Persian Empire around 400 BC." (Thomas Brunty alleged that Mithra began to be worshiped around 1200 BCE.[489]) Tony Bushby wrote:

> Tischendorf's conclusion also supports Professor Bordeaux's Vatican findings that reveal the allegory of Jesus Christ derived from the fable of Mithra, the divine son of God (Ahura Mazda) and messiah of the first kings of the Persian Empire around 400 BC. His birth in a grotto was attended by magi who followed a star from the East. They brought "gifts of gold, frankincense and myrrh" (as in Matt. 2:11) and the newborn baby was adored by shepherds. He came into the world wearing the Mithraic cap, which popes imitated . . . until well into the 15th century.
>
> Mithra, one of a trinity, stood on a rock, the emblem of the foundation of his religion, and was anointed with honey. **After a last supper with Helios and 11 other companions, Mithra was crucified on a cross, bound in linen, placed in a rock tomb and rose on the third day** or around 25 March (the full moon at the spring equinox, a time now called Easter after the Babylonian goddess Ishtar). The fiery destruction of the universe was a major doctrine of Mithraism - a time in which Mithra promised to return in person to Earth and save deserving souls. Devotees of Mithra partook in a sacred communion banquet of bread and wine, a **ceremony that paralleled the Christian Eucharist and preceded it by more than four centuries**.[490]

Again, as was his custom, Justin Martyr blamed this on the devil, saying, "Which the wicked devils have imitated in the mysteries of Mithras, commanding the same thing to

[487] Melloson Allen, "10 Ways the Bible Was Influenced by Other Religions."
[488] Jim Walker, "Did a historical Jesus exist?"
[489] Thomas Brunty, "Forgotten Christ," film by Agata Brunty, *Sensoria Productions*, 15 Mar. 2014, youtube.com, 20 Dec. 2014 <https://www.youtube.com/watch?v=zpDN2802YzA>.
[490] Bushby, "The Forged Origins of the New Testament."

be done."[491] Mithra was called "The Truth" and "The Light," and his special day of worship was Sunday.[492]

Viklund wrote:

> By all accounts, the Roman cult of Mithras was a rival of the early Christian Church. Thus the Mithras cult shared the fate of the Gnostic movement. **When in the fourth century, the Christian Church emerged the victor; the Mithras cult was eventually suppressed, and was later forbidden.** Its followers were persecuted, its temples destroyed, and Christian churches were erected upon the ruins. If the Mithraic Church ever possessed any writings, they have not survived. . .
>
> As a consequence of the precession of the equinoxes . . . the conditions of 4000 years ago (c. 2000 BCE) had changed in such a way that the sun at the vernal equinox rose in Aries instead of in Taurus. At some point in history, our ancestors must have made this discovery, and this probably was the basis of the widely spread idea about the killing of the bull. When they made this discovery, they killed a bull as a symbol of the entrance into a new era or perhaps only in order to appease the heavenly gods. The bull (Taurus) died and the ram (Aries) was born. . .
>
> At the dawn of Christianity, the vernal equinox had moved yet another sign, from Aries to Pisces. It seems likely that people at that time had the lamb (Aries) slaughtered and that the fish became the symbol of the new (Piscean) age. This is probably the basis of the bull (Taurus) slaughter done by Mithras and the reason why Jesus (the lamb or Aries) is slaughtered on the cross.[493]

Krishna/Chrishna/Christna/Chrisna/Kreeshna

The Indian god Krishna (c. 900 BCE, according to some sources) was another god whose life and death resembled that of Jesus'. Doane listed forty-six similarities between Jesus and Krishna; and Edward Moor, author of "Hindu Pantheon" and "Oriental Fragments," wrote that **both Krishna's name and his general story "extended to the time of Homer," about 900 years before Jesus was born and more than a hundred years before the prophet Isaiah wrote (meaning Krishna, resembling Jesus, was worshiped before Isaiah wrote his prophecies that were supposedly about Jesus).**[494] (One source says Krishna was born on the 19th or 21st of July 3228 BCE.[495]) Acharya S noted that a "number of the world's leading *Christian* Indianists . . . as well as numerous *Indian* scholars, have contended that the Krishna tale *predates* the Christian era by

[491] Justin Martyr, *The First Apology*, Ch. 66, newadvent.org, copyright 2009 by Kevin Knight, web, 26 Jan. 2015.
[492] Weigall (Putnam and The Book Tree), 145. See also: Joseph and Murdock, 47.
[493] Viklund, "The Jesus Parallels."
[494] John P. Lundy, *Monumental Christianity or The Art and Symbolism of the Primitive Church* (New York: J. W. Bouton, 1876), 151; and *Asiatick Researches; or, Transactions of the Society Instituted in Bengal, for Inquiring into the History and Antiquities, the Arts, Sciences, and Literature, of Asia* (London, 1806), Vol. I, 273. See also: Doane, XXVIII.
[495] Edward L. Winston, "Skeptic Project," conspiracies.skeptic.com, 29 Nov. 2007, web, 13 June 2015.

centuries at least."[496] **The *Sanskrit Dictionary*, "compiled more than two thousand years ago" (quote from Doane in the year 1882 CE, meaning it was compiled before the time of Christ), gives the story of Krishna's virgin birth and his escape from Kansa, who sought the infant's life.**[497] Sir William Jones, a Christian writing in the eighteenth century, also stated that the *Sanscrit Dictionary*, **which was, again, more than 2,000 years old, relates the whole story of Krishna, who was crucified and rose again, returning to his divine father.**[498] That should convince anyone that the stories regarding Krishna were not copied from Christianity.

Krishna's mother was Devaki (Devanagui), who was an "immaculate virgin" who had produced eight sons older than Krishna, and was "overshadowed" (Lk. 1:35) by Vishnu to conceive Krishna.[499] Krishna "came to die on earth for our salvation,"[500] and his death was by crucifixion on a tree with arrows, from which he was resurrected.[501] According to Dameron, Krishna was endowed with

> omniscience and omnipresence from the time of his birth . . . cures the lame and the blind, casts out demons, washed the feet of the Brahmans, and, **descending into the lower regions, hell, liberates the dead**, and returns to Vaicontha, the paradise of Vishnu. Chrisna was the god Vishnu in human form — **he crushes the serpent's head**.[502]

Upon his birth Krishna was laid in a manger, and shepherds and shepherdesses attended him. Like Moses, he was placed in a reed basket and deposited into the river. He battled evil forces and, again, crushed the serpent's head, healed the sick, and raised the dead. A woman anointed his head with expensive oils. **He was raised from death in three days, and went to heaven in his bodily form.**[503] Jones wrote the following about Krishna:

> The Indian incarnate God Chrishna, the Hindoos believe, had a virgin mother of the royal race, **who was sought to be destroyed in his infancy [from the reigning tyrant who killed all male children under the age of two] about nine hundred years before Christ**. It appears that he passed his life in working miracles, and preaching, and was so humble as to wash his friends' feet; at length, dying, but rising from the dead, he ascended into heaven in the presence of a multitude.[504]

---

[496] Acharya S, *Suns of* God, 154-155.
[497] Doane, XXIII.
[498] Acharya S, *Suns of God*, 206.
[499] Bennett, 100.
[500] Dameron, 54.
[501] Dameron, 52; and Bennett, 106.
[502] Dameron, 52.
[503] Acharya S, *Suns of God*, 151-152. See also: Bennett, 100.
[504] Kersey Graves, *The World's Sixteen Crucified Saviors* (New York: University Books, 1971), 86. See also: Acharya S, *Suns of God*, 205-206.

Krishna was placed in a *celestial* manger at his birth; and some say he was crucified between two thieves, although that and his virgin birth are questioned by others.[505] These two thieves may represent Sagittarius and Capricorn, who rob the sun of his energy and vitality as winter begins to arrive.[506] Also, in a Canaanite myth, El begets the stars of dawn and dusk, Shahar and Shalim.[507] Dawn and dusk were daily thieves of the Day Star, Jesus, who was crucified between them (Lk. 23:39-43). As Allegro explained it:

> Each morning, <u>before the sungod withdraws his penis from the earth's vaginal sheath, a rival to the heavenly father slips from the nuptial chamber</u> and heralds the coming dawn. This star is second only to the sun and moon in brightness, and <u>usurps some of their glory</u> by lightening the eastern sky in the morning and holding back the veil of night until the moon rises. This star they called Venus. . . Thus Pliny: Before the sun revolves, a very large star named <u>Venus</u> . . . whose alternative names in themselves indicate its <u>rivalry with the sun and moon</u> — when in advance and <u>rising before dawn it receives the name of Lucifer,</u> and being another sun and bringing the dawn, whereas <u>when it shines after sunset it is named Vesper,</u> as prolonging the daylight, or as being deputy for the moon.[508]

Perhaps Lucifer was the thief who refused to repent on the cross and Vesper asked Jesus to remember him when he came into his kingdom (Lk. 23:39-43).

Confucius

Confucius (born 501 BCE), like many other god-men, was of noble birth. It was prophesied that he "would be a king without throne or territory."[509] Angels appeared at his birth, and heavenly music was heard. **He had seventy-two disciples, twelve of whom were always with him, being witnesses to everything he said and did and commissioned to take up his doctrine after his death.**[510] Confucius was the first (that we know) to say "Love your neighbor as yourself" (in 551 BCE) and that people shouldn't do to others what they don't want done to them, which he said was the foundational principle of everything. (Tarico noted that Rabbi Hillel the Elder, before Jesus, verbalized the Golden Rule and said it was the "whole Torah";[511] and she wrote that the rule appears "in some form in virtually every religious or secular moral philosophy."[512]) Confucius also said to "never revenge injuries."[513]

---

[505] Acharya S, *Suns of God*, 206.
[506] Acharya S, *Suns of God*, 272.
[507] John Gray, *The Legacy of Canaan: The Ras Shamra Texts and Their Relevance to the Old Testament* (Leiden: E. J. Brill, 1965), 14, 158-159, 185. See also: Murdock, *Did Moses Exist?* 249.
[508] Allegro, 110-111.
[509] Doane, XII.
[510] Doane, XII.
[511] Valerie Tarico, "Here are 9 'facts' you know for sure about Jesus that are probably wrong," rawstory.com, 30 June 2015, web, 2 July 2015.
[512] Tarico, "In Defense of Cherry Picking the Bible."

Buddha

Doane listed forty-eight similarities between Jesus and Gautama Buddha,[514] whose birth Max Mūller placed at 656 BCE and Sir William Jones at 1000 BCE[515] (Wikipedia says c. 563 BCE or c. 480 BCE[516]), and John Jackson noted the similarities between Buddha and Jesus as follows:

> The close parallels between the life-stories of Buddha and Christ are just as remarkable as those between Krishna and Christ. **Buddha was born of a virgin named Maya, or Mary.** His birthday was celebrated on December 25. He was visited by wise men who acknowledged his divinity. **The life of Buddha was sought by King Bimbasara**, who feared that some day the child would endanger his throne. **At the age of twelve, Buddha excelled the learned men of the temple in knowledge and wisdom.** His ancestry was traced back to Maha Sammata, the first monarch in the world. (Jesus' ancestry is traced back to Adam, the first man in the world.) **Buddha was transfigured on a mountain top. His form was illumined by an aura of bright light.** (Jesus was likewise transfigured on a mountain top.) . . . After the completion of his earthly mission, **Buddha ascended bodily to the celestial realms.**[517]

Dameron added regarding Buddha that he lived 2,540 years ago (as of the nineteenth century CE, and long before Christ), that shepherds attended his birth, and that his mother (although married) was an immaculate virgin named "Maya deva" (great Mary). Dameron noted also that Buddha was "endowed with the same powers and performs wonders like that of Chrisna, and he also crushes the serpent's head."[518] Because Krishna, Buddha, and Jesus bore many similarities in their lives, Dameron was prompted to write:

> **It may be contended that Chrisna and Buddha were characters taken from that of Jesus of Nazareth. But ample proof is at hand to show that either of these religions extends far back into the night of time beyond the birth of Christ or the beginning of the Christian era.**[519]

Regarding Buddha's transfiguration, Gerald Massey said (and I mentioned this earlier) that there was a specific reason that Jesus went up onto the mountain "after six days" (Mk. 9:2). Massey wrote: "The sixth day was celebrated as that of the change and

---

[513] Confucius, "Lecture III, B.C. 500-300," 85, sacred-texts.com, web, n.d., 7 Aug. 2014. See also: Matthew Tindal: *Christianity as Old as the Creation: or, The Gospel, a Republication of the Religion of Nature* (London: 1732); "Confucius - Biography," *The European Graduate School: Graduate &Postgraduate Studies*, egs.edu, 1997-2012, web, 7 June 2015; and Doane, XXXVI.

[514] Doane, XXIX.

[515] Bennett, 107.

[516] "Gautama Buddha," wikipedia.org, 18 Mar. 2015, web, 18 Mar. 2015.

[517] Jackson, 17-18.

[518] Dameron, 53.

[519] Dameron, 53-54.

transfiguration of the solar god in the lunar orb, which he re-entered as the regenerator of light."[520] He continued:

> in the Hindu myth of the ascent and transfiguration on the Mount, the Six Glories of the Buddha's head are represented as shining out with the brilliance that was blinding to mortal sight. These Six Glories are equivalent to the six manifestations of the Moon-God in the six Upper Signs, or, as it was set forth, in the Lunar Mount. During six months, the Horus, or Buddha, as Lord of Light in the Moon, did battle with the Powers of Darkness by night, whilst the Sun itself was fighting his way through the Six Lower Signs.[521]

Yahweh and Jesus

We all know these two gods; however, I want to point out a few facts that might be new information (to some) regarding Yahweh and his son. Since they, like Osiris and Horus, are sometimes interchangeable, I will discuss them together.

First, I believe the Bible presents Yahweh as a distinct god from the Canaanite high god, El. Dr. Steven Dimattei wrote:

> In the oldest literary traditions of the Pentateuch, it is El who regularly appears and not Yahweh, or Yahweh as El! The patriarchal narratives identify El as the deity to whom many of the early patriarchal shrines and altars were built. For example, we are informed in Genesis 33:20 that Jacob builds an altar in the old cultic center of the north, Shechem, and dedicates it to "El, god of Israel" ('el 'elohe yiśra'el). There is no ambiguity in the Hebrew here: 'el must be translated as a proper name, El. The textual tradition from which this text derives, the Elohist, ultimately remembers a time when El was the patron god of Israel. . .

> Thus there seems to be ample evidence in the biblical record to support the claim that as Yahweh became the supreme national deity of the Israelites, he began to usurp the imagery, epithets, and old cultic centers of the god El. This process of assimilation even morphed the linguistic meaning of the name El, which later came to mean simply "god," so that Yahweh was then directly identified as 'el— thus Joshua 22:22: "the god of gods is Yahweh" ('el 'elohim yhwh).

> Noteworthy also is the fact that unlike the god Baal, there is no polemic in the Bible against El, and all the old cultic centers of El, those in Jerusalem, Shechem, and Beersheba, were later accredited to Yahweh. Since the large majority of patriarchal narratives that speak of shrines and altars to El are found in the northern kingdom, such as Bethel and Shechem, and, on the other hand, many biblical texts seem to accredit Yahweh's origin to the southern Negeb, the current scholarly hypothesis is that the worship of El in the north and of Yahweh in the south eventually merged. This thesis finds further support in the incident of Jeroboam, who may have acted to reestablish the cult of Yahweh-El at Dan and

---

[520] Massey, *Gerald Massey's Lectures*, 65. See also: Acharya S, *Suns of God*, 340.
[521] Massey, *Gerald Massey's Lectures*, 75. See also: Acharya S, *Suns of God*, 340.

Bethel via his "golden bulls" . . . In sum, the <u>biblical literature, spanning as it does hundreds of centuries of cultural and cultic traditions, preserves divergent views, portraits, theologies, and origins of its god Yahweh.</u> [522]

Dr. Doron B. Cohen pointed out that, according to Deuteronomy 32:8-9, Yahweh was given Jacob as his inheritance when the most high god El set the boundaries for the nations.[523] Cohen noted that an ancient version of the Bible states that El (Elyon) allotted gods and lands to nations, and Yahweh was one of many gods in his pantheon.[524]

> **When the Most High [Elyon]** gave the nations each their heritage, when he partitioned out the human race, he **assigned the boundaries of nations according to the number of the <u>children of God</u>, but Yahweh's portion was his people, Jacob** was to be the measure of his inheritance. (*New Jerusalem Bible*, 1985)

(As Dr. Dimattei wrote, "At some point, it is ascertained, the cultic worship of Yahweh must have absorbed that of El, through which means Yahweh assimilated both the imagery and epithets once used of El."[525]) The English Standard Version (ESV) also translates this allotment as being a division according to the sons of God, and it states that Yahweh received Jacob as his "allotted heritage." Bob Seidensticker noted regarding this:

> Here we see **Elyon, the head of the divine pantheon, dividing humankind among his children, giving each his inheritance**. The idea of a divine pantheon with a chief deity, his consort, and their children (the council of the gods) was widespread through the Ancient Near East. Elyon (short for El Elyon) is the chief god, not just in Jewish writings but in Canaanite literature. **The passage concludes with Yahweh getting Israel as his inheritance**.
>
> We learn more about terms like "sons of the gods" by widening our focus to consider Ugaritic (Canaanite) texts. <u>Ugarit was a Canaanite city destroyed along with much of the Ancient Near East during the Bronze Age Collapse in roughly 1200 BCE, a period of widespread chaos from which Israelite civilization seems to have grown.</u>
>
> <u>The Ugaritic texts state that El and his consort Asherah had 70 sons, which may be the origin of the 70 nations (or 72) that came from Noah's descendants listed in Genesis 10.</u>[526]

So El divided the nations, and Yahweh received Israel as his inheritance. Hence, he is, as the Bible says, the god of Israel.

---

[522] Steven Dimattei, PhD, "#27. Are Yahweh and El the same god OR different gods? (Gen 14:22, 17:1, 21:33; Ex 6:2-3; Ps 82:1 vs Deut 32:8-9; Ps 29:1, 89:6-8)," contradictionsinthebible.com, 27 Jan. 2013, web, 23 Mar. 2015.
[523] Doron B. Cohen, ThD, *The Japanese Translations of the Hebrew Bible: History, Inventory and Analysis* (Leiden, Netherlands, and Boston: Brill Academic Publishers, Inc., 2013), 148.
[524] Cohen, *The Japanese Translations of the Hebrew Bible: History, Inventory and Analysis.*
[525] Dimattei, *Ibid.*
[526] Seidensticker, "Polytheism in the Bible."

As for the phrase "according to the number of the children of Israel" in the King James Version of the Bible, Robert Wright wrote:

> The King James edition got this phrase from the "Masoretic Text," a <u>Hebrew edition of the Bible that took shape in the early Middle Ages, more than a millennium after Deuteronomy was written.</u> Where the Masoretic Text—the earliest extant Hebrew Bible—got it is a mystery. <u>The phrase isn't found in either of the two much earlier versions of the verse now available: a Hebrew version in the Dead Sea Scrolls and a Greek version in the Septuagint,</u> a pre-Christian translation of the Hebrew Bible. . .
>
> Some scholars who have used the Dead Sea Scrolls and the Septuagint to reconstruct the authentic version of the verse say that <u>"children of Israel" was stuck in as a replacement for "sons of El."</u> With that lost phrase restored, a verse that was cryptic suddenly makes sense: **El—the most high god, Elyon—divided the world's people into ethnic groups and gave one group to each of his sons. And Yahweh, one of those sons, was given the people of Jacob.** Apparently at this point in Israelite history (and there's no telling how long ago this story originated) <u>Yahweh isn't God, but just a god—and a son of God, one among many.</u>[527]

It makes more sense that El was dividing the world among his sons (since Yahweh, a god, received a portion) than what modern Bibles, such as the King James Version, say, which is, as stated, that all the nations received a portion according to the number of Israel. We can see that the high god was transferring to lesser *gods*, as Yahweh inherited Israel as his special people. So the context is that the most high god was portioning out the world to his underling deities and not that Yahweh was portioning land to humans, which makes no sense at all in the context of the passage. (Of course, again, El and Yahweh have been equated. El, we saw, was the husband of Asherah, meaning Yahweh was the husband of Asherah if they eventually became the same god.[528])

Note the context of this passage by looking at the previous verses. Verse 7 says: "Remember the days of old, consider the years of many generations: ask thy father, and he will shew thee; thy elders, and they will tell thee" (Deut. 32:7). Thom Stark wrote:

> There are no allusions here to any El epithets, no identification of Yahweh as a "father of years," or even as "aged." Verse 7 asks Israel to remember an older tradition, one the young people will have to ask their father and elders about. <u>The old tradition says that when Elyon divided up the earth to give one nation to each of his sons as his inheritance, Yahweh's inheritance was Israel.</u> What is the point of saying this? Well verse 5 makes it clear: Israel is not being faithful to Yahweh. Vv. 16-17 expound on this: <u>Israel was ungrateful to Yahweh and decided to go after other gods,</u> despite how well Yahweh had treated them. The point of vv. 8-9 is to remind Israel that <u>according to their old traditions, Israel belonged to</u>

---

[527] Wright, 117.
[528] Victor Harold Matthews, "Judges and Ruth," *New Cambridge Bible Commentary* (Cambridge University Press, 2004), 79.

Yahweh; Israel was Yahweh's inheritance. They thus had no business looking to other gods for support. The world was rightly ordered by Elyon, and according to the divinely-established world order, Israel belonged to Yahweh. Other people belonged to other gods, but Israel belonged to Yahweh. By worshiping other gods, Israel was kicking against the divinely-established world order.
. . . El is the father and creator of the gods, of the earth, and of humankind. And this makes perfect sense of Elyon's function in Deut 32:8-9. But in Deuteronomy 32, **Yahweh is only ever identified as father and fashioner of his own allotted people, Israel**. This is how all patron deities were understood.[529]

This explains Yahweh's interest in Israel only. Other nations had their own gods. Moab, for instance, was ruled by the god Chemosh (Num. 21:29, Jdg. 11:24, Jer. 48:7). It also explains why we see in Romans 11:26 that "so all Israel shall be saved: as it is written, There shall come out of Sion the Deliverer, and shall turn away ungodliness from Jacob." Jacob was Yahweh's concern; and we see, in Revelation 7:4-8, the sons of Jacob being sealed to Yahweh. (The Bible is a purely Jewish book, which was later utilized by Christians just as the Jews had done with the writings of others.)

Verse 9 of Revelation 7 does say: "After this I beheld, and, lo, a great multitude, which no man could number, of all nations, and kindreds, and people, and tongues, stood before the throne, and before the Lamb, clothed with white robes, and palms in their hands." However, according to *The Catholic Encyclopedia*, the German scholar Eberhard Vischer believed and taught that the book of Revelation was:

originally a purely Jewish composition, and to have been changed into a Christian work by the insertion of those sections that deal with Christian subjects. From a doctrinal point of view, we think, it cannot be objected to. There are other instances where inspired writers have availed themselves of non-canonical literature. Intrinsically considered it is not improbable. The Apocalypse abounds in passages which bear no specific Christian character but, on the contrary, show a decidedly Jewish complexion.[530]

Crawford Howell Toy, DD, LLD, and Kaufman Kohler, PhD, wrote an article in *The Jewish Encyclopedia* saying:

The last book in the New Testament canon, yet in fact one of the oldest; probably the only Judæo-Christian work which has survived the Paulinian transformation of the Church. The introductory verse betrays the complicated character of the whole work. It presents the book as a "Revelation which God gave . . . to show unto his servants things which must shortly come to pass," and at the same time as a revelation of Jesus Christ to "his servant John." According to recent investigations, the latter part was interpolated by the compiler, who worked the

[529] Stark, "The Most Heiser: Yahweh and Elyon in Psalm 82 and Deuteronomy 32."
[530] Charles Herberman, PhD, LLD, et al., eds., *The Catholic Encyclopedia: An International Work of Reference on the Constitution, Doctrine, Discipline, and History of the Catholic Church*, Vol. I (New York: Robert Appleton Company, 1907), 599. See also: Eberhard Vischer, *Die Offenbarung Johannis: Eine Judisch Apokalypse in Christlicher Bearbeitung Mit einem Nachwort v. A. Harnack* (Leipsic: J.C. Hinrichs'sche, 1886).

two sections of the book—the main apocalypse (ch. iv.-xxi. 6) and the letters to the "seven churches" (i.-iii. and close of xxii.)—into one so as to make the whole appear as emanating from John, the seer of the isle of Patmos in Asia Minor (see i. 9, xxii. 8), known otherwise as John the Presbyter. The anti-Paulinian character of the letters to the seven churches and the anti-Roman character of the apocalyptic section have been a source of great embarrassment, especially to Protestant theologians, ever since the days of Luther; but the apocalypse has become especially important to Jewish students since it has been discovered by Vischer . . . that the main apocalypse actually belongs to Jewish apocalyptic literature.[531]

Bernard D. Muller wrote: "[Revelation] 7:9-17 was NOT a part of the original Jewish version. 7:9-17 was inserted (textually right after the 144,000 Jews had been pre-selected to be saved in heaven some time later) to show Christians are God's first choice."[532] Another thought to consider is that "all nations" could possibly refer only to all Jewish nations, who spoke in various tongues (Acts 2:5-6), and the passage in Revelation might be speaking of a first resurrection from each Jewish nation and then a final resurrection from the same group (Rev. 20:5-6). Based on all of the above, and the fact that the entire Old Testament and most of the New Testament concern themselves with the Israelites, we can surmise that **Yahweh was/is the Jewish tribal god**.

Yahweh, in Exodus 15:2, is also called Yah (Jah, as in "hallelujah"), an Egyptian moon god (see also Psalms 68:4, 18, 77:11, 89:8; and Isaiah 12:2, 26:4, and 38:11).[533] **The Egyptian god was actually known as *Nuk-Pa-Nuk*, or *I Am That I Am*,** a name Yahweh also claimed (Ex. 3:14).[534] This name was not, as the Old Testament declares, revealed by Yahweh to Moses but was in fact found written on a temple of Isis at Sais in Egypt. The name Jehovah was also a name the Egyptians considered sacred, and it too was later used by the Hebrews.[535] Godfrey Higgins wrote:

> From this, I think, we may fairly infer, that the Egyptians were of the same religion, in its fundamentals, as the Jews. . . The book of Esther appears to have been part of the chronicles of the kings of Persia, adopted by the Jews into their canon, evidently to account for their feast of Purim.[536]

Jehovah IEUE was a Chaldean god, and that name too was later used by the Hebrews.[537]

---

[531] "Revelation (Book of): Jewish Origin," *Jewish Encyclopedia: The unedited full-text of the 1906 Jewish Encyclopedia*, jewishencyclopedia.com, n.d., web, 2 Dec. 2014 <http://www.jewishencyclopedia.com/articles/12712-revelation-book-of>.

[532] Bernard D. Muller, "Revelation of John, the original Jewish version: Apocalypse composition, dating & authorship," n.d., web, 2 Dec. 2014 <http://historical-jesus.info/rjohn.html>.

[533] Murdock, *Did Moses Exist?* 420. See also: Jimmy Dunn, "Yah (Lah), the Other Egyptian Moon God," n.d. web, 13 Nov. 2014.

[534] Bonwick, 395. See also: Doane, VI.

[535] Higgins, *Anacalypsis*, 1, 329; and 2, 17. See also: Doane, VI.

[536] Higgins, *Anacalypsis*, 1, 17; 3, 152. See also: Ernst von Bunsen, *The keys of Saint Peter or The house of Rechab: connected with the history of symbolism and idolatry* (London: Longmans, Green, and Co., 1807), 38-39; and Doane, VI.

[537] Higgins, *Anacalypsis*, 1, 329; and 3, 152. See also: Doane, VI.

In the Bible Jesus is called by the name of the Egyptian creator god Amen: "These things saith Amen, the faithful and true witness, the beginning of the creatures of God" (Rev. 3:14 GEN). Note the following, with pertinent information capitalized:

Isaiah 65:16 (KJV) That he who blesseth himself in the earth shall bless himself in THE GOD OF TRUTH; and he that sweareth in the earth shall swear by THE GOD OF TRUTH;

Isaiah 65:16 (DR) In which he that is blessed upon the earth, shall be blessed in GOD, AMEN: and he that sweareth in the earth, shall swear by GOD, AMEN:

Putting these together we have: In which he that is blessed upon the earth, shall be blessed in THE GOD AMEN: and he that sweareth in the earth, shall swear by THE GOD AMEN:

In ancient times people thought if they knew a god's name, they could force him to do their bidding. Richard Stuart Gordon wrote:

The ancient Jews considered God's true name so potent that its invocation conferred upon the speaker tremendous power over His creations. To prevent abuse of this power, as well as to avoid blasphemy, the name of God was always taboo, and increasingly disused so that by the time of Jesus their High Priest was supposedly the only individual who spoke it aloud — and then only in the Holy of Holies upon the Day of Atonement.[538]

Rumpelstiltskin spun gold for a princess, asking nothing in return if she could discover his name; but if not, she had to sacrifice her firstborn to him. In Exodus 3:14 Moses tried to discover the name of the god calling to him. The response was "I am that/who I am." Yahweh wasn't about to give power to Moses by offering his name. Today, Christians call upon the god Amen (saying "Amen" at the end of their prayers) in an attempt to "spin straw into gold" or convince Amen/Jesus to grant their various wishes.

Amen (Amon, Amun, or Ammon) was a sun god and was known as the "ultimate creator of the world."[539] Jesus, as Amen, was a sun god and the creator, and his life "duplicates the trajectory of the Sun in the sky,"[540] which will be shown later. In "Hymn to Amen," composed sometime between 1600 and 900 BCE, we read that Amen

is the physician . . . The winds are driven back, the hurricane is repulsed. . . He delivereth the helpless one. . . He is perfect . . . **All the gods are three, Amen, Rā and Ptah, and there are none like unto them** . . . He breatheth breath into all nostrils. . . **His wife is the earth**, he uniteth with her, his seed is the tree of life, his emanations are the grain."[541]

---

[538] Richard Stuart Gordon, *The Encyclopedia of Myths and Legends* (London: Headline Book Publishing, 1993), 480-481.

[539] James P. Allen, *The Ancient Pyramid Texts*, 425. See also: Murdock, *Christ in Egypt*, 115.

[540] "Jesus Is the Sun God," hiddenmeanings.com, n.d., web, 27 Aug. 2014 <http://www.hiddenmeanings.com/supernova.html>.

[541] "Hymn to Amen," from Chapter XII, "Egyptian Hymns to the Gods," *The Literature of the Ancient Egyptians*, wisdomlib.org, 5 Feb. 2011, web, 21 May 2015.

Jesus is referred to as Shemesh (Mal. 4:2: **the word for "sun" in Hebrew is Shemesh**[542]). Shemesh/Shamash was an "Akkadian/Babylonian sun god," or "deity of justice."[543] He was called shepherd, king, god of light, king of judgment, ruler of men, and one who "puts an end to wickedness and destroys enemies" and "loosens the bonds of the imprisoned, grants health to the sick, and even revivifies the dead."[544]

Yaldabaoth (Father of Yahweh and Elohim)

The Secret Book of John (*The Apocryphon of John*), a dialogue between John and Jesus, was written sometime before 180 CE. We know this because Irenaeus referred to it in his *Adversus Haereses*.[545] As stated earlier, Celsus, writing around 170 CE, never heard of the books *Matthew, Mark, Luke, or John*."[546] Since the "first mention and quote by a Christian writer from either the Gospel of Mark, Matthew, Luke, or John cannot be found before 180 C.E,"[547] we know that *The Apocryphon of John* was written before or near the same time as the four Gospels. And in it we read the full story of the creation, fall, and redemption of man. It's a little different from the biblical version. The hero/villain in this story is Sophia's son, Yaldabaoth (who fathers Yahweh and Elohim). The following synopsis is taken from a translation made by Stevan Davies.[548]

Sophia wanted to have a child, but she didn't seek approval from her "masculine counterpart." Upon producing a boy, she called him Yaldabaoth. He didn't realize anyone else existed, so he proclaimed, "I am God . . . I am a jealous God and there is no God but me!" Sophia realized that she had lost light and power in her ugly, ignorant, evil son, and she became ashamed. She cast him away from her in a cloud so he wouldn't be seen, and she "repented and wept furiously." All the "divine realms (pleroma)" heard her and sought "blessing for her from the Invisible Virgin Spirit." The Spirit responded, and Sophia was elevated above Yaldabaoth but was not "restored to her own original realm."

Yaldabaoth got together with his "subordinate demons" and said, "Let's create a man according to the image of God And our own likeness So that his image will illuminate us." Once the man was created Yaldabaoth's "principal advisors" said to him, "Blow some of your Spirit in the man's face, Then his body will rise up." Yaldabaoth complied and the man came alive. The man (Adam) was good and more intelligent than his designers, so "They took him and cast him down Into the lowest depths of the material world." Barbelo (forethought) put a spirit named Epinoia in Adam to help him.

---

[542] "Shemesh," *My Hebrew Dictionary: Learn Hebrew Online*, dictionary.co.il, 2015, web, 16 June 2015.

[543] Murdock, *Did Moses Exist?* 394.

[544] Morris Jastrow, *The Religion of Babylonia and Assyria* (Boston: Ginn & Company, 1898), 70-72. See also: Murdock, *Did Moses Exist?* 396.

[545] "Apocryphon of John," wikipedia.org, 12 Feb. 2015, web, 18 Mar. 2015.

[546] Craig M. Lyons, MsD, DD, MDiv, "The Evolution of the Jesus Myth," *Bet Emet Ministries*, firstnewtestament.com, n.d., web, 4 June 2014.

[547] Craig M. Lyons, MsD, DD, MDiv, "Marcion and the Marcionites," *Bet Emet Ministries*, firstnewtestament.com, n.d., web, 4 June 2014, 5 June 2014.

[548] Stevan Davies, tr., "The Secret Book of John (The Apocryphon of John)," *The Gnostic Society Library*, gnosis.org, 2005, web, 18 Mar. 2015. See also: "The Gnostic Jesus: Sethian Creation," gnostic-jesus.com, n.d., web, 19 Mar. 2015.

Adam was now in the material world (Earth), and had a physical body (shadow of death) to imprison his soul. Yaldabaoth bound him with forgetfulness and put him in the Garden of Eden. Yaldabaoth knew Epinoia enlightened Adam, so he tried to remove her from Adam through Adam's rib cage. Yaldabaoth was able to "recover the Power that he had put into Adam" by taking out Epinoia, but she escaped; "Adam's perceptions were veiled And he became unconscious. As he (Yaldabaoth) said through his prophet: 'I will make their minds dull so that they do not see or understand.'" Yaldabaoth then created a woman and captured Epinoia in her. Eve (via Epinoia) "raised up the veil that dulled [Adam's] mind. He sobered up from the dark drunkenness And he recognized his own counterpart." He thought this woman had given him life, so he called her Eve.

Yaldabaoth wanted the couple to remain ignorant so they would worship him; therefore, he told them not to eat from the tree of knowledge of good and evil. Adam and Eve were "too terrified to renounce Yaldabaoth," but they did eat from the tree (possibly due to the coaxing of Jesus). They realized then that Yaldabaoth, their creator, was a false god. "When Yaldabaoth discovered that they had moved away from him He cursed his earth." He "gave the woman over so that the man might be her master, Because he did not know the secret of the divine strategy." He "showed his ignorance to his angels" and "cast both of them out of paradise Dressing them in heavy darkness."

Then Yaldabaoth raped Eve, who bore Elohim the older and Yahweh the younger. Elohim was evil while Yahweh was good. "Yaldabaoth deceptively named the two: Cain and Abel." Then "Adam had intercourse with the image of his foreknowledge" and Seth was born. Yaldabaoth made the first couple drink from the "waters of forgetfulness" so they wouldn't know their "true place of origin." Seth's children populated the world but "remained in this [fallen, ignorant] condition for a while In order that when the Spirit descends from the holy realms The Spirit can raise up the children and heal them from all defects And thus <u>restore complete holiness to the fullness of God</u>." At that point the spark that was lost from the pleroma into Adam and Eve would return to the heavenly realms.

After a time Yaldabaoth regretted having created man and everything else, since his creation didn't work like he wanted because Adam was smarter than he was and cost him some of his own power and light, so he brought a flood to destroy mankind. Noah was warned of Yaldabaoth's plot from another heavenly source. He tried to preach to people, but they didn't know him and therefore didn't believe him. However, Noah and "many other people" hid in "a cloud of light" and didn't die in the flood.

At the end of the book we find "The Providence Hymn," which states in part:

I am the Providence of everything.
<u>I became like my own human children</u>.
<u>I existed from the first</u>.
<u>I walked down every possible road</u>. . .
I entered the midst of darkness
<u>I came to the deepest part of the underworld</u>.

I let my face light up
      Thinking of the end of their time
I entered their prison
    The body is that prison
I cried out:
    "Anyone who hears,
      Rise up from your deep sleep!"
And the sleeping one awoke and wept
    Wiping bitter tears saying
    "Who calls me?"
    "Where has my hope come from
        As I lie in the depths of this prison?" . . .
    Stay awake!
    Rise out of the depths of the underworld!
I raised him up
I sealed him with the light/water of the five seals.
Death had no power over him ever again.
I ascend again to the perfect realm.
I completed everything and you have heard it."

Jesus entered into prison (human body), woke the "dead" (those bound in forgetfulness and ignorance in the "underworld," or on Earth), and set the captives free.

This revelation came to John in a "mystery" from the savior in heaven, and when it was finished "the Savior vanished." John found the other disciples of Jesus and told them what he had seen and heard. *The Apocryphon of John* is as believable as anything else in the Bible, and certainly old enough to be considered regarding any truth about Jesus.

Serapis Christ

Serapis was one of many dying and rising gods that flourished throughout the Mediterranean long before the rise of the Roman Empire. He was a blending of Osiris with the bull god, Apis, into human form. Apis was incarnated by a spark from the father god, and was the spirit of the father god. Thus, **by the fifth century BCE Egypt had developed a trinity of gods: father, son, and spirit.**[549] (We can't forget the Amen, Ra, and Ptah trinity either. Of course, Amen and Ra eventually merged as Amen-Ra. In the Hindu trinity Brahma was "the creator, Vishnu the preserver, and Siva the destroyer."[550])

The Egyptians built a temple (the Serapeum) to Serapis in Memphis; it was later (third century BCE) moved to Alexandria. The Alexandrian library, which Christians destroyed in 391 CE, was a part of this temple and contained 500,000 to 700,000 books of classical teaching, some of which no doubt spoke of Serapis and revealed that he was much like Jesus. Serapis was a healer and bestowed the gift of prophecy upon his followers. He was known as the Word or Logos. He was also called the Good Shepherd and, of course, the Christ. Because of his atoning sacrifice, he was resurrected. The sign

---

[549] Brunty, "Forgotten Christ." See also: Bennett, 152.
[550] Bennett, 93.

of the cross was a part of his worship, and his power was expressed through the signs of the Zodiac.[551]

One order of the cult of Serapis was a healing group known as the Therapeuts, often recognized as the early or first Christians, who melded Judaic rites and rituals with the worship of Serapis.[552] (I will speak more about the Therapeuts later.) Thus, **Christianity really began with the worship of the Egyptian god Serapis.** Emperor Hadrian (117-138 CE) **believed Serapis to be the peculiar god of the Christians, as did the Gentiles at the time.** In fact, a cross was found under the temple of Serapis in Alexandria.[553]

Ahmed Osman is a British Egyptologist born in Cairo. Also a lecturer, historian, author, and researcher, Osman wrote as follows:

> The cult of Serapis was to have sweeping success throughout Greece and Asia Minor, especially in Rome, where it became the most popular religion. There was a Serapis temple in Rome as early as 105 BC. Initiation into the Serapis cult included the rite of baptism, and Sir Alan Gardiner, the British Egyptologist, argued in the Journal of Egyptian Archaeology in 1950 that Egyptian baptism should be seen as analogous to Christian baptism, of which he commented: "In both cases a symbolic cleansing by means of water serves as initiation into a properly legitimated religious life." The cults of Serapis and Isis did not merely survive the emergence of Christianity, but in the 2nd century AD actually increased in popularity. Serapis and Christ existed side-by-side and were frequently seen as interchangeable. Some early Christians made no distinction between Christ and Serapis and frequently worshipped both, while paintings of Isis with her son Horus became identified by early Christians as portraits of Mary with her son Jesus. The rite of baptism, part of the initiation ceremony of the Serapis cult, was also adopted by the Church as part of its initiation ceremony.
>
> In AD 134, after a visit to Alexandria, the Emperor Hadrian wrote a letter to his elderly brother-in-law, Servianus, in which he commented: "In [Egypt] the worshippers of Serapis are Christians, and those who call themselves Bishops of Christ pay their vows to Serapis."[554]

J. A. Giles mentioned this as follows:

> The worshipers of Serapis (here) are called Christians (Chrestians), and those who are devoted to the god Serapis (I find), call themselves Bishops of Christ (Chrestus) are, in fact, devotees of Serapis. There is no chief of the Jewish synagogue, no Samaritan, no Christian (Chrestian) presbyter, who is not an astrologer, a soothsayer, or an anointer.[555]

---

[551] Brunty, "Forgotten Christ."
[552] Brunty, "Forgotten Christ."
[553] M. D. Aletheia, *The Rationalist's Manual* (London: Watts & Co. 1897), 65. See also: George W. Cox, MA, *The Mythology of the Aryan Nations*, Vol. II (London: Longmans, Green, and Co., 1870), 132. See also: Doane, XX.
[554] Ahmed Osman, "Out of Egypt: Christian Roots in the Alexandrian Cult of Serapis," dwij.org, 2001, web, 19 Dec. 2014 <http://dwij.org/forum/amarna/8_serapis_and_christianity.htm>.
[555] J. A. Giles, *Hebrew and Christian Records*, Vol. II (Ann Arbor: University of Michigan Library, 1877), 86.

And John G. Jackson wrote:

> Suetonius in his "Life of Claudius" relates that: "He (Claudius) drove the Jews, who at the instigation of Christas were constantly rioting, out of Rome." This is said to have taken place about fifteen years after the crucifixion of Jesus. So Christas could hardly have been Jesus Christ.[556]

That is, he couldn't have been the Jesus in the Bible. It's possible that Serapis (Chrestus/Christus/Christ) was the god of the Chrestians or Christians. He was, after all, the god worshiped by the Therapeuts, whom Eusebius called the first Christians.[557]

Apparently "no Bible contains the actual term Christian . . . until near the midpoint of the 5th century in the Codex Alexandrinus. Before that the term is Chrestian (or quite literally good men) a generic term used by many other groups."[558]

> The evidence . . . strongly implies that the earliest form of the term "Christian" does not occur until Codex Alexandrinus, at least the 5th century, and may in fact not enter the chronological record . . . until substantially later. In place of the term "Christian" . . . quite invariably, is found the term "Chrestian."[559]

Again (and "centuries before the purported birth of Jesus"[560]), the term "Christos" or "Chrestos" was used for Serapis, whose characteristics and story greatly resemble that of Jesus'. If Serapis was Osiris and Jesus was Serapis, Jesus was Osiris.

Alexander the Great, Plato, Pythagoras, Caesar, and Socrates

The Greek gods often mated with humans. Some accounts of virgin births regarded men born before the time of Jesus.

Olympias, the mother of Alexander the Great (21 July 356 BCE–10 or 11 June 323 BCE), claimed that he was the son of Zeus via virgin birth, and Alexander himself believed this,[561] declaring that Zeus-Amen was his father.[562] The god Amen told Olympias she would have a son who would avenge her, and her husband (Philip II of Macedon) was told not to have intimate relations with her until the boy was born.[563] **Although little is known about Alexander's youth, his "miraculous birth is well documented by historians,"** being "associated with great signs and wonders, such as a bright star gleaming over Macedonia that night and the destruction of the temple of

[556] Jackson, 8; quoting from G. Suetonius Tranquillus, *Lives of the First Caesars* (reprint 1796, New York: AMS Press, 1970).
[557] Eusebius, "Philo's Account of the Ascetics of Egypt," *Church History: Book II*, 17:10-24, newadvent.org, copyright 2009 by Kevin Knight, web, 10 July 2014.
[558] "Evidence for the historical existence of Jesus Christ," rationalwiki.org, n.d., web, 19 Dec. 2014 <http://rationalwiki.org/wiki/Evidence_for_the_historical_existence_of_Jesus_Christ>.
[559] "Early 'Chrestians,'" mountainman.com, n.d., web, 20 Dec. 2014.
[560] Catherine Giordano, "Jesus Who? The Historical Record Gives No Clue," catherinegiordano.hubpages.com, 12 July 2015, web, 12 July 2015.
[561] Joshua J. Mark, "Alexander the Great," *Ancient History Encyclopedia*, ancient.eu.com, 14 Nov. 2013, web, 6 June 2014.
[562] "Alexander the Great Biography: The Man and the Myth," *All About Egypt*, all-about-egypt.com, 2015, web, 29 Apr. 2015.
[563] Robert M. Price, "Pagan Parallels to Christ Part 1," Tony Sobrado, youtube.com, 30 June 2012, web, 29 Apr. 2015.

Artemis [Diana] at Ephesus."[564] According to Plutarch, Diana's temple caught fire and burnt while she was away assisting at Alexander's birth.[565] **Alexander, by the way, crossed the Pamphylian Sea in the same way that Moses crossed the Red Sea—dry-shod, as the waters opened up for him and made obeisance to him as the king.** Josephus mentioned this *in an attempt to sustain the belief that the same thing happened with Moses.*[566] The historian Callisthenes, who accompanied Alexander on this expedition, wrote that the sea not only opened but rose and elevated its waters, paying Alexander "homage as its king."[567] Perhaps, as British Admiral Francis Beaufort declared, the north winds depressed the sea and Alexander took advantage of the opportunity to rush across.[568] We must look for a scientific explanation for this tale, yet we should believe without doubt that a god was involved in the Jewish story?

The Greek philosopher Plato (428/427-348/347 BCE) was also considered the child of a virgin birth, being the son of Apollo. Church father Origen (in *Contra Celsus* 1.37) mentioned this, as did Jerome in *Against Jovianus* (Adv. Jov. 1.42).[569] Plato's mother, the virgin Perictione, was impregnated by Apollo in the form of a bull (or Taurus).[570]

Pythagoras was also supposedly the son of Apollo. His mother was Parthenis, and from her name we get the word "*parthenos*, which means virgin."[571]

Both Julius and Augustus Caesar were deemed sons of a god. According to a poem written by Virgil, Augustus sprang from Jove.[572] Augustus also wore the title "saviour of the human race," and one legend says he was "born nine months after his mother was 'visited' by the god Apollo." In 40 BCE Virgil prophesied that a virgin would give birth to a king. While it wasn't true, the **hoi polloi truly believed that in the year Augustus was born, the "Roman senate had ordered the murder of all other children."**[573]

Even Socrates (469 BCE) was considered a god. When he was born, "Magi came from the east to offer gifts . . . bringing gold, frankincense and myrrh."[574] According to Higgins, these three gifts were "what were always offered by the Arabian Magi to the sun."[575] The god Chrishna was presented with sandalwood and perfumes while Mithras, like Jesus and Socrates, was given gold, frankincense, and myrrh.[576]

Dr. Nugent wrote that the children of gods who mate with humans are called *Gaborim*, which comes from the same root word as the name Gabriel. Nugent stated:

[564] Mark, "Alexander the Great." See also: Price, "Pagan Parallels to Christ Part 1."
[564] Mark, "Alexander the Great."
[565] Plutarch, *Lives*, Vol. 2 (New York: Random House, 2001).
[566] Flavius Josephus, *Antiquities of the Jews*, Book II, Ch. XVI. See also: Doane, VI.
[567] Doane, VI.
[568] Doane, VI.
[569] Murdock, *Christ in Egypt*, 161-162. See also: Armstrong, 92.
[570] Graham, 303.
[571] Graham, 302-303.
[572] Doane, XII.
[573] Scaruffi, "Jesus and Christianity."
[574] Graham, 308. See also: Doane, XV; and Godfrey Higgins, *Anacalypsis, an Attempt to Draw Aside the Veil of the Saitic Esis,* Vol. II (London: Longman, et al., 1836), 96.
[575] Higgins, *Anacalypsis*, II (1836), 96.
[576] Thomas Inman, MD, *Ancient Faiths and Modern: A Dissertation upon Worships, Legends and Divinities In Central And Western Asia, Europe, And Elsewhere, Before The Christian Era. Showing Their Relations To Religious Customs As They Now Exist* (London: Trubner & Co., 1876), Vol. 2.

In the second century, Gabriel appears in the Epistula Apostolorum. . . One of the secrets [Jesus revealed to his apostles after he rose] is that he is actually Gabriel. After Gabriel took on flesh and united with Mary, then he becomes Jesus. The idea that Christ was an angel was extremely popular in the early church.[577]

Caves, Crosses, and Sacrificial Deaths

We saw earlier that the Old Testament patriarch Abraham was born in a cave. Eusebius wrote that Jesus was born in a cave and that Constantine erected a temple on the spot so Christians could worship there. Tertullian (200 CE) and Jerome (375 CE) stated the same and added that Adonis was believed by the pagans to have been born in the exact same cave. Chrishna, Bacchus, Apollo, Mithras, and Hermes were likewise born in caves. That element is, again, a part of the universal god mythos.[578] Not only are the events surrounding the births of gods similar, but the same is true of their deaths.

We know about the darkness and earthquakes that occurred when Jesus died, but these bizarre occurrences were recorded at the deaths of others as well. Prometheus was "with chains nailed to the rocks on Mount Caucasus, 'with arms extended,' as a saviour; and the tragedy of the **crucifixion was acted in Athens 500 years before the Christian era**."[579] We read the following regarding this crucifixion:

When *Prometheus* was crucified on Mount Caucasus, *the whole frame of nature became convulsed*. The earth did quake, thunder roared, lightning flashed, the wild winds rent the vexed air, the boisterous billows rose, and the dissolution of the universes seemed to be threatened.[580]

Prometheus, according to Seneca and Hesiod, and in the words of J. P. Dameron, was

nailed to an upright beam of timber, to which were affixed extended arms of wood, and this cross was situated near the Caspian Straits. At the final exit of this god . . . **the earth shook, the rocks were rent, the graves were opened**. . . the solemn scene closed, and the savior gave up the ghost.[581]

Likewise, when Romulus, one of Rome's founders, died, "the sun was darkened, *and there was darkness over the face of the earth for the space of six hours.*"[582] Romulus was received into heaven via a fiery chariot, just as was Elijah (2 Kings 2:11).[583] (The story of Romulus even resembles the tale regarding the two disciples who ran into Jesus on the Road to Emmaus [Lk. 24:13-16]. Julius Proculus, under oath, stated that "as he was travelling on the road," he saw Romulus "looking taller and comelier than ever, dressed in

---

[577] Nugent, "'Many of These Gods Come from the Stars.'"

[578] Doane, XVI.

[579] William W. Hardwicke, *The Evolution of Man: His Religious Systems, and Social Ethics* (London: Watts & Co., 1899), 218.

[580] *Potter's Aeschylus*, "Prometheus Chained," last stanza. See also: Doane, XXI.

[581] Dameron, 56.

[582] Higgins, *Anacalypsis*, I, 616, 617. See also: Doane, XXI.

[583] Graham, 247.

shining and flaming armour." He asked Romulus why he had abandoned the "whole city to bereavement and endless sorrow." Romulus responded that it "pleased the gods . . . that we, who came from them, should remain so long a time amongst men as we did; and, having built a city to be the greatest in the world for empire and glory, should again return to heaven." Romulus told Proculus to tell the Romans farewell and that "by the exercise of temperance and fortitude, they shall attain the height of human power; we will be to you the propitious god Quirinus." Plutarch wrote that the story "seemed credible to the Romans, upon the honesty and oath of the relater," and that "indeed, too, there mingled with it a certain divine passion, some preternatural influence similar to possession by a divinity; nobody contradicted it, but, laying aside all . . . detractions, they prayed to Quirinus and saluted him as a god."[584]) When Julius Caesar died, again, the sun was eclipsed and darkness prevailed "for the space of six hours."[585] We read the same regarding Aesculapis and Hercules.[586]

If the idea of a cross had not pre-existed the crucifixion of Christ, he would not have told his followers to take up their "cross" and follow him, as they wouldn't have understood the reference (Mt. 16:24). Church father Tertullian admitted this when, trying to justify his own beliefs, he wrote that the heathens consecrated the cross and from it derived the origin of their gods.[587] The Egyptian cross, the *ankh*, in fact, represented eternal life.[588] Marcus Minucius Felix, who was a Christian apologist sometime between 150 and 270 CE,[589] wrote of the Egyptians: "Your victorious trophies not only imitate the appearance of a simple cross, but also that of a man affixed to it."[590]

Felix, in *Octavius*, expressed indignation that the cross was considered strictly Christian, claiming that the pagan "trophies not only represent a simple cross *but a cross with a man upon it.*"[591] Tertullian, writing to pagans, said: "The origin of *your* gods is derived from *figures moulded on a cross*. All those rows of *images on your standards* are the appendages of crosses; those hangings on your standards and banners are the robes of crosses."[592] Tertullian further wrote: "There is not an image you erect but resembles a cross in part; so that we who worship an entire cross, if we do worship it, methinks have much the better on it of you who worship but half a cross."[593] In an attempt to defend and make palatable their beliefs, **early Christians depended upon the fact that the pagans already worshiped deities *who were just like Jesus*;** today, with the same motivation, some Christians deny these facts, while others declare that Yahweh wrote the tale in the

[584] Plutarch, *Lives of the Noble Grecians and Romans*, The Original Classic Edition, 21.
[585] Higgins, *Anacalypsis*, I, 616, 617. See also: Josephus, *Antiquities of the Jews*, Book XIV, Ch. XII, and Note; and Doane, XXI.
[586] Aletheia, *The Rationalist's Manual*, 65. See also: Cox, *The Mythology of the Aryan Nations*; and Doane, XX.
[587] Tertullian, *Ad Nationes*, I, Ch. XII, tr. Q. Howe, tertullian.org, 2007, web, 25 Aug. 2014 <http://www.tertullian.org/articles/howe_adnationes1.htm>.
[588] Murdock, *Christ in Egypt*, 339.
[589] "Marcus Minucius Felix," wikipedia.org, 30 June 2014, web, 25 Aug. 2014.
[590] Marcus Minucius Felix, *The Octavius of Minucius Felix*, Ch. XXIX, *Christian Classics Ethereal Library*, 2005, web, 25 Aug. 2014 <http://www.ccel.org/ccel/schaff/anf04.iv.iii.xxix.html>.
[591] Minucius Felix, *Octavius*, Ch. XXIX, newadvent.org, copyright 2009 by Kevin Knight, web, 12 Nov. 2014. See also: Doane, XX.
[592] *The Apology of Tertullian*, tr. William Reeve, AM (London, 1709), Ch. XVI. See also: Tertullian, *Ad Nationes*, Ch. XII, tr. Q. Howe, 2007; and Doane, XX.
[593] *The Apology of Tertullian*, Ch. XVI.

sky (because Gentiles also needed a "schoolmaster," Gal. 3:24), which is why many such stories abound (although the one about Jesus is the true one).

Kersey Graves wrote:

Nearly all the phenomena represented as occurring at the crucifixion of Christ are reported to have been witnessed also at the final exit of Senerus, an ancient pagan demigod, who <u>figured in history at a still more remote period of time</u>. And similar incidents are related likewise in the legendary histories of several other heathen demigods and great men partially promoted to the honor of Gods. In the time-honored records of the oldest religion in the world, it is declared, "<u>A cloud surrounded the moon; and the sun was darkened at noonday, and the sky rained fire and ashes during the crucifixion of the Indian God Chrishna</u>." In the case of Osiris . . . Mr. Southwell says, "As his birth had been attended by an eclipse of the sun, so his death was attended by a still greater darkness of the solar orb" . . .

And similar stories are furnished us by several writers of Caesar and Alexander the Great. With respect to the latter, Mr. Nimrod says, "Six hours of darkness formed his aphanasia, and his soul, like Polycarp's, was seen to fly away in the form of a dove." (Nimrod, vol. iii. p. 458.) "It is remarkable," says a writer, "what a host of respectable authorities vouch for an acknowledged fable — the preternatural darkness which followed Caesar's death." Gibbon alludes to this event when he speaks of "the singular defect of light which followed the murder of Caesar." He likewise says, "This season of darkness had already been celebrated by most of the poets and historians of that memorable age." (Gibbon, p. 452.) <u>It is very remarkable that Pliny speaks of a darkness attending Caesar's death, but omits to mention such a scene as attending the crucifixion of Christ</u>. Virgil also seeks to exalt this royal personage by relating this prodigy. (See his Georgius, p. 465.) Another writer says, "Similar prodigies were supposed or said to accompany the great men of former days." . . .

the **same story was told of the graves opening, and the dead rising at the final mortal exit of several heathen Gods and several great men long before it was penned as a chapter in the history of Christ.**[594]

These men were esteemed as gods after their sacrificial deaths. This is true also of Jesus.[595] We can't put him in a class of his own. If we wouldn't believe incredible accounts of the heroics of Hercules, why should we believe them about Jesus?

Think Think Think

I know some will read all that has been said here and contend that the older god-tales were *changed* after Jesus was born so they would sound the same. People go to great

---

[594] Kersey Graves, *The World's Sixteen Crucified Saviors: Or, Christianity Before Christ* (Library of Alexandria), Ch. 17, *The Secular Web: A Drop of Reason in a Pool of Confusion*, infidels.org, 1995-2014, web, 12 Nov. 2014.
[595] Doane, XII.

lengths, for instance, to prove that certain gods weren't born on December 25. Well, neither was Jesus. I have no doubt that these stories, *like the stories about Jesus*, were modified over the years to make them even more amazing. I have diligently sought the best sources I could and tried to use only what seemed to be supported by the evidence (remember, the Christians burnt a lot of the proof) and, when I could, found original sources. I certainly can't vouch for the truthfulness of *all* I have shared here (nor can I, or anyone, do so for the biblical record). But the point is that all the stories are alike, and Jesus was a Johnny-come-lately savior. Why would we dismiss all the *older stories of gods we know existed prior to Jesus* and latch onto this more recent one, when it sounds just like the others? Carl S. wrote:

> Depending on what major religion one belongs to, one believes: That Jesus, unaided, floated up from the Earth's surface, into the sky, and was never seen again, or, that his mother likewise, did the same, or, that Mohammed also floated up, but this time on a horse, or that the prophet Ezekiel, likewise, floated up into the sky, but in a chariot.[596]

(Or some might believe Jack went up into the sky via a beanstalk, where he found *his* "golden" happy ending.) Obviously, people believed fantastic stories about all the god-men. Otherwise, why were these men/gods worshiped or revered at all if the people worshiping them hadn't heard and didn't believe the imaginary stories told about them *at the time they began to be worshiped*, which was before Jesus was born?

Some may no doubt say that perhaps the Hebrews simply didn't write their stories down first, or maybe they did but the copies were lost or destroyed and it simply *appears* that the other stories were written first. While we might consider this possibility regarding the Flood or the giving of law, we certainly can't entertain that thought with regard to Jesus as a dying and rising savior—*we know for a fact that he was not the first.*

The questions I have are: How do we know which story to believe? Why pick one over the other? Why, especially, choose a newer story over an older one? Why not understand that *all* of these stories came from a common pool and are based on what the people saw and understood with regard to either the sky or the earth? Why not realize that the legends are meant to help people remember events or are the fabrications of ancient minds attempting to determine creation and causation in the world, and provide a way to alleviate grief over the loss of a loved one or fear of one's own death?

Graves said there have been at least thirty-four men who have been claimed to be gods. These men exhibited the same characteristics in their stories, and Dameron presented these characteristics as follows:

> Each of these saviors was born at midwinter and their births have excited the jealousy of some kingly tyrant, and, though themselves of royal descent, were born in caves or mangers, forced to pass their infancy in obscurity and not unfrequently cause the "massacre of all the innocents" in the district in which

---

[596] Carl S., "Everyone Is Lacking In Faith."

they are born. They are all miracle-workers, and are generally connected with some snake story, in which is represented the evil power which is adverse to them. They generally perform about the same class of miracles, preach the highest morals of the age in which they appear, and are benevolent and act the part of great reformers, and oppose the abuses of the times. They feed multitudes, cast out devils, heal the sick; finally they succumb to the powers of evil that oppose them; die a violent death, very often by crucifixion, descend to the lower regions to rescue lost souls, reascend to heaven and thenceforth become judges of the dead, mediators and redeemers of men, who offer up vicarious sacrifices to God for the sins of the people.[597]

According to Samuel Butler:

Christianity is a copycat religion created by Emperor Constantine (for political purposes) based upon a myth (The Persian savior god Mithra, crucified 600 B.C. ? 400 B.C.?), which was based on other similar myths . . . There were 16 mythical crucifixions before Christ. The belief in the crucifixion of Gods was prevalent in various oriental or heathen countries long prior to the reported crucifixion of Christ. Of the 16 crucifixions, most were born of a virgin and about half of them on December 25th.[598]

Butler listed these crucifixions as follows: (1) Chrishna of India, 1200 B.C[599]; (2) Hindoo Sakia, 600 B.C.; (3) Thammuz of Syria, 1160 B.C.; (4) Wittoba of the Telingonesic, 552 B.C.; (5) Iao of Nepaul, 622 B.C.; (6) Hesus of the Celtic Druids, 834 B.C.; (7) Quexalcote of Mexico, 587 B.C.; (8) Quirinus of Rome, 506 B.C.; (9) (Aeschylus) Prometheus, 547 B.C.; (10) Thulis Of Egypt, 1700 B.C.; (11) Indra of Tibet, 725 B.C.; (12) Alcestos of Euripides, 600 B.C.; (13) Atys of Phrygia, 1170 B.C.; (14) Crite of Chaldea, 1200 B.C.; (15) Bali of Orissa, 725 B.C.; and (16) Mithra of Persia, 600 B.C.[600]

It seems unreasonable to recognize all but one of these fables as myths and then declare that lone one to be the honest-to-goodness truth. As Allegro wrote: "The death and resurrection story of Jesus follows the traditional pattern of fertility mythology, as has long been recognized. The hero is miraculously born, dies violently, returns to the underworld, and is then reawakened to new life."[601] I know Christians have written, and continue to write, books and articles to prove why their flawed and contradictory (not to mention scientifically impossible) stories are true; but surely if a god wrote a book for us, that divine book shouldn't require mere men to bolster it by writing tons of books to explain why it's the real McCoy even though it's just like all the other stories. If there is a god, he/she/it wants us to use our reasoning skills and consider whether we are being duped.

---

[597] Dameron, 58-59. See also: Kersey Graves, *The World's Sixteen Crucified Saviors*, "Address to the Clergy," 1875, *The Secular Web: A Drop of Reason in a Pool of Confusion*, infidels.org, web, 9 Sept. 2014.
[598] Butler, "How Christianity Was Invented: The Truth!"
[599] Butler notes: "Some say he was hung upside down from a tree. Other sources say he died from an arrow shot into his foot. Does it matter? They are different versions of a myth, anyway."
[600] Butler, "How Christianity Was Invented: The Truth!"
[601] Allegro, 154.

CHAPTER SIX
RECYCLED MYTHS

There may or may not have been a man named Jesus, but Jesus as a deity has been long debunked and is anything but original. History is filled with gods that feature elements of the Jesus story, from Osiris' death, resurrection and promise of salvation, to Romulus' and Perseus' virgin birth, to Zalmoxis' promise of eternal life, to Inanna's crucifixion in the underworld, ascension and reign from Heaven. There is nothing new under the sun.

Seth Andrews, "Free Will," *The Thinking Atheist Blog*

The three letters I H S, surrounded with rays of glory, that are so often seen hanging in the Catholic churches and burying grounds, which are supposed to stand for Jesus Homineum Salvator, is none other than the identical name of Bacchus, Yes, exhibited in Greek letters, V H E, (see Hesychius on the word V H E, i.e., Yes, Bacchus, Sol, the Sun). And the feast of Bacchus was always celebrated by drinking wine and eating bread, from which the Christians derived the idea of the sacrament.[602]

James Palatine Dameron

The Essenes and Therapeutae did not follow Jesus. They created him! . . . Reworking old myths and syncretizing them to create new ones was a major preoccupation of the Gnostics.[603]

Dr. Craig Lyons

Before Judaism existed, other religions included aspects of Judaeo-Christian doctrines, including: baptisms, virgin births, saviors, crucifixions, resurrections, a great flood, a Trinity of gods,[604] seventh-day worship,[605] an afterlife, final judgment, the ark of the covenant, circumcision[606] (practiced in Egypt long before Joseph arrived,[607] and "proved by the ancient monuments";[608] it was "first documented in art form by the Egyptians . . . in an Egyptian tomb built for Ankhmabor in Saqqara and dating to around 2400 B.C."[609]), communion, Easter, Christmas, and Passover. These were Egyptian concepts, predating Judaism by many years.[610] Like the authors of the Old Testament, those of the New utilized fables from other sources. The New Testament writers also "re-fulfilled" the "prophecies" of the Old Testament, which were most likely written after

---

[602] Dameron, 93.

[603] Craig M. Lyons, MsD, DD, MDiv, "The Therapeutae and the Essenes as the Earliest Christians," *Bet Emet Ministries*, firstnewtestament.com, n.d., web, 4 June 2014.

[604] Murdock, *Christ in Egypt*, 53.

[605] Raymond O. Faulkner, *The Ancient Egyptian Coffin Texts*, I (Oxford: Aris & Phillips, 1973), 161, 168. See also: Murdock, *Christ in Egypt*, 114.

[606] Bob Brier and Hoyt Hobbs, *Daily Life of the Ancient Egyptians* (Westport/London: Greenwood Press, 1999), 69, 74. See also: Murdock, *Christ in Egypt*, 213, and *Did Moses Exist?* 164.

[607] Doane, X.

[608] Herodotus, Book II, Ch. 36. See also: Doane, X.

[609] "History of Circumcision," d.umn.edu, 21 Dec. 2004, web, 31 Jan. 2015 <http://www.d.umn.edu/~mcco0322/history.htm>.

[610] Joseph and Murdock, 88.

various events in Jewish history and purported to be prophecies. We will consider this midrashic literature first.

Double Fulfillment and Haggadah

Biblical prophets wrote about events that had already occurred and changed previous stories. The Jews understood this and didn't consider their fantasies to be historical. Tarico noted that today's scholars "believe that some Bible texts once thought to be prophecies (for example in the Book of Revelation) actually relate to events that were past or current at the time of writing."[611]

Alyssa Quint, who is pursuing a doctoral degree in Yiddish literature at Harvard, wrote:

> What academics heralded not too long ago as "intertextuality"—an author's practice of alluding to older texts by engaging their original meaning, then placing them within a new context and endowing them with a renewed significance—has been the linchpin of Jewish literature since the writings of the prophets.[612]

Quint used Ezekiel 36:26-29 as an example, and said that the meaning is that "God will remain true to his covenant—only the means will change, that is the application—from the literal and ritualistic, linked with the temple, to the spiritual, a moral renewal."[613] This the New Testament writers did, taking Old Testament text and bringing it to pass again with new characters and scenarios.

Tim Chastain wrote:

> Midrash is a method of interpreting the Old Testament used by various Jewish groups, before and after the time of Jesus, to <u>analyze Old Testament texts and derive new information from them</u>. Midrash is a mixture of interpretation and commentary that produces <u>significance not intended by the original text</u>—especially as it applies to the writer and his audience.[614]

Chastain noted that "The story of Jesus' temptation recalls the testing of Israel in the desert. <u>Jewish hearers would recognize this story as midrash—not history</u>," and "The terrible intention of Herod against the infant Jesus, who was sent to save God's people, recalls Pharaoh's attempt to kill the infant Moses, who led God's people out of Egypt."[615] The final example Chastain gave was Jesus' being the Word. He recalled that Genesis speaks of creation by the word of God ("God said"). Psalm 33:6 says, "<u>By the word</u> of the

[611] Tarico, "Here are 9 'facts' you know for sure about Jesus that are probably wrong."
[612] Alyssa Quint, "In the Beginning, the Prophet Was Poet," Beliefnet: Inspiration, Spirituality, Faith," beliefnet.com, n.d., web, 25 June 2014.
[613] Quint, "In the Beginning, the Prophet Was Poet."
[614] Tim Chastain, "Midrash in the New Testament," jesuswithoutbaggage.wordpress.com, 17 Feb. 2014, web, 11 Mar. 2015.
[615] Chastain, "Midrash in the New Testament."

LORD were the heavens made." Thus Jesus was the word that created the world. In Proverbs 8 Wisdom cries out and puts forth her "voice" (v. 1). She speaks as follows:

> Proverbs 8 (WEB): 22 "Yahweh possessed me in the beginning of his work, Before his deeds of old. 23 I was set up from everlasting, from the beginning, Before the earth existed. 24 When there were no depths, I was brought forth, When there were no springs abounding with water. 25 Before the mountains were settled in place, Before the hills, I was brought forth; 26 While as yet he had not made the earth, nor the fields, Nor the beginning of the dust of the world. 27 When he established the heavens, I was there; When he set a circle on the surface of the deep, 28 When he established the clouds above, When the springs of the deep became strong, 29 When he gave to the sea its boundary, That the waters should not violate his commandment, When he marked out the foundations of the earth; 30 Then I was the craftsman by his side. I was a delight day by day, Always rejoicing before him, 31 Rejoicing in his whole world. My delight was with the sons of men. 32 "Now therefore, my sons, listen to me, For blessed are those who keep my ways. 33 Hear instruction, and be wise. Don't refuse it. 34 Blessed is the man who hears me, Watching daily at my gates, Waiting at my door posts. 35 For whoever finds me, finds life, And will obtain favor from Yahweh. 36 But he who sins against me wrongs his own soul. All those who hate me love death."

Chastain wrote: "John chapter 1 likely reminded hearers of both Genesis and Proverbs. It enriched their idea of Jesus, but they would have understood it as midrash—not history." He summarized his thoughts as follows:

> The writers of Gospel materials were Jewish and used Jewish techniques. The audience was primarily Jewish as well and recognized midrash for what it was. But there is a sharp difference between New Testament hearers and post-New Testament readers. Shortly after the original leaders died the predominantly Gentile church no longer had as strong a connection to the Jewishness of the Gospels.
>
> We stand farther removed from the Jewish context of the New Testament than even the early Church Fathers did. We will inevitably be mistaken if we try to read New Testament midrash as history. Doctrines that some consider important, or even essential, are based on misreading midrash as historical reporting.

Again, the Jews took older stories and embellished them or wrote new, fictional accounts comparable to them. Robert M. Price wrote:

> The line is thin between extrapolating new meanings from ancient scriptures (borrowing the authority of the old) and actually composing new scripture (or quasi-scripture) by extrapolating from the old. By this process of midrashic expansion grew the Jewish *haggadah, new narrative commenting on old (scriptural) narrative by rewriting it. Haggadah* is a species of *hypertext*, and thus it cannot be fully understood without reference to the underlying text on which it

forms a kind of commentary. The earliest Christians being Jews, it is no surprise that they practiced haggadic expansion of scripture, resulting in new narratives partaking of the authority of the old. The New Testament gospels and the Acts of the Apostles can be shown to be Christian haggadah upon Jewish scripture. . . Christian exegetes have long studied the gospels in light of Rabbinical techniques of biblical interpretation including allegory, midrash, and pesher. The discovery of the Dead Sea Scrolls lent great impetus to the recognition of the widespread use among New Testament writers of the pesher technique whereby prophetic prooftexts for the divine preordination of recent events was sought. Slower (but still steady) in coming has been the realization of the wide extent to which the stories comprising the gospels and the Acts of the Apostles are themselves the result of haggadic midrash upon stories from the Old Testament (as we may call it here in view of the Christian perspective on the Jewish canon that concerns us). The New Testament writers partook of a social and religious environment in which currents of Hellenism and Judaism flowed together and interpenetrated in numerous surprising ways, the result of which was not merely the use of several versions of the Old Testament texts, in various languages, but also the easy switching back and forth between Jewish and Greek sources like Euripides, Homer, and Mystery Religion traditions.

Earlier scholars (e.g., John Wick Bowman), as many today (e.g., J. Duncan M. Derrett), saw gospel echoes of the ancient scriptures in secondary coloring here or redactional juxtaposition of traditional Jesus stories there. But the more recent scrutiny of John Dominic Crossan, Randel Helms, Dale and Patricia Miller, and Thomas L. Brodie has made it inescapably clear that virtually the entirety of the gospel narratives and much of the Acts are wholly the product of haggadic midrash upon previous scripture. . .

And the more apparent it becomes that most gospel narratives can be adequately accounted for by reference to scriptural prototypes, Doherty suggests, the more natural it is to picture early Christians beginning with a more or less vague savior myth and seeking to lend it color and detail by anchoring it in a particular historical period and clothing it in scriptural garb. We must now envision proto-Christian exegetes "discovering" for the first time what Jesus the Son of God had done and said "according to the scriptures" by decoding the ancient texts. Today's Christian reader learns what Jesus did by reading the gospels; his ancient counterpart learned what Jesus did by reading Joshua and 1 Kings. . . the result is a new perspective according to which we must view the gospels and Acts as analogous with the Book of Mormon, an inspiring pastiche of stories derived creatively from previous scriptures by a means of literary extrapolation.[616]

Same Sayings

Again, not only is the story of Jesus created from *Jewish* legends but also from religious legends and myths from *other* cultures. Even some of the *sayings* of older gods were repeated by Christ.

---

[616] Price, "New Testament Narrative as Old Testament Midrash."

Massey wrote:

For example, when speaking of his departure **Buddha, like the Christ, promises to send the Paraclete, even the spirit of truth, who shall bear witness of him and lead his followers to the truth**. The Gnostic Horus says the same things in the same character . . . The sayings of Krishna as well as those of the Buddha are frequently identical with those of the Christ. I am the letter A, cries the one. I am the Alpha and Omega (or the A.O.), exclaims the other. I am the beginning, the middle, and the end, says Krishna—"I am the Light, I am the Life, I am the Sacrifice." <u>Speaking of his disciples, he affirms that they dwell in him and he dwells in them.</u>[617]

Massey also noted:

To begin with, two of the sayings assigned by Matthew to Jesus as the personal teacher of men are these:—**"Lay not up for yourselves treasure upon earth,"** etc., and, **"If ye forgive men their trespasses your heavenly Father will also forgive you"**! **But these sayings had already been uttered by the feminine Logos called Wisdom, in the Apocrypha**. We find them in the Book of Ecclesiasticus; "Lay up thy treasure according to the Commandments of the Most High, and it shall bring thee more profit than gold," and "Forgive thy neighbour the hurt that he hath done thee, so shall thy sins also be forgiven when thou prayest"![618] [*Ecclesiasticus* was written by a Jewish scribe, Shimon ben Yeshua ben Eliezer ben Sira of Jerusalem, sometime around 200 to 175 BCE.[619]]

I cannot prove that sets of the sayings of the Lord, as Horus, were continued intact up to the time of Papias. Nor is that necessary. For, according to the nature of the hidden wisdom they remained oral and were not intended to be written down. They were not collected to be published as historic until the mysteries had come to an end or, on one line of their descent, were merged in Christianity. But <u>a few most significant ones may be found in the Book of the Dead</u>. In one particular passage the speaker says he has given food to the hungry, drink to the thirsty, clothes to the naked, and a boat to the shipwrecked; and, as the Osirified has done these things, the Judges say to him, "Come, come in peace," and he is welcomed to the festival which is called "Come thou to me." <u>Those who have done these things on earth are held to have done them to Horus, the Lord; and they are invited to come to him as the blessed ones of his father Osiris. In this passage we have not only the sayings reproduced by Matthew, but also the drama and the scenes of the Last Judgment represented in the Great Hall of Justice, where a person is separated from his sins, and those who have sided with Sut [Set/Seth] against Horus are transformed into goats.</u>[620]

Sadly, not even the Lord's Prayer is original to the New Testament. According to Massey:

---

[617] Massey, *Gerald Massey's Lectures*, No. 15.
[618] Massey, *Gerald Massey's Lectures*, No. 10.
[619] "Sirach," wikipedia.org, 25 Oct. 2104, web, 30 Oct. 2014.
[620] Massey, *Gerald Massey's Lectures*, No. 18.

It is claimed by Christian teachers that the Christ was incarnated as the especial revealer of the father who is in heaven, and that the revelation culminated on the Mount when he taught the fatherhood of God in the Lord's prayer. But the **Lord's prayer is no more original than is the Lord to whom it was last assigned. In the Jewish "Kadish" we have the following pre-Christian form of it, which is almost word for word the same**:—"Our father which art in heaven! Be gracious to us, O Lord our God! Hallowed be thy name! And let the remembrance of thee be glorified in heaven above and upon earth below! Let thy kingdom reign over us now and for ever! Thy holy men of old said, 'Remit and forgive unto all men whatsoever they have done against me!' And lead us not into temptation! But deliver us from the evil thing! For thine is the kingdom, and thou shalt reign in glory for ever and for ever."[621]

This prayer was said to have been spoken about 150 years before Christ.[622]

Jesus Story Better Developed

Again, some say that many aspects of the stories of these gods were added later, copying the more developed Christianity. But, as stated earlier, many ideas about Jesus (his virgin birth on December 25, his resurrection, Mary's perpetual virginity, the Assumption of Mary, etc.) were also added later. It's impossible to know how much, if anything, regarding Jesus is true or when many of the events or characteristics were added. **If even one of the earlier gods rose from the dead, one walked on water, one turned water to wine, one was crucified, etc., then the story of Jesus could be pieced together from these myths.** Those writing about Jesus would add something new, but it's hard to deny *all* of the evidence regarding these mythical gods.

It is true that the story of Jesus is far more detailed and evolved than earlier myths, and some therefore defend it as truth on that basis. But as Joshua Tilghman wrote:

In my opinion, the Jesus narrative is a more compacted and better developed death, burial and resurrection story of the savior god-man simply because it had the chance to develop in the Roman Empire under the direction of the emperor and the Church Fathers. When Constantine made Christianity a legally recognized religion, competing religions and claims were stamped out and eventually the main gist of the Christian narrative we have today was fleshed out under strict supervision.[623]

When I began to read the apocryphal works, I recognized that they weren't well written or developed. That, to me, said they weren't inspired, and I understood why the "wise" men who evaluated them chose not to include them in the New Testament. However, now I realize that the apocryphal works aren't developed because they haven't

[621] Gerald Massey, *Gerald Massey's Published Lectures*, The *"Logia of the Lord;"* or, *The Pre-Christian Sayings Ascribed to Jesus the Christ*, No. 27, *Gnostic and Historic Christianity*, gerald-massey.org.uk, n.d., web, 12 Nov. 2014.
[622] Rutherford H. Platt Jr., *The Forgotten Books of Eden* (1926), Ch. 23, Footnotes, sacred-texts.com, n.d., web, 11 Mar. 2015.
[623] Joshua Tilghman, "Horus and Jesus: Is There a Link Between the Two?" *The Spirit of the Scripture.com: Uncovering the Hidden Meanings of the Bible!*" spiritofthescripture.com, 1 Jan. 2013, web, 27 June 2014.

been tampered with as the canon has been. Lamenting the fact that many forgeries existed, Joseph Wheless wrote, "In view of these 'divine testimonies' of Pagan Oracles forged by pious Christians in proof of their Christ, need one wonder that the like testimonies in the Gospels themselves may be under suspicion of like forgery?"[624] Indeed.

Stories from Secular Literature

The New Testament writers didn't stop at appropriating other scriptures, as Robert Price pointed out. They relied on secular literature as well.

One striking example of a New Testament legend lifted from another writer is the tale of the demoniac in Mark 5:1-20. Price explained:

> Clearly . . . the core of the story derives from Odyssey 9:101-565. Odysseus and his men come to shore in the land of the hulking Cyclopes, just as Jesus and his disciples arrive by boat in the land of the Gerasenes . . . Goats graze in one landscape, pigs in the other. Leaving their boats, each group immediately encounters a savage man-monster who dwells in a cave. The demoniac is naked, and Polyphemus was usually depicted naked, too. The Cyclops asks Odysseus if he has come with intent to harm him, just as the Gerasene demoniac begs Jesus not to torment him. Polyphemus asks Odysseus his name, and the latter replies "Noman," while Jesus asks the demoniac his name, "Legion," a name reminiscent of the fact that Odysseus' men were soldiers. Jesus expels the legion of demons, sending them into the grazing swine, recalling Circe's earlier transformation of Odysseus' troops into swine. Odysseus contrives to blind the Cyclops, escaping his cave. The heroes depart, and the gloating Odysseus bids Polyphemus to tell others how he has blinded him, just as Jesus tells the cured demoniac to tell how he has exorcised him. As Odysseus' boat retreats, Polyphemus cries out for him to return, but he refuses. As Jesus is about to depart, the man he cured asks to accompany him, but he refuses. As MacDonald notes, sheer copying from the source is about the only way to explain why Jesus should be shown refusing a would-be disciple.[625]

Odysseus, of course, is the sun, taking its journey around the earth. He yearns to return to his wife, Penelope, who represents Virgo, or the virgin mother. Odysseus shoots his arrow through the twelve axes (months of the year), a feat only the sun can accomplish. Again we see here a separation of husband and wife and a longing to return to the virgin mother/wife.

---

[624] Wheless, *Forgery in Christianity*, 39.
[625] Price, "New Testament Narrative as Old Testament Midrash." Other similarities between Mark and Homer can be found here: "BORROWED STORIES AND CHARACTERS? -- MARK 1-10," n.d., web, 17 May 2015 <http://vridar.info/xorigins/homermark/mkhmrfiles/mkhmrpt1.htm#top>.

More Hebrew Syncretism

Graham wrote that "the Hebrews got *all* their metaphysical ideas from older races. **There is practically nothing in the Bible that cannot be found in other literatures.**"[626] For good measure let's look at a few stray concepts that I may not have mentioned elsewhere.

*   The long life spans of biblical characters in Genesis is not unique. From Babylonian cuneiform records we find that King Alulim lived to be 18,900 years old; King Alalmar, 36,000; Beroseus, 63,000. This has to do with numerology, as the figures all "add up to nine, a significant number even in Revelation. It should be obvious that these kings were personifications of great epochs, and so are the men of Genesis."[627]

*   The Hebrews were not the first to consecrate the seventh day of the week. The seventh day was dedicated to Apollo, the sun, which is where we get our Sunday.[628] **The word "sabbath" didn't even originate with the Hebrews but comes from the Babylonian "Sabattu," or day of rest, which was observed by the Babylonians "long before the Hebrews."**[629]

*   Egypt's *Book of the Dead*, Spell 53, speaks of the "bread of life," and the Sumerian *Inanna's Descent to the Underworld* (c. 1900-1600 BCE) talks about the "food of life" and the "water of life."[630]

*   Greek god Phoebus Apollo was the "God of Light, in whom is no darkness at all" (1 Jn. 1:5).[631]

*   Jacob's son Joseph, while down in Egypt, was caught up in the story of Potiphar's wife (Zuleika), a myth taken from "Tale of Two Brothers," an Egyptian fable.[632]

*   The Babylonian priesthood performed a "bloody magic ritual" to keep demons away from the home; they put sheep's blood on their doorframes as the Israelites did at the Passover (Ex. 12:1-24).[633]

*   Hermes, son of Zeus (and messenger of the gods, whence we get our word "hermeneutics"[634]), walked on water.[635] Hermes was the messenger (word) of the gods, also known as Thoth. He "authored the Hermetic Books, an astonishing 36,525 volumes

---

[626] Graham, 42.
[627] Graham, 83.
[628] Graham, 41.
[629] Graham, 41.
[630] Murdock, *Did Moses Exist?* 234-235. See also: Samuel Noah Kramer, *History Begins at Sumer* (Garden City, NY: Doubleday, 1959), 165.
[631] Edith Hamilton, "Phoebus Apollo," *Mythology* (New York: Hachette Digital, Inc., 2012), ebook.
[632] Graham, 139.
[633] Murdock, *Did Moses Exist?* 345. See also: Bernard M. Levinson, *Deuteronomy and the Hermeneutics of Legal Innovation* (Oxford: Oxford University Press, 1997), 58; and "The Exodus," wikipedia.org, 26 Jan. 2015, web, 30 Jan. 2015.
[634] Hans-Georg Gadamer, *Truth and Method*, 2nd ed., rev. ed., tr. Joel Winsheimer and Donald G. Marshall (New York: Continuum Publishing Group: 2006), 157.
[635] Dennis R. MacDonald, *The Homeric Epic and the Gospel of Mark* (New Haven: Yale University Press, 2000), 150.

of magic and wisdom, and Egyptian history."[636] The year has 365.25 days, so he had to write a book for each day. Jesus, of course, outdid him in *action*, not mere words. John 21:25 states: And there are also many other things which Jesus did, the which, if they should be written every one, I suppose that <u>even the world itself could not contain the books that should be written</u>. Amen.

*   The New Testament's abode of the dead, Hades, is the name of the Greek god of the dead, or King of the Underworld,[637] and the Scandinavian goddess Hel was ruler of the dead.[638]

*   **The Babylonian demon Lilith appears in Isaiah 34:14** (as well as in the Dead Sea Scrolls).[639]

*   **Jesus' "We have piped unto you, and ye have not danced" (Mt. 11:17) is taken from the words of Aesop (c. 620-560 BCE)**[640]: "when I piped you would not dance.[641]

*   The goddess Hestia was "the <u>first</u> and the <u>last</u> of the children of Zeus, the <u>beginning and end of the god's creation</u>." The legend was that Zeus "swallowed each of his children at the moment of birth, but was ultimately forced to disgorge them. Hestia, being the firstborn was the last to be regurgitated, and so merited this title."[642] (See Matthew 19:30; Colossians 1:15; and Revelation 3:14, 22:13.)

> Certainly everything in the Bible is not stolen from other myths. As Viklund wrote:

> I am not necessarily saying that other cultures or mythologies influenced Christianity. That might of course be the case in many instances, but hardly always. A better explanation is that they <u>all draw from a common heritage</u>. However, simply because everything is not necessarily borrowed from the pagans, this does not imply that the story told of Jesus in the Gospels is true. It does imply, however, that each story told of each son of God is a mythic story, and the story of Jesus as well. It seems unlikely that "every" Saviour God should have led his life in approximately the same way as all the others. That suggests to me that the Gospels are fictitious documents.[643]

Jim Walker wrote along this vein as follows:

> Did the Christians copy (or steal) the pagan ideas directly into their own faith? Not necessarily. They may have gotten many of their beliefs through syncretism or through independent hero archetype worship, innate to human story telling. If gotten through syncretism, <u>Jews and pagans could very well have influenced the</u>

---

[636] "Hermes," *Hermograph Press*, hermograph.com, 2015, web, 17 Apr. 2015.

[637] "Haides," theoi.com, n.d. web, 7 Apr. 2014.

[638] Walker, *Man Made God*, 285.

[639] Janet Howe Gaines, "Lilith: Seductress, Heroine or Murderer?" *Bible History Daily*, biblicalarchaeology.org, 4 Sept. 2012, web, 20 June 2014.

[640] "Aesop's Fables," taleswithmorals.com, June 2014, web, 9 June 2014.

[641] "The Fisherman Piping," *Aesop's Fables*, tr. George Fyler Townsend, classiclit.about.com, 2014, web, 9 June 2014.

[642] Allegro, 70.

[643] Viklund, "The Jesus Parallels."

first Christians, especially the ideas of salvation and beliefs about good and evil. Later, at the time of the gospels, other myths may [have] entered Christian beliefs such as the virgin birth and miracles. In the 4th century, we know that Christians derived the birthday of Jesus from the pagans. If gotten through independent means, it still says nothing about Christian originality because we know that pagans had beliefs about incarnated gods, long before Christianity existed. The hero archetypes still exist in our story telling today. As one personal example, as a boy I used to read and collect *Superman* comics. It never occurred to me at the time to see Superman as a Christ-figure. Yet, if you analyze Superman and Jesus stories, they have uncanny similarities. In fact the movie *Superman Returns* explicitly tells the Superman story through a savior's point of view without once mentioning Jesus, yet Christians would innately know the connection. Other movies like *Star Wars*, *Phenomenon*, *K-PAX*, *The Matrix*, etc. also covertly tell savior stories. So whether the first Christians borrowed or independently came up with a savior story makes no difference whatsoever. The point here only aims to illustrate that Christians did not originate the savior story.[644]

Again, Judaism and Christianity aren't unique; and the Israelites (as most people do) sponged from the cultures of the nations among whom they lived. As stated, virtually all of the Bible's events/people show up in more ancient literature. While some people may think only a symbol, birth date, or other inconsequential concept was borrowed, the truth is that Christianity's basic tenets are simply rehashed myths. The bottom line is that Judaism shared the myths of other cultures, and Christianity further developed the Jewish myths.

Church Fathers Defend Their Faith

Interestingly, while we might not like hearing that our religion is just like everybody else's, the early church fathers were adamant that what they taught was *nothing new* but was the same as was taught by others of their time. In fact, as mentioned earlier, they counted on that fact to bolster their own beliefs.

Christian father Justin Martyr, writing in the 100s CE, admitted that earlier documents contained stories similar to those in the New Testament. He wrote:

And the Sibyl and Hystaspes said that there should be a dissolution by God of things corruptible. And the philosophers called Stoics teach that even God Himself shall be resolved into fire, and they say that the world is to be formed anew by this revolution; but we understand that God, the Creator of all things, is superior to the things that are to be changed. If, therefore, on some points we teach the same things as the poets and philosophers whom you honour, and on other points are fuller and more divine in our teaching, and if we alone afford proof of what we assert, why are we unjustly hated more than all others? For while we say that all things have been produced and arranged into a world by God, we shall seem to utter the doctrine of Plato; and while we say that there will

---

[644] Jim Walker, "Did a historical Jesus exist?"

be a burning up of all, we shall seem to utter the doctrine of the Stoics: and while we affirm that the souls of the wicked, being endowed with sensation even after death, are punished, and that those of the good being delivered from punishment spend a blessed existence, we shall seem to say the same things as the poets and philosophers; and while we maintain that men ought not to worship the works of their hands, we say the very things which have been said by the comic poet Menander, and other similar writers, for they have declared that the workman is greater than the work.[645]

And **when we say also that the Word**, who is the first-birth of God, was produced without sexual union, and that He, Jesus Christ, our Teacher, **was crucified and died, and rose again, and ascended into heaven, we propound nothing different from what you believe regarding those whom you esteem sons of Jupiter**. For you know how many sons your esteemed writers ascribed to Jupiter: Mercury, the interpreting word and teacher of all; Æsculapius, who, though he was a great physician, was struck by a thunderbolt, and so ascended to heaven; and Bacchus too, after he had been torn limb from limb; and Hercules, when he had committed himself to the flames to escape his toils; and the sons of Leda, and Dioscuri; and Perseus, son of Danae; and Bellerophon, who, though sprung from mortals, rose to heaven on the horse Pegasus. [646]

Martyr also wrote:

It having reached the Devil's ears that the prophets had foretold the coming of Christ, the Son of God, he set the heathen Poets to bring forward a great many who should be called the sons of Jove. The Devil laying his scheme in this, to get men to imagine that the true history of Christ was of the same characters the prodigious fables related of the sons of Jove.[647]

As to the miracles of Apollonius, he noted:

How is it that the talismans of Apollonius have power in certain members of creation, for they prevent, *as we see*, the fury of the waves, and the violence of the winds, and the attacks of wild beasts, and whilst *our* **Lord's miracles** *are* *preserved by tradition alone, those of Apollonius are most numerous, and actually manifested in present facts*, so as to lead astray all beholders.[648]

The miracles of Apollonius, that could be seen, led people astray because they were from the devil, but the miracles of Jesus, "preserved by tradition alone," were performed for the purpose of *creating faith*. At least that's what we're supposed to believe.

Speaking of proof for the miracles of the Gospels as well as anything else they teach, Origen, writing in 225-235 CE, admitted that there was no proof for the teachings and events of the Gospels when he declared in answer to the critic Celsus that the Christians

---

[645] Justin Martyr, *The First Apology*, Chs. 20 and 21, 12 Nov. 2014.
[646] Justin Martyr, *The First Apology*, Ch. 21, 31 May 2014.
[647] Doane, XII.
[648] Justin Martyr, "Quaest," Ch. 24. See also: Doane, XXVII.

took it all on faith. Since the adversaries of Christianity were, Origen said, "making such a stir about our taking things on trust," he wrote that, due to various reasons, it was better for the common people to have simple faith rather than to try to reason; its being a "useful thing for the multitude, we admit that we teach those men to believe without reasons."[649] (Of course, if he had *been aware of any proof*, he would have offered it.)

With regard to the god Bacchus, Martyr wrote:

> The devils, accordingly, when they heard these prophetic words, said that Bacchus was the son of Jupiter, and gave out that he was the discoverer of the vine, and they number wine [or, the ass] among his mysteries; and they taught that, having been torn in pieces, he ascended into heaven.[650]

Obviously, before Jesus was considered the son of God, Bacchus was considered the son of a god. Before Jesus ascended to heaven, Bacchus ascended to heaven. Before Jesus turned water into wine, Bacchus had power over wine. Martyr admitted this. Julius Firmicius wrote that the "devil has his Christs."[651] This was his way of saying that, sure, the pagans believed and practiced the same as Christians, but the devil was cunning and made sure this happened in an effort to deceive people when the true savior came into the world.

Martyr continued:

> Moreover, the Son of God called **Jesus, even if only a man by ordinary generation, yet, on account of His wisdom, is worthy to be called the Son of God; for all writers call God the Father of men and gods**. And if we assert that the Word of God was born of God in a peculiar manner, different from ordinary generation, let this, as said above, be no extraordinary thing to you, who say that Mercury is the angelic word of God. But if any one objects that He was crucified, in this also He is on a par with those reputed sons of Jupiter of yours, who suffered as we have now enumerated. . . And if we even affirm that He was born of a virgin, accept this in common with what you accept of Perseus. And in that we say that He made whole the lame, the paralytic, and those born blind, we seem to say what is very similar to the deeds said to have been done by Æsculapius.[652]

(Perseus was the son of Zeus and the virgin Danae, who was impregnated with sunlight or a "golden shower."[653] This is reminiscent of the Spirit, wind, or breath that impregnated the virgin Mary.) Martyr further admitted that he and his fellow Christians "say things similar to what the Greeks say" but were hated, he said, "on account of the

---

[649] Origen, *Contra Celsus*, Book 1, Chs. ix, x, newadvent.org, copyright 2009 by Kevin Knight, web, 29 Oct. 2014. See also: Doane, XXVII.

[650] Justin Martyr, *The First Apology*, Ch. 54, 29 Oct. 2014.

[651] Doane, XX.

[652] Justin Martyr, *The First Apology*, Ch. 22, 31 May 2014.

[653] Justin Martyr, *Dialogue with Trypho*, 67. See also: Alexander Roberts and James Donaldson, eds. *Ante-Nicene Fathers: Translations of the Writings of the Fathers down to A.D. 325* (Buffalo: The Christian Literature Publishing Company, 1885), Vol. I, 231; and Murdock, *Christ in Egypt*, 158-159.

name of Christ."[654] Martyr went on to say that these fictitious gods resembling Jesus were "influenced by the demons" and were written "through the instrumentality of the poets."[655] He wrote (and there will be some repetition here):

> But those who hand down the myths which the poets have made, adduce no proof to the youths who learn them; and we proceed to demonstrate that they have been <u>uttered by the influence of the wicked demons,</u> to deceive and lead astray the human race. For having heard it proclaimed through the prophets that the Christ was to come, and that the ungodly among men were to be punished by fire, <u>they put forward many to be called sons of Jupiter . . . And these things were said both among the Greeks and among all nations</u> where they [the demons] heard the prophets foretelling that Christ would specially be believed in . . . but imitated what was said of our Christ . . . The <u>devils,</u> accordingly, when they heard these prophetic words, <u>said that Bacchus was the son of Jupiter . . . and they taught that, having been torn in pieces, he ascended into heaven.</u> And . . . they . . . gave out that <u>Bellerophon,</u> a man born of man, himself <u>ascended to heaven on his horse Pegasus.</u> And when they heard it said by the other prophet Isaiah, that <u>He should be born of a virgin, and by His own means ascend into heaven, they pretended that Perseus was spoken of.</u> And when they knew what was said, as has been cited above, in the prophecies written aforetime, Strong as a giant to run his course, <u>they said that Hercules</u> was strong, and had journeyed over the whole earth. And when, again, they learned that it had been foretold that <u>He should heal every sickness, and raise the dead, they produced Æsculapius.</u>[656]

Tertullian also blamed the devil:

> Who interprets the meaning of those passages which make for heresy? The <u>devil,</u> of course, whose business it is to pervert truth, who <u>apes even the divine sacraments in the idol-mysteries.</u> Some he <u>baptizes—his own believers,</u> his own faithful. He <u>promises the removal of sins by his washing,</u> and, if my memory serves, in this rite <u>seals his soldiers on their foreheads.</u> He <u>celebrates the oblation of bread,</u> brings on a <u>representation of the resurrection,</u> and buys a wreath at the point of the sword. Why, he actually <u>restricts his High Priest to one marriage.</u>[657]

What Martyr and Tertullian were saying was that all the concepts they mentioned were believed and/or practiced in worship to gods *before* they were practiced/believed in Christianity. The mythological religions these men reference are too similar not to have come from the same source as Judaeo-Christianity.

Dameron spoke of later instances when the devil was blamed for deities that resembled Christ.

---

[654] Justin Martyr, *The First Apology*, Ch. 24, 18 June 2014.
[655] Justin Martyr, *The First Apology*, Ch. 23, 31 May 2014.
[656] Justin Martyr, *The First Apology*, Ch. 54, 18 June 2014.
[657] Tertullian, *The Prescription Against Heretics*, Ch. XL, tr. and ed. S. L. Greenslade, *Early Latin Theology, Library of Christian Classics V* (1956), tertullian.org, 11 May 2001, web, 18 June 2014.

The learned philologists have been able to trace this coming messiah far back in the sacred books of the ancient Hindoos, written in the Sanscrit; which is the mother language of the Aryan race. They had their trinity and they had their savior; so did the Persians and so did the ancient inhabitants of Mexico. When the latter country was invaded by Cortez, the priest said, "The devil was ahead of us; how could these people know of Christ and the Virgin Mary unless the devil had told them of it."[658]

Speaking of the Trinity, Doane noted that "Rev. Father Acosta," referring to the Peruvian Trinity, wrote: "It is strange that the devil after his manner hath brought a Trinity into his idolatry, for the three images of the Sun called *Apomti, Churunti,* and *Intiquaoqui,* signifieth Father and Lord Sun, the Son Sun, and the Brother Sun."[659] Long before the Christian era, Manetho, an Egyptian priest, was given by an Oracle to Sesostris: "First, *God;* then the *Word;* and with them, the *Spirit.*"[660] **The New Testament writers didn't invent the Trinity.**

While much literature was produced to refute Christianity, most of these documents have been destroyed. However, thankfully, since the Christians attempted to respond to the naysayers, we have enough information to recognize that other gods resembling Jesus preceded him, and some were worshiped centuries before his arrival. The myth of Jesus is simply recycled from similar, and earlier, myths.

---

[658] Dameron, 51-52.
[659] Doane, XXXV.
[660] Doane, XXXV.

CHAPTER SEVEN
SOURCE OF ALL DEITY MYTHS

1 (For the Chief Musician. A Psalm by David.) The heavens declare the glory of God. The expanse shows his handiwork. 2 Day after day they pour forth speech, And night after night they display knowledge. 3 There is no speech nor language, Where their voice is not heard. 4 Their voice has gone out through all the earth, Their words to the end of the world. In them he has set a tent for the sun, 5 Which is as a bridegroom coming out of his chamber, Like a strong man rejoicing to run his course. 6 His going forth is from the end of the heavens, His circuit to its ends; There is nothing hidden from its heat.

Psalm 19
World English Bible

The fable of Christ and his twelve apostles . . . is a parody of the sun and the twelve signs of the Zodiac, copied from the ancient religions of the Eastern world. . . Every thing told of Christ has reference to the sun. His reported resurrection is at sunrise, and that on the first day of the week; that is, on the day anciently dedicated to the sun, and from thence called Sunday.[661]

Thomas Paine

Now perhaps we can see that this account "revealed" only to the Jews is but one of innumerable Creation myths and follows the usual formula. Its characters are identical with those of the Greek. The Lord God is Jupiter, Satan is Prometheus, Adam is Epimetheus, and Eve is Pandora. That the woman caused all the trouble is also part of the formula. In Egypt, Noom, the heavenly artist, creates a beautiful girl and sends her to Batoo, the first man, after which all peace for Batoo is ended. According to the Chinese Book of Chi-King, "All things were at first subject to man, but a woman threw us into slavery, by an ambitious desire for things. Our misery came not from heaven but from woman. She lost the human race." . . . Every race of antiquity had this story and in practically all of them some kind of fruit served as the temptation symbol. In Greece it was an apple; in India it was figs. The Hindus tell us that the God Siva sent woman a fig tree and prompted her to tempt her husband with the fruit. This she did, assuring the man it would confer on him immortality. . . Such is the honor of the gods. According to the Greeks, Zeus gave the Hesperides a tree that bore golden apples. As they could not resist the temptation to eat of them, Zeus placed Ladon, a serpent, in the garden to watch the trees. Finally, Hercules, a personification of evolutionary life, slew the serpent, matter, and gave the apples freely to the Hesperides. . . Such is the Bible's "revealed truth"—other races' mythology, the basis of which is cosmology.[662]

Lloyd M. Graham

Christ Jesus . . . is none other than the personification of the Sun, and . . . the Christians, like their predecessors the Pagans, are really Sun worshipers.[663]

T. W. Doane

[661] Thomas Paine, *The Complete Religious and Theological Works of Thomas Paine*, 382. See also: D. M. Murdock/Acharya S, "Were George Washington and Thomas Jefferson Jesus Mythicists?"
[662] Graham, 74.
[663] Doane, XXXIX.

If the stories in the Bible, and elsewhere, are not inspired by Yahweh, or another god, from where did gods and goddesses originate? As has been suggested, these mythical gods developed from the ancients' study of nature, particularly the sky. Genesis 1:14 (WEB) states that the lights in the sky are "to divide the day from the night" and "for signs, and for seasons, and for days and years." We spend our nights going to the movies or other events or staying inside watching TV, reading, or chatting online; but at the time these spiritual ideas were developed the best entertainment was nature. It was also their teacher and dispenser of punishments. If they didn't observe its signs they were in trouble. That's the reason we have the many "types" of Christ in the Hebrew Bible as well as in the mythology of other nations. Most gods are "cosmic, allegorical and mythical entities . . . anthropomorphized or personified."[664] This is called "astral religion, astrolatry, astromythology or astrotheology."[665]

Sun Gods

The ancients considered the sun the father and the moon the mother. The sun impregnated the moon to produce stars.[666] We see this in the biblical account of Joseph's dream about his family. Jacob, Joseph's father, was the sun; his mother, Rachel, was the moon; and Joseph and his eleven brothers were stars (Gen. 37:5-11). All heroes who vanquish villains are sun gods.

Clearly Samson was a "sun god," with long hair as his rays of strength, which is why the cutting of his hair weakened him.[667] Samson had seven locks of hair, obviously representing the "number of the planetary bodies."[668] (The "yellow hair of Apollo was also a symbol of the solar rays."[669]) When Samson lost his strength he was also blind; the sun in winter, when it loses its intensity or vigor by going down, is blind. Belle M. Wagner and Thomas H. Burgoyne wrote: "The Sun [as Samson], shorn of his glory, or solar force, at the autumnal equinox, stands upon the equator between the two pillars of the temple (or light and darkness), and pulls down the temple (or signs) into the southern hemisphere."[670] (See Judges 16:21-31. Yes, the Jews knew how to make up stories to teach lessons just as the Egyptians and Greeks did, and just as we do today.) This symbolism is why the New Testament says a woman is the glory of her husband; she reflects his light because, as the moon, she has no light of her own. Her hair (rays), like Samson's, is her only glory (1 Cor. 11:7, 15). Thus the bride (moon) would one day shine like the husband (sun) as she would be "clothed [covered] with the sun" (Rev. 12:1). She would reflect his glory on the earth when the male and female were reunited.

---

[664] Murdock, *Did Moses Exist?* 72.

[665] Murdock, *Did Moses Exist?* 72.

[666] Acharya S, *Suns of God*, 73.

[667] Murdock, *Did Moses Exist?* 396.

[668] Doane, VIII.

[669] Inman, 679. See also: Doane, VIII.

[670] Belle M. Wagner and Thomas H. Burgoyne, *The Light of Egypt; or the science of the soul and the stars*—Volume 2 (Denver, CO: Astro Philosophical Pub. Co., 1903), "Chapter IV: Astro-Theology," Kindle ed.

In 2 Kings 2:23-24 we find Elisha's encounter with a bunch of children who come out of the city to mock him by saying "Go up, thou bald head; go up, thou bald head." Elisha cursed the children, at which point "there came forth two she bears out of the wood, and tare forty and two children of them." Until recently I didn't understand the children's taunt. They weren't making fun of Elisha because he had no hair. They were telling him he was weak and needed to go "up" (rise higher in the sky, get more rays on his head, gain some strength). Elisha was, they thought, at winter (weak) and needed to head toward summer (get higher in the sky and gain power). He proved them wrong! (The two bears that mauled the children were probably Ursa Major and Ursa Minor.) [671]

Strength and weakness in the Bible often relate to the sun and the solstices. The father grows old and dies and then is reborn as the son. The sun is a "golden child" who is "born in the midst of his enemies" or in the dark of winter (Christmas). The ruler (or power) who attempts to kill the child represents the winter or "darkness" wanting to "get rid of any new light that might threaten his rule." The child is weak but grows stronger (increases in wisdom, stature, etc. [Lk. 2:52]). Because he is feeble the baby is "the almost extinguished flame." But he "regains his strength at spring and deposes his enemies," at which point he "sets out on his journey to the heights." The hero in all the biblical accounts, and other stories as well, is always the dawn or morning sun. He is the superman who vanquishes the bad guy (Satan, big bad wolf, zombie, vampire, monster, wicked witch, General Zod, Darth Vader, Scar/Taka, night, winter). It's the "greatest story ever told!......it is nature and it strikes a chord in our psyche."[672]

We see this battle begin early on in Genesis with the talking snake in the Garden of Eden. Genesis 3:15 states: "And I will put enmity between thee and the woman, and between thy seed and her seed; it shall bruise thy head, and thou shalt bruise his heel." This serpent who was to do battle with humans is Draco, or the dragon, who resides in the sky along with the constellation Hercules. "As Draco circles around the Pole, his head is either below or above Hercules' heel. The top position represents who is doing the bruising." So either Draco is bruising the heel of Hercules or Hercules is crushing Draco's head with his foot.[673] Of course, the sun god always wins the battle in the end. So we see the foot of Hercules "stepping on Draco's head, the dragon/snake who[m] Hercules has vanquished and perpetually gloats over for eternities."[674]

> During the time that Draco's star Thuban was the pole star, it would have appeared to ancient sky watchers that the Earth revolved around Draco. Dragons and other similar creatures often played a role in creation myths. In these stories the gods would often battle such creatures for control of the Earth. When defeated, the dragons were flung up into the skies.[675]

---

[671] "Its [sic] written in the stars," bibliodac.wordpress.com, 16 July 2014, web, 22 Mar. 2015.

[672] "Its [sic] written in the stars," Ibid.

[673] "Its [sic] written in the stars," Ibid.

[674] "Hercules (constellation)," wikipedia.org, 12 Mar. 2015, web, 22 Mar. 2015. See also: Mark R. Chartrand III, Skyguide: A Field Guide to the Heavens (Golden Books Publishing Co., 1982), 150.

[675] Kathy Miles, "Draco the Dragon," starryskies.com, 1995-2008, web, 22 Mar. 2015.

Thus, the serpent is thrown into the abyss. This is why a serpent is prevalent in all the ancient creation myths. Regarding Hercules, Gavin White argues that "the original name of Hercules – the 'Kneeler' . . . is a conflation of the two Babylonian constellations of the Sitting and Standing Gods."[676] Therefore, we have a father god who sits on a throne and a son god who stands at the right of the father.

The following passages exhibit that the Israelites worshiped the "host of heaven."

2 Kings 23:5 And he put down the idolatrous priests, whom the kings of Judah had ordained to burn incense in the high places in the cities of Judah, and in the places round about Jerusalem; them also that burned incense unto Baal, to the sun, and to the moon, and to the planets, and to all the host of heaven. . . 11 And he took away the horses that the kings of Judah had given to the sun, at the entering in of the house of the LORD, by the chamber of Nathanmelech the chamberlain, which was in the suburbs, and burned the chariots of the sun with fire.

Jeremiah 8:2 And they shall spread them before the sun, and the moon, and all the host of heaven, whom they have loved, and whom they have served, and after whom they have walked, and whom they have sought, and whom they have worshipped: they shall not be gathered, nor be buried; they shall be for dung upon the face of the earth.

Ezekiel 8:16 And he brought me into the inner court of the LORD'S house, and, behold, at the door of the temple of the LORD, between the porch and the altar, were about five and twenty men, with their backs toward the temple of the LORD, and their faces toward the east; and they worshipped the sun toward the east.

Acts 7:41 And they made a calf in those days, and offered sacrifice unto the idol, and rejoiced in the works of their own hands. 42 Then God turned, and gave them up to worship the host of heaven; as it is written in the book of the prophets, O ye house of Israel, have ye offered to me slain beasts and sacrifices by the space of forty years in the wilderness?

The "host of heaven" obviously refers to the heavenly bodies; and Genesis 2:1 says: "Thus the heavens and the earth were finished, and all the host of them." However, 1 Kings 22:19 (and 2 Chronicles 18:18) states: "I saw the LORD sitting on his throne, and all the host of heaven standing by him on his right hand and on his left." Nehemiah 9:6 states that the host of heaven *worshiped* Yahweh. Isaiah 34:4 says the host of heaven would one day be dissolved, echoing the warning that the gods would die like men (Ps. 82:7). It was these gods (the heavenly bodies) that made man (in their image), and we know that we are made of the same elements as they are. The "LORD" was the sun.

While we see condemnation for sun worship in the Bible, that doesn't negate the idea that this practice is the origin of all "god" worship. In reality, the god being worshiped is

---

[676] "Hercules (constellation)," *Ibid.* See also: Gavin White, *Babylonian Star-lore* (London: Solaria Publications, 2008), 199ff.

old Sol, and these god-man stories were the ancients' attempt to make everything on earth as it was in heaven. Today, of course, we think of the "host of heaven" as angels.

Precession of the Equinoxes

A Great Year is called a precession. This "year" lasts about 25,765 years. From our perspective, the stars and constellations rotate around our planet. The earth wobbles on its axis like a top and, as Sandra Weaver noted, traces out a "conical shape over a 25,625 years cycle."[677] In fact, the entire solar system curves through space. Above I said this precession takes 25,765 years. Obviously the timing is not exact. NASA, in its definition of the Great Year, says: "The period of one complete cycle of the equinoxes around the ecliptic, about 25,800 years."[678] This is also called a Platonic Year. Within this Year, we experience all of the signs of the Zodiac, each lasting about 2,160 years and called an age or aion.[679] (The signs are backward to the yearly cycle, as the stars move backwards across the sky.)

From 4300 to 2150 BCE the age was that of Taurus, or the Bull. Hence, we see the Egyptians, from their very beginning, worshiping the bull god, Apis. Weaver noted: "Bull worshiping cults began to form in Assyria, Egypt and Crete. The building of pyramids began signifying the bull through solidity, stability, and attempts at eternity. Figures on Egyptian pyramids and temples had bull's horns at this time."[680]

2150 BCE to 1 CE was the year of the Ram, or Aries. This is why Moses was incensed when the Israelites worshiped a golden *calf* (Ex. 32). However, they were being torn from *their* gods to a *new* one. When life wasn't working out, what did they do? They returned to what they knew. But Taurus was over, and it was time for Aries to rule. Whether the golden calf incident happened or not, the story itself reflects the thinking of the time. Remember that when Abraham was about to sacrifice Isaac, Yahweh provided a *ram* instead (Gen. 22:13). The Ram (Aries) would be the new sacrifice. The Jews to this day blow a ram's horn.[681]

When Jesus appeared on the scene at the time of the age of Pisces, or Fish, he fed people fish and called fishermen to be his disciples (Mt. 4:18, 15:34-36). Christians used the Fish, the sign of the sun's kingdom in Pisces, as their religious symbol. Did Yahweh make this happen or did the powers that be know what they were doing because they understood the Zodiac better than we and were simply following the tradition, attempting to make everything "done in earth, as it is in heaven" (Mt. 6:10)?[682] Weaver wrote:

[677] Sandra Weaver, "Precession of the Equinoxes Determines Astrological Ages and Mayan Great Ages," *Spiritual Growth Prophecies: Empowering Ways to Find Peace and Growth in a World of Chaos*, 2012-spiritual-growth-prophecies.com, 2008-2014, web, 21 Dec. 2014.
[678] "Great Year," *Aerospace Science & Technology Dictionary*, hq.nasa.gov, NASA SP-7, 1965, web, 21 Dec. 2014.
[679] Weaver, "Precession of the Equinoxes Determines Astrological Ages and Mayan Great Ages."
[680] Weaver, "Precession of the Equinoxes Determines Astrological Ages and Mayan Great Ages."
[681] "Religion, Bible, Can you handle the Truth? (Must Watch)," youtube.com, 10 Oct. 2013, web, 20 Dec. 2014 <https://www.youtube.com/watch?v=G4VRnXPDuXs>.
[682] "Religion, Bible, Can you handle the Truth? (Must Watch)."

Precession causes much more than changes in our view of the night sky. When a Mayan Great Cycle or Astrological Age changes it affects everything on earth including us, physically and psychologically. This may surprise you, but if you really think about it, the full moon has been proven to have dramatic effects at times on a person's mood. . .

The common thread that creates the uncanny resemblances between the Greek/Egyptian Astrological Ages and the Mayan Great Ages is the ancient people's knowledge of precession. Our ancestors were much closer to nature than we are today, and they realized over time that what happened in the cosmos above affected events on the earth and all life below.

I used to wonder why Yahweh, the god of the Old Testament, was cruel and hateful while Jesus, the god of the New Testament, was gentle and kind. My study of astrotheology has explained that conundrum. When Yahweh (whose name is not even mentioned in the New Testament) ruled, the sun was in the sign of Aries, the ram. Aries is ruled by Mars, "the fiery, destructive and warrior element, or force, in Nature." Therefore, the Jewish concept of a god at that time was "Lord of Hosts, a God mighty in battle, delighting in the shedding of blood and the smell of burnt offerings, ever marshalling the people to battle and destroying their foes and the works of his own hands; a god imbued with jealousy, anger, and revenge."[683] Bill Darlison stated that Taurus is an earth sign and represents the body, sensuality, and sexuality; therefore, religion expressed this during the reign of Taurus. Aries, on the other hand, being a fire sign, brought with it initiation into religion at the point of a knife (circumcision). Libra is the opposite sign to Aries, so justice and law were important during that age.[684] By the time of Christianity, however, 2,160 years had passed and the sun had "entered the sign Pisces, which is ruled by Jupiter, the beneficent father."[685] Thus, Jesus, unlike his malevolent father, was tender and merciful, and his message was one of peace and love. He lifted up the fallen (even adulterous women, bastards, and men with crushed and missing testicles [Deut. 23:1-2, Jn. 8:3-11]) and urged the people to put down their swords. Jesus was Joshua, like the son of "Nun," which means "fish," and the New Testament references fish twenty-eight times. Initiation into Christianity is through water, of course; and, Virgo's being the opposite of Pisces, celibacy is highly valued. Friday is the special day of Venus (Freya), who rules in Pisces; so we eat fish on Fridays.[686] It was a new age, as a new sign was in the skies; and the authors of the Piscean era's myths were, once again, attempting to make everything on the earth as it was in the heavens. Jesus said that "whatever things you will bind on earth will be bound in heaven, and whatever things you will release on earth will be released in heaven" (Mt. 18:18 WEB). In about 2150 CE the age of Aquarius will arrive. (Hopefully no new "god" will come at that time to take the place of Jesus.) Those following Jesus will fight to hang onto him, but he will probably disappear with the age.

[683] Wagner and Burgoyne, *The Light of Egypt, Ibid.*
[684] Darlison, "The New Age."
[685] Wagner and Burgoyne, *The Light of Egypt, Ibid.*
[686] Darlison, "The New Age."

Some say Aquarius is already here. Maybe that's why many today are becoming enlightened and are recognizing that Jesus is just another solar deity. O, the ever-changing, never-changing gods!

Dying and Rising Gods

The concept of a Messiah, or crucified god (with a virgin birth, descent into hell, and ascension into heaven), dying for his people, is, as I have stated, often found in ancient cultures, including Assyria, Egypt, Persia, and Babylonia, and is based on worship of the sun.[687] [688] According to Doane, "even among the Hindoos even in *Vedic* times," we find the story of a Messiah who dies for the people. (The *Rig-Veda* "hymns and invocations to the gods" are "older than any other books in the world."[689]) Doane wrote:

> *The sacrificer was mystically identified with the victim*, which was regarded as the ransom for sin, and the instrument of its annulment. **The *Rig-Veda* represents the gods as sacrificing the god *Purusha* [before Jesus was a twinkle in Yahweh's eye, or in the seventeenth century BCE[690]], the primeval male supposed to be coeval with the Creator.**[691]

Even Inanna, the Queen of heaven (or Ishtar), was, as mentioned previously, a dying and rising goddess. According to *The Descent of Inanna*, she descended to the depths of the underworld, where she was stripped, humbled, killed by being nailed up by demons, and resurrected.[692]

Doane noted that the ancients imagined the gods to be like humans; if they liked wine, maybe the gods would. They thought some gods were partial to plants and some to animals. They offered whatever seemed good to try to avert a calamity or appease the gods. Eventually, and especially because of their strange beliefs regarding blood, this led to animal and human sacrifice.[693] The sweet-smelling savor went up as the gods' favor came down when the people built their hope upon the bloody altars. As we learned earlier, primitive people believed that life was made of blood; therefore, a virile god needed blood—and lots of it. Blood made gods happy, and a happy god was likely to be predisposed to grant the people three, or more, wishes. If the gods were happy, crops would grow and livestock would be healthy and fat.

Tertullian noted that "Osiris also, whenever he is buried, and looked for to come to life again, and with joy recovered, is an emblem of the regularity wherewith the fruits of

---

[687] Acharya S, *Suns of God*, , 357-358, 364-365, 404.

[688] Robert Taylor, AB, *The Diegesus* (Whitefish, MT: Kessinger Publishing, 1992; facsimile of 1829 ed.), 9.

[689] Bennett, 77.

[690] Armstrong, 28.

[691] Doane, XX.

[692] Richard Carrier, PhD, *On the Historicity of Jesus: Why We Might Have Reason to Doubt* (Sheffield, England: Sheffield Phoenix Press, 2014), Kindle ed. See also: Stephanie Dalley, *Myths from Mesopotamia: Creation, the Flood, Gilgamesh, and Others* (Oxford; New York: Oxford University Press, 2000).

[693] Doane, XX.

the ground return, and the elements recover life, and the year comes round."[694] Jesus has been identified with the dying and rising Phoenix of Egypt. This bird supposedly died and rose again from his ashes (just as Jesus did, 1 Cor. 15:42-49). More than that, the Phoenix remained dead for three days before rising again.[695] Tammuz and Attis, as we know, also died and rose, and their resurrection, like Christ's, was in the spring.[696] Obviously these resurrection stories relate to the renewal of life in spring, which is why even today we celebrate the resurrection of Jesus with bunnies and eggs in the spring. Even the rising of Baal from the dead symbolized the "return to life and fecundity."[697]

Not only does the precession of the equinoxes affect religious beliefs and practices, but even every change in the Zodiac in each year is reflected in religious teaching. At the beginning of autumn we see Scorpio in the sky. He is the Judas, or kiss of death, to the sun. After this the sun falls below (crosses or "passes over") the equator. It continues to fall until December 22, at which point it is still (as far as we can tell) in the Southern Cross. The sun continues to refuse to move at all through December 23 and 24. Thus it is *dead* for *three days*. If a person is dead for three days he is "positively, absolutely, undeniably, and reliably . . . most sincerely dead."[698] If he comes to life again at this point, he has *resurrected*, or been *born again*. And the sun, of course, not only rises on the third day but also ascends into (returns to) heaven. This passing over the equator is Passover, of course, so in the spring Jews celebrate the sun with this feast; and Christians celebrate Easter, which is why they get up early to see the *sunrise*. The spring, as we know, brings revitalization of life.

No matter how it is sliced up and delivered, Christianity is sun worship.[699] It is as pagan as any other religion. Just as the sun "dies" for three days in winter, it "hangs for three days upon the celestial cross formed by the ecliptic and the equator" in the spring.[700] (The cross is the "emblem or symbol of the *Sun*, of *eternal life*, or *generative powers*."[701]) Viklund wrote:

> At the winter solstice, the sun begins its journey to the north. Two thousand years ago, the constellation of Virgo rose on the eastern horizon at every winter solstice. In the old sun-worshipping societies, people could observe the Sun being born again, and every year it was "born" in Virgo. Indubitably, many nations have regarded the sun as a god. It is equally certain that the return of the sun at the winter solstice was an important event accompanied with ceremonial festivals. Therefore, it must be reasonable to assume that people in the sun-worshipping societies interpreted the sun's rising in the constellation of Virgo as

[694] Tertullian, *Against Marcion*, Book 1, Ch. 13.

[695] Murdock, *Christ in Egypt*, 426.

[696] Murdock, *Did Moses Exist?* 375. See also: "Attis," wikipedia.org.

[697] Aicha Rahmouni, *Divine Epithets in the Ugaritic Alphabetic Texts*, tr. J. N. Ford (Leiden: E. J. Brill, 2008), 57-58. See also: Murdock, *Did Moses Exist?* 412.

[698] Harold Arlen, "Ding Dong! The Witch Is Dead," *The Wizard of Oz*, Dir. Victor Fleming, Metro-Goldwyn-Mayer, 1939, film.

[699] Jordan Maxwell, "Similarity between jesus and mithras and sun," youtube.com, 9 Mar. 2008, web, 11 Sept. 2014.

[700] Graham, 346.

[701] John William Colenso, *The Pentateuch and the Book of Joshua Critically Examined*, Part VI (London: Longmans, Green, and Co., 1872), 113-115. See also: Doane, XXXIII.

if the Virgin gave birth to the Sun, which was worshipped as a god. Consequently, the Virgin gave birth to the God or to the Son of God.[702]

This is ancient knowledge, and it is not just now surfacing even in our day. In 1903 Wagner and Burgoyne expressed these ideas as follows:

Then comes the flight to escape Kronos, or Saturn (ruling Capricorn [which begins December 21 and is the "stable of the Goat, in the manger of which the young Savior of the world is born"], who kills the young babes. There is a period of silence in the God's history while the Sun is in transit through the signs of Capricorn and part of Aquarius. That is, he is hidden or obscured by the clouded skies of this period. We hear of him but once again until he, the Sun-God, or Savior, is thirty years old, or has transited thirty degrees of space. He has entered the sign of Aquarius (symbolical of the Man). . .

The devil (or winter) with his powers of darkness, is defeated and man saved. The final triumph is the crucifixion in Aries, the vernal equinox, about the 21st of March, quickly followed by the resurrection, or renewal of life. Then the God rises into heaven, to sit upon the throne at the summer solstice, to bless his people. We read, that, the Savior of mankind was crucified between two thieves. Very good. The equinoctial point is the dividing line between light and darkness, winter and summer. . .

The three days in the tomb are the three months, or three signs, before the vernal equinox, or the resurrection, the rising out of the South to bring salvation to the northern portion of our Earth.[703]

Sex and Regeneration

The cross was prominent in fertility cults long before Christianity. It is not therefore simply an icon representing the death of Jesus. Nor is the fish symbol many proudly display. As Cezary Jan Strusiewicz wrote, the "ancient cultures generally had a tendency to revere anything vaguely genitalia related."[704]

Annie Besant (1847-1933)[705] wrote:

The cross is, in fact, nothing but the refined phallus, and in the Christian religion is a significant emblem of its pagan origin; it was adored, carved in temples, and worn as a sacred emblem by sun and nature worshipers, long before there were any Christians to adore, carve, and wear it.[706]

---

[702] Viklund, "The Jesus Parallels."

[703] Wagner and Burgoyne, *The Light of Egypt, Ibid.*

[704] Cezary Jan Strusiewicz, "6 Famous Symbols That Don't Mean What You Think," cracked.com, 2 July 2012, web, 27 Jan. 2015.

[705] "Annie Besant," wikipedia.org, 23 June 2015, web, 1 July 2015.

[706] Annie Besant, *The Freethinker's Text-book, Part II: Christianity: Its Evidences. Its Origin. Its Morality. Its History* (London: R. Forder, 1893), 357.

The **cross within a circle** (sun cross or solar cross), which has come to us from ancient paganism, **represents eternal life as well as the origin of life**. John William Colenso noted that the "self-evident conclusion" is:

> the symbol is merely a phallic emblem, the cross and the circle (oval or crescent), being used to represent the **male and female organs**,—a fact respecting which there can be no doubt whatever in the minds of those who have studied the question thoroughly, and traced the symbol in its various modifications.[707]

Today, in our supposedly enlightened world, **Christians still worship not only the sun but also human sexuality**, casting their hopes on a created savior who was born of a god's mating with a human female. Even the church steeple, or obelisk, is a phallic symbol. Dr. Charles G. Berger, in *Our Phallic Heritage*, wrote:

> All pillars or columns originally had a phallic significance, and were therefore considered sacred. Pan, the goat god and god of sensuality, was often represented as an obelisk. The obelisk is a long pointed four sided shaft, the uppermost portion of which forms a pyramid. The word "obelisk" literally means "Baal's shaft" or "Baal's organ of reproduction."[708]

Aasha Wilson noted that it is "widely understood that the obelisk is a phallic symbol honoring and celebrating regeneration of the sun god Ra."[709] **Thus, the church building (representing Christians, or the female aspect of Christ) is attached to the steeple (the penis of Christ, that has come into the female body to dwell).** Actually, Christ was the "little head"—the son, the junior, the fruit/spittle/word that shot forth from the Father, the point at the end, the head of the corner, the capstone of the shaft (Lk. 20:17).

While we may shrink back from such thoughts, this was standard fare for fertility cults. Even the fish symbol is sexual.

> Along with being a generative and reproductive spirit in mythology, the fish also has been identified . . . with reincarnation and the life force. Sir James George Frazer noted in his work, "Adonis, Attis, Osiris: Studies in the History of Oriental Religion" (Part Four of his larger work, "The Golden Bough") that among one group in India, the fish was believed to house a deceased soul, and that as part of a fertility ritual specific <u>fish is eaten in the belief that it will be reincarnated in a newborn child.</u>

> Well before Christianity, the fish symbol was known as "the Great Mother," a pointed oval sign, the "vesica piscis" or Vessel of the Fish. "Fish" and "womb" were synonymous terms in ancient Greek, "delphos." Its <u>link to fertility, birth,</u>

---

[707] Colenso, 114.

[708] Charles G. Berger, MD, *Our Phallic Heritage* (Greenwich Book Publishers, 1966). See also: Cathy Burns, PhD, *Masonic and Occult Symbols Illustrated* (Sharing, 1998), 341.

[709] Aasha Wilson, "Are Church Steeples Pagan? YES! They Symbolize the Male Sex Organ," *Yah's Elect Network: Bringing People Out of the Dark and Into the Light of the Way of Yahushuwa!* godselectpeople.ning.com, 30 Oct. 2012, web, 8 Jan. 2015.

feminine sexuality and the natural force of women was acknowledged also by the Celts, as well as pagan cultures throughout northern Europe. Eleanor Gaddon traces a "Cult of the Fish Mother" as far back as the hunting and fishing people of the Danube River Basin in the sixth millennium B.C.E. Over fifty shrines have been found throughout the region which depict a fishlike deity, a female creature who "incorporates aspects of an egg, a fish and a woman which could have been a primeval creator or a mythical ancestress..." The "Great Goddess" was portrayed elsewhere with pendulous breasts, accentuated buttocks and a conspicuous vaginal orifice, the upright "vesica piscis" which Christians later adopted and rotated 90-degrees to serve as their symbol. . .

From its focus of worshipping a god-man born of a virgin to the selection of holidays and symbols, Christianity appropriated the metaphors of earlier pagan religions, grafting them into its own account of the creation and beyond. Few Jesus worshippers are aware of this. Even fewer know that when they flaunt the "Ichthus" ["offspring son of the ancient sea goddess Atargatis"] . . . as a representation which originated in Christianity, they are in fact, displaying a more ancient symbol indicative of female anatomy and reproductive potency -- the very sign of the Great Mother.[710]

"The fish [is] also a central element in other stories, including the Goddess of Ephesus (who has a fish amulet covering her genital region), as well as the tale of the fish that swallowed the penis of Osiris, and was also considered a symbol of the vulva of Isis."[711] Once again, we remember the divine goddess and the ancient ideas about the making of babies, and realize that all religions are based on natural phenomena. We are also reminded of the male's need to reunite with the female. Allegro noted that the "Christian doctrine of the fatherhood of God stems not from the paternal relationship of Yahweh to his chosen people but from the naturalistic philosophy that saw the divine creator as a heavenly penis impregnating mother earth."[712] Being half human and half divine (some say fully human and fully divine), Jesus connected Father Heaven to Mother Earth—ending the separation of male and female and, therefore, the death (male and female together produce *life*). This sheds light on the Gnostic apostle Paul's concept of resurrection—transforming from a natural, earthy being (Adam/Israel/Jerusalem) to become a spiritual, heavenly being (Christ/Israel of God/new Jerusalem) [1 Cor. 15]. (We'll consider this further later on.)

Nursery Tales

It's time to consider the purpose of the stories about humans being swallowed by whales or fish. These fables were written to express the black night's swallowing up the day, with the three days (inside the fish) representing the time in winter when the sun

---

[710] "True Origin of Christian 'FISH' Symbol Might Outrage, Shock Jesus Worshippers," godlessgeeks.com, n.d., web, 27 Jan. 2015.
[711] "True Origin of Christian 'FISH' Symbol Might Outrage, Shock Jesus Worshippers," *Ibid.*
[712] Allegro, 7.

stands still for three days in the "bowels of the Earth."[713] (This also represents the three months of winter.) These were "big fish" stories, or fables to teach lessons. Most legends and fairy tales are based on this idea.

I already mentioned Rumpelstiltskin as a gospel motif, but I'll say a bit more here. Only a god can make gold out of straw, so in this story Rumpelstiltskin is obviously a god. The princess represents humanity and its plight, of course. She is between a rock and a hard place and needs a savior. This particular savior is both good and kind, as most gods are. He will provide the gold upon the incantation of his name (one must call upon the name of the Lord to be saved, Rom. 10:13), but if the princess fails to call she is doomed. And what is the price she must pay? The loss of her firstborn child, of course!

While we might not have noticed as children, the "Little Red Riding Hood" story was written to symbolize the daily/yearly event of the sun's fight with darkness. The weak little girl (red evening sun or late fall sun) who came to comfort the old grandmother (Earth) found the grandmother swallowed by the big bad wolf (night or winter). But when the big strong woodsman (bright morning sun or summer sun) arrived, he cut open the big bad wolf and let out the grandmother.[714]

The story of Pinocchio is easily recognized as a "gospel" story. Pinocchio was made of wood. He had a wooden heart, which is basically the same as a heart of stone. Yahweh said he would take away Israel's stony heart and give her a heart of flesh (Ezek. 36:26). When he did this, Israel was to rise from the dead and come alive. Yahweh said he would cause breath to come into Israel and her dry bones would rise and she would live. Pinocchio, if he was a *good* little boy, could be a real *living* boy. He could "repent" so to speak and have true life.

When Sleeping Beauty, who was living under a *curse*, reached the *age of accountability*, she pricked her finger and *died*. But in the *fullness of time* a *handsome prince* came along, kissed her, and *brought her to life again*. And, of course, *they lived happily ever after*.

Even the tale of Cinderella is a sun myth. Cinderella was ragged and dull, hidden behind her sisters (clouds) and evil stepmother (night). But the prince (morning sun) took her as his bride and she became the beautiful, adored one.[715] In one version of this story, pigeons peck out the eyes of the wicked stepsisters and they live as blind beggars while Cinderella spends the remainder of her life in the lap of luxury at the palace of the prince.[716] Sound familiar? It should. Yahweh found Israel in her blood, cleaned her up, and put linen and silk clothes upon her, along with bracelets and necklaces, gold and silver, and even a crown—all while he brought troubles and pain upon the nations who were Israel's enemies (Ezek. 16:1-14).

Isn't this also the Christian fable? We are lost and undone, worthless and forgotten; but our shining prince comes riding in on his white horse and rescues us. Then we, rather than our tormentors, are the special ones, the beautiful and glorious bride of Christ

---

[713] Doane, IX.
[714] Doane, IX.
[715] Doane, Appendix C.
[716] J. Frater, "The Hidden Meanings behind Fairy Tales," *Drama Start*, drama-in-ecce.com, Nov. 2010, web, 14 Nov. 2014.

decked out with gold and various jewels. We rule in our golden kingdom alongside him, and live happily ever after, forever and ever, as we banish our tormenters, and all other "unworthies," far from us in the darkness of the dungeon. (This is even the story of Delta Dawn. Trusting in a promise, she waits for her "mysterious, dark-haired man" to "take her to his mansion in the sky."[717])

Professor Max Müller wrote: "The *divine myth* became an *heroic legend*, and the *heroic legend* fades away into a *nursery tale*. Our nursery tales have well been called the modern *patois* of the ancient sacred mythology of the Aryan race."[718] When we get to the bottom of all the legends and myths, we discover that all religion is about honoring or worshiping whatever or whoever provides life and health—and makes the crops grow. And that is the sun.

The Zodiac and the Numbers Twelve and Seventy

Astrology and numerology play a huge role in the beliefs of Christianity just as they do in other religions. We see this in the Bible by its varied use of particular numbers, such as twelve and seventy.

> The number 12 is significant in Sumerian culture, which was the first to observe the 12 moon cycles throughout the year and to split up the Zodiac into 12 constellations, each representing a god. The Sumerians passed on the significance of 12 and the Zodiac to the Greeks, the Greeks to the Romans, and the Romans to the Western world.[719]

Carmen Turner-Schott wrote: "In the Jewish temple of Jerusalem it is believed that the twelve signs of the zodiac were inlaid in its floor. According to Josephus, stamps were even issued with the zodiac signs on them and they were representative of the twelve tribes of Israel."[720] The sun (Jesus) is in the center of twelve stars, just as both Ishmael and Jacob had twelve sons; there were twelve tribes of Israel and twelve apostles; new Jerusalem has twelve foundations and a wall with twelve gates and twelve angels; and the woman in Revelation 12:1 has twelve stars in her crown (Gen. 25:16, 35:22, 49:28; Rev. 21:12, 14). The Hindus have twelve Aditya and the Scandinavians twelve Aesirs of Asgard. Both Osiris and Marduk had twelve helpers.[721] A Buddhist's life is "composed of 12 stages."[722] The months of the year are twelve. The days are divided into twelve during the day and twelve at night. Both Rome and Greece worshiped twelve gods, there were "12 adventures of Gilgamesh" and "12 labors of Hercules"; and

---

[717] Harvey, Alex, and Larry Collins. "Delta Dawn." 1972. Song.
[718] Max Müller, MA, *Chips from a German Workshop, Vol. 2: Essays on Mythology, Traditions, and Customs* (New York: Charles Schribner and Company, 1872), 260. See also: Richard Heber Newton, *Sermons in All Souls monthly, 1888-1891* (East Hampton, NY), 12; and Doane, IX.
[719] Robert Engelbach, "On the Sacred Path with Gilgamesh and Enkidu," spiritofthescripture.com, 29 Jan. 2015, web, 29 Jan. 2015.
[720] Carmen Turner-Schott, MSW, LISW, "The Shining Star of Bethlehem: Signs in the Sky," *About Astrology*, astrology.about.com, n.d., web, 19 June 2014.
[721] Graham, 316.
[722] Engelbach, "On the Sacred Path with Gilgamesh and Enkidu."

Gnosticism had its "twelve governors."[723] Even the Egyptian "lakes of fire" were attended by twelve gods.[724] At the age of twelve, Jesus worked in his Father's house (Lk. 2:41-49). This relates to the sun, noted by Murdock as follows: "In the solar mythos, the 'age' of 12 refers to the sun at high noon, the twelfth hour of the day when the 'God Sun' is doing his 'heavenly father's work' in the 'temple' or 'tabernacle' of the 'most high.'"[725] In Vedic hymns, the sun is referred to as the "son of the sky," Lord, Savior, Redeemer, and Preserver of mankind.[726] **Heaven and earth were considered to be the "parents of all things" and were male and female divinities.**[727] (They had a domestic squabble and all hell broke loose, but they got back together for the sake of their son.)

It takes little effort to discover that the number twelve in the Bible relates to the Zodiac and the twelve months of the year. Revelation 21:18-20 leaves no doubt, as the **description of the walls of the new Jerusalem presents all twelve birthstones of the months.** Graham listed these as follows: March, Jasper; April, Sapphire; May, Chalcedony; June, Emerald; July, Onyx; August, Carnelian; September, Chrysolite; October, Beryl; November, Topaz; December, Ruby; January, Garnet; and February, Amethyst.[728] The traditional birthstones bear out this truth.[729]

Viklund explained the use of the number twelve with regard to the disciples of Jesus:

> It might also be said that the Son of God had twelve companions, or disciples if you like, in the shape of the twelve zodiacal constellations which the sun passes on its journey in the sky. The Sun God Mithras is in most cases depicted together with the twelve signs of the Zodiac. The two equinoxes (vernal and autumnal) and the two solstices (summer and winter) form a cross in the circle of the zodiac (mentioned by Plato), and so the Sun God can be said to be fettered on this cross, as he must constantly follow the path of the cross. All these ideas are probably the basis of the corresponding Christian conceptions.[730]

According to Robert Engelbach,

> In numerology, the number 12 is related to Pisces. The (12th) Tarot card is The Hanged Man. It represents the completed cycle of experience and when an individual reincarnates as the number 12 they have completed a full cycle of experience and learned of the possibility of regeneration toward a higher consciousness.[731]

Thus, the "figure on Card 12 has made the ultimate surrender – to die on the cross of his own travails – yet he shines with the glory of divine understanding. He has sacrificed

---

[723] Murdock, *Christ in Egypt*, 261, 277.

[724] E. A. Wallis Budge, *A Guide to the Egyptian Galleries* (British Museum, 1909), 182. See also: Murdock, *Christ in Egypt*, 272.

[725] Murdock, *Christ in Egypt*, 214.

[726] Doane, XXXIX.

[727] Doane, XXXIX.

[728] Graham, 375.

[729] "Birthstone," wikipedia.org, 25 Jan. 2015, web, 26 Jan. 2015.

[730] Viklund, "The Jesus Parallels."

[731] Engelbach, "On the Sacred Path with Gilgamesh and Enkidu."

himself, but he emerges the victor."[732] Pisces is the "Alpha and Omega, the beginning and the end, the first and the last" (Rev. 22:13). We pass through the waters to be born, and cross over the river at death to be resurrected or born again. Pisces is the end of the yearly cycle, but (in geometric or retrograde order) the beginning of the astrological age.

The numbers seven and seventy-two also figure prominently in the biblical story, as they do in most other religious myths. This is also, and of course, for astrological reasons.

The number seven relates to the sun, moon, and five anciently known planets.[733] We see this number often in antiquity. In the Bible we find: seven days of creation; seven plus seven years Jacob worked for Rachel; seven years of plenty and famine; seven days of unleavened bread; seven-day walk around the walls of Jericho; seven demons of Mary Magdalene; seven sons of Sceva; seven men full of the Holy Ghost; seven churches, seven stars, seven candlesticks, seven seals, seven thunders (Gen. 2:2, 29:20-28, 41:29-30; Ex. 12:15; Mk. 16:9; Acts 6:3, 19:14; Heb. 11:30; Rev. 1:4, 1:20, 5:1-5, 10:3-4). This number is used in a sacred sense in the seven doors to the Mithraic caves, seven prophetic rings of the Brahmans, seven Persian spirits, seven Chaldean archangels, seven branches on the Assyrian tree of life, seven gates of Thebes, Pan's flute with seven pipes, Apollo's lyre of seven strings, seven arms of the Hindu god, and seven stages of Mount Meru, among other instances.[734] Josephus expounded on the Jewish use of astrology as follows:

When Moses distinguished the tabernacle into three parts, and allowed two of them to the Priests, as a place accessible and common, he denoted the land and the sea: for these are accessible to all. But when he set apart the third division for God, it was because heaven is inaccessible to men. And when he ordered twelve loaves to be set on the table, he denoted the year, as distinguished into so many months. And when he made the candlestick, of seventy parts, he secretly intimated the *Decani,* or seventy divisions of the planets. And as to the seven lamps upon the candlesticks, they referred to the course of the planets, of which that is the number. And for the veils, which were composed of four things, they declared the four elements. For the fine linen was proper to signify the earth; because the flax grows out of the earth. The purple signified the sea; because that colour is dyed by the blood of a sea shell-fish. The blue is fit to signify the air; and the scarlet will naturally be an indication of fire. Now the vestment of the High Priest being made of linen, signified the earth; the blue denoted the sky; being like lightning in its pomegranates, and in the noise of the bells resembling thunder. And for the ephod it shewed that God had made the universe of four [elements:] and as for the gold interwoven, I suppose it related to the splendor by which all things are inlightened. He also appointed the breast-plate to be placed in the middle of the ephod, to resemble the **earth: for that has the very middle place of the world**. And the girdle which encompassed the High Priest round, signified the ocean: for that goes round about and includes the universe. Each of the sardonyxes declares to us the sun and the moon: those I mean that were in the nature of buttons on the High Priests shoulders. And for the **twelve stones, whether we understand by them the months; or whether we understand the**

---

[732] Engelbach, "On the Sacred Path with Gilgamesh and Enkidu."
[733] Doane, II.
[734] Doane, II and III.

like number of the signs of that circle which the Greeks call the _Zodiack_, we shall not be mistaken in their meaning.[735]

Josephus obviously recognized the religion of the Jews as being based on the earth and the sky, or the Zodiac, and the elements and seasons.

Murdock noted that Philo saw the "70 as seven multiplied by 10, astrotheologically the number 70 represents the . . . 72 divisions of the zodiacal circle into five degrees each, a motif like the 12, which is found commonly in many mythologies, such as concerns the gods of Egypt, Greece and Rome."[736] Murdock wrote that the number seventy-two is "frequently shortened to 70. The 72 descendants [of Jacob, also said to be seventy, Ex. 1:5] and 70 elders or disciples would symbolize the same mythical theme."[737] (Seventy elders went up with Moses, Aaron, Nadab, and Abihu to eat lunch with Yahweh [Ex. 24:9-11].) According to the Ugaritic tablets, El and Asherah (known as Ashtoreth or Astarthe in the Old Testament) had seventy sons, who were the Elohim.[738] (Again, Asherah was spoken of as the consort of Yahweh, equating El with Yahweh and Baal. If Baal and Yahweh were El's sons, this is to be expected, as Yahweh and his son Jesus are also equated.) The Elohim, we discovered, were the gods who created the world in Genesis. Job 38:7 speaks of the **morning stars, or sons of Elohim**, singing together and shouting for joy; and, again, El judged among his sons (Ps. 82:1). Psalm 82 is a reprimand to the sons of El for not judging righteously. They were gods but they weren't doing what El wanted—defending the fatherless and delivering the needy. (In myths the **main god is usually the sun and the lesser gods are stars**. In Numbers 29, seventy bullocks were sacrificed. Seventy bulls were also sacrificed in the myth of Baal "centuries before the Bible was composed."[739] All the gods, or Elohim, needed a sacrifice.) Remember that the ancients thought the stars possessed power over the lives of humans; it was determined whether a child would be great based on what the heavens "declared" at the time of the child's birth. Perhaps the whole point of El's (Sol's) anger was that the stars weren't doing a good job of meting out good fortunes to the deserving.

One of El and Asherah's sons, by the way, was called "king" and was "identified with Venus as the morning star," and Yahweh's son Jesus is also called the morning star (Rev. 2:28, 22:16). "Thus, we have a God the Father of the Morning Star over 1000 years before Jesus supposedly walked the earth."[740] Venus is called Lucifer in Isaiah 14:12; thus Jesus is recognized as Lucifer (he is both sinner and saint, both Adam and Christ, the one who must die and the one to be resurrected). I know all of this is confusing. If it weren't, we would all have figured it out long ago. The Bible is extremely, and possibly intentionally, baffling. The main reason we don't know about astrotheology is that we have not been taught; the information has been hidden from us.

---

[735] Flavius Josephus, _Antiquities of the Jews_, 3, 7, 7.
[736] Murdock, _Did Moses Exist?_ 234.
[737] Murdock, _Did Moses Exist?_ 234.
[738] John Gray, _The Legacy of Canaan_ (Leiden, Netherlands: E. J. Brill, 1957), 78. See also: Murdock, _Did Moses Exist?_ 403.
[739] Murdock, _Did Moses Exist?_ 403, 405.
[740] Murdock, _Did Moses Exist?_ 406.

More Magic Numbers

Not only the numbers seventy and twelve are important to the Judaeo-Christian religion, but forty and thirty are also significant in the Bible. The number forty figures prominently not only in the Bible but also in other, and older, literature ("Semitic mythology centuries before the time of Moses or Jesus" and in the *Epic of Gilgamesh*).[741] This number "in ancient myth apparently represents the time it takes for certain seeds to germinate after they have been planted in the spring."[742] With regard to the Israelites' wandering in the desert for forty years, this would represent "a period of 40 from the barren soil of the desert germinating into the land of 'milk and honey.'"[743] The Israelites died in the wilderness and were "resurrected" after forty years into the Promised Land, just as Jesus/Adam "died," was "buried," and then was "resurrected" after forty years in the year 70 CE. (See my book *We Are Emmanuel* for a full explanation of this claim.)

As for the number thirty, Zoroaster, Horus, Jesus, and John the Baptist all began their work at the age of thirty; Joseph stood before Pharaoh at thirty years of age (Gen. 41:46); Judaic priests had to be thirty years old (Num. 4:3); the Israelites mourned the death of Moses for thirty days (Deut. 34:8); Samson had thirty companions (Jdg. 14:10); at thirty, Ezekiel began to see visions from Yahweh (Deut. 34:8); and Judas betrayed Jesus for thirty pieces of silver (Mt. 26:14-15). This number is likely related to the days of the month.[744]

Another astrological element of the gods is the four points of the Zodiac. In Ezekiel 1:4-10 the prophet speaks of four creatures having four faces—man, lion, ox, and eagle. (Revelation lists the beasts as lion, calf, man, and eagle, Rev. 4:7.) Baal also had four faces—"lion, bull, dragon and human."[745] Also related is Macrobius' "four solar aspects of Hades, Zeus, Helios and Dionysus."[746] Murdock wrote:

> Ezekiel's four beasts evidently symbolize the fixed points of the zodiac, the man equated with Aquarius, the ox or cherub with Taurus, the lion with Leo and the eagle with Scorpio. These points represent the signs immediately after the winter solstice, vernal equinox, summer solstice and autumnal equinox, respectively."[747]

The Zodiac and Ezekiel's Wheel

The biblical prophet Ezekiel, in the first chapter of the book bearing his name, spoke of a wheel within a wheel and four living creatures. This was supposed to be the word and vision from God, but it can be seen within the Zodiac. Graham wrote:

---

[741] Murdock, *Did Moses Exist?* 240.
[742] Murdock, *Did Moses Exist?* 240.
[743] Murdock, *Did Moses Exist?* 240.
[744] Revelation, "Number 30 In the Bible | What's the Significance of Age 30 in the Bible?" revelation.co, 6 Jan. 2013, web, 12 Nov. 2014.
[745] Sally Tomlinson, *Demons, Druids and Brigands on Irish High Crosses* (Ann Arbor, MI: ProQuest, 2007), 270.
[746] Murdock, *Did Moses Exist?* 426.
[747] Murdock, *Did Moses Exist?* 427.

These four creatures, a man and ox, lion and eagle are but Aquarius, Taurus, Leo and Scorpio, the four cardinal points of the stellar zodiac, and hence of the creative process. All antiquity knew about them, and every race made use of them in its art and mythology. Why then should it be a revelation to Ezekiel? Among the Orphics they were . . . Dragon, Bull, Lion, and Eagle. The Chaldeo-Babylonians called them Oustour, the Man; Kirub, the Bull; Nirgal, the Lion; and Nathga, the Eagle. In the Hindu pantheon they are the cosmic Maharajas, otherwise known as the Asuras, Kinnaras and Nagas; also the Avengers, the Winged Wheels, the Locapalas or supporters of the world. As the latter they were respectively Indra, the East; Yama, the South; Varuna, the West; and Kuvara, the North. There is a drawing by Levi of these four animals enclosed in a six-pointed star, with the Hebrew name *Adoni* over it. In India there is a similar picture with the word *Adonari* over it, hence the *Adoni* of the scriptures. . .

The complexity, a "wheel within a wheel" and many other wheels, is but the zodiac itself, with its cosmogonical, precessional, annual and diurnal cycles within it. The "whirlwind" is its ceaseless motion. The ancient symbol of this was the swastika . . . The Ancients called it "The Wheel of Fir." The "eyes" of the wheel are symbols of the creative intelligence within this complexity. The four beasts "had the likeness of a man"; in plain words, they are Man, Aquarius, the evolving Life Principle. This is the one and only factor in Creation, the God of religion being but a priestly necessity.[748]

Buddha was the "Wheel king," and the Babylonian Shamash is pictured with a "wheel behind him, and the spokes of the wheel are made of stars instead of eyes."[749] The Assyrian god Asshur is pictured inside a wheel, and the Assyrians believed Asshur's life was in the wheel. Today, the four beasts are the Catholic Church's four angels—Gabriel, Michael, Uriel, and Raphael; and, "when humanized, Matthew, Mark, Luke, and John."[750]

Identity Theft

The gods have many names, and a different name doesn't necessarily imply a different god. It's often difficult to distinguish them as they practice identity theft. It's therefore hard to recognize that they are all sun gods and many of them are the same god.

It's easy to see the resemblance between Adonai (a name used about 439 times in the Bible)[751] and Adonis. El Shaddai (*Shadday* in Hebrew), God's name in Exodus 6:3 (where he says that was always his name until he decided to go by Yahweh), is also the name of a storm god, who was a "West Semitic god, another of the many Canaanite Elohim, possibly one of El's sons."[752]

The Chaldeans referred to Dionysus/Bacchus as Iao (Jah, also used for Yahweh). The *Jehovah Encyclopedia Britannica* notes that Yaho is an ancient Semitic

---

[748] Graham, 253-254.
[749] Graham, 254.
[750] Graham, 254-255.
[751] Michal Hunt, "The Many Names of God," agapebiblestudy.com, 2003, web, 13 Nov. 2014.
[752] Murdock, *Did Moses Exist?* 408-409.

and mystic name for God, and that Yah is an abbreviated form. The names Yah and Yaho were both used by the Hebrews; however, the **Chaldeans made use of the names Yaho and Ia or Ya(h) prior to the Jews' application of these appellations**.[753] Iao was a triune god, and the **Phoenicians also worshiped a trinity of gods named Iao. Iah (Yah) was also moon god to the Egyptians**.[754] (Yahweh is "often called Sabaoth" as well.[755] See Romans 9:29 and James 5:4.)

The Dead Sea Scrolls refer to Yahweh as Iao, and Tertullian confirmed that the Valentinian Gnostics called God Iao.[756] Macrobius and Plutarch "identified the solar Iao with Bacchus, who . . . was equated by Diodorus with Yahweh."[757] Bacchus is also associated with Adonis.[758]

Gray wrote that responsible scholars are increasingly recognizing that "Yahweh, the god of a militant tribal group, was first subordinated to El the Canaanite high god before he took over his attributes and functions as King and creator."[759] As Murdock noted, it seems the Jewish scribes found as many gods as they could and rolled them into one to make their god superior to all others.[760] She further wrote that if Dionysus, Adonis, and Iao are indeed the sun, but are "identified with Yahweh," then "we can conclude that the Jewish tribal god too is a typical solar deity, as found in numerous cultures dating back to remote antiquity, in the very eras and areas in which he flourished as a tribal god."[761]

Ritual Baptism

The Bible speaks of being baptized into the death of Christ (Rom. 6:3-12). But baptism, as has been noted, didn't originate in the New Testament. DeRobingne Mortimer Bennett wrote that the Brahmans, long before the advent of Christianity, sprinkled infants at the age of nine days and also "hastily" baptized those who were dying in order that the "dying man would be cleansed from the effects of sin."[762] R. L. Vos noted: "The washing of the corpse with water is an ancient solar rite, the object being the removal of impurity and the bringing about of resurrection, just as the sun rises from the primeval waters or, which amounts to the same thing, from the horizon."[763]

The practice of baptizing the "dead" is thus quite ancient and is, again, based on events of the sky. Buddha administered baptism for the remission of sins.[764] Brahman priests also performed baptisms for the forgiveness of sins. The Brahman priest rubbed

[753] *Jehovah Encyclopedia Britannica*, Vol. 12, 1958 edition, 995.
[754] "Yaho/Yah/Iao/Yahweh/Jehovah," jesus-messiah.com, n.d., web, 12 Nov. 2014.
[755] Murdock, *Did Moses Exist?* 432.
[756] Alexander Roberts and James Donaldson, eds., *Ante-Nicene Christian Library*, Vol. 15 (Edinburgh: T & T Clark, 1870), 140. See also: Murdock, *Did Moses Exist?* 433.
[757] Murdock, *Did Moses Exist?* 435.
[758] Plutarch, *Plutarch's Miscellanies and Essays*, Vol. 3, ed. William W. Goodwin (Boston Little, Brown and Company, 1889), 310. See also: Murdock, *Did Moses Exist?* 435.
[759] John Gray, *The Legacy of Canaan*, Dead Sea Scroll fragment 4Q120, Rockefeller Museum, Jerusalem, 161. See also: Murdock, *Did Moses Exist?* 407.
[760] Murdock, *Did Moses Exist?* 415.
[761] Murdock, *Did Moses Exist?* 436.
[762] Bennett, 594.
[763] R. L. Vos, *The Apis Embalming Ritual* (Leuven: Peeters Publishers, 1993), 31. See also: Murdock, *Christ in Egypt*, 250.
[764] Acharya S, *Suns of God*, 311.

mud on the sinner, "plunged him three times into the water," and said: "O Supreme Lord, this man is impure, like the mud of this stream; but as water cleanses him from this dirt, *do thou free him from his sin.*"[765] Likewise, Zoroaster baptized himself for purification; and when he came up out of the water, the "archangel Vohu Mana appears to him . . . and commissions him to bear the tidings of the one God Ahura Mazda, whereupon the evil one Ahriman tempts him to abandon this call."[766] The Jews, before the time of Christ, baptized new converts, but only after their Babylonian captivity, meaning that the ritual was borrowed "from their heathen oppressors."[767] **The poet Ovid (43 BCE) spoke of baptism *for the remission of original sin* when he wrote: "Ah, easy Fools, to think that a whole Flood Of water e'er can purge the Stain of Blood."**[768] In Egypt the baptizer was Anubis, Inpu, or Anpu; in Babylon he was the "water god Oannes"; and in Christianity he was Ioannes or John. These men all relate to the Zodiacal sign of Aquarius, the Water Bearer. The Catholic Church set John the Baptist's birthday at June 24 (six months prior to that of Jesus), which is when Aquarius begins to be seen in the sky. This is the time of the summer solstice, after which the days become shorter until the winter solstice (when Jesus was supposedly born), so John indeed decreased while Jesus increased (Jn. 3:30). Interestingly, sometimes Aquarius appears to be decapitated, just as the baptizers Anubis and John were.[769]

Dr. Richard A. Gabriel wrote: "The Egyptians believed that each morning the sun passed through the waters of the ocean before being reborn, emerging purified and revitalized. [Remember, water was life-giving semen.] The ritual baptism of the pharaoh each morning symbolized this event and renewed life and vigor of the recipient."[770] (Thus, the sky is the origination of yet another ritual.) James Bonwick noted that the water used in these Egyptian rites "absolutely cleansed the soul, and the person was said to be regenerated."[771] Often in Egyptian baptism, as in Christian baptism, the recipient was given a "new name."[772]

Tertullian, casting aspersions upon "pagan baptisms" in the worship of Isis and Mithras, exalted Christian baptism by saying that "if the mere nature of water, in that it is the appropriate material for washing away, leads men to flatter themselves with a belief in omens of purification, how much more truly will waters render that service through the authority of God."[773] While Tertullian wanted to downplay previous baptisms, he made it clear that such had been practiced. And, as usual, he, as well as Justin Martyr, blamed the previous baptisms on imitations by demons, to prevent belief in the *true* baptism.[774]

---

[765] Doane, XXXI.

[766] Price, "New Testament Narrative as Old Testament Midrash."

[767] Albert Barnes, *Notes*, Vol. 1, 41, as quoted by Doane, XXXI.

[768] Ovid, *Fast*, II, 45. See also: Doane, XXXI.

[769] Herbert Julius Hardwicke, *The Popular Faith Unveiled* (London: 1884),195. See also: Murdock, *Christ in Egypt*, 253-254.

[770] Richard A. Gabriel, *Gods of Our Fathers: The Memory of Egypt in Judaism and Christianity* (Greenwood Publishing Group, 2002), 184. See also: Murdock, *Christ in Egypt*, 233.

[771] Bonwick, 416. See also: Murdock, *Christ in Egypt*, 244.

[772] Murdock, *Christ in Egypt*, 244.

[773] Alexander Roberts and James Donaldson, *Ante-Nicene Fathers*, III (New York: Charles Scribner's Sons, 1903), 671. See also: Murdock, *Christ in Egypt*, 245.

[774] Taylor, *Diegesis*, 232. See also: Doane, XXXI.

Ancient Egyptian worshipers practiced two types of baptism; as with Christianity, one was in water and the other in the spirit.[775] The Egyptians also believed in the baptism of fire mentioned in the New Testament (Mt. 3:11, Lk. 3:16). The dead were conducted through this "Lake of Fire, in a form of baptism by fire."[776] As in Christianity, the wicked were cast into the Lake of Fire. And, again, as in Christianity, even those who were holy were also baptized with fire, as fire purifies one (Mt. 3:11). Remember, the ancients expected to return to their mother's womb. And, according to Allegro, in Sumerian mythology, **when a scribe wanted to represent the concept of "love," he "drew a simple container with a burning torch inside, to indicate the fermenting heat of gestation in the womb."[777] Thus God is both "love" and a "consuming fire"** (Heb. 12:29, 1 Jn. 4:8), defender and prosecutor, executioner and scapegoat, satan and savior.

Speaking of the Lake of Fire, the Bible teaches the salvation of all (at least all of Israel, over which Yahweh reigned, if not the whole world[778]). Revelation 11:15 states: "The kingdoms of this world are become the kingdoms of our Lord, and of his Christ; and he shall reign for ever and ever." As Graham wrote:

> But think not this is exclusively Hebrew knowledge. Older far than this is the Hindu story of Vishnu pacifying humanity and pardoning the devils Siva threw into the bottomless pit, after which all will dwell with the gods again on Mount Meru. What then becomes of the doctrine of eternal punishment? Even Origen pronounced this doctrine false and well he might for it is but mythological double talk and nothing more. . . Do you not see then the necessity of knowing something more than the literal word? This is neither fact nor history; it is priestly perversion thereof.[779]

Graham also related the Persian view of eternal salvation, stating that these people believed good folks would enter "this happy abode (the regenerated earth)," while others would be purified by being baptized into the lake of fire and then, basically, live happily ever after.[780] Carried by Anubis, Egyptians passed through (were baptized in) a purifying lake, arriving at their eternal abode.[781] Everybody has to be immersed in the waters—maneuver up the *narrow* way (through the fallopian tubes)—to get back to the Promised Land (Mt. 7:14, 1 Cor. 10:2). This is also why people were baptized to begin a new walk in life, and it's why stories of baptism into death were written and why one must make his/her way through the River Styx after death in order to obtain the glorious afterlife. When winter (sin, death, darkness) has passed, coming up out of the watery grave of Pisces is the newborn or reborn sun. Aquarius, the Water Bearer (John the Baptist), baptizes the sun in the Piscean waters, and the sun then rises in Aries as the lamb of God.

---

[775] Murdock, *Christ in Egypt*, 247.

[776] Murdock, *Christ in Egypt*, 242.

[777] Allegro, 13.

[778] Sometimes in the Bible the word "world" refers only to Israel or the Roman world (Lk. 2:1, Gal. 4:3-5, Col. 2:20). It is not the purpose of this book to determine whether the Bible teaches the salvation of Israel only or the whole world.

[779] Graham, 387.

[780] Graham, 405.

[781] Jan Assmann, *Death and Salvation in Ancient Egypt*, tr. David Lorton (Ithaca, NY: Cornell University Press, 2005), 32-33.

The Amazing Sun

Truly the sun was the first god of mankind, and other gods have been based on it. **The sun walks on water and rides on the clouds; gives life and produces the harvest; is the light of the world; dies at the winter solstice to be reborn on December 25; is both kind and cruel; rules the good day while the darkness governs the evil night; is no respecter of persons; is dependable and faithful to rise every morning; and, if he turns his face from us, we die. As Psalm 19 states, the heavens declare God's glory and his work, speech, and knowledge.** They are a voice that goes to the end of the world, with nothing hidden from the sun, the "bridegroom coming out of his chamber."[782]

With regard to sun worship, Dameron wrote of Hercules:

Parkhurst, in his Greek Lexicon, says: "It is well known that by Hercules was meant the sun or solar light, and his twelve famous labors referred to his passage through the zodiacal signs." And that the Garden of the Hesperides was the Garden of Eden, and the serpent's head was crushed beneath the heel of Hercules; all of which goes to show that the <u>ancient theology taught by Moses was the same as that which existed in India, Egypt, China, Assyria, Babylon, Persia, Arabia, Asia Minor and Palestine; with the Greeks, Romans, Celts, Gauls, modern Europeans, Australians, ancient Mexicans and Peruvians, which had its origin with the pre-historic man long before the continents took their present shape</u>. The legends among the savage as well as the civilized man, point to the antique garb, with its shreds and patches of ever increasing theological complications, for the benefit of modern fanaticism, and the edification of those who are content to take the word of priestcraft, instead of thinking and investigating for themselves.[783]

Tertullian admitted that Jesus was a sun god when he said, "You say we worship the sun; so do you."[784] Stella Woods confirmed this as follows:

The Bible tells us that three wise men came from the east, following a star that led them to Bethlehem to celebrate the birth of Jesus the Messiah. [Peter] Joseph claims that the star in the east was Sirius, the brightest star in the sky, which on December 24th aligns with the three brightest stars in the constellation of Orion (Orion's belt). The stars were referred to by many ancient cultures as the Three Kings. You may recall . . . that the great pyramids of Egypt were built in exact alignment with these three stars, to channel the star energy on the earthly plane. And <u>when Sirius (the brightest star) lined up with the Three Kings, they pointed to the place of sunrise on December 25th – the symbolic birth place of the sun or son</u>.[785]

---

[782] For a thorough study of this issue, see *Solar Mythology and the Jesus Story: A Primer on Astrotheology*, solarmythology.com, 8 Dec. 2013, web, 18 June 2014.
[783] Dameron, 56.
[784] J. Chapman, "Tertullian," *The Catholic Encyclopedia* (New York: Robert Appleton Company, 1912); newadvent.org, 2012, web, 18 June 2014.
[785] Stella Wood, "Winter Solstice–Sun on the Southern Cross," June 2008, pdf, 19 June 2014.

The Jews, however, promoted their sun myths as truths. Graham wrote:

> The Greeks were not so gullible. <u>So let us see the difference between the Hebrew mythologists and the pagan ones. The purpose of the latter was the preservation of truth and enlightenment of man through the Zodiacal Night.</u> To this end they wrote their tales in such a way that no intelligent man could be deceived by them; they purposely made their myths incredible and their gods immoral that no religion might be founded on them. <u>They did not say they walked and talked with Zeus, or that he commanded them to write. They made no claim to divine revelation or inspiration; they wrote with a simple naiveté that charms but does not seduce. The Hebrews, on the other hand, wrote with malice aforethought; their purpose was not the preservation of truth and human enlightenment but the obscuration of truth and the enslavement of the mind to priestly rule.</u> They were religion makers, and to this end they claimed divine authority; they even put their preposterous claims into the mouth of their monstrous God and declared he said them. Having no material or national power of their own, they invented a conceptual one to intimidate their neighbors and to cripple the Gentile race. And how they have succeeded![786]

Emperor Constantine was the first to prescribe Sunday, the day of the sun, as a day of worship for Christians. Eusebius wrote:

> <u>He [Constantine] ordained, too, that one day should be regarded as a special occasion for prayer</u>: I mean that which is truly the first and chief of all, the day of our Lord and Saviour. . . <u>Accordingly he enjoined on all the subjects of the Roman empire to observe the Lord's day, as a day of rest</u> . . . his desire was to teach his whole army zealously to <u>honor the Saviour's day</u> (**which derives its name from light, and from the sun**).[787]

Arthur Weigall noted that the Church made Sunday sacred

> <u>largely because it was the weekly festival of the sun</u>; for it was a definite Christian policy to take over the pagan festivals endeared to the people by tradition, and to give them a Christian significance. But, as a solar festival, <u>Sunday was the sacred day of Mithra</u>; and it is interesting to notice that since <u>Mithra was addressed as *Dominus*, "Lord", Sunday must have been "the Lord's Day" long before Christian times.</u>[788]

Thus the sun, which had been freely worshiped by the Jews, continued to be the deity of Christians; and as long as it shines, life continues for man and his earth.

I know some will say, "Yes, God wrote all about his son in the heavens." But which god? And which son? Again, why would the one true deity be the new kid on the block who looks like all the other fake kids who came before him?

---

[786] Graham, 275-276.
[787] Eusebius, *Life of Constantine*, IV, Ch. 18.
[788] Weigall (Putnam and The Book Tree), 145.

CHAPTER EIGHT
GNOSTIC CHRIST

None of the early schools of Christianity resembled the literalist Christianity that we know today. The so-called "historical" Christianity . . . was invented over the course of three and a quarter centuries, until the Council of Nicea set it in stone and covered up its early roots, while Christian monks burned whole libraries of books, killed priestesses, destroyed temples, forbade the study of philosophy and closed the schools, thus by eradicating the classical world's knowledge helped to bring on the Dark Age. [789]

Barbara G. Walker

When I am told that a woman called Mary said that she was with child without any co-habitation with a man, and that her betrothed husband Joseph said that an angel told him so [in a dream!] I have a right to believe them or not; such a circumstance requires a much stronger evidence than their bare word for it; but we have not even this - for neither Joseph nor Mary wrote any such matter themselves; it is only reported by others they said so - it is hearsay upon hearsay, and I do not choose to rest my belief upon such evidence.

Thomas Paine

Jesus is a mythical figure in the tradition of pagan mythology and almost nothing in all of ancient literature would lead one to believe otherwise. Anyone wanting to believe Jesus lived and walked as a real live human being must do so despite the evidence, not because of it.

C. Dennis McKinsey, Bible critic, *The Encyclopedia of Biblical Errancy*

The word "gnosis" means "knowledge of spiritual matters; mystic knowledge."[790] Gnostic metaphorical views were pushed aside by a literal view of the Christian scriptures; but despite what some say, Gnosticism was an "early branch of Christianity" rather than a heretical offshoot.[791] Timothy Freke said Gnostics "filled the universe" in the first and second centuries CE.[792] And Bill Darlison wrote:

Indeed, it is no longer unthinkable for us to invert the customary view of the relationship between 'historic' and 'esoteric' Christianities. It seems increasingly likely that the former was a perversion of the latter, that the attempt to establish historical credentials for the Jesus story came some time after the theory itself originated in the fertile imagination of some esoteric group, whose poetic account of the spiritual journey was transformed into history by people who had either misunderstood the story, or who were motivated by more cynically pragmatic political or ecclesiastical considerations.[793]

[789] Walker, *Man Made God*, 139.
[790] "Gnosis," dictionary.com, 2014, web, 12 Nov. 2014.
[791] Jacobovici, "Jesus' Marriage to Mary the Magdalene Is Fact, Not Fiction."
[792] "Osiris & Christianity - The Christian Adoption of Egyptian Iconography, Symbolism, and Myth," dir. Roel Oostra, CTC/Cresset Communications, 2003; youtube.com, 12 June 2013, web, 2 Jan. 2015, film.
[793] Bill Darlison, *Gospel and the Zodiac: The Secret Truth about Jesus* (London/New York: Overlook Books, 2008), Kindle ed.

Gnostics "represent the losers in the Christian orthodoxy game. After the fourth century, the <u>Church burnt Gnostic holy books and the people who believed in them</u>";[794] the Gnostics were persecuted, and the Church "<u>outlawed all other histories of Jesus but the four official ones.</u>"[795] While the Church canonized only four Gospels, many more existed (several still available today), some of which present an allegorical view of the Christ. John Allegro wrote that "it was the more original cult that was driven underground by the combined efforts of the Roman, Jewish, and ecclesiastical authorities; it was the supreme 'heresy' which came on, made terms with the secular powers, and became the Church of today."[796] The winners write the history and do their best to deny evidence that contradicts their view; however, I believe the New Testament teaches that Christ offered his blood sacrifice not literally on Earth but figuratively in the sky, as did other sun gods. In this chapter I present mainly non-biblical evidence for this claim.

Jesus the Sky God

Dr. Craig Lyons stated that Jesus began as a sky god, performing his deeds in the heavenly realm just like all other deities (and the Bible, of course, declares that Jesus could not be priest or offer sacrifices on Earth, Heb. 8:4, which we will discuss below), but was later literalized by Ignatius as well as Irenaeus and some other early Christians.[797] Lyons further noted:

The gospel figure of Jesus is a Jewish adaptation of the mythical godman found under many different names in ancient pagan mystery religions: in Egypt he was Osiris, in Greece Dionysus, in Asia Minor Attis, in Syria Adonis, in Italy Bacchus, in Persia Mithras. All the major elements of the Jesus story, and there are hundreds of them, from the virgin birth to the crucifixion and resurrection, can be found in earlier stories of pagan godmen that existed thousands of years prior to the time of the New Testament "Jesus". The idea of a suffering God atoning by his death for the sins of men, descending into the abodes of darkness and rising again to bring life and immortality to light, is found in the oldest records of the human race in every part of the world. It is originally in all cases a personification of the Sun . . .

The reason why all these narratives are so similar, with a godman who is crucified and resurrected, who does miracles and has 12 disciples, is that these stories were based on the movements of the sun through the heavens, an astrotheological development that can be found throughout the planet because the sun and the 12 zodiac signs can be observed around the globe. In other words, Jesus Christ and all the others upon whom this character is predicated are personifications of the sun, and the Gospel fable is merely a rehash of a

---

[794] Jacobovici, "Jesus' Marriage to Mary the Magdalene Is Fact, Not Fiction."
[795] Scaruffi, "Jesus and Christianity."
[796] Allegro, xxi.
[797] Bushby, "The Forged Origins of the New Testament."

mythological formula (the "Mythos,") revolving around the movements of the sun through the heavens. For instance, many of the world's crucified godmen have their traditional birthday on December 25th. This is because the ancients recognized that (from an earthcentric perspective) the sun makes an annual descent southward until December 21st or 22nd, the winter solstice, when it stops moving southerly for three days and then starts to move northward again. During this time, the ancients declared that "God's sun" had "died" for three days and was "born again" on December 25th. The evidence is overwhelming once you begin to look at it . . .

<u>Contrary to popular belief, the ancients were not an ignorant and superstitious lot who actually believed their deities to be literal characters. Indeed, this slanderous propaganda has been part of the conspiracy to make the ancients appear as if they were truly the dark and stupid that was in need of the "light of Jesus."</u> The reality is that the ancients were no less advanced in their morals and spiritual practices, and in many cases were far more advanced, than the Christians in their own supposed morality and ideology, which, in its very attempt at historicity, is in actuality a degradation of the ancient Mythos. Indeed, unlike the "superior" Christians, the true intelligentsia amongst the ancients were well aware that their gods were astronomical and atmospheric in nature.[798]

Crossified Man

The ancients thought the sun couldn't be at peace as it moved toward winter and didn't shine as long and as brightly. It lost its strength and was afflicted. James Lewis Spence wrote: "As the days began to shorten and the nights to lengthen it was thought that [Set] stole the light from the sun-god."[799] As Murdock noted, that makes Set a "*thief in the night* who robs Osiris/Horus of his strength and life."[800] Plato (living about 400 years before Christ) spoke about a "crucified divine man floating in space."[801] Albert Parsons wrote regarding this idea:

Light is thrown upon his meaning by an ancient figure of the Galaxy in the form of a man, with the axis of the poles represented by a perpendicular spear resting on the feet and issuing forth from the top of the head, while the equator is represented by another <u>spear run horizontally through the body</u>. This is only extending the axial and equatorial lines of the earth from our position at the centre of the Galaxy to its limits in both directions. Thus is the <u>divine man crossified in space</u>. The obliquity of the ecliptic, as the result of the disaster which tilted the earth's axis, is indicated in this ancient figure by a <u>spear thrust diagonally upward through the side of the divine man</u>.[802]

[798] Craig M. Lyons, MsD, DD, MDiv, "Finding the Truth about the Christ in the 'Jesus Story' of the New Testament," *Bet Emet Ministries*, christianityasamysteryreligion.com, n.d. web, 11 June 2014.

[799] James Lewis Spence, *Ancient Egyptian Myths and Legends* (New York: Dover, 1990), 100. See also: Murdock, *Christ in Egypt*, 72.

[800] Murdock, *Christ in Egypt*, 72.

[801] Albert R. Parsons, *New Light from the Great Pyramid* (New York: Metaphysical Publishing Company, 1893), 219. See also: Murdock, *Christ in Egypt*, 355.

[802] Parsons, 219. See also: Murdock, *Christ in Egypt*, 355-356.

Long before Christianity existed, people considered the sun to be "hung on a cross" at the time of the equinoxes. Murdock wrote that "in numerous Egyptian scriptures, the <u>sun is depicted as 'crossing over' the sky, by its movement essentially making the sign of the cross</u>."[803] Just as other gods were crucified "in the heavens," again, evidence points to a heavenly crucifixion of Christ. But even if it could be proven (it can't) that a literal man named Jesus was hung on a cross and people literally thought it was for our sins, that wouldn't change the truth of the scientific evidence. It would simply point out that humans were attempting to portray on the earth what goes on in the sky.

Passover

Santos Bonacci explained astrotheology as follows:

Astrotheology is the holy science that combines astrology, astronomy and theology. This holy science shows that in fact all myths, all story's [sic], the bible and all other holy scriptures, and even nursery rhymes are based on the movement and interaction of the seven lights we see in the sky. These seven lights we know as the Sun, the Moon, Mercury, Venus, Mars, Jupiter and Saturn. They are the lights our eyes can see wandering in front of the fixed background of the stars. These are the main characters that create patterns in the sky, which have an effect on our lives here on Earth or Terra. "As above, so below".

The brightest of these seven lights is the Sun also known as "Helios" in Greece and as "Helios Atum" in ancient Egypt. "Atum" sounds like "atom" and it is in fact the same because the sun is an atom. It has an electric light core and electron bodies floating around it.

Plato said that the Sun is "the cause of our knowledge, without it we cannot see". So the Sun is the teacher of the sense of the sight and the ruler of our eyes. The Sun is the "lucent" one, or "Lucifer".

In ancient Egyptian mythology, the name of the "Sun" god was "Ra", the one who "ra"diates. In churches, you will often see the letters "IHS" on books, altars, baptismal fonts etc. always pictured with a symbol of the sun around it. IHS stands for the Greek letters "iota", "eta" and "sigma". Writing in our alphabet, "IHS" equals "JHS" or "JHC". [Hence we hear some exclaim "Jesus H. Christ!"] The pronunciation of this word is "JES", which is a shorthand for "Jesus". Jesus and the sun are the same. Jesus is the sun! Jesus Christ is God's sun. The sun is the risen savior. So this "IHS" is a Christogram, amonogram which is an abbreviation of the name of "Jesus". The early Christians were called: "Helionostics" which means "Those who have knowledge of the Sun".

In Hebrew "yes", or "jes" means fire or the sun! <u>The name of the sun in Hebrew is Michael, or Emanuel.</u> In India, it is: Krishna, Brahma, Shiva or Jes-Christna. In

---

[803] Murdock, *Christ in Egypt*, 342. See also: Faulkner, *The Ancient Egyptian Coffin Texts*, I, 226.

Egypt, it is: Ra, Horus, Seth, Atum, Aman. In the "Nag Hammadi" teachings is written that: "Christ is the true life and the sun of life".[804]

Bonacci noted that the Bible speaks of God's being love, light, and fire. The sun, of course, is all of these: it is pure love as it gives its life and strength to save us, without it we would be blinded and grope in darkness, and its heat keeps us from freezing to death. This is why, Bonacci said, the first couple had to be clothed. When they ate from the tree of knowledge (in the fall harvest time), they were judged (on the scales of Libra) and began their descent into winter and cold weather, which meant they needed clothes in order to keep warm. The sun, or Helios, is Hel; but it is also El (Elyon, Helion, Hellion). It is, again, both good and bad, having a dual nature just as Yahweh of the Bible does. [805]

Bonacci explained that the word "God" is an acronym standing for "Generation, Operation, Dissolution" (GOD). God is "creator, preserver, destroyer." Everyone is born, performs or acts in the world, and then dissolves. It is important to work and provide for ourselves because if one doesn't work in the day (or warm weather) he dies when the night (winter) comes. That's the nature of life. One must "work out" his own salvation and earn his keep (Phil. 2:12, 2 Thess. 3:10).[806]

Bonacci spoke of Jesus' being crucified in Egypt (Rev. 11:8) and pointed out that this is so because Egypt represents death. Yahweh was, as noted, always calling his people out of Egypt. They were to rise from their bondage and be free after they passed through the waters (Aquarius/Pisces) in baptism. Capricorn is a Goat. The sun in the Goat climbs the mountain out of Egypt, maneuvers through the Piscean waters, and passes over the equator. And Jesus (Jes/Yes) is the light, love, or fire (sun) that all must pass through to get to their source (Jn. 14:6). The sun in Capricorn moves through Aquarius to Pisces, then rises at the spring equinox, at which point the sun and moon are equal ("Equinox" means equal night) since the day and night are then of the same length. Therefore, the female has become male and the two are joined in harmony with no power struggle.[807] The god and goddess are no longer estranged.

According to Bonacci, Jews teach biblical myths to their children only until they are twelve years old. Then they explain the true esoteric meaning behind the stories.[808] It is time that we recognize that the fables we were taught have caused us to look through a "glass, darkly" (1 Cor. 13:12). As adults, we need to move beyond fairy tales.

Early Christian Writings

Again, some early Christian writings portray Jesus as being crucified in the heavens rather than on Earth. These were written as early as were the canonical works.

---

[804] Greg Prescott, MS, ed., "The Sun, Sunspots and Consciousness," *in5d Esoteric Metaphysical Spiritual Database*, in5d.com, 25 Jan. 2015, web, 8 Mar. 2015.
[805] Santos Bonacci, "The Key to the Holy Science," "Nexus" 2011, posted by E. P. James MacAdams, youtube.com, 19 Apr. 2012, web, 8 Apr. 2015 <https://www.youtube.com/watch?v=E5maozgL23U>.
[806] Bonacci, "The Key to the Holy Science."
[807] Bonacci, "The Key to the Holy Science."
[808] Bonacci, "The Key to the Holy Science."

In *The Acts of John*, dated circa 150-200 CE, **Jesus tells John that his crucifixion was "only in appearance" and that the "true cross, shining in the heavens" was not the "wooden one of Golgotha but the wonderful 'cross of light.'"**[809] This book continues to say:

> 101 <u>Nothing, therefore, of the things which they will say of me have I suffered</u>: nay, that suffering also which I showed unto thee and the rest in the dance, <u>I will that it be called a mystery</u>. . . <u>Thou hearest that I suffered, yet did I not suffer</u>; that I suffered not, yet did I suffer; that I was pierced, yet <u>I was not smitten</u>; hanged, and <u>I was not hanged</u>; that <u>blood</u> flowed from me, and it <u>flowed not</u>; and, in a word, what they say of me, that befell me not, but what they say not, that did I suffer. Now what those things are I signify unto thee, for I know that thou wilt understand. Perceive thou therefore in me the praising . . . of the (or a) Word (Logos), the **piercing of the Word, the blood of the Word, the wound of the Word, the hanging up of the Word, the suffering of the Word, the nailing (fixing) of the Word, the death of the Word**. And so speak I, separating off the manhood. <u>Perceive thou therefore in the first place of the Word; then shalt thou perceive the Lord, and in the third place the man, and what he hath suffered.</u> 102 When he had spoken unto me . . . <u>he was taken up, no one of the multitudes having beheld him.</u> And when I went down <u>I laughed them all to scorn, inasmuch as he had told me the things which they have said concerning him; holding fast this one thing in myself, that the Lord</u> **contrived all things symbolically** . . . for their conversion and salvation.[810]

The Word existed in the beginning, creating the world (Jn. 1:1-3). **It was the seed (Yahweh's seed, semen, fruit) that Yahweh planted in the world.** It was abused and died, or was rejected of men, but it sprouted in the hearts of honest souls, and *rose* to produce fruit (Lk. 8:11). (Isaiah 53:3 says that "<u>He is despised and rejected</u> of men," while Jeremiah 8:9 states that "they have <u>rejected the word</u> of the LORD.") The Word went forth from Yahweh's mouth and didn't return to him void just as Jesus came to do the will of his Father and then return to his Father's house (Is. 45:23, 55:11; Jn. 5:30). Jesus explained all of this in Mark 4:13-20. Psalm 19:4 states: "Their <u>voice has gone out through all the earth, Their words to the end of the world</u>. In them he has set a tent for the sun, 5 Which is as a <u>bridegroom coming out of his chamber</u>, Like a strong man rejoicing to run his course." When reading this rhetoric about the heavens, it is impossible not to think of this: "But I say, Have they not heard? Yes verily, <u>their sound went into all the earth, and their words unto the ends of the world</u>" (Rom. 10:18). The Word, not a literal bridegroom, went into all the world.

The Word increased, as John said Jesus would (Jn. 3:30, Acts 6:7). The Word was trampled underfoot (Mt. 7:6). The Word was "clothed with a vesture dipped in blood"

[809] Jean Doresse, *The Secret Books of the Egyptian Gnostics* (Vermont: Inner Traditions International, 1986), 95. See also: Murdock, *Christ in Egypt*, 356.
[810] "Gnostic Scriptures and Fragments: The Acts of John," *The Gnostic Society Library*, 1994-2014, web, 21 Nov. 2014 <gnosis.org/library/actjohn.htm>.

(Rev. 19:13). The Word would be the judge in the last day, but all judgment had been committed to Jesus (Jn. 5:22, 12:48). The Word "was made flesh" only as it dwelt in "earthen vessels" (Jn. 1:14, 2 Cor. 4:6-7). Again, **Yahweh's "Son" was his fruit, his seed, his word**. He planted that seed into Israel, the "virgin daughter of Zion" (hence we have a virgin birth), who later became the "mother of us all" (Lam. 2:13, Mt. 1:23, Gal. 4:26). How did that happen? It happened because the seed planted in the virgin Israel was the Word planted in the hearts of people in the New Testament. Burton L. Mack wrote: "In the Hellenistic tradition of education, sowing seed was understood as a metaphor taken from agriculture. In the tradition of gnostic thought, however, sowing seed was a metaphor implying sexual union and conception."[811] James B. Jordan wrote:

> in Biblical symbolism the land represents Israel and the sea represents the gentiles. The land is above the sea, with mountains on it reaching up toward heaven. The land is a "priestly" territory between God's heaven and the rest of the world. Throughout the Old Testament the gentiles are often spoken of in terms of the sea, or are reached by crossing waters of one sort or another. This land-sea symbolism is applied consistently in the book of Revelation to distinguish the Jews and Judaizers from the gentiles.[812]

> Revelation 21:1 And I saw a new heaven and a new earth: for the first heaven and the first earth were passed away; and there was no more sea. [No more darkness, no more night, no more winter, no more death.]

Salvation was of the Jews (the land); they were "intercessors" or "advocates" between the sky and the sea (Jn. 4:22). And, as Ray C. Stedman wrote, Israel "brought forth the Christ."[813] The intercessor was removed, and the sea was then in contact with God (and no longer sea). Thus, **not only was Israel the virgin who gave birth, but she was the advocate between Yahweh and the other nations. The Bible declares Jesus to be the advocate, but Jesus was Israel, the firstborn of Yahweh and the one who paid for the sin of the world** (Ex. 4:22, Mt. 23:35-38, 1 Jn. 2:1).

Like *The Acts of John*, *The Gospel of Peter* presents the story of Christ as non-literal.[814] These writings should not be dismissed simply because some council decided they were uninspired. We can discern the first-century mentality by reading them.

As stated previously, **Justin Martyr noted that Christians believed nothing different from what pagans believed regarding the sons of Jupiter. That means that Martyr, like the pagans, didn't believe in a physical dying and rising god**.

Murdock wrote:

> this springtime/Easter resurrection myth occurred in Greek mythology with the tale of Kore/Persephone descending into the underworld to reside with Hades, leading to the death of winter. Her reemergence out of the underworld

---

[811] Mack, 265-266.
[812] James B. Jordan, "Biblical Horizons: #133: 153 Large Fish," biblicalhorizons.com, Sept. 2000, web, 25 Mar. 2014.
[813] Ray C. Stedman, "Woman and the Serpent," *Authentic Christianity*, raystedman.org, 4 Mar. 1990, web, 26 Feb. 2015.
[814] Murdock, *Christ in Egypt*, 486.

represented the springtime renewal of life on Earth—thus, *Persephone's resurrection symbolized eternal life*, precisely as did that of Jesus *and Osiris.*

Comprising the entombment for three days [the winter solstice when the sun stands still and appears dead], the descent into the underworld, and the resurrection, the spring celebration of "Easter" represents the period of the vernal equinox, when the sun is "hung on a cross" composed of the days and nights of equal length. After a touch-and-go battle for supremacy with the night or darkness [prince of darkness], the sun emerges triumphant, being "born again" or "resurrected" as a "man," moving towards "his" full strength at the summer solstice.[815]

Again, many gods supposedly died and rose in the sky, as many early Christians believed about Jesus. *Christian Mythology Unveiled* reveals:

Now it is not a little extraordinary that **some of the earlier Christian sects maintained that Christ was crucified in the sky**. Here is a direct demonstration that the Brahmin crucifixion is, wholly and radically, an astronomical allegory of the equatorial crossings of the sun at the Equinoxes; and that the Christian fable is identically the same, but the <u>scientific meaning is lost, through the fraud of priestcraft, and the ignorance it fosters</u>.[816]

When Christianity first took root, many people, as stated, flat-out refused to believe in a literal god-man. Marshall Gauvin wrote:

A large body of opinion in the early Church denied the reality of Christ's physical existence. In his "History of Christianity," Dean Milman writes: "The Gnostic sects denied that Christ was born at all, or that he died," and Mosheim, Germany's great ecclesiastical historian, says: "<u>The Christ of early Christianity was not a human being, but an 'appearance,' an illusion, a character in miracle, not in reality—a myth</u>.[817]

Arthur Drews noted that the Gnostics "believed only in a metaphysical and ideal, not an historical and real, Christ."[818] And Dameron wrote:

It is evident that the Gnostics had a better and more correct knowledge of the teachings . . . than those who claim to be founders of the **modern Christianity, which did not have its rise until in the third century**; and we should be willing to give to them the credit of being as honest as any other sect.[819]

---

[815] Murdock, *Christ in Egypt*, 390.

[816] Mitchell Logan, *Christian Mythology Unveiled in a Series of Lectures* (Kessinger Publishing, 2004), 117. See also: Acharya S, *Suns of God*, 285.

[817] Marshall Gauvin, "Did Jesus Christ Really Live?" *The Historical Library*, infidels.org, 1922, web, 27 Aug. 2014. See also: Acharya S, *Suns of God*, 373.

[818] Arthur Drews, *Witnesses to the Historicity of Jesus*, tr. Joseph McCabe (London: Watts, 1912), 57. See also: Acharya S, *Suns of God*, 373.

[819] Dameron, 90.

Jim Walker noted:

> In the book *The Jesus Puzzle*, the biblical scholar, Earl Doherty, presents not only a challenge to the existence of an historical Jesus but reveals that early pre-Gospel Christian documents show that the concept of Jesus sprang from non-historical spiritual beliefs of a Christ derived from Jewish scripture and Hellenized myths of savior gods. Nowhere do any of the New Testament epistle writers describe a human Jesus, including Paul. None of the epistles mention a Jesus from Nazareth, an earthly teacher, or as a human miracle worker. Nowhere do we find these writers quoting Jesus. Nowhere do we find them describing any details of Jesus' life on earth or his followers. Nowhere do we find the epistle writers even using the word "disciple" (they of course use the term "apostle" but the word simply means messenger, as Paul saw himself). Except for a few well known interpolations, Jesus always gets presented as a spiritual being that existed before all time with God, and that knowledge of Christ came directly from God or as a revelation from the word of scripture. Doherty writes, "Christian documents outside the Gospels, even at the end of the first century and beyond, show no evidence that any tradition about an earthly life and ministry of Jesus were in circulation."[820]

The Gnostics created the Christ of the New Testament but didn't intend that he be taken literally. They presented an ideal, but **"they did not reckon with the ignorant Gentile literalists who were to follow them."**[821] Church father Origen in fact taught that the "virgin birth of Christ in the womb of Mary was not primarily to be understood as a literal event but as the birth of the divine Wisdom in the soul."[822] Graham wrote that **it was around the third or fourth century BCE that Hebrew mythology began to be taken literally and around the third or fourth century CE that "Christian mythology lost its symbolic meaning and likewise became a priestly religion. Both began as mythology and ended in dogmatic theology."**[823] Higgins noted that the Roman Church began as a Gnostic religion, stating that "every thing which has been disguised by being charged to the Gnostics is found there, without a single exception."[824]

Higgins wrote regarding the church father Irenaeus:

> Irenaeus was evidently a Gnostic. If he were not, how came he to place the Zodiac on the floor of his church? a part of which, not worn away by the feet of devotees, is yet remaining. He was of the sect of the Christ *not* crucified. How is all this to be accounted for, except that what the first Christian fathers all taught was true, namely that there was an *esoteric* and an *exoteric* religion? . . . Gnosticism was the secret religion of the conclave. **They had Jesus of Bethlehem for the people, Jesus of Nazareth for the conclave and the**

---

[820] Jim Walker, "Did a historical Jesus exist?" See also: Earl Doherty, "The Jesus Puzzle," Canadian Humanist Publications, 1999.
[821] Graham, 286.
[822] Armstrong, 100.
[823] Graham, 243-244.
[824] Higgins, *Anacalypsis*, II (1878), 129.

cardinals. For the people, they had and have _Jesus crucified_, for the conclave, Jesus _not_ crucified.[825]

Irenaeus wrote that Jesus was not crucified under Herod and Pilate but that he lived to be fifty years old. Higgins said this information came to Irenaeus upon word from Polycarp, "who had it from St. John himself and from _all the old people of Asia_."[826] If this is true, it seems to place Jesus with men like Alexander the Great, who were made into bigger-than-life-heroes after they died, and Jesus' story fits well into the pagan mythos.

Pagan Easter

Barbara Walker considered the story of Jesus' death and resurrection to be pagan:

Modern scholarship has shown that Easter is not a Christian institution. Every detail is of pagan origin. The divinely fathered savior, born of a virgin at the winter solstice, followed by 12 zodiacal disciples, sacrificed at the spring equinox, buried in a new tomb, resurrected amid general rejoicing, bringing salvation and eternal life to those who worship him and/or sacramentally consume his flesh and blood—all these are purely pagan concepts. When early Christian fathers were told that their Jesus was just one more copy of many sacrificial saviors going the rounds in the Roman Empire, they could hardly deny it. They could think of no better rebuttal than to say that the devil knew in advance about the coming of Jesus and so invented all these other religions many centuries earlier, in imitation of the true religion, in order to confuse people.[827] This improbability was much used, before the Church succeeded in wiping out the memory of such earlier faiths, in opposition to the obvious probability of the imitation having gone in the other direction.[828]

Christians know that Easter and Christmas customs stem from paganism. But they refuse to consider that the _foundations_ upon which the festivals rest may be pagan and that Yahweh and Christ are mythical characters—sun, moon, and/or fertility gods.

Historical Jesus

We talked about Jesus earlier with regard to evidence for his life that can be gleaned from his contemporaries, discovering that nobody spoke of him. Today's biblical scholars, however, generally say he existed, although some disagree.

Not only do most scholars say Jesus lived, but they often become upset if someone suggests he didn't. According to Rabbi Tovia Singer, even agnostic New Testament scholars don't like it when someone claims Jesus didn't walk the earth. Singer noted that the reason for this is that these scholars are biased. When someone suggests Jesus wasn't

[825] Higgins, _Anacalypsis_, II (1878), 129.
[826] Higgins, _Anacalypsis_, II (1878), 129.
[827] Walker, _Man Made God_, 165. See also: Homer Smith, _Man and His Gods_ (Boston: Little, Brown & Co., 1952), 83.
[828] Walker, _Man Made God_, 165.

real, that person is saying to these scholars: "You have devoted your entire life to studying Bugs Bunny. It means your life has been a waste." Singer continued: "You're now saying that their life has been studying Casper the Friendly Ghost."[829]

When the New Testament was compiled, many apparently argued that Christ had not "come in the flesh," prompting John to argue vehemently against them (1 Jn. 4:3, 2 Jn. 1:7). The Jew Trypho in the second century disbelieved and said to Justin Martyr: "But Christ if he is come, and is anywhere, is unknown . . . But you, having got an idle story by the end, do form yourself an imaginary Christ, and for his sake you foolishly and inconsiderately rush headlong into dangers."[830] Later, mythicists such as French scholar Charles François Dupuis and Count Volney; British Robert Taylor, Godfrey Higgins, J. M. Robertson, and Gerald Massey; and German Arthur Drews spoke against a historical Jesus. By the end of the nineteenth century J. P. Lundy admitted that most of the mythicist arguments were true, although he held onto Jesus as the Christ while claiming that earlier dying and rising gods were "prototypes."[831]

Irishman Thomas L. Brodie, a Dominican priest mentioned previously, has also questioned (since the 1970s) whether Jesus lived.[832] In 2012 he wrote *Beyond the Quest for the Historical Jesus* in which he clarified his beliefs, stating that

> the New Testament account of Jesus is essentially a rewriting of the Septuagint version of the Hebrew Bible, or, in some cases, of earlier New Testament texts. Jesus' challenge to would-be disciples (Luke 9.57-62), for example, is a transformation of the challenge to Elijah at Horeb (1 Kings 19), while his journey from Jerusalem and Judea to Samaria and beyond (John 2.23-4.54) is deeply indebted to the account of the **journey of God's Word** in Acts 1-8.[833]

Historical researcher Michael Paulkovich claims that Jesus is a "mythical character." **Paulkovich investigated the writers of 126 authors who lived and wrote in the first through the third centuries CE and found no verifiable mention of Jesus.** He noted:

> "When I consider those 126 writers, all of whom should have heard of Jesus but did not - and Paul and Marcion and Athenagoras and Matthew with a tetralogy of opposing Christs, the silence from Qumram and Nazareth and Bethlehem, conflicting Bible stories, and so many other mysteries and omissions - I must conclude that Christ is a mythical character," he writes.

> "Jesus of Nazareth" was nothing more than urban (or desert) legend, likely an agglomeration of several evangelic and deluded rabbis . . .

---

[829] Rabbi Tovia Singer, "Did Jesus Actually Exist? Rabbi Tovia Singer's Evidence and Conclusion will Surprise You," youtube.com, 21 Feb. 2015, web, 1 Mar. 2015.

[830] Herbert Cutner, *Jesus: God, Man or Myth? An Examination of the Evidence* (San Diego: Book Tree, 2000), 89.

[831] "Jesus: God, Man or Myth by Herb Cutner," stellarhousepublishing.com, 2015, web, 25 May 2015. See also: Cutner, *Jesus: God, Man or Myth? An Examination of the Evidence*.

[832] Patrick Counihan, "Irish priest proves Jesus never existed: Church bans him from teaching and speaking to media," *Signs of the Times*, sott.net, 21 Jan. 2013, web, 1 Mar. 2015.

[833] Thomas L. Brodie, *Beyond the Quest for the Historical Jesus* (Sheffield, England: Sheffield Phoenix Press Ltd, 2012), description of book on Amazon.

Even in the Bible Paulkovich says Paul, often credited with spreading what would become Christianity, never refers to Jesus as a real person.

"Paul is unaware of the virgin mother, and ignorant of Jesus' nativity, parentage, life events, ministry, miracles, apostles, betrayal, trial and harrowing passion," he writes.

"Paul knows neither where nor when Jesus lived, and considers the crucifixion metaphorical." . . . [We will consider Paul's writings later.]

He continues: "Christian father Marcion of Pontus in 144 CE denied any virgin birth or childhood for Christ - Jesus' infant circumcision was thus a lie, as well as the crucifixion!

"Reading the works of second century Christian father Athenagoras, one never encounters the word Jesus . . . Athenagoras was thus unacquainted with the name of his savior it would seem."[834]

Jim Walker asserted:

No one has the slightest physical evidence to support a historical Jesus; no artifacts, dwelling, works of carpentry, or self-written manuscripts. . . There occurs no contemporary Roman record that shows Pontius Pilate executing a man named Jesus. Devastating to historians, there occurs not a single contemporary writing that mentions Jesus. All documents about Jesus came well after the life of the alleged Jesus from either: unknown authors, people who had never met an earthly Jesus, or from fraudulent, mythical or allegorical writings. . . Courts of law do not generally allow hearsay as testimony, and nor does honest modern scholarship. Hearsay does not provide good evidence, and therefore, we should dismiss it. . .

Authors of ancient history today, of course, can only write from indirect observation in a time far removed from their aim. But a valid historian's own writing gets cited with sources that trace to the subject themselves, or to eyewitnesses and artifacts. For example, a historian today who writes about the life of George Washington, of course, can not serve as an eyewitness, but he can provide citations to documents which give personal or eyewitness accounts. None of the historians about Jesus give reliable sources to eyewitnesses, therefore all we have remains as hearsay.[835]

Dr. Richard Carrier's conclusion regarding the historicity of Jesus is that

the Jesus figure was originally conceived of as a celestial being known only through private revelations and hidden messages in scripture; then stories placing this being in earth history were crafted to communicate the claims of the gospel

[834] Jonathan O'Callaghan, "'Jesus NEVER existed': Writer finds no mention of Christ in 126 historical texts and says he was a 'mythical character'," dailymail.com, 1 Oct. 2014, web, 1 Mar. 2015.
[835] Jim Walker, "Did a historical Jesus exist?"

allegorically; such stories eventually came to be believed or promoted in the struggle for control of the Christian churches that survived the tribulations of the first century.[836]

Carrier also wrote: "I have no vested interest in proving Jesus didn't exist. . . I suspect he might not have, but then that's a question that requires rigorous and thorough examination of the evidence before it can be confidently declared."[837]

Valerie Tarico presented five reasons she doesn't believe Jesus lived: (1) no secular evidence supports a belief in Jesus; (2) the earliest New Testament authors were unclear as to the events of his life, which became more detailed in later writings; (3) the stories in the New Testament make no claim of being first-hand accounts; (4) the Gospels are contradictory to one another; and (5) modern scholars who claim Jesus existed see him as totally different people.[838]

D. M. Murdock wrote:

The "Jesus Christ" of the New Testament is a fictional compilation of characters, not a single historical individual. A compilation of multiple "people" is no one. When the mythological and midrashic layers are removed, there remains no historical core to the onion. The evidence reveals that the gospel story is myth historicized, not history mythologized.[839]

Despite all of the above, it's possible that a man, or several men (as Murdock noted), in the first century, and in the prior century, were heralded as a Messiah. Maybe a man named Jesus lived in the first century and he was simply turned into a godlike being by his followers. Even Santa Claus lived once upon a time.

Angie Mosteller wrote that St. Nicholas was a "godly man known for his charity and generosity."[840] Born in the third century to devout Christians who had prayed for a long time for a child, Nicholas was devoted to Yahweh by his parents. They died during a plague when Nick was young, leaving him a huge inheritance that he used to honor Yahweh. He was so respected for his goodness that he became Archbishop of Myra at an early age, meaning he possessed "wisdom and maturity beyond his years."[841] Nicholas was one of the bishops that attended the Council of Nicea in 325 CE. Mosteller wrote that Nicholas couldn't have "known that his name would one day be more recognized than any other in attendance at this council that developed the famous Nicene Creed." After Nick died, on January 6, a "tradition of gift giving was begun in his honor." Another name for Nicholas, Kris Kringle, is the "English form of the German name for 'Christ

[836] Carrier, *On the Historicity of Jesus: Why We Might Have Reason to Doubt*, description of book on Amazon.

[837] Richard Carrier, PhD, *Proving History: Bayes's Theorem and the Quest for the Historical Jesus* (Amherst, NY: Prometheus Books, 2012), 8.

[838] Valerie Tarico, "5 reasons to suspect that Jesus never existed," salon.com, 1 Sept. 2014, web, 1 Mar. 2015.

[839] D. M. Murdock, "Jesus Christ is a mythical figure," freethoughtnation.com, 28 Oct. 2014, web, 26 Feb. 2015.

[840] Angie Mosteller, "Who Is Santa and What Does He Have to Do with Christmas?" crosswalk.com, 12 Dec. 2011, web, 4 Dec. 2014.

[841] Mosteller, "Who Is Santa and What Does He Have to Do with Christmas?"

Child.'" In the United States Kris is the same as "St. Nicholas, St. Nick, Santa Claus and even the English name Father Christmas."[842] Christmas truly *is* about Santa Claus.

Still, Santa doesn't come down my chimney every year and eat my cookies and drink my milk. He doesn't leave me gifts I have requested, and he doesn't answer my "prayers." However, many are convinced that he flies all around the world in one night, scooting up and down chimneys, and bringing Christmas joy and toys. But those people are children. "When I was a child, I spake as a child, I understood as a child, I thought as a child: but when I became a man, I put away childish things" (1 Cor. 13:11). Although St. Nicholas was a good man, as adults we know he was/is not magical. As "Daffodil" wrote: Santa is used by parents to control kids. Be good or Santa won't bring you anything! Religion is used the same way. Believe in God or you won't get to heaven! . . . Religion is a form of control. It's all an elaborate lie, begun long ago, to explain nature and control others."[843]

Nick is an example of how some myths take form. A person makes his mark on the world, he dies, and then he becomes far greater than he was in real life. Dameron wrote:

> The tendency in all ages has been to deify their great and good men when dead, and to make saints out of them, which has, no doubt, given rise to a multiplicity of gods and demigods, similar to those of the old Greek and Roman mythology, who at one time were men, and these sages, statesmen and warriors became the tutelar deities of their country, to whom the people made offering as a mark of reverence and to get them to use their influence in their behalf, which has tended to confuse the idea of one universal God, and to give to that God a human form.[844]

Santa, who "knows if you've been bad or good"[845] (rewarding or giving fiery coals based on behavior reported on his "list"), is no more incredible than other gods. Dameron bemoaned the fact that the "sublime teachings of [Christ, Chrishna, and Buddha] have become adulterated so that it is hard to recognize them as they are now taught by their disciples and priests."[846] Just as Nicholas became the immortal Santa, perhaps Jesus (or some other Hebrew man or combination of men) became the immortal Christ.

John M. Allegro, who translated some of the Dead Sea Scrolls, said that the <u>historical Jesus was a leader of a sect of Nazarenes who were Essenes in the first century BCE</u>. Allegro stated that these people lived out in the desert by the Dead Sea for 200 years, until the Romans dispersed them in the year 68 CE. <u>Their leader, a "teacher of righteousness," was crucified in about 88 BCE</u>. According to Allegro, the Nazarenes were not people from Nazareth (which wasn't even a city at the time of Christ but was a village near Mt. Carmel where the Essenes shared a communal life[847]).[848] Perhaps this story became mythicized in the New Testament.

---

[842] Mosteller, "Who Is Santa and What Does He Have to Do with Christmas?"

[843] Daffodil, "Losing My Faith in Kansas, Part 2," exchristian.net, 22 Apr. 2015, web, 23 Apr. 2015.

[844] Dameron, 54.

[845] John Frederick Coots and Haven Gillespie, "Santa Claus Is Coming to Town," recorded by Harry Reser, Decca, 1934, wikipedia.org, 16 Jan. 2015, web, 23 Jan. 2015.

[846] Dameron, 54.

[847] Nottingham, "The Mystery of the Essenes."

According to Ted Nottingham, the Essenes believed and practiced almost identically to the early Christians described in the New Testament: Both Jesus and the teacher of righteousness were revered as suffering servants who preached penitence, love of one's neighbor, chastity, and humility. Both adjured their followers to obey the Law of Moses. Both were called Messiah, Redeemer, and Master. Both opposed the priests and were condemned and murdered. Both founded a group of believers who expected their leader to return and judge the world. Both shared an identical sacred, ritual meal with their followers (the Essenes thought their Messiah was present in spirit for this just as Christians today do). Both enjoyed a communal life, having all goods in common with those among whom they lived. Both predicted the fall of Jerusalem. Both practiced baptism. The teacher of righteousness led a council of twelve men with three special priests, while Jesus had twelve apostles, his three favorites being Peter, James, and John. Jesus said the meek would inherit the earth, and the Essenes considered themselves to be meek and thought they would inherit the earth. The Essenes believed that by their leader's knowledge everything was brought into being and was established for his purposes and that apart from him nothing was accomplished (Jn. 1:3, Col. 1:16-17). Both groups fasted and prophesied. The Essenes believed themselves to be the light shining in darkness, and they taught that anyone who loved was born of God and dwelt in God, and that God dwelt in him or her (Jn. 14:23; 1 Jn. 2:8-11, 4:7, 5:1).[849] There is nothing supernatural about any of this, so it's believable that this teacher of righteousness lived and taught in the sect of the Nazarenes. And the apostle Paul was accused of being a "ringleader of the sect of the Nazarenes" (Acts 24:5), which was an Essene sect.

While the mythical Christ was created by the Church to control and rule the people, that doesn't mean a real man (or men) didn't exist and teach some of the doctrines we find in the Gospels. Jim Walker summed up his thoughts on the historicity of Jesus as follows:

> Unfortunately, belief and faith substitute as knowledge in many people's minds and nothing, even direct evidence thrust on the feet of their claims, could possibly change their minds. We have many stories, myths and beliefs of a Jesus but if we wish to establish the facts of history, we cannot even begin to put together a knowledgeable account without at least an eyewitness account or a contemporary artifact that points to a biological Jesus.

> Of course a historical Jesus *might* have existed, perhaps based loosely on a living human even though his actual history got lost, but this amounts to nothing but speculation. However we *do* have an abundance of evidence supporting the mythical evolution of Jesus. Virtually every major detail in the gospel stories occurred in Hebrew scripture and pagan beliefs, long before the advent of Christianity. We simply do not have a shred of evidence to determine the historicity of a Jesus "the Christ." We only have evidence for the *belief* of Jesus.[850]

---

[848] The Hall of Records, "John Allegro: Who Was Jesus?" 17 Apr. 2009, web, 30 Jan. 2015 <https://www.youtube.com/watch?v=w8PDt2IKS4k>.
[849] Nottingham, "The Mystery of the Essenes."
[850] Jim Walker, "Did a historical Jesus exist?"

CHAPTER NINE
GNOSTIC NEW TESTAMENT

As Socrates tells us, the first gods that the Greeks worshiped were the cosmic bodies. These are realities; it remained for the Hebrews to replace them with a conceptual unreality.[851] "Every woman" [Exodus 3:22] is Virgo, the plant kingdom, which does and must steal from Egypt, earth, its raiment and its jewels, substance and vitamins, to clothe and feed itself biologically. This it is that God approves and not the Jewish people.[852]

Lloyd M. Graham

There is nothing in all the universe save consciousness and energy, and these two deities [Yahweh and Satan] are but their personifications. Collectively, they are one, the cursing God of the higher planes and the accursed Satan of the lower—and neither of them possesses moral qualities.[853]

Lloyd M. Graham

Despite what some might think, some of the writers of the New Testament taught Gnostic doctrine. These include the apostle Paul and the author of Hebrews.

The Apostle Paul

Paul's writings, at least in some instances, present a Gnostic view of the crucified savior. He claimed to have received his gospel not from eyewitnesses of a literal man named Jesus but from a "revelation of Jesus Christ" (Gal. 1:11-12). Paul was, according to Graham, "the Moses of the New Testament." Thus even Paul is a reiteration or type. Moses took up the salvation of the Jews when Joseph's time ended, and Paul became the main leader in Christianity. Graham wrote:

Just as Moses was reared an Egyptian but became the leader of the Jews, so Paul was reared a Jew but became the leader of the Gentiles. Just as Moses became the lawgiver of the Jews, so Paul became the lawgiver of the Christians. As God spoke to Moses from a burning bush, so Christ spoke to Paul from a blinding light. As Moses was told to go to Sinai to receive power and do great works, so Paul was told to go to Damascus for like reasons. Moses built a tabernacle, Paul a church. Moses preached biologic rightness, Paul, moral righteousness. . . The cue to this parallel is given in Acts, which gives Paul's history. Chapter 7 recounts the whole story of Moses that we may see the connection.[854]

According to Princeton professor Elaine Pagels, Paul taught Gnosticism and "became known in the second century as the 'apostle of the heretics.'"[855] Some early authors

---

[851] Graham, 148.
[852] Graham, 170.
[853] Graham, 67.
[854] Graham, 410.
[855] Elaine Hiesey Pagels, *The Gnostic Paul: Gnostic Exegesis of the Pauline Letters* (Philadelphia: Fortress Press, 1975), 157.

160

(including Clement and Peter) declared Paul himself to be a heretic.[856] Piero Scaruffi wrote:

> For a long time gnostics have been viewed as opposed to "Pauline Christianity", Christianity as it is today. But now we know that the gnostics actually revered Paul and considered [him] one of theirs. We also know that **only seven of the 13 letters attributed to Paul are authentic** and one can suspect that the other six were written to prove something that was not proven in the original seven. (**Some of the letters appear for the first time with Irenaeus, in 190.**)[857] [858]

Scaruffi noted that if these six fake Epistles are removed, "**the originals are strikingly similar to gnostic literature and not a single attack against the gnostics remains.**"[859] Dameron claimed that Paul was "well versed in the mysterious doctrines of the Gnostics,"[860] and Irenaeus "by the late second century" became the "challenger of 'the gnostic Paul'"[861] while Tertullian called Paul "the heretics' apostle."[862] Irenaeus, Tertullian, Hippolytus, and Origen fought strongly against Gnosticism.[863] (Irenaeus, like Paul, seems to have swayed back and forth enough that people see him as both a Gnostic and an antiGnostic. Perhaps his goal, also like Paul's, was to be "all things to all men" [1 Cor. 9:19-23].) Pagels wrote that Irenaeus, and Tertullian (despite calling Paul a heretic), affirmed that Paul denounced Gnosticism, and people have accepted their word for it.[864] However, the Valentinian sect of the Gnostics claimed that "Paul's own secret wisdom tradition" was Gnostic.[865] Although Irenaeus and Tertullian argued that no "secret" teachings of Paul existed and that the claim was an "insult to Paul,"[866] these "non-existent" teachings were later found at Nag Hammadi.[867] And Pagels wrote:

> When we compare the heresiological accounts with the newly available evidence, we can trace how two antithetical traditions of Pauline exegesis have emerged from the late first century to the second. Each claims to be authentic, Christian, and Pauline: but one reads Paul *antignostically*, the other *gnostically*. Correspondingly, we discover two conflicting images of Paul: on the one hand,

[856] Scaruffi, "Jesus and Christianity."
[857] Scaruffi, "Jesus and Christianity."
[858] Dr. Richard Carrier stated that 95 percent of scholars agree that only seven of Paul's letters are authentic, while the others are forgeries. Richard Carrier, PhD, "Richard Carrier: Acts as Historical Fiction," youtube.com, 13 Mar. 2014, web, 9 Jan. 2015 <https://www.youtube.com/watch?v=B5MUUP4l6l4>.
[859] Scaruffi, "Jesus and Christianity."
[860] Dameron, 88.
[861] Hiesey Pagels, 162.
[862] Tertullian, *Against the Valentinians*, I.4. See also: Michael Kaler, *Paul and Pseudepigraphy*, ed. Stanley E. Porter and Gregory P. Fewster (Leiden, Netherlands/Boston: Brill, 2013), 337.
[863] Elaine Pagels, *The Gnostic Paul; Gnostic Exegesis of the Pauline Letters* (New York: Continuum International Publishing Group, 1992), 2-4. See also: Hisey Pagels, 157.
[864] Hiesey Pagels, 162.
[865] Hiesey Pagels, 4.
[866] Hiesey Pagels, 4.
[867] Pagels, 2-4. See also: "The Prayer of the Apostle Paul," tr. Dieter Mueller, *The Nag Hamadi Library*, bibliotecapleyades.net, n.d., web 18 June 2015.

the antignostic Paul familiar from church tradition, and, on the other, the gnostic Paul, teacher of wisdom to gnostic initiates![868]

Pagels said the Valentinians claimed that most Christians mistakenly read the scriptures in a literal fashion while *they* "through their initiation into gnosis, learn to read [Paul's] letters (as they read all the scriptures) on the *symbolic* level, as they say Paul intended. Only this pneumatic reading reveals 'the truth' instead of its mere outward 'image.'"[869] Pagels sees the literal view of the New Testament as worshiping the creature instead of the creator (Rom. 1:21-32). This makes sense in that, according to Numbers 23:19, God is not a "son of man" while Jesus stated many times that he *was* a son of man (Mt. 8:20, 9:6, 10:23, et al.). Therefore, if one worships a son of man, he isn't worshiping God but a creature of God.

Dameron wrote: "According to the Chaldean doctrine found in the Kabala, the Jehovah of the Jews was one of the emanations of the divine essence, and was androgynous, being male and female, like all angels, double-sexed."[870] Although it was Yahweh's will for all people to be one, the early Christians were separated as Adam and Eve had been (Christ restored this union, Gal. 3:28). An "unnatural" separation (Rom. 1:26-27) had occurred between the "pneumatics" (who viewed the Bible metaphorically) and the "psychics" (who viewed it literally). The "elect" understood that when Paul spoke of this "unnatural" behavior he was referring to the disunity of the believers and the separation that Christ came to destroy.[871] We know **Christ's purpose was to get his parents back together, to restore heaven and earth, to join the physical world to the spiritual one**. The story itself (of a miraculous birth and resurrection) was just a way of explaining that, but it was turned into "history."

Graham noted that the "Gnostic and pagan doctrine was the source of Pauline Christianity. In it lies the true esoteric basis, a universal principle available to all."[872] Graham continued:

> Christianity began not in Rome nor yet in Jerusalem, but in Antioch in Syria—and it was operative before the time of Christ. It took three hundred years to blend its two components, and now we live by a synthetic faith whose name and purpose derive from the Greeks and whose theology and psychology derive from the Hebrews. Its morality derives from neither exclusively but from humanity in general, and this is the one good apple in the whole rotten barrel.
>
> **Paul preached neither Jesus nor Christ but Christhood, that deified consciousness developed within the individual** rather than from a Christ without. This was the method of the schools of the Mysteries, their long, arduous and dedicated work of initiation resulted in a spirituality that can never be

---

[868] Hiesey Pagels, 5.
[869] Hiesey Pagels, 6.
[870] Dameron, 32.
[871] Hisey Pagels, 17.
[872] Graham, 411-412.

achieved vicariously. Rightly understood, this is the heart of all religions but the literalists destroyed it. . .

It has been said that Paul was the real founder of Christianity, but not the Christianity that came down to us. His was Gnostic Christianity, the other but a priestly perversion of this. Paul, however, was a combination of both: priestly zeal, and knowledge he could not absorb because of his racial heritage. He too was a victim of Jewry, and therefore burdened with its false theology and conviction of sin. Thus <u>he was a man torn between two philosophies</u>. While he spoke as a Gnostic, there is much that is deep and profound in his words, but <u>alas, he could not escape his heritage</u>.[873]

Earl Doherty summed up Paul's philosophy as follows: "We are led to conclude that, in Paul's past, there was no historical Jesus. Rather, the <u>activities of the Son</u> about which God's gospel in scripture told, as interpreted by Paul, <u>had taken place in the spiritual realm</u> and were accessible only through revelation."[874] Philosopher Adam Randolph wrote that a literal reading of the Scriptures is "for those who cannot, or cannot yet, understand the metaphorical, secret teachings. The metaphorical is reserved for those who are elect"[875] (1 Cor. 2:6-7).

The Gnostics recognized that their scriptures were being stolen and distorted, and they spoke out against both crimes. Massey noted:

The <u>Gnostics complained</u>, and truly maintained, that their mysteries had been made mundane in the Christian Gospels; that celestial persons and celestial scenes, which could only belong to the pleroma—could only be explained by the secret wisdom or gnosis—had been transferred to earth and translated into a human history; <u>that their Christ, who could not be made flesh, had been converted into an historical character</u>; that their Anthropos was turned into the Son of Man—according to Matthew—Monogenes into the Only-begotten, according to John, their Hemorrhoidal Sophia into the woman who suffered from the issue of blood, the mother of the seven inferior powers into Mary Magdalene possessed by her seven devils, and the twelve Æons into the twelve Apostles. Thus, the Gnostics enable us to double the proof which can be derived directly and independently from Egypt. They claim that the miracle of the man who was born blind, and whose sight was restored by Jesus, was their mystery of the Æon, who was produced by the Only-begotten as the sightless creature of a soulless Creator. Irenæus, in reporting this, makes great fun of the Word that was born blind! He did not know that this Gnostic mystery was a survival of the Egyptian myth of the two Horuses, one of whom was the blind Horus, who exclaims in his blindness—"I come to search for mine eyes," and has his sight restored at the coming of the Second Horus—the light of the world. Nor did he dream that the two-fold Horus would explain why the <u>blind man in our Gospels should be single in one version and two-fold in another account of the same miracle</u>. **The Gnostic Horus came to seek and to save the poor lost mother, Sophia, who had**

[873] Graham, 412-413.
[874] Jim Walker, "Did a historical Jesus exist?" See also: Doherty, "The Jesus Puzzle," 83.
[875] Adam Randolph, "The Resurrection of Paul," unpublished paper, 2014, viewed 30 Aug. 2014.

wandered out of the pleroma, and the Gnostics identified this myth with the statement assigned to Jesus when he said **he had only come after that <u>lost sheep</u> which was gone astray [the <u>mother, Israel, Yahweh's estranged wife</u>]**. For, as <u>Irenæus says, they explain the wandering sheep to mean their mother.</u> This shows how the character of the Christ was limited to the mould of the Mythos and the likeness of Horus. But the lost sheep of the House of Israel has not yet found Jesus.[876]

Paul's Gnostic Resurrection

As an example to explain the differences between these two warring factions (Gnosticism or "priestly perversion"), psychics believed their dead bodies would be reconstituted in a literal and physical resurrection, while the Gnostic pneumatics recognized the resurrection as the "process of receiving gnosis,"[877] or, as Irenaeus proclaimed, the Gnostics "maintain that 'the resurrection from the dead' is knowing the truth that they proclaim."[878] The *Gospel of Truth*, a Gnostic gospel written between 140 and 180 CE,[879] states:

> As one's ignorance disappears when he gains knowledge, and as darkness disappears when light appears, so also incompleteness is eliminated by completeness. Certainly, <u>from that moment on, form is no longer manifest</u>, but will be dissolved in fusion with unity. For now their works lie scattered. In time unity will make the spaces complete. By means of unity each one will understand itself. <u>By means of knowledge it will purify itself</u> of diversity with a view towards unity, <u>devouring matter within itself like fire and darkness by light, death by life.</u> . . It is thus that <u>each one has acted, as if he were asleep, during the time when he was ignorant</u> and thus <u>he comes to understand, as if he were awakening</u>. And happy is the man who comes to himself and awakens. Indeed, blessed is he who has opened the eyes of the blind.[880]

Paul (in the New Testament) may not have always presented a cohesive view, but his description of the resurrection of the dead in 1 Corinthians 15 clarifies that the resurrection was indeed a spiritual awakening, confirming that the Christ was not an earthly man but was only a spiritual being. Here is the text from Young's Literal Translation.

> 1 Corinthians 15:42 So also is the rising again of the dead: it is sown in corruption, it is raised in incorruption; 43 it is sown in dishonour, it is raised in glory; it is sown in weakness, it is raised in power; 44 <u>it is sown a natural body,</u>

---

[876] Massey, *Gerald Massey's Lectures*, No. 21. See also: Gerald Massey, *The Natural Genesis* (New York: Cosimo, Inc., 2007), Vol. 2, 428; and David Rankin, *Tertullian and the Church* (New York: Cambridge University Press, 1995), 79.

[877] Hisey Pagels, 29.

[878] Hisey Pagels, 29.

[879] "Gospel of Truth," wikipedia.org, 5 Oct. 2014, web, 11 Jan. 2015.

[880] "The Gospel of Truth," tr. Robert M. Grant, *The Gnostic Society Library*, gnosis.org, n.d., web, 11 Jan. 2014 <http://gnosis.org/naghamm/got.html>; from Robert M. Grant, *Gnosticism* (New York: Harper & Brothers, 1961), as quoted in Willis Barnstone, *The Other Bible* (San Francisco: Harper & Row, 1984).

it is raised a spiritual body; there is a natural body, and there is a spiritual body; 45 so also it hath been written, "The first man Adam became a living creature," the last Adam is for a life-giving spirit, 46 but that which is spiritual is not first, but that which was natural, afterwards that which is spiritual. 47 The first man is out of the earth, earthy; the second man is the Lord out of heaven; 48 as is the earthy, such are also the earthy; and as is the heavenly, such are also the heavenly; 49 and, according as we did bear the image of the earthy, we shall bear also the image of the heavenly. 50 And this I say, brethren, that flesh and blood the reign of God is not able to inherit, nor doth the corruption inherit the incorruption;

Verse 47, above, says: "The first man is out of the earth, earthy; the second man is the Lord out of heaven." It is difficult to understand how someone can read that the second man is the Lord out of heaven and then teach that the second man is a reconstituted, re-created biological body of John Doe or Suzy Homemaker. The natural man was Adam but not the physical body of some man named Adam. Jesus, if he lived at all on the earth, would have been a descendant of Adam/Israel and carried Adam's biological DNA, so he was the natural Adam too and born under the death curse. Jesus too was earthy if being earthy means having a physical body! Thus, there could be no distinction between Adam and Christ! Two bodies are mentioned here: the body of flesh (Adam's body, the Israelites, the earthly kingdom, the carnal man, the earth, the human) and the body of Christ (the spiritual kingdom, the spiritual aspect of man, the sky or heaven, the god). **There was a natural body of Yahweh's people that was morphing into a spiritual body of Yahweh's people.** Max R. King wrote that "out of the decay of Judaism arose the spiritual body of Christianity that became fully developed or resurrected by the end-time. Hence, this is the primary meaning of Paul's statement, 'It is sown a natural body; it is raised a spiritual body. There is a natural body and there is a spiritual body.'"[881] King also noted: "The natural body, receiving its death blow at the cross and beginning then to wax old and decay (Heb. 8:13), became a nursery or seed-body for the germination, growth, and development of the spiritual body by means of the gospel."[882] The truth is, the body that was killed and buried was the old covenant body of Israel, God's firstborn son, Adam. Once again, God was saying to "Egypt": "Let my people go" (Ex. 5:1). He warned further: "and if thou refuse to let him go, behold, I will slay thy son, even thy firstborn" (Ex. 4:23). The firstborn, the natural man (Egypt/Israel [Rev. 11:8]), was finally being slain.

Ezekiel 37:12 states: "I will open your graves, and cause you to come up out of your graves, and bring you into the land of Israel." Peter Enns wrote regarding this passage:

If moving from the land into exile is to move from life to death, returning to the land is (all together now) to be brought back to life, to be raised from the dead (as Ezekiel's prophecy lays out for us).

---

[881] Max R. King, *The Spirit of Prophecy* (Colorado Springs: Bimillennial Press, 2002), 199-200.
[882] King, *Ibid.*

And that is where we find "resurrection" in the Old Testament: returning to the land, where God and his temple are, where there is peace and security, the land promised to Abraham (Genesis 12), the land "flowing with milk and honey."

Physical resurrection of individuals isn't the hot topic of conversation in the Old Testament. Revival of a nation is.[883]

The natural Adam was being transformed into, or conformed to, the spiritual Adam. Carnal Adam was finally going to bite the dust—return to dust as Yahweh told him he would do. But in his dying, a new body was to emerge. That was the body of Christ. There is a natural body and a spiritual body, and the natural was disappearing while the spiritual was rising. Adam, the natural man, became Christ, the spiritual man of Yahweh. The natural, earthy body became the spiritual, heavenly body. Mack confirmed that "The Corinthians had understood the Christ myth, not in terms of a bodily resurrection 'from the dead,' but in terms of translation, metamorphosis, or exaltation into a purely spiritual mode of existence."[884] As Valerie Tarico wrote:

The earliest Christian texts, the letters of Paul, suggest that the eternal body is "pneuma" or spirit, but later New Testament writers inclined toward physical resurrection of both Jesus and believers, though with renewed, perfected bodies. This view was affirmed by Church fathers and is now the predominant Christian belief.[885]

The resurrected Christ was not human. 1 Corinthians 2:7 says, "we speak the wisdom of God in a mystery." And Paul said he would "travail in birth" until Christ was "formed" in his fellow Christians, and we read that the "mystery" was "Christ in you" (Gal. 4:19, Col. 1:27). The book of Revelation speaks of a woman's travailing in birth. She is "clothed with the sun, and the moon under her feet, and upon her head a crown of twelve stars . . . pained to be delivered" (Rev.12:1-2). This is the mother. She is being reunited here with her spouse and has her crown of glory (her children) upon her head. Author Peter Gandy said that Paul existed "before the literal story" and that Paul spoke of "the Christ within."[886] Referencing Galatians 1:16, Timothy Freke agreed, saying that "there is no literal Jesus at this time" and Paul spoke of the Son's being "revealed *in* me" rather than "*to* me."[887] Pagels added that **Jesus was not spoken of as "the" son of God until the year 160 CE, and that the book of John seems to have been written for the purpose of declaring this claim of divinity.**[888]

Viklund noted regarding the god Adonis: "they say that for a long time certain rites of initiation are conducted: first, that they weep for [Adonis], since he has died; second,

[883] Peter Enns, "Brief Bible thought: is there resurrection from the dead in the Old Testament?" 9 Feb. 2015, web, 26 Feb. 2015.
[884] Mack, 133.
[885] Valerie Tarico, "10 reasons Christian heaven would actually be hell," rawstory.com, 31 Jan. 2015, web, 31 Jan. 2015.
[886] "Osiris & Christianity - The Christian Adoption of Egyptian Iconography, Symbolism, and Myth."
[887] "Osiris & Christianity - The Christian Adoption of Egyptian Iconography, Symbolism, and Myth."
[888] "Osiris & Christianity - The Christian Adoption of Egyptian Iconography, Symbolism, and Myth."

that they rejoice for him because he has risen from the dead."[889] Adonis was called a bridegroom as "his resurrection involved a sacred marriage with the Goddess, a tradition also found in early Christianity, before Church fathers eliminated it."[890] I don't think this idea was completely obliterated, as we find ample proof in the New Testament that Jesus, like Adonis who came hundreds of years before him, married the glorious goddess who came down from the sky (Rev. 21:2, 9). Thus the god was reunited with his goddess.

Place of the Skull

Jesus was crucified at Golgotha, or "the place of the skull" (Mt. 27:33-37). Christ's purpose was to purify the "conscience" (in the skull). Adam and Eve were naked before their fall and naked afterwards (nothing changed except in their minds). The believers in Christ were to "repent" or "have a change of mind" (Acts 3:19). They were to "kill the beast" or overcome the "natural man," thus becoming a spiritual, or resurrected man.

The scheme of redemption is metaphorical. A man standing upright with his arms out is a cross. Tertullian, when declaring that others (besides Christians) worshiped a cross, wrote: "If you position a man with his arms outstretched, you shall have created the image of a cross."[891] Within the skull of that man is a natural man, Adam. That Adam (Jesus) had to be crucified or destroyed so that the new Adam, the anointed man, the Christ, could rise. (This is why anyone in the new Christ would be greater than John [Mt. 11:11, Jn. 3:30].) That was the crucifixion of the *son of man* (not the son of God), an "invisible, spiritual, cosmic event of the mind."[892] Of course, upon this crucifixion and resurrection the person *became* a child/son of God and a "new man" (Eph. 2:15, 4:24; Col. 3:10).

Again, resurrection in the New Testament is spiritual. That's why a person crucified the "Son of God" afresh when he turned back to his old ways (Heb. 6:6). When a person is enlightened, all darkness is gone and his eye is single (Lk. 11:34). He rises from his grave and is alive. His spirit is renewed and he experiences a new, resurrected life. This is the resurrection that Paul described in 1 Corinthians 15. Again, **Yahweh's "Son" was his fruit, his seed, his word that was planted in the heart of man**. Proverbs 15:4 says that a "wholesome tongue is a tree of life: but perverseness therein is a breach in the spirit." A breach is a fracture, a brokenness. When Israel lived perversely like the nations about her, she partook of the forbidden fruit, which broke her connection to her only true source of wisdom. Lamentations 2:13 states: "O daughter of Jerusalem? what shall I equal to thee, that I may comfort thee, O virgin daughter of Zion? for thy breach is great like the sea: who can heal thee?" The "house of Jacob" (Israel, the virgin daughter herself) would eventually be the "repairer of the breach" (Is. 58:12). Isaiah 30:26 says that the "light of the moon shall be as the light of the sun, and the light of the sun shall be sevenfold, as the light of seven days, in the day that the LORD bindeth up the breach of his people, and

---

[889] Viklund; Origen, *Comments on Ezekiel*, 8:12; quoted by Richard Carrier.
[890] Walker, *Man Made God*, 136-137. See also: Walker, *The Woman's Encyclopedia of Myths and Secrets*, 465.
[891] Tertullian, *Ad Nationes*, I, XII.
[892] Bill Donahue, "What is the Crucifixion?" hiddenmeanings.com, n.d., web, 26 June 2014.

healeth the stroke of their wound." Again, the bride (moon) would shine like the husband (sun). She would reflect his glory on the earth with her crown of children on her head. Adam was the old Israel, and Christ was the new Israel.

Those who walk in the light of Yahweh eat from the tree of life (Christ). Christians must, then, crucify the *natural* man, the man who is selfish, prideful, and ego-ridden. That's the only way, if one wishes to follow the teachings of the New Testament, to reach a resurrected state. Joshua Tilghman wrote:

> You, too, must learn to defeat the ego just as Jesus defeated Satan. You are also meant to carry your cross and be crucified (your ego) at Golgotha, the place of the skull! It's all in your head. You must conquer the mind, meaning the ego, and then become the Christ that Paul labors to form in you![893]

The number of man (Adam), according to Revelation 13:18, is 666. That is also the number of the beast. The Koine Greek number for the name "Jesus," as has been stated, is 888.[894] When the natural, earthly Adam (man) died, the beast died with him, and the Christ arose. That is the teaching of 1 Corinthians 15. Romans 1:3-4 states that Jesus was "made of the seed of David according to the flesh; And declared to be the Son of God with power, according to the spirit of holiness, by the resurrection from the dead." **Resurrection made him the son of God** with power. According to the flesh, he was of the seed of David. He was Israel. He was the natural man. **He was the Christ *only* in the resurrection**. According to the Bible, Adam was made in the image of God and Jesus was the image of God (Gen. 1:26, Col. 1:13-15), but both were men. Making a man in the belly of a woman is no different from making a man from dirt. Both were humans if they existed at all (they were human characters in the biblical story).

Dr. Tony Nugent, ordained Presbyterian minister, former professor in the Department of Theology and Religious Studies at Seattle University, and, as mentioned previously, a scholar of world religions, wrote:

> Jewish Christians, the first Christians, didn't believe in the virgin birth. They believed that Joseph was the biological father of Jesus. Part of their Christology was "adoptionism"–they thought Jesus was adopted as the unique son of God at some time later in life. There were disagreements about when – Mark suggests the baptism, **Paul suggests the resurrection**. . . Eventually we get the gospel of John which pushes the sonship of Jesus back to the beginning of time. . . But Matthew and Luke think that the sonship of Jesus began at birth.[895]

Obviously the writers disagreed with one another. While Nugent stated that Paul's belief was that a literal Jesus became the son of God upon his resurrection (and, in the story, perhaps he did), Paul's teaching in 1 Corinthians 15 presents a Christ's coming into being

---

[893]Joshua Tilghman, "Jesus, the Zodiac, and Higher Consciousness," *The Spirit of the Scripture.com: Uncovering the Hidden Meanings of the Bible!* spiritofthescripture.com, 8 Sept. 2012, web, 27 June 2014.

[894] John Henry, ThD, "Jesus = 888," reason.landmarkbiblebaptist.net, n.d., web, 10 June 2014.

[895] Tony Nugent, PhD, "Jewish angels and Roman gods: The ancient mythological origins of Christmas," interview with Valerie Tarico, salon.com, 12 Dec. 2014, web, 26 Dec. 2014.

at the final resurrection of the dead, not the resurrection of a man named Jesus (1 Cor. 15:43-47). This is important—it's the spiritual significance of the mythical *story*. In the story, when Jesus was crucified he said, "It is finished" (Jn. 19:30). But it was *not* finished—not until *Israel* was "crucified," not until *Israel* was reduced to ashes (with not one stone left on another [Mt. 24:2]), not until *Israel* rose from the dead. Adam was Jesus was Israel (1 Cor. 15:42-58). The soul that *sinned* (Adam) is the soul that *died* (Israel) and the soul that was *resurrected*" (Christ) (Ezek. 18:4, 20).

Paul stated that Christ appeared to Peter and then to "the twelve, afterwards he appeared to above five hundred brethren at once . . . afterwards he appeared to James, then to all the apostles. And last of all — as to the untimely birth — he appeared also to me" (1 Cor. 15: 5-8). Although Paul *never* saw the risen Christ, he made no distinction in the way *he* "saw" Christ and the way the others he mentioned saw Christ. Paul's intent was to express support for a Christ in *heaven*. Hebrews 8:4 states that if Christ "were [or "had been," BBE] on earth" he couldn't be priest; and Paul made sure people accepted his claim of Christ's being in heaven, from where he *did* have authority as priest and could offer sacrifices. Jesus said that anywhere two or three people gather in his name, he is right there with them (Mt. 18:20). Do people actually see him? No. Did Paul see him? No, he saw a blinding light; and later he had a vision (Acts 9:3, 7; 18:9; 22:6). So what might we assume about how others "saw" Jesus after his resurrection (if indeed he was historic and walked on the earth before his supposed resurrection)? (Paul considered his seeing a *light* to be like everybody else's seeing Jesus, yet he strangely never mentioned that Stephen claimed to see *Jesus* in the heavens [Acts 7:56].)

Raphael Lataster, author and lecturer at the University of Sydney, wrote:

The first problem we encounter when trying to discover more about the Historical Jesus is the lack of early sources. **The earliest sources only reference the clearly fictional Christ of Faith**. These early sources, compiled decades after the alleged events, all stem from Christian authors eager to promote Christianity – which gives us reason to question them. The authors of the Gospels fail to name themselves, describe their qualifications, or show any criticism with their foundational sources – which they also fail to identify. Filled with mythical and non-historical information, and heavily edited over time, the Gospels certainly should not convince critics to trust even the more mundane claims made therein.

Paul's Epistles, written earlier than the Gospels, give us no reason to dogmatically declare Jesus must have existed. Avoiding Jesus' earthly events and teachings, even when the latter could have bolstered his own claims, Paul only describes his "Heavenly Jesus." Even when discussing what appear to be the resurrection and the last supper, his only stated sources are his direct revelations from the Lord, and his indirect revelations from the Old Testament. In fact, Paul actually rules out human sources (see Galatians 1:11-12).

Also important are the sources we don't have. There are no existing eyewitness or contemporary accounts of Jesus. All we have are later descriptions of Jesus' life events by non-eyewitnesses, most of whom are obviously biased. Little can be gleaned from the few non-Biblical and non-Christian sources, with only Roman scholar Josephus and historian Tacitus having any reasonable claim to be writing about Jesus within 100 years of his life. And even those sparse accounts are shrouded in controversy, with disagreements over what parts have obviously been changed by Christian scribes (the manuscripts were preserved by Christians), the fact that both these authors were born after Jesus died (they would thus have probably received this information from Christians), and the oddity that <u>centuries go by before Christian apologists start referencing them</u>.

Agnosticism over the matter is already seemingly appropriate, and support for this position comes from independent historian Richard Carrier's recent defense of another theory — namely, that the **belief in Jesus started as the belief in a purely celestial being (who was killed by demons [like Inanna] in an upper realm), who became historicized over time**. To summarize Carrier's 800-page tome, this theory and the traditional theory – that Jesus was a historical figure who became mythicized over time – both align well with the Gospels, which are later mixtures of obvious myth and what at least sounds historical.

The Pauline Epistles, however, overwhelmingly support the "celestial Jesus" theory, <u>particularly with the passage indicating that demons killed Jesus, and would not have done so if they knew who he was</u> (see: 1 Corinthians 2:6-10). Humans – the murderers according to the Gospels – of course would still have killed Jesus, knowing full well that his death results in their salvation, and the defeat of the evil spirits.[896]

We read in *Ascension of Isaiah*:

The Lord will indeed descend into the world in the last days (he) who is to be called Christ after he has descended and become like you in form, and <u>they will think that he is flesh and a man</u>. And the <u>god of that world will stretch out his hand against the Son</u>, and they will lay their hands upon him and hang him upon a tree, <u>not knowing who he is</u>. And thus <u>his descent</u>, as you will see, <u>will be concealed even from the heavens so that it will not be known who he is</u>. And when he has plundered the angel of death, he will rise on the third day.[897]

And all the angels of the firmament, and <u>Satan, saw him and worshiped</u>. And there was much sorrow there as they said, "How did our Lord descend upon us, and we did not notice the glory which was upon him, which we (now) see was upon him from the sixth heaven?" And he ascended into the second heaven, and he was not transformed, but all the angels who (were) on the right and on the left, and the throne in the middle, worshiped him, and praised him, and said, "<u>How did our Lord, remain hidden from us as he descended, and we did not notice?</u>"[898]

[896] Raphael Lataster, "Did historical Jesus really exist? The evidence just doesn't add up," washingtonpost.com, 13 Dec. 2014, web, 19 Dec. 2014.
[897] James H. Charlesworth, ed. "Martyrdom and Ascension of Isaiah," *The Old Testament Pseudepigrapha*, Vol. 2 (Peabody, MA: Hendrickson Publishers Marketing, LLC, 1983), 170.
[898] Charlesworth, "Martyrdom and Ascension of Isaiah."

This fits well with the biblical declaration that it was the princes of this world who killed Jesus, not knowing who he was (1 Cor. 2:8).

Tilghman wrote:

Jesus' life as it is related to the sun's travels through the zodiac is a depiction of the soul's birth and death on the physical plane as it relates to attaining Christ consciousness. It is the plan of salvation for every human being should they choose to undertake the journey of crucifying their ego.

We must also remember that the Gospel stories depict Jesus' ministry as taking place in one year. The sun travels through the 12 houses of the Zodiac in one year. Coincidence? I think not. Remember, even Enoch, another Christ figure and type, was taken by God at 365 years old. 365 days represents the completion of the solar year.

With all the Zodiacal signs complete we can see a rebirth of the physical man into a spiritual man. This is the goal for anyone undertaking the advanced spiritual journey.[899]

While stories depicting a dying and rising god appear in the New Testament, that doesn't necessarily mean the authors of the accounts believed them to be true, except perhaps in a metaphorical sense. Paul's writings reveal this truth. And the idea, when taken allegorically, is not a bad concept: Heaven and earth are one. We can agree on that.

<h3 align="center">Heinous Human Sacrifice</h3>

No good father-god would literally kill his son; such heinous behavior is unthinkable. If true it would reduce Christianity to a cult of human sacrifice. As Alvin Kuhn wrote:

If the Christ was in most real truth crucified in space, the physical timber on Golgotha's ghastly height, hewn and sawed and nailed, might be accepted with enlightenment as pure symbol of cosmic process. But as it stands in common thought among Christian people it is a gruesome sign of the most abject stultification of the godlike principle of intelligence known to history.[900]

It is, of course, true that ancient people were savagely sacrificing people to the gods long before Christianity came into existence. The following depicts this monstrous ritual:

The human sacrifice ritual around the Mediterranean, birthplace of Christianity, was virtually identical in important aspects to the Passion portrayed in the gospel story. This ritual often required a sacred king, whose death, it was believed, would propitiate a god and ensure good fortune and fecundity. During a national

[899] Joshua Tilghman, "The Conclusion of Jesus, the Sun, and the Zodiac," *The Spirit of the Scripture.com: Uncovering the Hidden Meanings of the Bible!* spiritofthescripture.com, 12 Sept. 2012, web, 27 June 2014.
[900] Alvin Boyd Kuhn, *Who is this King of Glory?* (New Jersey: Academy Press, 1944), 214. See also: Acharya S, *Suns of God*, 268.

crisis, it was deemed necessary for the king to sacrifice his own son or sons, "to die for the whole people," for the same reason.[901]

In the ancient **Semitic <u>sacred-king sacrifice</u>, which was the <u>same as the Passion of Christ but which preceded Christianity by centuries and millennia</u>**, the proxy of the god was <u>first anointed as king and high priest</u>. Next, he was <u>clothed in a purple cloak and crown, and led through the streets with a scepter</u> in his hand. The <u>crowd adored him, and then he was stripped and scourged</u>. Finally, in the <u>third hour</u> [see Mark 15:25], he was <u>killed, collected and sprinkled upon the congregation</u> in order to ensure their future fertility and fecundity. At that point, the <u>faithful crowd ritually cried, "his blood be upon us and our children!"</u> (Mt. 27:25) After the sacrificial victim's death, the <u>women mourned, wailed and tore their hair</u> at their loss, and <u>his body was eventually removed at sunset, buried in a sepulcher and covered with a stone</u>. Adonis and Tammuz are two of the pre-Christian Near Eastern gods in whose names were practiced such sadistic rites, echoed in the New Testament.[902]

Yahweh even insisted on human sacrifice in the Old Testament, as seen here:

Leviticus 27 (BBE): 28 But <u>nothing which a man has given completely to the Lord</u>, out of all his property, <u>of man or beast</u>, or of the land which is his heritage, may be given away or got back in exchange for money; <u>anything completely given is most holy</u> to the Lord. 29 <u>Any man given completely to the Lord may not be got back: he is certainly to be put to death</u>.

Later, we read that Yahweh commanded human sacrifice in order to destroy his people.

Ezekiel 20 (BBE): 25 Wherefore <u>I gave them also statutes that were not good</u>, and judgments whereby they should not live; 26 And <u>I polluted them in their own gifts, in that they caused to pass through the fire all that openeth the womb, that I might make them desolate</u>, to the end that they might know that I am the LORD.

Even the idea of eating flesh and drinking blood, the eucharist (communion, Lord's supper), didn't originate with Christianity, as has been shown. Again, the ancients thought that if they drank the blood or ate the flesh of brave or strong men, they themselves would take on these men's characteristics. Hence, if we eat Christ's body and drink his blood, we *become* Christ—we are a part of him (Jn. 6:56). According to *The Gospel of Thomas*, even Jesus spoke of this. He said: "Blessed is the lion which <u>becomes man</u> when consumed by man; and cursed is the man whom the lion consumes, and the <u>lion becomes man</u>."[903]

---

[901] Frazer, *The Golden Bough*, 341. See also: Acharya S, *Suns of God*, 276-277.

[902] Edouard Dujardin, *Ancient History of the God Jesus* (London: Watts, 1938), 55-56. See also: Acharya S, *Suns of God*, 276-277.

[903] James M. Robinson, ed., *The Gospel of Thomas*, tr. Thomas O. Lamdin, *The Gnostic Society Library* (San Francisco: HarperCollins, 1990) <http://gnosis.org/naghamm/gthlamb.html>.

E. A. Wallis Budge (1857-1934), an English Egyptologist and prolific author of books pertaining to the ancient Near East,[904] explained this as follows:

> The notion that, by eating the flesh, or particularly by drinking the blood, of another living being, a man absorbs his nature or life into his own, is one which appears among primitive peoples in many forms. It lies at the root of the widespread practice of drinking the fresh blood of enemies—a practice which was familiar to certain tribes of the Arabs before Muhammad . . . The flesh and blood of brave men also are, among semi-savage or savage tribes, eaten and drunk to inspire courage.[905]

Budge wrote the words above regarding "a passage from the pyramid of the Egyptian ruler Unas, in which Unas is depicted as 'eating' all the gods, thereby taking on their magical powers and eternal life."[906] Allegro wrote that those who ate Bacchus "took on his power and character as the Christians 'carried in their bodies the death of Jesus, so that the life of Jesus might be manifested in their bodies' (II Cor 4:10)."[907]

Every Sunday Christians metaphorically vampirize and cannibalize on Jesus' "blood" and "flesh" in an attempt to become like him or, really, to *be* him as it is the only way to have Christ dwelling inside one and experience his immortality and, hence, receive his "magical powers" (Jn. 6:53-58, 14:12; 1 Cor. 11:23-34). According to Genesis 3:22 and as Allegro noted, Yahweh stated that Adam had become like one of "us" (the Elohim) and Yahweh was concerned that Adam would eat of the tree of life and live forever. Therefore, according to verses 23-24, Yahweh drove the man out of the garden and made it so that he/they could never return. Within the doctrines of Christianity, the tree of life is available and people live forever by feasting on this metaphorical "tree" (Jesus). Hence, Christians eat Christ in order to obtain his characteristics.

However, while human sacrifice did occur, when a *god* was sacrificed it was in the heavens. And Jesus could not have literally fulfilled the Judaeo-Christian demands for a *human* scapegoat sacrifice (if indeed Yahweh wanted such a heinous offering) since he was not qualified as a priest to offer a sacrifice to Yahweh on the earth. For various reasons (and based on the biblical texts), he could not have been an earthly savior, and his crucifixion on the earth for the sins of the world can't be valid.[908]

The Book of Hebrews

According to the Law of Moses, Jesus couldn't have offered his life or his blood for the sins of people on the earth because he was not of the priestly tribe of Levi (Heb. 7:14). But the book of Hebrews gives another reason. There were still priests on the earth offering sacrifices in the "worldly sanctuary," and the way into the most holy place

---

[904] "E. A. Wallis Budge," wikipedia.org, 2014, web, 12 Nov. 2014.

[905] E. A. Wallis Budge, *The Egyptian Book of the Dead* (Dover, NY, 1967), lxxi. See also Acharya S, *Suns of God*, 275.

[906] Acharya S, *Suns of God*, 275.

[907] Allegro, 86.

[908] For a while I will be quoting from my book *We Are Emmanuel: How Man Became God.*

couldn't be manifested as long as they were performing their duties (Heb. 8:4; 9:1, 8). No matter how good Jesus was or how much he bled out, he couldn't offer a sacrifice on the earth. Any offering he made would have been rejected. His death on a literal cross couldn't have atoned for sins, and he didn't carry blood in a bucket to heaven. If Jesus didn't literally carry his blood to heaven, that means his blood was not *real* but *symbolic*. If his blood was symbolic, his death should have been symbolic too. Even the text says that Jesus "through the eternal Spirit offered himself without spot to God" (Heb. 9:14).

> Hebrews 9 (GEN): 22 And almost all things are by the Law purged with blood, and without shedding of blood is no remission. 23 It was then necessary, that the similitudes of heavenly things should be purified with such things: but the heavenly things themselves are purified with better sacrifices than are these. 24 For Christ is not entered into the holy places that are made with hands, which are similitudes of the true Sanctuary: but is entered into very heaven, to appear now in the sight of God for us,

While the Law might have allowed the shedding of blood for purification, that wasn't the way it was to be in the kingdom of Christ. He would offer a heavenly sacrifice; **he was in fact in heaven at that time offering his sacrifice**. And, again, it wasn't literal blood.

Christian teaching itself expresses that the blood sacrifice took place in heaven, not on Earth. Hebrews 10:12 says that Jesus "offered one sacrifice for sins." Where did he make this sacrifice? According to the New Testament, priests were on the earth years after Jesus died on the cross; but Jesus was in heaven, where, at the time of the writing of the book of Hebrews, the new covenant had not been ratified and iniquities had not been forgiven (Heb. 8:4-13). However, Jesus was a "priest forever," and he offered his sacrifice *in heaven, being slain from the foundation of the world* (Heb. 7:21, 27; Rev. 13:8). Jesus couldn't be crucified on Golgotha in a specific time period if he was crucified from the foundation of the world. The author of Hebrews expressed that Jesus was not a priest on the earth because *had he been here he could not have been priest* (Heb. 8:4). Regarding this passage Jim Walker wrote: "Furthermore, the epistle to the Hebrews (8:4), makes it explicitly clear that the epistle writer did not believe in a historical Jesus: 'If He [Jesus] had been on earth, He would not be a priest.'"[909] Again, the Bible says that Christ "through the eternal Spirit offered himself without spot to God" (Heb. 9:14). He did not, however (pardon my repetition), carry his literal blood into a literal place called heaven to sprinkle it on a literal altar. His sacrifice was therefore considered even by the writers of the New Testament to be spiritual (heavenly), not literal (Heb. 9:23).

The Allegory

As written in my book *We Are Emmanuel*, and according to Eusebius, Philo of Alexandria (c. 20 BCE–c. 50 CE), a "Hellenistic Jewish philosopher,"[910] wrote that the

---

[909] Jim Walker, "Did a historical Jesus exist?"
[910] "Philo," wikipedia.org, 15 Jan. 2015, web, 20 Jan. 2015.

early Christians (known as Therapeuts, who, as we learned earlier, worshiped Serapis Christ) "explain the philosophy of their fathers in an <u>allegorical manner, regarding the written words as symbols of hidden truth which is communicated in obscure figures</u>. They have also writings of ancient men, who were the founders of their sect, and who left many <u>monuments of the allegorical method</u>." Eusebius said these writings were probably the "Gospels and the writings of the apostles, and probably some expositions of the ancient prophets, such as are contained in the Epistle to the Hebrews, and in many others of Paul's Epistles."[911] Eusebius continued to quote Philo:

> <u>They expound the Sacred Scriptures figuratively by means of allegories</u>. For the whole law seems to these men to resemble a living organism, of which the <u>spoken words constitute the body</u>, while the <u>hidden sense stored up within the words constitutes the soul</u>. . . But that <u>Philo, when he wrote these things, had in view the first heralds of the Gospel and the customs handed down from the beginning by the apostles, is clear to every one</u>.[912]

Origen, who fought Gnosticism, nevertheless agreed: "The learned may penetrate into the significance of all oriental mysteries, but the <u>vulgar can only see the exterior symbol. It is allowed by all who have any knowledge of the scriptures that everything is conveyed enigmatically</u>."[913] Dameron believed Jesus was schooled in Gnosticism, stating that "his code of ethics is purely Buddhistic; his mode of action and walk of life Essenian."[914] Dameron wrote further that Gnosticism was the "purest form of primitive Christianity . . . who derived their doctrine from the oriental philosophy."[915]

Dr. Craig Lyons wrote that "contrary to what Rome would have us believe about a 'literal' Christ," the **earliest believers considered Christ to be an allegory, believing in a "salvation of a dying and rising god; not literally but only allegorically."**[916] Lyons continued: "A person attains salvation by learning . . . of their spiritual essence: that they are a divine spark of light or spirit of God . . . In allegorical terms their soul was asleep and they were unaware of their true spiritual essence."[917] This fits well with Paul's view of the death of Adam and resurrection of the Christ (1 Cor. 15), as well as with the following: "Awake thou that sleepest, and arise from the dead, and Christ shall give thee light" (Eph. 5:14). The early Christians were said to be members of Christ's body: "of his flesh, and of his bones" (Eph. 5:30). That sounds literal, but we know it wasn't intended to be so; therefore, it should come as no surprise that the <u>biblical story (at least through the lens of Christianity) may be metaphorical in all aspects</u>. The kingdom of God is said to be *within* the Christian (Lk. 17:21); also, as Paul declared, Christ was a "spiritual"

[911] Eusebius, "Philo's Account of the Ascetics of Egypt." See also my book *We Are Emmanuel*, 115.
[912] Eusebius, "Philo's Account of the Ascetics of Egypt."
[913] Origen, *Contra Celsus*, as found in Alfred Boyd Kuhn, PhD, *Who Is This King of Glory?: A Critical Study of the Christos-Messiah Tradition* (San Diego: The Book Tree, 2007), 70.
[914] Dameron, 51.
[915] Dameron, 50.
[916] Craig M. Lyons, MsD, DD, MDiv, "Gnosticism: What Did Gnostics Believe?" *Bet Emet Ministries*, firstnewtestament.com, n.d., web, 4 June 2014.
[917] Lyons, "Gnosticism: What Did Gnostics Believe?"

Rock (1 Cor. 10:4). And, no, Christians don't *literally* eat and drink him. However, if they did, it would be no more repulsive than a god's demanding literal human blood to appease his anger and nearly insatiable need for vengeance. That (as well as dumb animal blood sacrifices) sounds more like what a devil might require. ("Pound me the witch drums."[918])

Closing of the Breach

One aspect of this natural-to-spiritual imagery is that the earth was becoming the sky, the human a god, the female a male. The breach was going to be closed.

In *The Gospel of Thomas* Jesus states that he plans to make women male so they can enter his kingdom.

> (114) Simon Peter said to him, "Let Mary leave us, for women are not worthy of life." Jesus said, "I myself shall lead her in order to make her male, so that she too may become a living spirit resembling you males. For every woman who will make herself male will enter the kingdom of heaven."[919]

Of course, this didn't make it into the canon, but it is nevertheless evident that, within early Christian thoughts, male and female would be reunited as one being, the new, androgynous last Adam, or Christ. Christ then would be "all in all" (1 Cor. 15:28, Eph. 1:23). As Clement of Alexandria wrote, the "'Sun of Righteousness,' who drives His chariot over all, pervades equally all humanity."[920]

Jesus (of the house of Jacob) fixed the rift between his parents, thus closing the breach, ending their separation, and bringing reconciliation. They got back together for their offspring. Jesus' mother, who had been so lewd the Philistines were ashamed of her, committed fornication with the Egyptians and the Assyrians, and fornicated from the land of Canaan to Chaldea, pouring her prostitution on "everyone who passed by" (Ezek. 16:15-29), finally came home. The new Jerusalem, the "mother of us all" (Gal. 4:26), descended and Yahweh's tabernacle was with men (Rev. 21:2-4). Heaven came down and joined the earth. The old heaven and old earth were gone, and in their place was only one entity, with no more sea (adversary, foreign lover) to separate the divine couple (Rev. 21:1). Again, Lamentations 2:13 states that the breach between Yahweh and his "virgin daughter" Israel was "great like the sea: who can heal thee?" Jesus was the only one who could build a bridge across the sea, and crush the serpent, dragon, devil, or Satan. He was the knight in shining armor who killed the monster in the waters surrounding the castle, rebuilt the bridge across the moat, and brought everybody home safe and sound. "In that

---

[918] Marilyn Manson, "Cupid Carries a Gun," opening theme song for TV show *Salem*, genius.com, 2015, web, 11 June 2015. On *Salem*, the devil needs a human sacrifice in order to manifest himself, and the mother (Mary Sibley) of the boy to be sacrificed is told she is honored like the Virgin Mary, and that any betrayal she feels is like the betrayal the "other Mary" must have felt since "The angel of the annunciation failed to mention that she would end up weeping at the foot of the cross beneath her slaughtered son." *Salem*, TV series, created by Brannon Braga and Adam Simon, 2014-present, Season 2, Episode 9, "Wages of Sin," 31 May 2015.

[919] Robinson, *The Gospel of Thomas*.

[920] Clement of Alexandria, *Exhortation to the Heathen*, "Chapter 11. How Great are the Benefits Conferred on Men Through the Advent of Christ," tr. William Wilson, ed. Kevin Knight, newadvent.org, 2009, web. 26 Feb. 2015.

day the LORD with his sore and great and strong sword shall punish leviathan the piercing serpent, even leviathan that crooked serpent; and he shall slay the dragon that is in the sea" (Isa. 27:1). At this point, of course, the *old Israel* had become *Egypt*, or the sea that was no more (Jn. 8:44, Gal. 4:24-28, Rev. 11:8).

Remember, the brother of the mother in ancient times was the male figure in a child's life. In Amos 6:10 the uncle of a dead man was to go into a burned house and get the man's bones. In the New Testament we read about "Paul's sister's son" and "Marcus, sister's son to Barnabas," presumably because these nephews were close to their uncles (Acts 23:16, Col. 4:10). If an indigent widow (widow indeed) has children or *nephews*, Christianity demands that both provide for her (1 Tim. 5:4). In ancient times the "only recognized bonds of blood relationship depended on motherhood . . . The bonds were maternal because no paternal relationships were perceived or even guessed."[921]

An interesting concept appears with regard to the god Adonis as well as Osiris—an idea we have mentioned, which is that the gods enjoy incestuous relationships. We saw it with Ishtar and Tammuz; and the mother of Adonis was the reincarnated Aphrodite or Venus, and was the consort of Adonis and therefore both his mother and his lover.[922] Isis mothered Horus through Osiris and became both the mother and lover of Horus. Isis was also the sister of Osiris,[923] hence his sister and his lover. Also, Horus and Osiris may be identical gods, making Isis the wife of God and the mother of God.[924] Brahma, Abraham, and Zeus married their sisters. And who can forget: "I am come into my garden, my sister, my spouse" (Sng of Sngs 5:1)? We might also remember that Yahweh called Israel both his daughter and his wife (Jer. 3:8, Lam. 2:13). As we know, the Virgin Mary was both the wife of God (Yahweh) and the mother of God (Jesus). This is carried over into the relationship the New Testament bears out between Christ and his church. He is the older brother and the bridegroom, as well as the father (Is. 9:6); and the church (or new Jerusalem) is both the mother of all, which would include the Christ since he is the Christian's brother, and the bride of Christ (Jn. 3:29, Gal. 4:26, Rev. 21). Barbara Walker noted that the "female who is both Bride of God and Mother of God, like Mary, dates all the way back to Paleolithic cultures before biological fatherhood was understood."[925] Another interesting tidbit is that Mary Magdalene was, in some stories, the midwife at the birth of Jesus, the one who anointed him with oil (making him the Christ), and, in some Gnostic literature, the lover of Jesus.[926] In fact, Jacobovici wrote regarding Mary:

> In our Lost Gospel, she is depicted as a Galilean Phoenician priestess that abandons idolatry after meeting and falling in love with Jesus. They marry, but she's not simply "Mrs. Jesus." She is a partner in redemption referred to as the "Daughter of God" and "The Bride of God." Our Lost Gospel states that Jesus

---

[921] Walker, *Man Made God*, 63.
[922] Walker, *Man Made God*, 163.
[923] Bennett, 146. See also: "Osiris," wikipedia.org, 18 Jan. 2015, web, 30 Jan. 2015.
[924] "Osiris & Horus," ambrosiasociety.org., 2009, web, 7 Nov. 2014.
[925] Walker, *Man Made God*, 177.
[926] Walker, *Man Made God*, 170. See also: Clement A. Miles, *Christmas Customs and Traditions* (New York: Dover, 1976), 107.

and Mary had two children and it witnesses to the idea that, for their earliest followers, <u>Jesus and his wife Mary were co-deities</u> embroiled in the politics of their times.[927]

Origen thought Mary Magdalene was immortal, calling her "titles later bestowed on the Virgin Mary, such as Ecclesia (the Church), Jerusalem and 'Mother of Us All.'"[928] Thus, just as we have a fanciful story of a fake male savior, so we have a fake tale of a female savior. One stuck while the other didn't.

Again, today we know that females have male DNA in their brains that may have come not only from their fathers but from older brothers who left it in the womb of their mothers. This makes older brothers a part of their younger siblings.[929] So, physically and biologically, a sister and brother are connected in much the same way as a father and child. The point is that once a child is born, no force on Earth can destroy the bond between the child's family members. Children bind parents, they bind siblings, and they bind in-laws. The entire family (or human race) is connected, particularly in this son of the most powerful god who is now brother, father, and husband to humanity and a bridge between humans and gods. And, according to Romans 8:38-39, nothing can "separate us from the love of God, <u>which is in Christ Jesus our Lord</u>."

Once the couple (Yahweh and Mary, Asherah, or Israel; heaven and earth; male and female; spirit and body or matter) made that baby (who was a part of them both), it was a done deal—signed, sealed, and delivered; no power could separate them. Men finally found a way, through the divine mother, for their male god to make a baby god and become a creator and sustainer of life. The purpose of marriage is intimacy and consequent offspring. Companions can be had without marriage, but sex and babies are why we marry. (Yahweh was married to sister wives Judah and Israel, and Jesus married his ecclesia.) **Immortality was thus gained** in the closing of the breach, as **sex produces life while separation produces death**. And, with the return of the goddess (Matronit, Sophia, Holy Spirit, Asherah, Shekinah, Mary the mother of Jesus, Mary Magdalene the whore-turned-bride, Ecclesia, New Jerusalem, Israel, Matter, or Mother Earth), and the birth of the baby who closed the breach, Yahweh was no longer sexually frustrated, his wrath was assuaged, and our home became happy again. Allegro wrote: "When the penis slides into the vagina . . . 'harmony' has been achieved."[930] The Bible begins with a separation and ends with a reunion; thus death turned to life. That's the whole story.

Allegro continued:

It has seemed strange to scholars that Pluto, the god of the underworld, should elsewhere be reckoned as a god of fertility. It is true that much of our western

---

[927] Jacobovici, "Jesus' Marriage to Mary the Magdalene Is Fact, Not Fiction."

[928] Walker, *Man Made God*, 171. See also: Marjorie Malvern, *Venus in Sackcloth* (Carbondale: Southern Illinois University Press, 1975), 60.

[929] This is called microchimerism, and the cells from a fetus reside in a woman's cells and organs for the rest of her life, and are therefore transferred to later children. So a man's nieces and nephews could be a part of him. Robert Martone, "Scientists Discover Children's Cells Living in Mothers' Brains: the connection between mother and child is ever deeper than thought," scientificamerican.com, 12 Dec. 2012, web, 16 Nov. 2014.

[930] Allegro, 104.

classical and Semitic tradition has led us to think of Hades as a place of dull lifelessness, or even of retributive torture of the damned. More original, as we have seen, is the conception of the <u>earth's bowels as the seat of creation where all life is conceived and after death recreated</u>. In the <u>subterranean oven, the god's seminal fluid is processed into living matter</u>, and the Word made flesh.[931]

Thus, as Job said, we return to our mother's womb, possibly to be reborn (Jn. 9:2-3).

Destruction of Evidence

While we still see some Gnosticism within the New Testament, for the most part, as Massey noted, Gnostic doctrine was replaced by literalism and a human Christ.

> The gospel according to John is the link of connection between the true Gnosis and the false history of the other gospels. It shows the very ground on which the mythos alighted to be made mundane, and that is why it was kept secret, and withheld until the middle of the second century or so, by which time the doctrine of the Christ made flesh was considered safe, and sure to supersede the teachings of the Gnostics with the gospel of historic Christianity.[932]

Unfortunately, to hide the truth, Christians burnt what they could of the Gnostic scriptures. Edward Carpenter noted that "they took special pains to destroy the pagan records and so obliterate the evidence of their own dishonesty."[933] Graham wrote that "the early Christians heated their baths with the Ancient Wisdom. And what knowledge they may have contained!"[934] These barbarous Christians even burnt Hebrew scrolls, including "twelve thousand volumes of the Talmud."[935] With the evidence destroyed, they could "substitute their own absurdities. And to substantiate them they altered words and inserted verses that did not exist in the original texts."[936] Massey wrote:

> And when Eusebius recorded his memorable boast that he had virtually made "all square" for the Christians, it was an ominous announcement of what had been done to keep out of sight the mythical and mystical rootage of historic Christianity. The <u>Gnostics had been muzzled, and their extant evidences, as far as possible, masked.</u> He and his co-conspirators did their worst in destroying documents and effacing the tell-tale records of the past, to prevent the future from learning what the bygone ages could have said directly for themselves. <u>They made dumb all Pagan voices that would have cried aloud their testimony against the unparalleled imposture then being perfected in Rome. They had almost reduced the first four centuries to silence on all matters of the most vital importance for any proper understanding of the true origins of the Christian Superstition. The mythos having been at last published as a human history</u>

---

[931] Allegro, 153.
[932] Massey, *Gerald Massey's Lectures*, No. 30.
[933] Graham, 444.
[934] Graham, 444.
[935] Graham, 444.
[936] Graham, 444–445.

everything else was suppressed or forced to support the fraud. Christolatry is founded on the Christ, who is mythical in one phase and mystical in the other; Egyptian (and Gnostic) in both, but historical in neither.[937]

Barbara Walker noted: "Even St. Augustine (City of God, 4.31) deemed it 'expedient' to make people believe certain things that are false and to conceal other things that the 'vulgar crowd' should not know."[938]   And: "Through the centuries, religious 'fathers' have deliberately forged, fabricated and dissembled the beliefs demanded of their 'children,' for, as St. Gregory Nazianzen (330-389/390) allegedly wrote to St. Jerome (c. 347-420), the people are childlike, and 'the less they understand, the more they admire.'"[939]

Although evidence was burnt, the New Testament, particularly Paul's writings and the book of Hebrews, expresses a metaphorical view of Christ, a sun god like his predecessors. The New Testament presents a narrative to explain spiritual concepts. Even Jesus said he spoke in parables to those who couldn't understand (Mt. 13:13). We need to move beyond fables and recognize the allegory. Unfortunately, as Randolph stated, the "literal, and banal, way of reading won the day through the Christian tradition."[940]

Summary

When the Bible itself presents the Christ as having performed his redemptive duties in the heavenly realm, we ought to accept the book's own teaching if we value its content at all. Based on the biblical text and the information contained herein, it seems evident that the story of Jesus Christ, like similar stories before it, is a myth based on the Zodiac and the heavenly bodies. Murdock wrote:

> To summarize, in the solar myth the "death" of the "old sun" occurs as the days decrease in length towards the winter solstice—the word "solstice" meaning "sun stands still"—as for three days the sun appears not to be moving south or north. Hence, it is considered "dead" in the "Tomb" or "cave," and did not "return to life" until three days later, at midnight on December 24th, when it began its northerly journey again. Therefore, the ancients said the sun was born, reborn or resurrected on December 25th.[941]

On the night of December 24 the Egyptians performed a ritual in which they "carried from a sanctuary the image of a new-born child, the Sun, and shouted that "the Virgin has born," and that the "light is increasing."[942] The Gnostics called the winter solstice "Harpokrates," or "Horus the child."[943] This confirms that Horus (from where we get the

---

[937] Massey, *Gerald Massey's Lectures*, No. 3. See also: Graham, 445.

[938] Walker, *Man Made God*, 31.

[939] Walker, *Man Made God*, 31. See also: Tom Harpur, *The Pagan Christ* (Toronto: Thomas Allen Publishers, 2004), 182.

[940] Adam Randolph, "The Resurrection of Paul."

[941] Murdock, *Christ in Egypt*, 83.

[942] Stefan Weinstock, "A New Greek Calendar and Festivals of the Sun," *The Journal of Roman Studies*, Vol. 38, Parts 1 & 2, 1948, 42. See also: Murdock, *Christ in Egypt*, 90.

[943] Heinrich Karl Brugsch, *Thesaurus Inscriptionun Aegyptiacarum* (Austria: Akademische Druck, 1968), 419. See also: Murdock, *Christ in Egypt*, 106.

words "horizon" and "hours") was the newborn son that appeared at the winter solstice. And since Horus bore many characteristics of another "son of God" (Jesus), we may deduce the same of Jesus. Man's first enemy was darkness, so our ancestors longed for the life-giving rays of the newborn sun; if only the sun could shine perpetually, all darkness (and evil and death) would dissipate.[944]

Acharya S wrote in *Suns of God*:

The miraculously announced infant is born of a virgin (Virgo) in a cave or stable at the winter solstice ("Christmas"). His birth is attended by wise men (Three Kings in Orion's Belt) following a star in the East (Sirius) and bearing gifts. His life is threatened by a tyrant (Leo "the King"), who pursues him and slaughters many male newborns (stars). The solar babe escapes and grows up doing miracles, achieving manhood at the summer solstice, after which he heals the sick and raises the dead. He is baptized in the Jordan (Eridanus constellation) by Oannes the Dipper (Aquarius), and overcomes the "Prince of Darkness" (the night sky and winter). The sun god gathers around him 12 principle disciples or helpers (signs of the Zodiac), who preach the "good news." The solar hero is betrayed (Scorpio), killed, often by crucifixion ("crossified" at the equinoxes), side-wounded (Sagittarius) and buried in a cave (winter solstice [when the sun stands still as if dead for three days]). Three days later, the sun god rises again, leaving an empty tomb, and eventually ascends to heaven.[945]

Annie Besant, summarizing the thinking of Charles Dupuis, added further to this idea:

the hero is born about December 25th, without sexual intercourse, for the sun, entering the winter solstice, emerges in the sign of Virgo, the heavenly virgin. His mother remains ever-virgin, since the rays of the sun, passing through the zodiacal sign, leave it intact. His infancy is begirt with dangers, because the new-born sun is feeble in the midst of the winters' fogs and mists, which threaten to devour him; his life is one of toil and peril, culminating at the spring equinox in a final struggle with the powers of darkness. At that point the day and the night are equal, and both fight for the master; though the night veil the sun, and he seems dead; though he has descended out of sight, below the earth, yet **he rises again triumphant, and he rises in the sign of the Lamb, and is thus the Lamb of God, carrying away the darkness and death of the winter months**. Henceforth, he triumphs, growing ever stronger and more brilliant. He ascends into the zenith, and there he glows, "on the right hand of God," himself God, the very substance of the Father, the brightness of his glory, and the "express image of his person," "upholding all things" by his heat and his life-giving power; thence he pours down life and warmth on his worshippers, giving them his very self to be their life; his substance passes into the grape and the corn, the sustainers of health; around him are his twelve followers, the twelve signs of the zodiac, the twelve months of the year; his day, the Lord's Day, is Sunday, the day of the Sun, and his yearly course, ever renewed, is marked each year by the

---

[944] "ASTRO-THEOLOGY: THE 'SUN' ON THE CROSS...OR...THE 'SON' ON THE CROSS?" paganizingfaithofyeshua.freeservers.com, n.d., web, 4 June 2015.
[945] Acharya S, *Suns of God*, 458.

renewed memorials of his career. <u>The signs appear in the long array of sun-heroes, making the succession of deities, old in reality, although new-named.</u>[946]

Although Arthur Drews confirmed that "The Gospels do not contain the history of an actual man, but only the myth of the god-man Jesus, clothed in a historical dress,"[947] the early Christians destroyed nearly all evidence of the mythic nature of Christianity. This destruction was so complete by the fifth century that Archbishop Chrysostom boasted that every "trace of the old philosophy and literature of the ancient world has vanished from the face of the earth."[948] Besides that, we know that the documents we have today known as the New Testament are not original, and we have no idea who even wrote the Gospels.[949] Also, the Gospels in the canon are a remnant of what was written in the "first few centuries BCE and AD/CE," and they "bear the marks of extensive interpolation, revision and reinterpretation added by Church authorities centuries later" and are "hardly more reliable than fairy tales."[950] And, finally, not one historian—not one—living at the time Jesus supposedly lived ever spoke of him. *Not one.* Barbara Walker wrote:

> The earliest literature concerning [Jesus Christ] was written by Paul, who never knew him or anyone else who might have known him and who never heard anything about his life story. <u>Paul mentioned none of these now-so-familiar details, which were added much later by unknown writers who pretended to bear the names of various disciples and who sprinkled their writings with mythic data gathered from sacred-king traditions</u> of contemporary Greek, Roman, Egyptian, Persian and Levantine salvation cults.[951]

The biblical texts are fabrications. The Bible says as much, calling both covenants an allegory (Gal. 4:24-26). These stories were not originally meant to be taken literally. Many of the men who wrote their own doctrine and destroyed the writings of others may have genuinely thought they were doing a service to the world. Others no doubt discovered that they could gain power, prestige, and a pretty penny by twisting and perverting the scriptures into a means to deceive, manipulate, and frighten uneducated, ignorant people into believing lies about a god who would punish them if they weren't obedient to religious leaders. No matter what the motivation was, these early myth-makers destroyed anything and everything that stood in their way. And today blinded Christians declare the writings of Jews and the Roman Empire to be the word of God. It doesn't occur to many even to look at the other literature that might help them comprehend the fraud that occurred. They accept the lies of the Jews and the Romans hook, line, and sinker, and guide their lives accordingly, even to the point of condemning and ostracizing their own loved ones.

---

[946] Besant, 343-344.
[947] Graham, 282.
[948] Doane, 436. See also: Graham, 281.
[949] Graham, 281.
[950] Walker, *Man Made God*, 145.
[951] Walker, *Man Made God*, 144-145.

CHAPTER TEN
OUR LEGACY

Pure inspiration is confined to no particular person, age or nation. . . Everything that moves anywhere in . . . Nature sustains a relation more or less intimate to the spirit which animates the world. Every creature enjoys a living communion with the all-animating principle; and the relations which subsist between the little worm and the creation of worlds are just as intimate in principle as those enjoyed by man.[952]

James Palatine Dameron

Christianity is a cult of human sacrifice. . . not a religion that repudiates human sacrifice. It is a religion that celebrates a single human sacrifice as though it were effective.[953]

Dr. Sam Harris

The doctrine of original sin, which lies at the foundation of Christianity, is illogical and unjust. To hold all mankind . . . responsible for the indiscretion of Eve for eating an apple that was placed on a tree to tempt her . . . and that, to atone for this original sin, besides being driven out of the Garden of Eden, which science has shown to be a myth, God had to send His only son Jesus to be crucified between two thieves, to ransom all men, condemned and lost in consequence of the indiscretion of Adam and Eve, who did a good thing by eating the apple that opened their eyes to their ignorance and nakedness, is contrary to all reason and common sense.[954]

James Palatine Dameron

But, after all, who knows, and who can say whence it all came, and how creation happened? The gods themselves are later than creation, so who knows truly whence it has arisen? 7. **Whence all creation had its origin, he, whether he fashioned it or whether he did not, he, who surveys it all from highest heaven, he knows or maybe even he does not know.**[955]

Ecclesiastes 3 (BBE): 19 Because the fate of the sons of men and the fate of the beasts is the same. As is the death of one so is the death of the other, and all have one spirit. Man is not higher than the beasts; because all is to no purpose. 20 All go to one place, all are of the dust, and all will be turned to dust again. 21 **Who is certain that the spirit of the sons of men goes up to heaven, or that the spirit of the beasts goes down to the earth**? 22 So I saw that there is nothing better than for a man to have joy in his work — because that is his reward. Who will make him see what will come after him?

If there is a god, I'm pretty sure he/she/it isn't the one in the bible. That god is too exclusive just as are all of the other man-made gods. The Hebrew/Jewish/Christian god is nothing more than another tribal mythical god as with all of the other Ancient Near

---

[952] Dameron, 48.
[953] Sam Harris, PhD, "Sam Harris demolishes Christianity," youtube.com, 20 Jan. 2012, web, 7 Feb. 2015.
[954] Dameron, 76-77.
[955] *Rigveda*, X, 129, 6-7, tr. A. L. Basham, *The Wonder That Was India* (London, 1954), 247-248. See also: "Mircea Eliade 'From Primitives to Zen': 'Who Can Say Whence It All Came and How Creation Happened?'" *Myths of Creation and of Origin: Myths of the Creation of the World*, mircea-eliade.com, n.d., web, 22 Dec. 2014.

East religions of the past. A universal creator would be exactly that—god of everyone and everything, no exclusivity at all! How he would deal with us after we die is up to him. If we live the best life we can and try to treat others with love, how could he not accept that?[956]

Dale Stanford

The Bible and Christianity don't stand up under scrutiny. There are too many glaring contradictions and inconsistencies, incoherent reasoning and moral repugnances, ethical sidesteps and magical presuppositions. As a spiritual entity it is corrupt and self-serving, ego-centered, narcissistic.[957]

Craig Lee Duckett

We are incapable of knowing either what [God] is or whether he is.[958]

Blaise Pascall

It seems to me that the idea of a personal god is an anthropological concept which I cannot take seriously.[959]

Albert Einstein

The Hindus consider the *Vedas* to be inspired, the Japanese the *Shinto*, the Muslims the *Koran*, the Jews the *Tanakh*, and the Christians the Old and New Testaments.[960] Christians have, for more than 2,000 years, proclaimed their savior to be "the way, the truth, and the life" (Jn. 14:6); and they have lived their lives based on Jewish/Roman literature telling them so. But why would the Jews and Romans above all others have a direct line to the creative force of the universe? If all Christians seriously considered this question, I believe they would be atheistic with regard to Yahweh just as they are concerning Zeus and other fake gods. The Judaeo-Christian myth tells the story of a god who was separated from his wife but reconciled. It is a sensual romance that teaches us a good lesson, which is that unity is necessary to happiness and fulfillment. While I appreciate the message, I can't ignore the truths I have learned that have helped me to see that the Judaeo-Christian tale is a myth like all other deity legends. Therefore, as those before me left their understanding of spiritual matters for me to read, I must leave mine for those who come behind me.

That Old-Time Religion

We have compared the god-men of the Bible to the gods of other cultures and found them to be virtually identical. Again, the truth seems to be that the Jews collected all the god stories they could find and claimed them as tales about their own god, and the Christians did likewise. As Barbara Walker wrote:

---

[956] Dale Stanford, facebook.com, 21 Aug. 2014, web, 21 Aug. 2014.
[957] Craig Lee Duckett, "The World Simply Does Not Behave the Way Described in the Bible."
[958] Armstrong, 297, 299. Pascal (1623-1662) was a French theologian, physicist, and mathematician.
[959] Albert Einstein, "Religion and Science," *New York Times Magazine* (9 Nov. 1930), 1-4. See also: Albert Einstein, *The World as I See It* (New York: Philosophical Library, 1949), 24-28; and "Albert Einstein on: Religion and Science," sacred-texts.com, n.d., web, 22 Apr. 2015.
[960] Watts, "Jesus: His Religion or the Religion About Him."

the Bible is a highly diversified collection of writings, put together more or less at random over many centuries and extensively edited, revised, added to, subtracted from, mistranslated and misunderstood in a variety of ways. To regard any of it as historically accurate is simply a delusion that can be maintained only with considerable damage to the faculty of reason. . .

scholars know now that the Old Testament contains innumerable lies, mistakes, contradictions and bits of plagiarism; for the writers were not really creative authors. They were copiers and collectors of earlier texts, which they often garbled or misunderstood. They didn't create their own unique creation myth; they *adapted* it from many earlier sources.[961]

Graham noted:

The Jews would have us believe their entire book is a revelation from this God, yet how can it be since all the other races had the same material? Here we repeat, there is scarcely anything in their scriptures that cannot be found in the literature of older races. This they will deny, tracing as they do their lineage back to Adam, but their antiquity is as mythological as their history, so also their calendar . . . As for revelation, there is no such thing. All knowledge is humanly acquired sometime.[962]

The stories we have inherited reflect the mindset of the ancients as they attempted to grapple with theological issues and curiosity about their origin and the calamities and good fortune that came their way. While we may never have a clear answer as to who first began propagating many of these legends, we have no choice but to accept that the biblical account borrowed from other traditions. Dennis Bratcher observed:

Since the Israelites shared the cultural milieu of the Middle East, it would not be surprising, as pervasive as these myths were in that area, that they would use some of this imagery. . . While the specific origin of many of the symbols of apocalyptic writings cannot be traced, several basic elements . . . have a common background in Canaanite and Middle Eastern culture.[963]

Tarico wrote:

Preliterate people handed down their best guesses about gods and goodness by way of oral tradition . . . Their notions of what was good . . . and how to live in moral community with each other were free to evolve as culture and technology changed. But the advent of the written word changed that. As our Iron Age ancestors recorded and compiled their ideas into sacred texts, these texts allowed their understanding of gods and goodness to become static. The sacred texts of

---

[961] Walker, *Man Made God*, 39-40, 99.

[962] Graham, 231.

[963] Dennis Bratcher, "Speaking the Language of Canaan: The Old Testament and the Israelite Perception of the Physical World: How the Scriptures Appropriate Non-Hebraic World Views," *Christian Resource Institute: The Voice: Biblical and Theological Resources for Growing Christians,* cresourcei.org, 2013, web, 16 Feb. 2014.

Judaism, Christianity and Islam forbid idol worship, but over time the texts themselves became idols, and many modern believers practice—essentially—book worship, also known as bibliolatry. . .

Adherents who think their faith is perfect, are not just naïve or ill informed. They are developmentally arrested, and in the case of the world's major religions, they are anchored to the Iron Age, a time of violence, slavery, desperation and early death.

Ironically, the mindset that our sacred texts are perfect betrays the very quest that drove our ancestors to write those texts. Each of the men who wrote part of the Bible, Quran, or Gita took his received tradition, revised it, and offered his own best articulation of what is good and real. We can honor the quest of our spiritual ancestors, or we can honor their answers, but we cannot do both.[964]

Tarico's words are enlightening. Our ancestors changed their scriptures as their knowledge advanced, but many today remain stuck at an outdated level of discernment because they refuse to move past the philosophies of the ancients.

Curtis Hinson wrote:

In the twenty-first century, one ought to be able to worship any deity or no deity freely, but without the expectation of suspension of criticism from those outside a given view. If faith is humanistic, that is, if it contributes to human well-being and advancement, then it has value for those who practice it. If a faith causes harm and oppression, however, if it causes "Othering"[965] (in the Lacan/Levinas sense), then it cannot be seen as a positive contribution to the world or to its adherents.

Genocide, rape, and slavery are all described with varying levels of approval or disapproval attributed to God and the Israelites. The Israelites had a tribalistic worldview that allowed the juxtaposition of atrocities with a benevolent tribal God. The Torah contains what may be beautiful theological metaphors—yet cannot be accepted uncritically as a whole without severe cognitive and moral disconnect. With a more ancient view of canon (such as the concept even existed in proto-form), this was not an obstacle at all. Different genres (some of which are extant in modern literature), parallel but disagreeing narratives, and internal disagreements or clashes were expected, as a less literalistic and more oral view of the (then mostly oral) tradition made this a non-conflict.

In the modern, Western Christian view, particularly the fundamentalist flavor thereof, where the canon is forced to harmonize where it was never intended to harmonize, across internal theological development, three different languages, and several centuries of history and many more centuries of textual transmission

---

[964] Tarico, "These are the 12 worst ideas religion has unleashed on the world."

[965] "Othering is the process of casting a group, an individual or an object into the role of the 'other' and establishing one's own identity through opposition to and, frequently, vilification of this Other." Yiannis Gabriel, "The Other and Othering - A Short Introduction," *Stories, music, psychoanalysis, politics, reviews, the odd cooking recipe . . .* , yiannisgabriel.com, 10 Sept. 2012, web, 12 Jan. 2015.

and translation, the resulting God cannot be respected as God without suspension of moral judgment and an absolute privileging of text and theology. Those of us who do not share this privileging are in no account compelled to suspend criticism. The constructed god is an assault on human progress.[966]

As Tarico noted, while this "focus on the written word . . . has allowed Christianity and Islam to become more powerful than any religion in history . . . it has also allowed both traditions to become stagnant and cruel."[967]

Our forebears recognized the need to evolve. Perhaps they did the best they could with the information available to them. I truly believe that is so of some of them. They were simply attempting to understand their world. Let's not degrade their legacy by refusing to further their knowledge. They left us a heritage of a curious mind and a heart to discover new truth. What legacy will we leave our children? Do we want them to cling to outdated, ignorant ideas, or do we want them to add their own more enlightened thoughts to what we already have? We must set the example! Maybe that "old-time religion" *shouldn't* be "good enough for me."[968] Of course, the truth may be that the ancients knew more than we do and we should move back beyond the time when the Jews and Catholics literalized the myths and return to the truths we can glean from nature.

Hats Off to the Israelites

American Jew Marcus Eli Ravage wrote the following mocking words to Christians:

Our tribal customs have become the core of your moral code. Our tribal laws have furnished the basic groundwork of all your august constitutions and legal system. Our legends and our folk-tales are the sacred lore which you croon to your infants. Our poets have filled your hymnals and your prayer-books. Our national history has become an indispensable part of the learning of your pastors and priests and scholars . . . Our ancient little country is your Holy Land. Our national literature is your Holy Bible. What our people thought and taught has become inextricably woven into your very speech and tradition, until no one among you can be called educated who is not familiar with our racial heritage.

Jewish artisans and Jewish fishermen are your teachers and your saints, with countless statues carved in their image and innumerable cathedrals raised to their memories. A Jewish maiden is your ideal of motherhood and womanhood. A Jewish rebel-prophet is the central figure in your religious worship. **We have pulled down your idols, cast aside your racial inheritance, and substituted for them our God and our traditions**. No conquest in history can even remotely compare with this clean sweep of our conquest over you.[969]

[966] Curtis Hinson, message to the author, 12 Jan. 2014.
[967] Tarico, "In Defense of Cherry Picking the Bible."
[968] "(Give Me That) Old-Time Religion," traditional gospel song, 1873, written down by Charles Davis Tillman, 1889, wikipedia.org, 20 Jan. 2015, web, 23 Jan. 2015.
[969] Marcus Eli Ravage, "A Real Case Against Jews," *Century Magazine* (New York: The Century Co., 1928), Vol. 115, No. 3, Jan. 1928, 346ff. See also: Graham, 276-277; and Murdock, *Did Moses Exist?* 497.

Graham wrote regarding Ravage's words: "So true are [Ravage's] mocking words, that every Christian in Christendumb should hang his head in shame."[970] We have given up our own ancestry and culture, replacing it with that of the Jews. As Mack wrote: "What do you suppose [the people of Southeast Asia] thought when they first learned about Adam and Abraham and the Christ, and then discovered that their own ancestors, heroes, and gods would now have to lurk in the shadows as demigods and forest spirits?"[971] We (by that I mean I) have wasted our lives poring over ancient Hebrew (and Roman) writings while totally ignoring our own heritage. May this stop now!

The Facts of Life

When people are faced with insurmountable evidence against their beliefs, they often say, "I walk by faith," as if that takes away any obligation to reason or provide evidence for their beliefs. Blind faith seems to be considered a virtue. As Carl S. wrote: "We frequently find social stigma attached to someone who is 'lacking in faith,' as if believing in anything, however outrageous, is acceptable if it is sincerely believed in. What's so special about that?" He continued to say that if we don't have faith maybe the reason is that we can't force ourselves to trust without evidence and our lack of faith is therefore the "positive, mature attitude to maintain."[972]

Let's imagine we never heard of angry Yahweh or lowly Jesus. We know nothing of a talking snake, original sin, or a god's mating with a human then killing his son because he couldn't stand the humans *he* made and he just *had* to take his vengeance on *someone*. We're reading the Bible for the *first time*. Can we *believe* this book full of magic and wizardry like other fables, legends, and fairy tales that we *know* to be false? *Should* we believe it? If my crazy neighbor Noah tells me God is going to pour down water to drown the world and I therefore need to get into his boat, or my fanatical cousin Lot rants about how God is going to rain down fire and brimstone so I need to get out of the city, why in the name of sanity would I believe either of them? Why should I be *expected* by a rational god to believe them? I hope my readers will be honest and admit that they wouldn't believe their cousin or neighbor any more than I would believe mine and that such non-belief is *rational* and *wise*! When I was little my two oldest sisters told my next oldest sister and me that if we made horses out of corn stalks and corn silk and put them in Mommy's sewing machine drawer overnight, when we woke up they would be real, live horses. We believed our sisters because we were innocent and gullible and had tons of *faith*. But we *shouldn't* have! And nobody should be rewarded for being ignorant enough to accept nonsense just because another human being says it did or will happen.

We must look at the *facts* (as **knowledge surpasses faith**); the facts do not justify faith in the Judaeo-Christian gods. At the time the Christ myth came into being, people were superstitious. (Even the New Testament declares that [Acts 17:22].) They were

---

[970] Lloyd M. Graham, *Deceptions and Myths of the Bible* (New York: Skyhorse Publishing, 1979), 276.
[971] Mack, 295.
[972] Carl S. "Everyone Is Lacking In Faith."

already accustomed to honoring fake gods and goddesses. Naturally one more wasn't a problem for them. But it should be for us.

Despite all that has been said here, we can surely learn from the myths of the Bible (as we can and do from all myths—that is their purpose). Eckhart Tolle wrote, "The man on the cross . . . is every man and every woman."[973] He further noted that "Christ can be seen as the archetypal human, embodying both the pain and the possibility of transcendence."[974] Bill Darlison put it this way:

> The person on the cross is you. It is I. It is Everyman, and Everywoman. Crucifixion is not just an archaic and barbaric punishment for a few unfortunate lawbreakers; it is a condition of life. Crucifixion is the perfect metaphor for the human situation because, unlike most types of execution, it delivers a slow, lingering, painful death. What's more, it takes place for all of us on Golgotha, Calvary, 'the place of the skull' (Golgotha is Aramaic for 'skull', Calvary is 'skull' in Latin) which is itself an image of life stripped down to its skeletal essentials. We are all poised in pain on the cross of life. None escapes, and all attempts to insulate ourselves from life's pains are fruitless. . . The message of Easter is not that once upon a time a single individual's death paid the price of sin and he was rewarded by having his corpse reanimated. . . The story of the literal crucifixion and literal resurrection from physical death of a single human being is biologically impossible, historically implausible, and, in the way that it is often presented, it is morally questionable. But the story of our own resurrection from spiritual death while we are still alive is the most important and liberating message we will ever hear.[975]

Not only is the crucifixion/resurrection the story of our lives; in fact, it's the sequence of each day. We wake up with a clean slate to greet the morning sun; we struggle to make it through the day; then we lie down at night, either in peace or torture based on what happened that day (or, at least, how we dealt with the day's happenings); either way, we close our eyes in our "little death"[976] of sleep. Arthur Schopenhauer said, "Each day is a little life: every waking and rising a little birth, every fresh morning a little youth, every going to rest and sleep a little death."[977] John A. Sanford wrote: "The world-creating Logos could be seen in the movements of the heavenly bodies, in the majesty of the skies, in the great ocean with its abundance of life . . . in the tiniest unit of life."[978] The story is written in the sky, in the seasons, in the womb, and in the stages of growth/aging of each individual (Gen. 1:14; Ps. 19:1-6, 84:11; Mal. 4:2; Rom. 1:20; Rev. 22:16). We come into the world naked and unashamed, we play our part, we fall into a deep sleep, and we return innocently to our source (even if it is only as dust in the wind). We have our

---

[973] Eckhart Tolle, *A New Earth: Awakening to Your Life's Purpose* (New York: Penguin Group, 2005), 102.

[974] Tolle, 144.

[975] Bill Darlison, "Two Thieves," *Roads for Traveling Souls*, billdarlison.blogspot.com, 18 Apr. 2014, web, 7 May 2015.

[976] George R. R. Martin, *A Dance with Dragons (HBO Tie-in Edition): A Song of Ice and Fire: Book Five: A Novel* (New York: Bantam Books, 2015), 450.

[977] Arthur Schopenhauer, "Arthur Schopenhauer Quotes," brainyquotes.com, n.d., web, 10 Apr. 2015.

[978] John A. Sanford, *Mystical Christianity: A Psychological Commentary on the Gospel of John* (New York: The Crossroad Publishing Company, 1994), 23.

spring, summer, fall, and winter. And, again, we must work in the spring and summer (day/youth/strength) so that when our fall (evening/old age/weakness) comes, we can harvest and eat; if not, we will either freeze to death, being unclothed, or we will die of starvation in our winter—we will be naked and hungry (we will go down in shame). As the Psalmist said, we labor in sorrow for seventy years and then are cut off and fly away (Ps. 90:10). We live our seventy weeks, or our seventy years, with our seventy family members, bearing whatever cross is ours, and then we face our 70 CE (Ex.1:5, Dan. 9:24). Just as with the biblical characters Adam and Jesus, the only way to "return to God" is to die. This process is repeated throughout the biblical texts in various ways. It is the cycle of life.

So, even if we conclude that the Bible, like all ancient scriptures, was written by men, that doesn't mean it offers nothing beneficial. Surely we are all a part of the energy, force, intellect, or whatever exists that holds us all together. No, I don't believe that power is a personal, male, mind-reading, bloodthirsty, vengeful god who destroys "the blameless and the wicked" (Job 9:22). Still, *both the blameless and the wicked do die*! Some creative force brought us all into being, some force will take us out, and we are indeed unified with the universe. That, we can agree on. Maybe what we call *God* is simply consciousness, or "the life force";[979] thus it truly is in everything and everybody, as the Bible (and the Egyptian god Aten) says (Acts 17:28, Col. 1:16-20).

We Are Free

We don't need a devil to blame our bad deeds on, a savior to pay for them, or a magic fairy godfather/godmother to grant our wishes and allow us to live in his/her fancy kingdom with a golden street (if we only believe with all of our little hearts that it is so). The Bible came to us via myths, some clever magic may have been performed to help us believe it, and it was originally nothing but a metaphor. If we would use the Bible for good, that would be wonderful. Unfortunately, Christianity and other Abrahamic religions promote disunity, discord, hate, and war. We criticize, ostracize, and kill one another over whose myth is the truest—over which superhero (Superman, Batman, or Spider-Man) is the greatest. It was supposedly the *Word* that reconciled man to Yahweh. He spoke and it was so. As Isaiah 55:11 says, "God's word went forth from his mouth, didn't return to him void, but accomplished what he wanted and prospered in the thing to which he sent it." Jesus was, after all, the savior of the *world*, not just believers (Jn. 4:42, 1 Jn. 4:14). Of course, some say the *world* is Israel only (Jews and the dispersed Israelites), and that salvation was accomplished in the first century CE never to be repeated (Gen. 17:5-14, 35:10-11; Deut. 32:9; Ps. 147:19-20; Isa. 11:11-12, 61:9; Jer. 31:31; Ezek. 37:21-28; Mic. 5:8; Mt. 4:15, 10:6, 15:24, 19:28; Lk. 1:32-33; Jn. 1:10-11, 7:35; Acts 2:36, 6:1-2, 21:21, 23:6, 24:15, 28:20; Rom. 4:11-19, 11:25-27; 1 Cor. 10:11; Eph. 2:11-12; Heb. 9:15; 1 Pet. 1:5; 1 Jn. 2:18; Jude 1:15-19; Rev. 21:3, 12). If indeed

---

[979] Eben Alexander, MD, *Proof of Heaven: A Neurosurgeon's Journey into the Afterlife* (New York: Simon & Schuster, Inc., 2012), 156.

Jesus was the savior of Israel only—since Israel was Yahweh's inheritance and the only people over whom he had authority—or this salvation happened in the past and won't be repeated, we who are living today and/or are not Israelites can happily ignore Yahweh's promises and death threats. But, as I noted in footnote number 778 (p. 142), it isn't the purpose of this book to determine whether the Bible teaches the salvation of Israel only or the whole world. Therefore (assuming Yahweh eventually took all humanity under his wing), **according to the Bible, the Word accomplished its purpose of reconciliation. So, believers or non-believers, we can all relax. Mommy and Daddy are back together and all is right with our world.** Robert Farrar Capon wrote:

> Christianity is the proclamation of the end of religion, not of a new religion, or even the best of all possible religions. And therefore if the cross is the sign of anything, it's the sign that God has gone out of the religion business and solved all the world's problems without requiring a single human being to do a single religious thing.[980]

Mommy is back home, Daddy is sexually satisfied, and life goes on "forever and ever."

I was lying in bed one night thinking about how I have drastically changed my religious views, and suddenly I had what I would call, for lack of a better term, a spiritual experience. It dawned on me that no god put a man and woman in a pit with a monstrous snake, no god drowned innocent children and newborn puppies or ripped apart mothers to abort their babies, no god picked a "pet" among his children to fight and kill his other children over a piece of ground, no god murdered his own son because of his unforgiving nature, and no god is going to burn anyone. No god like that exists! When that thought struck me, the most amazing relief came over me. I felt what seemed like chains begin to break apart all over my body, falling at my feet. As I watched I realized that they weren't chains after all but brown scales; and they literally covered every inch of me to the point that they *were* my body. I had been hidden or disguised by them so that my true body wasn't apparent. I watched the scales fall and listened as they clinked onto the floor. And what emerged was a smooth pink body that radiated a soft white glow. I *was* light, glowing and producing heat. I was wispy as a feather and could float into the air. I was at peace. I felt joy. I was reborn. I was free. I believe the *truth* has set me free.

See, I have visions too. But I don't plan on teaching them as doctrine and attempting to gather a following based on them. Robert M. Price said that

> as long as the individual prophet is the only one to believe as he does, we call him insane. We say he has a delusion, because he is the only one navigating by this compass, on these particular seas. . . And <u>after a while, when enough people believe it, we no longer call it a delusion. We call it a religion.</u>[981]

---

[980] Robert Farrar Capon, *The Mystery of Christ . . . & why we don't get it* (Grand Rapids, MI: Wm. B. Eerdmans Publishing Co., 1993), 62.
[981] Robert M. Price, "He Really Is Santa Claus," robertmprice.mindvendor.com, 1996, 2007, web, 10 Apr. 2015.

Karen Armstrong wrote, "As an epileptic, I had flashes of vision that I knew to be a mere neurological defect: had the visions and raptures of the saints also been a mere mental quirk?"[982] Shouldn't we consider the possibility that biological, psychological, political, and environmental issues might have come into play with regard to the visions and god-encounters of the ancients?

I don't have an answer to whether a *god* exists or what he/she/it might be like. Martin Luther "doubted the possibility of proving the existence of God."[983] Even Mother Teresa had her reservations about his existence.[984] The fact that people say they have *faith* proves they don't have *knowledge* of a god, and especially the god Yahweh. **Religions are based on faith, and faith is not fact; if we could call a god's existence a *fact*, then *faith* would disappear.** I believe the *Bible* is about nature. It's about sex. It's about love. It's about life. And life eventually comes to an end. When we die we go either to the tomb-womb of Mother Earth or to some realm or dimension we know nothing about, perhaps to be resurrected through reincarnation in a new spring or to live "somewhere out there" (or maybe we remain right here but operate on a different frequency or vibration).

Again, *I don't know* whether there is a god or what happens after this life, and neither does anyone else. *And we all know we don't know.* I think it's time we admit this truth. Obviously, I have a hope that our consciousness continues after death. Events in my life make me believe we *may* be eternal. But my visions (yes, I have had my share), encounters, revelations, and beliefs are mine alone, and should be given no more credence than any other person's. I don't expect anyone to accept them as true; likewise, I have no obligation to take on the beliefs of anyone else, whether the person be a prophet, priest, preacher, or poet. Our faith, or lack of faith, is personal; and we have every right to our own thinking on spiritual matters. As someone said, "Religion is like a penis. It's fine to have one and it's fine to be proud of it, but please don't whip it out in public and start waving it around. And *please* don't try to shove it down my child's throat."

So, as for what I say, everyone is free to ignore it, ponder it, or research the matter on his or her own. If what I've said seems false, may all reject it; if it rings true, I hope all will consider it. Surely I have presented enough evidence to at least prompt the reader to do a thorough study of the life and times of the Israelite god Yahweh and a more in-depth and impartial investigation of his so-called book. At the least, **I pray that Christians will think twice before judging and condemning their fellow man based on the "high and holy" thinking of a people who didn't even know human trafficking was wrong.**

The Clock's Running

I'll end this book with a few words from Frank Sinatra that appeared in *Playboy Magazine* in 1963.[985] He first stated:

---

[982] Armstrong, xviii-xix.

[983] Armstrong, 278.

[984] Michelle Singer, "Letters Reveal Mother Teresa's Secret," cbsnews.com, 23 Aug. 2007, web, 14 Nov. 2014.

[985] "Frank Sinatra's views on organized religion were decades ahead of his time," deadstate.org, 29 Aug. 2014, web, 8 Nov. 2014.

I believe in you and me. I'm like Albert Schweitzer and Bertrand Russell and Albert Einstein in that I have a respect for life — in any form. I believe in nature, in the birds, the sea, the sky, in everything I can see or that there is real evidence for. If these things are what you mean by God, then I believe in God. . . Now don't get me wrong. I'm for decency — period. I'm for anything and everything that bodes love and consideration for my fellow man. . . I've got no quarrel with men of decency at any level. But I can't believe that decency stems only from religion.[986]

Then he went on to say:

Have you thought of the chance I'm taking by speaking out this way? Can you imagine the deluge of crank letters, curses, threats and obscenities I'll receive after these remarks gain general circulation? Worse, the boycott of my records, my films, maybe a picket line at my opening at the Sands. Why? Because I've dared to say that love and decency are not necessarily concomitants of religious fervor.[987]

The interviewer from *Playboy* said, "If you think you're stepping over the line, offending your public or perhaps risking economic suicide, shall we cut this off now, erase the tape and start over along more antiseptic lines?" Sinatra responded: "No, let's let it run. I've thought this way for years, ached to say these things. Whom have I harmed by what I've said? What moral defection have I suggested? No, I don't want to chicken out now. Come on, pal, the clock's running."[988]

The clock's running. Darlison wrote that, like Jesus, we are all crucified between two thieves, those thieves being our past and our present.

What do these bandits steal? They steal our life. <u>They are the past and the future, the twin thieves of everyone's life</u>. . . The past consumes us with regret, remorse, revenge, nostalgia, habit; the future eats away at our life with anxiety, uncertainty, procrastination, fear. . . We enter into the life of promise today. Now. It's now or never. By destroying, or transforming, those twin thieves of our lives we enter into a whole new way of being, resurrected life, when the tomb which held us fast is broken open . . . This is the consistent message of the world's spiritual traditions. This is the perennial philosophy.[989]

As I said earlier, it wasn't the wizard who brought Dorothy Gayle back home; but the truth is, it really wasn't the kind and pretty Glinda either. It was Dorothy herself who had the power to transform her life. She didn't need to follow the Yellow Brick Road to the Emerald City to find a powerful being to grant her wish. She could make it home on her own. And she was happier in her own little house with her family and friends in good old Kansas. Dorothy finally realized that the life she was given was enough for her; likewise,

[986] "Frank Sinatra's views on organized religion were decades ahead of his time."
[987] "Frank Sinatra's views on organized religion were decades ahead of his time."
[988] "Frank Sinatra's views on organized religion were decades ahead of his time."
[989] Darlison, "Two Thieves."

our current earthly lives should be enough for us. Let's not ignore our vital present in order to weep over our sinful past and dream of a future castle in the sky in a city of gold. Despite what we may have been told, this is not a dress rehearsal; this is the main event. My friend John Marra wrote, "Since this is the only life any of us can actually be certain of, let's try to fill it with all the love, joy, and happiness we possibly can because it's so precious."[990]

The clock's running! If there is more after this life, great; but destroying one another in search of an ideal that may never come to fruition cannot be the right way to live. All religions, including Christianity, separate humans from one another when even the biblical scriptures urge unity. I hope it won't take much more time before we realize that when we leave here we *may* go the way of every monkey, squirrel, and cockroach; therefore, our time, money, and energies should be used to help one another live a better life now (here, on Earth, in Kansas or wherever we may be), because *we don't know* what is beyond the grave. Even if we exist after this life, it may not be as the people we are now (or as people at all). The only legacy we may have is whatever we create in the *here* and *now*. Let's make the only life we know we have one of acceptance of *all people*, regardless of their religious views or way of life that may be different from ours. As my friend Dale Stanford said, any god who might be out there watching us will surely honor that behavior.

This book could be my undoing in the eyes of many—the last straw for some or the final nail in my coffin; and my friends and loved ones will no doubt wonder why I don't pretend I still believe in Yahweh and Jesus rather than bringing disrespect upon myself and creating shock waves in my personal environment. The answer is the same as it would be if I had been worshiping Baal, Mithra, Chrishna, or Hercules, and I suddenly discovered that my god wasn't real. Would I keep quiet then and feign belief in a pagan god just because the crowd was worshiping him? No, I wouldn't. I can't profess to worship a god I consider to be pagan (no matter how many others believe in him), nor can I worship a human being (Jesus, if he was truly a historical figure). I also can't, and in my opinion shouldn't, keep quiet. I must raise my voice along with the voices of others who are breaking the shackles of superstition and paganism. So my readers can feel sorry for me, they can pray for me, they can even turn me over to Satan. But let's let it run.

---

[990] John Marra, facebook.com, 24 June 2015, web, 24 June 2015.

BIBLIOGRAPHY

Abelard, Miles R. *Physicians of No Value*. Winter Park, FL: Reality Publications, 1979.

Acharya S. *The Christ Conspiracy: The Greatest Story Ever Sold*. Kempton, IL: Adventures Unlimited, 1999.

Acharya S. *Suns of God: Krishna, Buddha and Christ Unveiled*. Kempton, IL: Adventures Unlimited Press, 2004.

Aesop. "The North Wind and the Sun." Aesopfables.com. N.d. Web. 26 May 2015.

"Aesop's Fables." Taleswithmorals.com. June 2014. Web. 9 June 2014.

"Akhenaten." Wikipedia.org. 30 Jan. 2015. Web. 31 Jan. 2015.

"Albert Einstein on: Religion and Science." Sacred-texts.com. N.d. Web. 22 Apr. 2015.

Aletheia, M.D. *The Rationalist's Manual*. London: Watts & Co. 1897.

Alexander, Eben, MD. *Proof of Heaven: A Neurosurgeon's Journey into the Afterlife*. New York: Simon & Schuster, Inc., 2012.

"Alexander the Great Biography: The Man and the Myth." *All About Egypt*. All-about-egypt.com. 2015. Web. 29 Apr. 2015.

Allegro, John M. *The Sacred Mushroom and the Cross: A study of the nature and origins of Christianity within the fertility cults of the ancient Near East*. Garden City, NY: Doubleday & Company, Inc., 1970.

Allen, James P. *The Ancient Egyptian Pyramid Texts*. Atlanta: Society of Biblical Literature, 2005.

Allen, Melloson. "10 Ways the Bible Was Influenced by Other Religions." Listverse.com. 30 June 2013. Web. 5 Apr. 2014.

Andrews, Seth. "Free Will." Thethinkingatheist.com/blog. 28 Apr. 2014. Web. 20 Nov. 2014.

Angus, S. *The Mystery-Religions*. New York: Dover, 1975.

"Annie Besant." Wikipedia.org. 23 June 2015. Web. 1 July 2015.

"Apocryphon of John." Wikipedia.org. 12 Feb. 2015. Web. 18 Mar. 2015.

The Apology of Tertullian. Tr. William Reeve, AM. London: 1709.

Aratus (c. 310-240 BCE). *Phaenomena* 1-5.

Aristotle, *De Partibus Animalium I and De Generatione Animalium I*. Tr. C. M. Balme. Oxford: Oxford University Press, 1992.

"Arius." Wikipedia.org. 19 Feb. 2015. Web. 4 Mar. 2015.

Arlen, Harold. "Ding Dong! The Witch Is Dead." *The Wizard of Oz*. Dir. Victor Fleming. Metro-Goldwyn-Mayer, 1939. Film.

Armstrong, Karen. *A History of God: The 4,000-Year Quest of Judaism, Christianity and Islam*. New York: Ballantine Books, 1993.

Asiatick Researches; or, Transactions of the Society Instituted in Bengal, for Inquiring into the History and Antiquities, the Arts, Sciences, and Literature, of Asia (London, 1806), Vol. I.

Assmann, Jan. *Death and Salvation in Ancient Egypt*. Tr. David Lorton. Ithaca, NY: Cornell University Press, 2005.

"ASTRO-THEOLOGY: THE 'SUN' ON THE CROSS...OR...THE 'SON' ON THE CROSS?" Paganizingfaithofyeshua.freeservers.com. N.d. Web. 4 June 2015.

"Aten." Wikipedia.org. 28 Jan. 2015. Web. 31 Jan. 2015.

"Aten, god of Egypt." Siteseen Ltd. June 2014. Web. 31 Jan. 2015.

"Attis." Wikipedia.org. 9 Jan. 2015, Web. 25 Jan. 2015.

"Baali." Strong's H1180. Blueletterbible.org. 2015. Web. 22 Jan. 2015.

Bailey, Jared. *Crimes of Humanity*. Lulu.com, 2014.

"Bali." Strong's 1180. Biblehub.com. 2015. Web. 11 Apr. 2015.

Barker, Dan. *Losing Faith in Faith: From Preacher to Atheist*. Madison, WI: FFRF, Inc., 1992.

Barnes, Albert. *Notes*. Vol. 1.

Barnstone, Willis. *The Other Bible*. San Francisco: Harper & Row, 1984.

Baron, Salo Wittmeyer. *A Social and Religious History of the Jews*. 10 vols. 2nd ed. New York, 1952-1967, I.

Baronius, Caesar, Cardinal. *Annales Ecclesiastici*. Tome vii, Fol. Antwerp, 1597.

Baum, Frank. *The Wizard of Oz*. Dir. Victor Fleming. Metro-Goldwyn-Mayer, 1939. Film.

Bennett, DeRobingne Mortimer. *The Gods and Religions of Ancient and Modern Times . . . .* 1880.

Berger, Charles G., MD. *Our Phallic Heritage*. Greenwich Book Publishers, 1966.

Berry, Gerald. *Religions of the World*. New York: Barnes & Noble, 1955.

Besant, Annie. *The Freethinker's Text-book, Part II: Christianity: Its Evidences. Its Origin. Its Morality. Its History*. London: R. Forder, 1893.

"Biblical Contradictions." *Evil Bible.com: Fighting Against Immorality in Religion*. Evilbible.com. N.d. Web. 8 Sept. 2014.

Bihu, L. E. "Midianite Elements in Hebrew Religion." *Jewish Theological Studies*.

"Birthstone." Wikipedia.org. 25 Jan. 2015. Web. 26 Jan. 2015.

Bonacci, Santos. "The Key to the Holy Science." "Nexus" 2011. Posted by E. P. James MacAdams. Youtube.com. 19 Apr. 2012. Web. 8 April 2015 <https://www.youtube.com/watch?v=E5maozgL23U>.

Bonwick, James. *Egyptian Belief and Modern Thought*. London: C. Kegan Paul & Co., 1878.

The Book of Jasher. Tr. from Hebrew to English, 1840. Salt Lake City: J. H. Parry & Company, 1887.

"Book of Jasher (Pseudo-Jasher)." Wikipedia.org. 11 Oct. 2014. Web. 22 Jan. 2015.

Bordeaux, Edmond S. "The Whole of Church History is Nothing but a Retroactive Fabrication." *How The Great Pan Died* [Vatican archivist]. USA: Mille Meditations, MCMLXVIII.

"BORROWED STORIES AND CHARACTERS? -- MARK 1-10." N.d. Web. 17 May 2015 <http://vridar.info/xorigins/homermark/mkhmrfiles/mkhmrpt1.htm#top>.

Botterweck, G. Johannes. *Theological Dictionary of the Old Testament*, 2:338.

"Brahma and Saraiswati." *Leventy Leven: A Trip Around the World*. Leventyleven.com. 14 Sept. 2013. Web. 26 June 2014.

Bratcher, Dennis. "Enuma Elish: 'When on High . . . ' The Mesopotamian/Babylonian Creation Myth." *Christian Resource Institute: The Voice: Biblical and Theological Resources for Growing Christians*. Cresourcei.org. 2013. Web. 16 Feb. 2014.

Bratcher, Dennis. "Speaking the Language of Canaan: The Old Testament and the Israelite Perception of the Physical World: How the Scriptures Appropriate Non-Hebraic World Views." *Christian Resource Institute: The Voice: Biblical and Theological Resources for Growing Christians*. Cresourcei.org. 2013. Web. 16 Feb. 2014.

Brier, Bob, and Hoyt Hobbs. *Daily Life of the Ancient Egyptians*. Westport/London: Greenwood Press, 1999.

Briffault, Robert. *The Mothers II*. New York: Macmillan, 1927.

Brodie, Thomas L. *Beyond the Quest for the Historical Jesus.* Sheffield, England: Sheffield Phoenix Press Ltd, 2012.

Brugsch, Heinrich Karl. *Thesaurus Inscriptionun Aegyptiacarum*. Austria: Akademische Druck, 1968.

Brunty, Thomas. "Forgotten Christ." Film by Agata Brunty. *Sensoria Productions*. 15 Mar. 2014. Youtube.com. 20 Dec. 2014 <https://www.youtube.com/watch?v=zpDN2802YzA>.

B'sorah HaEv'rim: The Goodnews according to the Hebrews. Reconstructed by James Scott Trimm. Pdf. Jacksonsnider.com. N.d. Web. 17 Jan. 2015.

Budge, E. A. Wallis. *The Egyptian Book of the Dead*. Dover, NY, 1967, LXXI.

Budge, E. A. Wallis. *Gods of the Egyptians, II*. New York: Dover, 1969.

Budge, E. A. Wallis. *A Guide to the Egyptian Galleries*. British Museum, 1909.

Budge, E. A. Wallis. *A Guide to the First and Second Egyptian Rooms*. British Museum, 1904.

Burns, Cathy, PhD. *Masonic and Occult Symbols Illustrated*. Sharing, 1998.

Bushby, Tony. *The Crucifixion of Truth*. Buddina Queensland, Australia: Joshua Books, 2004.

Bushby, Tony. "The Forged Origins of the New Testament." March 2007. Extracted from *Nexus Magazine*, Vol. 14, No. 4 (June - July 2007). Nexusmagazine.com. Web. 22 June 2014.

Butler, Samuel. "How Christianity Was Invented: The Truth!" Beyondallreligion.net. 21 Jan. 2012. Web. 13 Aug. 2014.

"Canaanite Myth: The Baal Epic." Theologywebsite.com. 1997-2009. Web. 26 Nov. 2014 <http://www.theologywebsite.com/etext/canaanite/baal.shtml>.

"Canon of the New Testament." *Catholic Encyclopedia*. New York: Robert Appleton Company, 1913.

Capon, Robert Farrar. *The Mystery of Christ . . . & why we don't get it*. Grand Rapids, MI: Wm. B. Eerdmans Publishing Co., 1993.

Carlile, Richard, ed. *The Republican*. London: R. Carlile, 1824. Vol. X.

Carrier, Richard, PhD. *Hitler Homer Bible Christ: The Historical Papers of Richard Carrier 1995-2013*. Richmond, CA: Philosophy Press, 2004.

Carrier, Richard, PhD. *On the Historicity of Jesus: Why We Might Have Reason to Doubt*. Sheffield, England: Sheffield Phoenix Press, 2014. Kindle ed.

Carrier, Richard, PhD. *Proving History: Bayes's Theorem and the Quest for the Historical Jesus*. Amherst, NY: Prometheus Books, 2012.

Carrier, Richard, PhD. "Richard Carrier: Acts as Historical Fiction." Youtube.com. 13 Mar. 2014. Web. 9 Jan. 2015 <https://www.youtube.com/watch?v=B5MUUP4l6l4>.

Cassels, Walter Richard. *Supernatural Religion: Introduction. Miracles. The Synoptic gospels*. Longmans, Green and Company, 1875.

"Catholic and Protestant Bibles." Cathtruth.com. N.d. Web. 6 Apr. 2014.

The Century, XXXVIII. London: T. Fisher Unwin, 1889.

"Cham." Biblehub.com. N.d. Web. 15 Dec. 2014 <http://biblehub.com/hebrew/2526.htm>.

Changooly, Joguth Gunder. *Life and Religion of the Hindoos with a Sketch of My Life and Experience*. Boston: Crosby, Nichols, Lee and Company, 1860.

Chapman, J. "Tertullian." *The Catholic Encyclopedia*. New York: Robert Appleton Company, 1912. Newadvent.org. 2012. Web. 18 June 2014.

Charlesworth, James H., ed. "Martyrdom and Ascension of Isaiah." *The Old Testament Pseudepigrapha*, Vol. 2. Peabody, MA: Hendrickson Publishers Marketing, LLC, 1983.

Chartrand, Mark R. III. *Skyguide: A Field Guide to the Heavens*. Golden Books Publishing Co., 1982.

Chastain, Tim. "Midrash in the New Testament." Jesuswithoutbaggage.wordpress.com. 17 Feb. 2014. Web. 11 Mar. 2015.

Clement of Alexandria. *Exhortation to the Heathen*. "Chapter 11. How Great are the Benefits Conferred on Men Through the Advent of Christ." Tr. William Wilson. Ed. Kevin Knight. Newadvent.org. 2009. Web. 26 Feb. 2015.

Cline, Eric H. "The Garden of Eden." Bibleinterp.com. Oct. 2009. Web. 21 Feb. 2014. Reprinted with permission of the National Geographic Society from the book *From Eden to Exile: Unraveling Mysteries of the Bible*, 2007.

Clodd, Edward. *Magic in Names and Other Things*. London: Chapman & Hall, Ltd., 1920.

"Code of Hammurabi." Wikipedia.org. 14 Jan. 2015. Web. 14 Nov. 2014.

Codex Sinaiticus. Dr Constantin von Tischendorf. London: British Library.

"Codex Sanaiticus: Experience the oldest Bible." Codexsinaiticus.org. N.d. Web. 9 Mar. 2014.

Cohen, Doron B., ThD. *The Japanese Translations of the Hebrew Bible: History, Inventory and Analysis*. Leiden, Netherlands, and Boston: Brill Academic Publishers, Inc., 2013.

Colenso, John William. *The Pentateuch and the Book of Joshua Critically Examined*, Part VI. London: Longmans, Green, and Co., 1872.

Collins, Tina Rae. *The Gathering in the Last Days*. New York: M. F. Sohn Publications, 2012.

Collins, Tina Rae, PhD. *We Are Emmanuel: How Man Became God*. New York: M. F. Sohn Publications, 2014.

The Coming Into Day (*Book of the Dead*). "Chapter 125: The Judgement of the Dead." Richard-hooker.com. 1997. Web. 31 Dec. 2014 <http://richard-hooker.com/sites/worldcultures/EGYPT/BOD125.HTM>.

Confucius. "Lecture III, B.C. 500-300." Sacred-texts.com. Web. N.d. 7 Aug. 2014.

"Confucius - Biography." *The European Graduate School: Graduate & Postgraduate Studies*. Egs.edu. 1997-2012. Web. 7 June 2015.

"Contradictions in the Bible." *The Skeptic's Annotated Bible*. Skepticsannotatedbible.com. N.d. Web. 27 June 2014.

Conway, Moncure Daniel, ed. *Writings of Thomas Paine—Vol. 4 (1794-1796): the Age of Reason*. Public domain, 1796.

Conybeare, Frederick C. *Philo about the Contemplative Life*. Oxford: Clarendon Press, 1895.

Coots, John Frederick, and Haven Gillespie. "Santa Claus Is Coming to Town." Recorded by Harry Reser. Decca. 1934. Wikipedia.org. 16 Jan. 2015. Web. 23 Jan. 2015.

"Council of Trent." Wikipedia.org. 25 Dec. 2014. Web. 10 Jan. 2015.

Counihan, Patrick. "Irish priest proves Jesus never existed: Church bans him from teaching and speaking to media. *Signs of the Times*. Sott.net. 21 Jan. 2013. Web. 1 Mar. 2015.

Cox, George W., MA. *The Mythology of the Aryan Nations*, Vol. II. London: Longmans, Green, and Co., 1870.

Cutner, Herbert. *Jesus: God, Man or Myth? An Examination of the Evidence*. San Diego: Book Tree, 2000.

Daffodil. "Losing My Faith in Kansas, Part 2." Exchristian.net. 22 Apr. 2015. Web. 23 Apr. 2015.

Dahl, Ken. "Confusing Our Potential With Our Significance." Facebook.com. 11 Jan. 2015. Web. 13 Jan. 2015.

Dahl, Ken. *What Is God and How Does It Work? A Call For Honesty About Reality and Religion*. 2014.

Dalley, Stephanie. *Myths from Mesopotamia: Creation, the Flood, Gilgamesh, and Others*. Oxford; New York: Oxford University Press, 2000.

Dameron, James Palatine. *Spiritism; The Origin of All Religions*. San Francisco. Self-published, 1885.

DarkMatter2525. "Still the Good Guys?" Youtube.com. 12 May 2013. Web. 1 Feb. 2015.

DarkMatter2525. "You Send Yourself to Hell." Youtube.com. 10 Mar. 2014. Web. 1 Feb. 2015.

Darlison, Bill. *Gospel and the Zodiac: The Secret Truth about Jesus*. London/New York: Overlook Books, 2008. Kindle ed.

Darlison, Bill. "The New Age." UKUnitarians. Youtube.com. 26 Apr. 2014. Web. 24 Apr. 2015.

Darlison, Bill. "Two Thieves." *Roads for Traveling Souls*. Billdarlison.blogspot.com. 18 Apr. 2014. Web. 7 May 2015.

Davies, Stevan, tr. *The Secret Book of John* (*The Apocryphon of John*)." *The Gnostic Society Library*. Gnosis.org. 2005. Web. 18 Mar. 2015.

Deurer. "The Osiris Legend." Egyptartsite.com. 1996-2010. Web. 22 Jan. 2015.

Dimattei, Steven, PhD. "#27. Are Yahweh and El the same god OR different gods? (Gen 14:22, 17:1, 21:33; Ex 6:2-3; Ps 82:1 vs Deut 32:8-9; Ps 29:1, 89:6-8)." Contradictionsinthebible.com. 27 Jan. 2013. Web. 23 Mar. 2015.

Dimont, Max I. *Jews, God, and History*. 2nd ed. Ed. and rev. Ethel Dimont. New York: Signet Classics, 1990. Ebook.

"Diodorus Siculus." Britannica.com. 2015. Web. 16 Jan. 2015.

Doane, Thomas W. *Bible Myths and Their Parallels in Other Religions*. The Truth Seeker, 1882. Chapter VI.

Doane, Thomas W. *Bible Myths and Their Parallels in Other Religions Being a Comparison of the Old and New Testament Myths and Miracles with Those of Heathen Nations of Antiquity Considering Also Their Origin and Meaning*. USA: public domain, 1882, 1910.

Doherty, Earl. "The Jesus Puzzle." Canadian Humanist Publications, 1999.

Donahue, Bill. "What is the Crucifixion?" Hiddenmeanings.com. N.d. Web. 26 June 2014.

Doresse, Jean. *The Secret Books of the Egyptian Gnostics*. Vermont: Inner Traditions International, 1986.

Drews, Arthur. *Witnesses to the Historicity of Jesus*. Tr. Joseph McCabe. London: Watts, 1912.

Duckett, Craig Lee. "The World Simply Does Not Behave the Way Described in the Bible." *25 Reasons Why I Am No Longer a Christian*. 2007-2012. Web. 28 Aug. 2014.

Dujardin, Edouard. *Ancient History of the God Jesus*. London: Watts, 1938.

Dunn, Jimmy. "Yah (Lah), the Other Egyptian Moon God." N.d. Web. 13 Nov. 2014.

Dupuis, Charles François. *The Origin of All Religious Worship*. New Orleans, 1872.

"E. A. Wallis Budge." Wikipedia.org. 2014. Web. 12 Nov. 2014.

"Early 'Christians.'" Mountainman.com. N.d. Web. 20 Dec. 2014.

Easttom, William C. II. "Quotes About Hell." Tentmaker.org. 2014. Web. 14 Aug. 2014.

Eichenwald, Kurt. "The Bible: So Misunderstood, It's a Sin." Newsweek.com. 23 Dec. 2014. Web. 10 Jan. 2015.

Einstein, Albert. Obituary in *New York Times*. 19 April 1955.

Einstein, Albert. "Religion and Science." *New York Times Magazine*. 9 Nov. 1930.

Einstein, Albert. *The World as I See It*. New York: Philosophical Library, 1949.

Elmsley, Peter. *The Vatican Censors*. Oxford. N.d.

Encyclopaedia Biblica. London: Adam & Charles Black, 1880, 1899. Vols. II and III.

Encyclopedias: Their History Throughout the Ages. 1966.

Engelbach, Robert. "On the Sacred Path with Gilgamesh and Enkidu." Spiritofthescripture.com. 29 Jan. 2015. Web. 29 Jan. 2015.

Enns, Peter. "Brief Bible thought: is there resurrection from the dead in the Old Testament?" 9 Feb. 2015. Web. 26 Feb. 2015.

Euripides. Tr. Michael Cacoyannis. Play.

"Eusebius." Wikipedia.org. 12 Jan. 2015. Web. 25 Jan. 2015.

Eusebius. *The Church History*. Book 5. Section 28.

Eusebius. *Life of Constantine*, I, II, III, IV. Tr. Ernest Cushing Richardson. From *Nicene and Post-Nicene Fathers*, Second Series, Vol. 1. Ed. Philip Schaff and Henry Wace. Buffalo, NY: Christian Literature Publishing Co., 1890. Rev. and ed. for New Advent by Kevin Knight. Newadvent.org. 2009. Web. 9 Apr., 2015.

Eusebius. "Philo's Account of the Ascetics of Egypt." *Church History: Book II*, 17:10-24. Newadvent.org. Copyright 2009 by Kevin Knight. Web. 10 July 2014.

Eusebius. *Praeparatio Evangelica* (*Preparation for the Gospel*), Vol. 15. Tr. E. H. Gifford. Oxonii: Typographeo Academico/H. Frowde, 2903, 15.720.

"Evidence for the historical existence of Jesus Christ." Rationalwiki.org. N.d. Web. 19 Dec. 2014 <http://rationalwiki.org/wiki/Evidence_for_the_historical_existence_of_Jesus_Christ>.

"The Exodus." Wikipedia.org. 26 Jan. 2015. Web. 30 Jan. 2015.

"Facts about the Bible." Ministerbook.com. 2012. Web. 6 Nov. 2014 <http://ministerbook.com/topics/facts-about-bible/>.

Farb, Peter. *Word Play*. New York: Alfred A. Knopf, 1974.

Farley, John M., ed. *The Catholic Encyclopedia*. New York: Encyclopedia Press, Inc., 1913, Vols. I, III, VI, VII, VIII.

Farrar, Frederic W. *The Life of Christ*. London: Cassell, 1874.

"Father Eusebius-Forger." Christianity-Revealed.com. Also Jdstone.org. 2000-2014. Web. 30 Oct. 2014. 12 Nov. 2014.

Faulkner, Raymond O. *The Ancient Egyptian Coffin Texts*, I. Oxford: Aris & Phillips, 1973, 1974.

Faulkner, Raymond O. *The Ancient Egyptian Pyramid Texts*. Oxford: Clarendon Press, 1969.

Felix, Marcus Minucius. *Octavius*. Chapter XXIX. Newadvent.org. Copyright 2009 by Kevin Knight. Web. 12 Nov. 2014.

Felix, Marcus Minucius. *The Octavius of Minucius Felix*, Chapter XXIX. *Christian Classics Ethereal Library*. 2005. Web. 25 Aug. 2014 <http://www.ccel.org/ccel/schaff/anf04.iv.iii.xxix.html>.

Finkelstein, Israel, and Neil Asher Silberman. *The Bible Unearthed*. Simon and Schuster/Touchstone, 2002.

"The Fisherman Piping." *Aesop's Fables*. Tr. George Fyler Townsend. Classiclit.about.com. 2014. Web. 9 June 2014.

Fossum, Jarl. "The Myth of the Eternal Rebirth: Critical Notes on G.W. Bowersock, Hellenism in Late Antiquity." *Vigiliae Christianae* 53.3. 1999.

"Frank Sinatra's views on organized religion were decades ahead of his time." Deadstate.org. 29 Aug. 2014. Web. 8 Nov. 2014.

Frater, J. "The Hidden Meanings behind Fairy Tales." *Drama Start*. Drama-in-ecce.com. Nov. 2010. Web. 14 Nov. 2014.

Frazer, James G. *Adonis, Attis, Osiris: Studies in the History of Oriental Religion*. London: MacMillan and Co., 1906.

Frazer, James G. *The Golden Bough*. Collier, NY, 1963. London: Penguin Classics, 1996.

Freke, Timothy, and Peter Gandy. *The Jesus Mysteries*. New York: Harmony Books, 1999.

Fromm, Eric. *The Anatomy of Human Destructiveness*. New York: Holt, Rinehart & Winston, 1973.

Gabriel, Richard A. *Gods of Our Fathers: The Memory of Egypt in Judaism and Christianity*. Greenwood Publishing Group, 2002.

Gabriel, Yiannis. "The Other and Othering - A Short Introduction." *Stories, music, psychoanalysis, politics, reviews, the odd cooking recipe . . .* Yiannisgabriel.com. 10 Sept. 2012. Web. 12 Jan. 2015.

Gadamer, Hans-Georg. *Truth and Method*, 2nd ed., rev. ed. Tr. Joel Winsheimer and Donald G. Marshall. New York: Continuum Publishing Group, 2006.

Gaines, Janet Howe. "Lilith: Seductress, Heroine or Murderer?" *Bible History Daily*. Biblicalarchaeology.org. 4 Sept. 2012. Web. 20 June 2014.

Gardner, Laurence. *Bloodline of the Holy Grail: The Hidden Lineage of Jesus Revealed*. Rockport, MA: Element Books Ltd., 1997.

Gasparo, Guilia Sfameni. *Soteriology and Mystic Aspects in the Cult of Cybele and Attis*. Leiden: E. J. Brill, 1985.

Gately, Iain. *Drink: A Cultural History of Alcohol*. New York: Gotham Books, 2008.

"Gautama Buddha." Wikipedia.org. 18 Mar. 2015. Web. 18 Mar. 2015.

Gauvin, Marshall. "Did Jesus Christ Really Live?" *The Historical Library,* 1922. Infidels.org. N.d. Web. 27 Aug. 2014.

Gershwin, George and Ira. "It Ain't Necessarily So," 1935; performed by Louis Armstrong and Ella Fitzgerald in the opera "Porgy & Bess." Polygram Records, 1957.

Gibbon, Edward. *Rome*, Vols. II and III. Philadelphia, 1876.

Giles, J. A. *Hebrew and Christian Records*, Vol. II. Ann Arbor: University of Michigan Library, 1877.

Gilgamesh, Horus. "Obey Your Masters: Why Didn't Jesus Outlaw Slavery?" Awkwardmomentsbible.com. N.d. Web. 13 Aug. 2014.

Gill, N. S. "The God El." Ancienthistory.about.com. 2014. 11 Nov. 2014.

Gilmore, Ryan. "Ancient Confession Found: 'We Invented Jesus Christ.'" Uk.prweb.com. 8 Oct. 2013. Web. 11 Apr. 2015.

Giordano, Catherine. "Jesus Who? The Historical Record Gives No Clue." Catherinegiordano.hubpages.com. 12 July 2015. Web. 12 July 2015.

"(Give Me That) Old-Time Religion." Traditional gospel song. 1873. Written down by Charles Davis Tillman. 1889. Wikipedia.org. 20 Jan. 2015. Web. 23 Jan. 2015.

Gmirkin, Russell E. *Gerossus and Genesis, Manetho and Exodus: Hellenistic Histories and the Date of the Pentateuch*. New York/London: T & T Clark International, 2006.

"Gnosis." Dictionary.com. 2014. Web. 12 Nov. 2014.

"The Gnostic Jesus: Sethian Creation." Gnostic-jesus.com. N.d. Web. 19 Mar. 2015.

"Gnostic Scriptures and Fragments: The Acts of John." *The Gnostic Society Library*. 1994-2014. Web. 21 Nov. 2014 <gnosis.org/library/actjohn.htm>.

Goelet, D. Ogden. *The Egyptian Book of the Dead: The Book of Going Forth by Day - The Complete Papyrus of Ani Featuring Integrated Text and Full-Color Images*. San Francisco: Chronical Books, 2008.

Goldziher, Ignaz. *Muslim Studies*. Ed. S. M. Stern. Tr. C. R. Barber and S. M. Stern. Chicago: Aldine Publishing Company, 1966.

Gordon, D. H., and N. L. Torrey. *History in the Encyclopedia*. New York, 1947.

Gordon, Richard Stuart. *The Encyclopedia of Myths and Legends*. London: Headline Book Publishing, 1993.

"Gospel of the Hebrews." Wikipedia.org. 18 Jan. 2015. Web. 24 Jan. 2015.

The Gospel of the Holy Twelve. Tr. G. J. R. Ouseley. Thenazareneway.com. N.d. Web. 19 May 2014.

"The Gospel of Truth." Tr. Robert M. Grant. *The Gnostic Society Library*. N.d. Web. 11 Jan. 2015 <http://gnosis.org/naghamm/got.html>.

"Gospel of Truth." Wikipedia.org. 5 Oct. 2014. Web. 11 Jan. 2015.

"The Gospel Story Quiz." Exchristian.net. N.d. Web. 29 Dec. 2014 <http://www.exchristian.net/3/>.

Graham, Lloyd M. *Deceptions and Myths of the Bible*. New York: Bell Publishing Company and Skyhorse Publishing, 1979.

Grant, Robert M. *Gnosticism*. New York: Harper & Brothers, 1961.

Graves, Kersey. *Bible of Bibles*. Kila, MT: Kessinger Publishing.

Graves, Kersey. *The World's Sixteen Crucified Saviors*. New York: University Books, 1971.

Graves, Kersey. *The World's Sixteen Crucified Saviors*. "Address to the Clergy," 1875. *The Secular Web: A Drop of Reason in a Pool of Confusion*. Infidels.org. Web. 9 Sept. 2014.

Graves, Kersey. *The World's Sixteen Crucified Saviors: Or, Christianity Before Christ*. Library of Alexandria, Chapter 17. *The Secular Web: A Drop of Reason in a Pool of Confusion*. Infidels.org, 1995-2014. Web. 12 Nov. 2014.

Gray, John. *The Legacy of Canaan*. Dead Sea Scroll fragment 4Q120. Rockefeller Museum, Jerusalem.

Gray, John. *The Legacy of Canaan*. Leiden, Netherlands: E. J. Brill, 1957.

Gray, John. *The Legacy of Canaan: The Ras Shamra Texts and Their Relevance to the Old Testament*. Leiden: E. J. Brill, 1965.

"Great Year." *Aerospace Science & Technology Dictionary*. Hq.nasa.gov. NASA SP-7, 1965. Web. 21 Dec. 2014.

"Greek/Hebrew Definitions: Strong's #4325: *mayim*." Bibletools.org. 1992-2015. Web. 28 Jan. 2015.

"Haides." Theoi.com. N.d. Web. 7 Apr. 2014.

The Hall of Records. "John Allegro: Who Was Jesus?" 17 Apr. 2009. Web. 30 Jan. 2015 <https://www.youtube.com/watch?v=w8PDt2IKS4k>.

Hamilton, Edith. "Phoebus Apollo." *Mythology*. New York: Hachette Digital, Inc., 2012. Ebook.

Hardwicke, Herbert Julius. *The Popular Faith Unveiled*. London, 1884.

Hardwicke, William W. *The Evolution of Man: His Religious Systems, and Social Ethics*. London: Watts & Co., 1899.

Harpur, Tom. *The Pagan Christ*. Toronto: Thomas Allen Publishers, 2004.

Harris, Sam, PhD. "Sam Harris demolishes Christianity." Youtube.com. 20 Jan. 2012. Web. 7 Feb. 2015.

Harris, Sam, PhD. "Sam Harris - Morality and the Christian God." Atheism-is-Unstoppable. Youtube.com. 30 Nov. 2013. Web. 31 Jan. 2015.

Harris, Stephen L. *The New Testament*, 6th ed. Boston: McGraw Hill, 2009.

Harvey, Alex, and Larry Collins. "Delta Dawn." 1972. Song.

Hávamál. Poetic Edda. Stanzas 137-163.

"*Hávamál*." Wikipedia.org. 4 Mar. 2015. Web. 15 Apr. 2015.

Haven. Based on Stephen King's *The Colorado Kid* (2005). 2010-present. TV series.

Hefner, Alan G. "Baal." *Encyclopedia Mythica*. Pantheon.org. 3 Mar. 1997. Rev. 11 Jan. 2004. Web. 31 Dec. 2014.

Henry, John, ThD. "Jesus = 888." Reason.landmarkbiblebaptist.net. N.d. Web. 10 June 2014.

Herberman, Charles, PhD, LLD, et al., eds. *The Catholic Encyclopedia: An International Work of Reference on the Constitution, Doctrine, Discipline, and History of the Catholic Church*, Vol. I. New York: Robert Appleton Company, 1907.

"Hercules." Wikipedia. org. 20 Oct. 2014. Web. 12 Nov. 2014.

"Hercules (constellation)." Wikipedia.org. 12 Mar. 2015. Web. 22 Mar. 2015.

Hermes." *Hermograph Press*. Hermograph.com. 2015. Web. 17 Apr. 2015.

Herodotus. Vol. 8. Tr. A. D. Godley. Cambridge, MA: Harvard University Press, 1920.

Herodotus. Book II. Chapter 36.

Herzog, Ze'ev. "Deconstructing the walls of Jericho." Haaretz.com. 29 Oct. 1999. Web. 1 June 2014.

Higgins, Godfrey. *Anacalypsis, an Attempt to Draw Aside the Veil of the Saitic Esis,* Vol. II. London: Longman, et al., 1836.

Higgins, Godfrey. *Anacalypsis: An Attempt to Draw Aside the Veil, or The Saitic Esis*, Vols. I, II, III. London: J. Burns, 1878.

Hinson, Curtis. Message to the author. 12 Jan. 2015.

"History embalmed: Aten." Siteseen Ltd. July 2014. Web. 31 Jan. 2015.

"History of Circumcision." D.umn.edu. 21 Dec. 2004. Web. 31 Jan. 2015 <http://www.d.umn.edu/~mcco0322/history.htm>.

Hitler, Adolph. Speech on 12 April 1922. Ed. Norman H. Baynes. *The Speeches of Adolf Hitler*. April 1922-August 1939, Vol. 1. Oxford University Press, 1942.

Hitler's religious beliefs and fanaticism (Selected quotes from Mein Kampf). Comp. Jim Walker. 28 Nov. 1996. Ed. 7 July 2001 <http://www.nobeliefs.com/hitler.htm>.

Hooke, S. H. *Middle Eastern Mythology*. Harmondsworth: Penguin Books Ltd., 1963.

Houck, C. M. "Jonah and the Whale Myth." *Time Frames and Taboo Data Blog*. Timeframesandtaboodata.com. 2011. Web. 18 June 2014.

The Human Odyssey. Facebook.com. 19 Oct. 2014. Web. 7 Nov. 2014.

Hunt, Michal. "The Many Names of God." Agapebiblestudy.com. 2003. Web. 13 Nov. 2014.

"Hymn to Amen." Chapter XII. "Egyptian Hymns to the Gods." *The Literature of the Ancient Egyptians*. Wisdomlib.org. 5 Feb. 2011. Web. 21 May 2015.

Index Expurgatorius Vaticanus. Ed. R. Gibbings. Dublin, 1837.

Ingersoll, Robert G. "The Liberty of Man, Woman, and Child." *Superstition and Other Essays*. Prometheus Books, 2004.

Inman, Thomas, MD. *Ancient Faiths and Modern: A Dissertation upon Worships, Legends and Divinities in Central and Western Asia, Europe, and Elsewhere, Before the Christian Era, Showing Their Relations To Religious Customs As They Now Exist*. Vol. II. London: Trubner & Co; New York: J. W. Bouton, 1876.

"Is the original Bible still in existence?" Gotquestions.org. 2002-2014. Web. 20 Nov. 2014 <http://www.gotquestions.org/original-Bible.html>.

"Its [sic] written in the stars." Bibliodac.wordpress.com. 16 July 2014. Web. 22 Mar. 2015.

Jackson, John G. *Pagan Origins of the Christ Myth*. Cranford, NJ: American Atheist Press, 1989.

Jacobovici, Simcha. "Jesus' Marriage to Mary the Magdalene Is Fact, Not Fiction." *The Blog*. Huffingtonpost.com. 26 Nov. 2014. Web. 27 Nov. 2014.

Jastrow, Morris. *The Religion of Babylonia and Assyria*. Boston: Ginn & Company, 1898.

Jefferson, Thomas. Letter to John Adams. 11 Apr. 1823.

Jehovah Encyclopedia Britannica. Vol. 12. 1958 edition.

Jeremias, Joachim. *The Parables of Jesus*, rev. ed. London: SCM Press, 1972.

Jerome. *Commentary on Ephesians 3*.

"Jesus: God, Man or Myth by Herb Cutner." Stellarhousepublishing.com. 2015. Web. 25 May 2015.

"Jesus Is the Sun God." Hiddenmeanings.com. N.d. Web. 27 Aug. 2014 <http://www.hiddenmeanings.com/supernova.html>.

"Job was a type of Christ." *Catholic Radio Dramas*. Catholicradiodramas.com. 2014. Web. 16 Mar. 2014.

Johnson, Edwin. *Antiqua Mater: A Study of Christian Origins*. London: Trubner & Co., Ludgate Hill; Edinburgh and London: Ballantine Press, 1887.

Jones, Stephen E., PhD. *Creation's Jubilee*. Fridley, MN: God's Kingdom Ministries, 2009.

Jordan, James B. "Biblical Horizons: #133: 153 Large Fish." Biblicalhorizons.com. Sept. 2000. Web. 25 Mar. 2014.

Joseph, Peter, and D. M. Murdock. *The Zeitgeist Sourcebook, Part 1: The Greatest Story Ever Told: Zeitgeist the Movie*. 2010.

Josephus, Flavius. *Antiquities of the Jews*, 1, 1, 3; 2, 16; 3, 7, 7; 14, 12, and Note.

Kaler, Michael. *Paul and Pseudepigraphy*. Ed. Stanley E. Porter and Gregory P. Fewster. Leiden, Netherlands/Boston: Brill, 2013.

Keeler, Bronson. *A Short History of the Bible*. California: Health Research, 1965.

King, Edward. *Antiquities of Mexico*, Vol. VI. London: 1830-31, 1848.

King, Max R. *The Spirit of Prophecy*. Colorado Springs: Bimillennial Press, 2002.

Kramer, Samuel Noah. *History Begins at Sumer*. Garden City, NY: Doubleday, 1959.

Kruger, C. Baxter, PhD. *Jesus and the Undoing of Adam*. Jackson, MS: Perichoresis Press, 2001.

Kuhn, Alvin Boyd. *Who is this King of Glory?* New Jersey: Academy Press, 1944.

Kuhn, Alfred Boyd, PhD. *Who Is This King of Glory? A Critical Study of the Christos-Messiah Tradition*. San Diego: The Book Tree, 2007.

Lane, Eugene N. *Cybele, Attis and Related Cults*. Leiden, Netherlands: E. J. Brill, 1996.

Larrington, Carolyne, tr. *The Poetic Edda*. Oxford World's Classics, 1999.

Larson, Martin A. *The Story of Christian Origins*. Washington: Village, 1977.

Lataster, Raphael. "Did historical Jesus really exist? The evidence just doesn't add up." Washingtonpost.com. 13 Dec. 2014. Web. 19 Dec. 2014.

Laubach, Douglas L. *The Parallax from Hell: Satan's Critique of Organized Religion & Other Essays*. Bloomington, IN: iUniverse, 2012.

Leedom, Tim., ed. *The Book Your Church Doesn't Want You to Read*. Dubuque, IA: Kendall/Hunt, 1993.

Leeming, David Adams, PhD. *Mythology: The Voyage of the Hero*. New York: Oxford University Press, 1998.

Leick, Gwendolyn. *The A to Z of Mesopotamia*. Scarecrow Press, 2010.

"The Letters of Jerome." *Library of the Fathers*. Oxford Movement, 1833-45, Vol. 5.

Levinson, Bernard M. *Deuteronomy and the Hermeneutics of Legal Innovation*. Oxford: Oxford University Press, 1997.

Lichtheim, Miriam. *Ancient Egyptian Literature: Volume I: The Old and Middle Kingdoms*. 1980.

"List of Christian denominations." Wikipedia.org. 23 Jan. 2015. Web. 22 June 2014.

Loftus, John W. "Asherah, the Israelite Goddess." *Debunking Christianity*. Debunkingchristianity.blogspot.com. 6 Aug. 2013. Web. 31 Dec. 2014.

Loftus, John W. "Why I Am An Atheist." *Debunking Christianity*. Debunkingchristianity.blogspot.com. 5 June 2013. Web. 16 June 2014.

Logan, Mitchell. *Christian Mythology Unveiled in a Series of Lectures*. Kessinger Publishing, 2004.

Longman, Tremper III, and Raymond B. Dillard. *An Introduction to the Old Testament*, 2nd ed. Grand Rapids, MI: Zondervan, 2006.

Lundy, John P. *Monumental Christianity or The Art and Symbolism of the Primitive Church*. New York: J. W. Bouton, 1876.

Lyons, Craig M., MsD, DD, MDiv. "The Evolution of the Jesus Myth." *Bet Emet Ministries*. Firstnewtestament.com. N.d. Web. 4 June 2014.

Lyons, Craig M., MsD, DD, MDiv. "Finding the Truth about the Christ in the 'Jesus Story' of the New Testament." *Bet Emet Ministries*. Christianityasamysteryreligion.com. N.d. Web. 11 June 2014.

Lyons, Craig M., MsD, DD, MDiv. "Gnosticism: What Did Gnostics Believe?" *Bet Emet Ministries*. Firstnewtestament.com. N.d. Web. 4 June 2014.

Lyons, Craig M., MsD, DD, MDiv. "Jesus Turned Water into Wine at the Wedding Feast at Cana: Truth or Sun-Myth Retold?" *Bet Emet Ministries*. Christianityasamysteryreligion.com. N.d. Web. 31 May 2014.

Lyons, Craig M., MsD, DD, MDiv. "Marcion and the Marcionites." *Bet Emet Ministries*. Firstnewtestament.com. N.d. Web. 5 June 2014.

Lyons, Craig M., MsD, DD, MDiv. "The Therapeutae and the Essenes as the Earliest Christians." *Bet Emet Ministries*. Firstnewtestament.com. N.d. Web. 4 June 2014.

MacDonald, Dennis R. *The Homeric Epic and the Gospel of Mark*. New Haven: Yale University Press, 2000.

Mack, Burton L. *Who Wrote the New Testament? The Making of the Christian Myth*. San Francisco: HarperOne, 1996.

MacKensie, Donald A. *Myths of Babylonia and Assyria* (1915). "Myths of Tammuz and Ishtar." Chapter V. Sacred-texts.com. N.d. Web. 15 Nov. 2014 <http://www.sacred-texts.com/ane/mba/mba11.htm>.

Malvern, Marjorie. *Venus in Sackcloth*. Carbondale: Southern Illinois University Press, 1975.

Mangan, Lucy. "Bible Hunters: the Search for Bible Truth; The Good Wife - TV Review." 14 Feb. 2014. Web. 22 Nov. 2014 <http://www.theguardian.com/tv-and-radio/2014/feb/14/bible-hunters-the-good-wife-tv-review>.

Manson, Marilyn. "Cupid Carries a Gun." Opening theme song for TV show *Salem*. Genius.com. 2015. Web. 11 June 2015.

"Marcus Minucius Felix." Wikipedia.org. 30 June 2015. Web. 25 Aug. 2014.

Mark, Joshua J. "Alexander the Great." *Ancient History Encyclopedia*. Ancient.eu.com. 14 Nov. 2013. Web. 6 June 2014.

Mark, Joshua J. "Inanna." *Ancient History Encyclopedia*. Ancient.eu. 15 Oct. 2010. Web. 23 Apr. 2015.

Mark, Joshua J. "Sargon of Akkad." *Ancient History Encyclopedia*. Ancient.eu.com. 2 Sept. 2009. Web. 6 June 2014.

Mark2pt0. "Denial and Jealousy." Exchristian.net. 14 Apr. 2015. Web. 15 Apr. 2015.

Marra, John. Facebook.com. 24 June 2015. Web. 24 June 2015.

Martin, George R. R. *A Dance with Dragons (HBO Tie-in Edition): A Song of Ice and Fire: Book Five: A Novel*. New York: Bantam Books, 2015.

Martin, William. *The Parent's Tao Te Ching: A New Interpretation: Ancient Advice for Modern Parents*. New York: Marlowe & Company, 1999.

Martone, Robert. "Scientists Discover Children's Cells Living in Mothers' Brains: the connection between mother and child is ever deeper than thought." Scientificamerican.com. 12 Dec. 2012. Web. 16 Nov. 2014.

Martyr, Justin. *Dialogue with Trypho*, 67.

Martyr, Justin. *The First Apology*. Newadvent.org. Copyright 2009 by Kevin Knight. Web. 31 May 2014. 18 June 2014. 29 Oct. 2014. 12 Nov. 2014. 26 Jan. 2015, 22 Mar. 2015.

Martyr, Justin. "Quaest," Ch. 24.

Maspero, G. *Popular Myths of Ancient Egypt*. New York: University Books, 1967.

Massey, Gerald. *Ancient Egypt: Light of the World*, II. Whitefish, MT: Kessinger Publishing, 2002.

Massey, Gerald. *Gerald Massey's Lectures*. New York: A&B Publishers, 1992.

Massey, Gerald. *Gerald Massey's Published Lectures*. The "Logia of the Lord;" or, The Pre-Christian Sayings Ascribed to Jesus the Christ, No. 27. Gerald-massey.org.uk. *Gnostic and Historic Christianity*. N.d. Web. 12 Nov. 2014.

Massey, Gerald. *The Natural Genesis*, Vol. 2. New York: Cosimo, Inc., 2007.

Matthews, Victor Harold. "Judges and Ruth." *New Cambridge Bible Commentary*. Cambridge University Press, 2004.

"Maveth." Strong's H4194. Blueletterbible.org. 2015. Web. 12 May 2015.

Maxwell, Jordan. "Similarity between jesus and mithras and sun." Youtube.com. 9 Mar. 2008. Web. 11 Sept. 2014.

"Men have nipples because every fetus is a female until the Y chromosome kicks in." Omgfacts.com. 3 Mar. 2014. Web. 8 Nov. 2014.

Mendham, Joseph, and J. Duncan. *The Literary Policy of the Church of Rome,* 2nd ed. London, 1830, 1840.

Mercer, Samuel. *The Pyramid Texts*. London: Longmans, Green & Co., 1952.

Mercer, Samuel A. B. *The Pyramid Texts*. London: Longmans, Green & Co., 1952 <www.sacred-texts.com/egy/pyt/index.htm>.

Mettinger, Tryggve N. D. *The Riddle of Resurrection: "Dying and Rising Gods" in the Ancient Near East*. Philadelphia: Coronet Books, 2001.

Meyer, Marvin W. *The Ancient Mysteries: A Sourcebook of Sacred Texts*. Philadelphia: University of Pennsylvania Press, 1987.

Miles, Clement A. *Christmas Customs and Traditions*. New York: Dover, 1976.

Miles, Kathy. "Draco the Dragon." Starryskies.com. 1995-2008. Web. 22 Mar. 2015.

Miller, Adam. "Psychedelic Messiah." Youtube.com. 3 Nov. 2014. Web. 17 Nov. 2014 <https://www.youtube.com/watch?v=Rbflahul_vM#t=14>.

Miller, Robert J., ed. *The Gospel of Thomas*. Tr. Stephen Patterson and Marvin Meyer. *The Complete Gospels: Annotated Scholars Version*. Polebridge Press, 1992, 1994.

Mintz, Josh. "Were Jews ever really slaves in Egypt, or is Passover a myth?" *Jewish World Blogger*. 26 Mar. 2012. Web. 23 Mar. 2015. Reprinted on haaretz.com. 24 March 2015 (Nisan 4, 5775).

"Mircea Eliade 'From Primitives to Zen': 'Who Can Say Whence It All Came and How Creation Happened?'" *Myths of Creation and of Origin: Myths of the Creation of the World*. Mircea-eliade.com. N.d. Web. 22 Dec. 2014.

Moeller, Bill. "The shocking discovery about evangelical Christianity that I made after becoming a father." Salon.com (originally appeared at AlterNet). 8 Aug. 2014. Web. 10 Aug. 2014.

Moore, A. "8 Biblical Concepts and Stories That Originated Outside of The Bible." Atlantablackstar.com. 3 Feb. 2014. Web. 13 Aug. 2014.

"Moses." Wikipedia.org. 22 Jan. 2015. Web. 30 Jan. 2015.

Mosteller, Angie. "Who Is Santa and What Does He Have to Do with Christmas?" Crosswalk.com. 12 Dec. 2011. Web. 4 Dec. 2014.

"Mot (Semitic god)." Wikipedia.org. 20 Jan. 2015. Web. 6 Mar. 2015.

Muller, Bernard D. "Revelation of John, the original Jewish version: Apocalypse composition, dating & authorship. N.d. Web. 2 Dec. 2014 <http://historical-jesus.info/rjohn.html>.

Müller, Max, MA. *Chips from a German Workshop, Vol. 2: Essays on Mythology, Traditions, and Customs*. New York: Charles Schribner and Company, 1872.

Murdock, D. M. *Christ in Egypt: The Horus-Jesus Connection*. Seattle: Stellar House Publishing, 2009.

Murdock, D. M. *Did Moses Exist? The Myth of the Israelite Lawgiver*. Seattle: Stellar House Publishing, 2014.

Murdock, D. M. *The Gospel According to Acharya S.* Seattle: Stellar House Publishing, 2009.

Murdock, D. M. "Jesus Christ is a mythical figure." Freethoughtnation.com. 28 Oct. 2014. Web. 26 Feb. 2015.

Murdock, D. M. (Acharya S). "Were George Washington and Thomas Jefferson Jesus Mythicists?" Truthbeknown.com. 2015. Web. 4 July 2015.

Neumann, Erich. *The Origins and History of Consciousness*. London: Routledge, 1999.

New Catholic Encyclopedia (NCE). New York: McGraw-Hill, 2002. "Gospel of John," 1080; NCE, Vol. XII.

Newton, Richard Heber. *Sermons in All Souls monthly, 1888-1891*. East Hampton, NY.

Neyrey, Jerome. Weston School of Theology. Cambridge, Massachusetts. "The Four Gospels." *U.S. News & World Report*, 10 Dec. 1990.

Nottingham, Ted. "The Mystery of the Essenes." Youtube.com. 15 Nov. 2010. Web. 30 Jan. 2015.

Nugent, Tony, PhD. "Jewish angels and Roman gods: The ancient mythological origins of Christmas." Interview with Valerie Tarico. Salon.com. 12 Dec 2014. Web. 26 Dec. 2014.

Nugent, Tony, PhD. "'Many of These Gods Come From Stars': The Fascinating True Story of Angels, Virgin Birth and Jesus: A religious scholar shares his thoughts on the mythologies of Christmas." Interview with Valerie Tarico. Alternet.org. 10 Dec. 2014. Web. 26 June 2015.

O'Callaghan, Jonathan. "'Jesus NEVER existed': Writer finds no mention of Christ in 126 historical texts and says he was a 'mythical character'." Dailymail.com. 1 Oct. 2014. Web. 1 Mar. 2015.

Ochs, Carol. *Behind the Sex of God*. Boston: Beacon Press, 1977.

"Odin's Discovery of the Runes." *Norse Mythology for Smart People*. Norse-mythology.org. 2012-2015. Web. 15 Apr. 2015.

Origen. *Comments on Ezekiel*, 8:12; quoted by Richard Carrier.

Origen. *Contra Celsus*, Book 1, Chapters IX, X. Newadvent.org. Copyright 2009 by Kevin Knight. Web. 29 Oct. 2014.

"Origen." Wikipedia.org. 21 Feb. 2015. Web. 4 Mar. 2015.

"Osiris." Wikipedia.org. 18 Jan. 2015. Web. 30 Jan. 2015.

"Osiris & Christianity - The Christian Adoption of Egyptian Iconography, Symbolism, and Myth." Dir. Roel Oostra. CTC/Cresset Communications. 2003. Youtube.com. 12 June 2013. Web. 2 Jan. 2015. Film.

"Osiris & Horus." Ambrosiasociety.org. 2009. Web. 7 Nov. 2014.

Osman, Ahmed. "Out of Egypt: Christian Roots in the Alexandrian Cult of Serapis." Dwij.org. 2001. Web. 19 Dec. 2014 <http://dwij.org/forum/amarna/8_serapis_and_christianity.htm>.

Ovid. *Fast*, II.

Pagan Origins of the Christ Myth. Pocm.info. N.d. Web. 16 Jan. 2015 <http://pocm.info/pagan_ideas_god.html>.

Pagels, Elaine. *The Gnostic Gospels*. New York: Random House, 1979.

Pagels, Elaine. *The Gnostic Paul; Gnostic Exegesis of the Pauline Letters*. New York: Continuum International Publishing Group, 1992.

Pagels, Elaine Hiesey. *The Gnostic Paul: Gnostic Exegesis of the Pauline Letters*. Philadelphia: Fortress Press, 1975.

Paine, Thomas. *Age of Reason*. Part 1, Section 4.

Paine, Thomas. *Age of Reason* (1796). From *The Writings of Thomas Paine*, Vol. IV. Ed. Moncure Daniel Conway. Part I, Chapter II, "Of Missions and Revelations."

Paine, Thomas. *The Complete Religious and Theological Works of Thomas Paine*.

Palmer, A. Smythe. *Babylonian Influence on the Bible and Popular Beliefs*. London: David Nutt, 1897.

Palmer, Jim. Status update. Facebook.com. 14 Aug. 2014. Web. 14 Aug. 2014.

Parsons, Albert R. *New Light from the Great Pyramid*. New York: Metaphysical Publishing Company, 1893.

Pausanias. *Description of Greece*. Tr. W.H.S. Jones, et al. New York: G. P. Putnam's Sons, 1926, 4.36.7.

"Philo." Wikipedia.org. 15 Jan. 2015. Web. 20 Jan. 2015.

Platt, Rutherford H. Jr. *The Forgotten Books of Eden* (1926). Chapter 23. Footnotes. Sacred-texts.com. N.d. Web. 11 Mar. 2015.

Plutarch, *Isis & Osiris*, 65:387C.

Plutarch. *Lives*, Vol. 2. New York: Random House, 2001.

Plutarch. *Lives of the Noble Grecians and Romans*. The Original Classic Edition.

Plutarch, *Moralia*. Tr. Frank Cole Babbitt. Cambridge, MA: Harvard University Press, and London: William Heinemann Ltd., 1936.

Plutarch. *Plutarch's Miscellanies and Essays*, Vol. 3, ed. William W. Goodwin. Boston: Little, Brown and Company, 1889.

Potter's Aeschylus. "Prometheus Chained." Last stanza.

"The Prayer of the Apostle Paul." Tr. Dieter Mueller. *The Nag Hamadi Library*. Bibliotecapleyades.net. N.d. Web. 18 June 2015.

Prescott, Greg, MS, ed. "The Sun, Sunspots and Consciousness." *In5d Esoteric Metaphysical Spiritual Database*. In5d.com. 25 Jan. 2015. Web. 8 Mar. 2015.

Price, Robert M., PhD. "He Really Is Santa Claus." Robertmprice.mindvendor.com. 1996, 2007. Web. 10 Apr. 2015.

Price, Robert M., PhD. "Jonathan Z. Smith: Drudgery Divine. On the Comparison of Early Christianities and the Religions of Late Antiquity," *Journal for Higher Criticism*. Institute of Higher Critical Studies. Spring 1996. Web. 22 Mar. 2015 <depts.drew.edu/jhc/jzsmith.html>.

Price, Robert M., PhD. "New Testament Narrative as Old Testament Midrash." *Theological Publications*. Robertmprice.mindvendor.com. 2004. Web. 25 June 2014.

Price, Robert M., PhD. "Pagan Parallels to Christ Part 1." Tony Sobrado. Youtube.com. 30 June 2012. Web. 29 Apr. 2015.

Pseudo-Callisthenes, I.30–33.

Quint, Alyssa. "In the Beginning, the Prophet Was Poet." Beliefnet: Inspiration, Spirituality, Faith." Beliefnet.com. N.d. Web. 25 June 2014.

"Quran on Human Embryonic Development." Scienceislam.com. N.d. Web. 15 Nov. 2014.

Rahmouni, Aicha. *Divine Epithets in the Ugaritic Alphabetic Texts*. Tr. J. N. Ford. Leiden: E. J. Brill, 2008.

Rainbow Warrior. "Brahma and Abraham: Divine Covenants of Common Origin." Academia.edu. 2014. Web. 25 June 2014.

Randolph, Adam. "The Resurrection of Paul." Unpublished paper. 2014. Viewed 30 Aug. 2014.

Rankin, David. *Tertullian and the Church*. New York: Cambridge University Press, 1995.

Ravage, Marcus Eli. "A Real Case Against Jews." *Century Magazine*. New York: The Century Co., 1928. Vol. 115, No. 3, Jan. 1928.

Rawson, Philip. *The Art of Tantra*. Greenwich, CT: New York Graphic Society, 1973.

Rawson, Philip. *Erotic Art of the East*. New York: G. P. Putnam's Sons, 1968.

"Real Proof that Jesus was NOT real." Maythetruthbeknown. Youtube.com. 28 May 2008. Web. 10 Mar. 2015.

Rehmus, Ed. "The Cream of Christ." Ecphorizer.com. N.d. Web. 10 Jan. 2015.

"Religion, Bible, Can you handle the Truth? (Must Watch)." Youtube.com. 10 Oct. 2013. Web. 20 Dec. 2014 <https://www.youtube.com/watch?v=G4VRnXPDuXs>.

Remsburg, John E. "Silence of Contemporary Writers." *The Christ*. Positiveatheism.org. 2000. Web. 27 Aug. 2014 <http://www.positiveatheism.org/hist/rmsbrg02.htm>.

Revelation. "Number 30 In the Bible | What's the Significance of Age 30 in the Bible?" Revelation.co. 6 Jan. 2013. Web. 12 Nov. 2014.

"Revelation (Book of): Jewish Origin." *Jewish Encyclopedia: The unedited full-text of the 1906 Jewish Encyclopedia*. Jewishencyclopedia.com. N.d. Web. 2 Dec. 2014.

Reyes, E. Christopher. *In His Name*, Vols. 3 and 4. Bloomington, IN: Trafford Publishing. 2014.

Rigveda. Tr. A. L. Basham. *The Wonder That Was India*. London, 1954.

"Rigveda." Wikipedia.org. 21 Dec. 2014. Web. 22 Dec. 2014.

Roberts, Alexander, and James Donaldson, eds. *Ante-Nicene Christian Library*, Vol. 15. Edinburgh: T & T Clark, 1870.

Roberts, Alexander, and James Donaldson, eds. *Ante-Nicene Fathers*, Vol. III. New York: Charles Scribner's Sons, 1903.

Roberts, Alexander, and James Donaldson, eds. *Ante-Nicene Fathers: Translations of the Writings of the Fathers down to A.D. 325*, Vol. I. Buffalo: The Christian Literature Publishing Company, 1885.

Robinson, B. A. "Translation Errors and Forgeries in the Bible." Religioustolerance.org. 3 Oct. 2003. Web. 22 June 2015.

Robinson, James M., ed. *The Gospel of Philip*. Tr. Thomas O. Lamdin. *The Gnostic Society Library*. San Francisco: HarperCollins, 1990 <http://gnosis.org/naghamm/gthlamb.html>.

Robinson, James M., ed. *The Gospel of Philip*. Tr. Wesley W. Isenberg. *The Gnostic Society Library*. San Francisco: HarperCollins, 1990 <http://gnosis.org/naghamm/gop.html>.

Robinson, James M., ed. *The Gospel of Thomas*. Tr. Thomas O. Lamdin. *The Gnostic Society Library*. San Francisco: HarperCollins, 1990 <http://gnosis.org/naghamm/gthlamb.html>.

Roush, Doug. "The Code of Hammurabi." *Truth Magazine*. Vol. XLV: 1. January 4, 2001.

Rowling, J. K. *Harry Potter*. Warner Brothers. 2001-2011. Film.

Rudd, Steve. "Rejected Books." Bible.ca. N.d. Web. 24 Jan. 2015.

Runyon, Michael. "How I Figured Out Christianity Is Not Real." Exchristian.net. 11 Nov. 2013. Web. 29 Dec. 2014.

Russell, Brian D. *The Song of the Sea: The Date of Composition and Influence of Exodus 15:1-21*. New York: Peter Lang, 2007.

Rutherford, Robert. Facebook.com. 1 Feb. 2015. Web. 1 Feb. 2015.

Rutherford, Robert. Photos. Facebook.com. Web. 6 Jan. 2015.

S., Carl. "Everyone Is Lacking In Faith." Exchristian.net. 24 Jan. 2015. Web. 24 Jan. 2015.

S., Carl. "Three Wise Men and One Wise Guy." Exchristian.net. 13 Jan. 2015. Web. 14 Jan. 2015.

St. Hilary of Poitiers. *De Trinitate*, Book 2, Paragraph 2, Line 6.

Salem. TV series. Created by Brannon Braga and Adam Simon. 2014-present. Season 2, Episode 9, "Wages of Sin." 31 May 2015.

Sanford, John A. *Mystical Christianity: A Psychological Commentary on the Gospel of John*. New York: The Crossroad Publishing Company, 1994.

Scaruffi, Piero. "Jesus and Christianity." Scaruffi.com. 2010. Web. 3 Jan. 2015.

Schmidt, Orlando P. *A Self-verifying Chronological History of Ancient Egypt*. Ohio: George C. Shaw, 1900.

Schmidt, Wilhelm. *The Origin of the Idea of God*. 1912.

Schniedewind, William M., and Joel H. Hunt. *A Primer on Ugaritic: Language, Culture and Literature*. Cambridge: Cambridge University Press, 2007.

Schopenhauer, Arthur. "Arthur Schopenhauer Quote." Brainyquotes.com. N.d. Web. 10 April 2015.

Segal, Norman. *The Good News of the Kingdoms*. Australia, 1995.

Seidensticker, Bob. "Polytheism in the Bible." Patheos.com. 13 Feb. 2013. Web. 8 Feb. 2015.

"Shemesh." *My Hebrew Dictionary: Learn Hebrew Online*. Dictionary.co.il. 2015. Web. 16 June 2015.

Shore, John. "If hell is real, then love has no meaning." *John Shore Trying God's Patience Since 1958*." Patheos.com. 7 Jan. 2015. Web. 8 Jan. 2015.

Siculus, Diodorus. *The Antiquities of Egypt*. New Brunswick, NJ: Transaction Publishers, Rutgers, 1990, 1.94.

Siculus, Diodorus. *Library of History*, 1.94. Oldfather, C. H. *Diodorus of Sicily, The Library of History*. Books I - ii. 34. Loeb Classical Library #279, 1933, 1998.

Singer, Michelle. "Letters Reveal Mother Teresa's Secret." Cbsnews.com. 23 Aug. 2007. Web. 14 Nov. 2014.

Singer, Tovia, Rabbi. "Did Jesus Actually Exist? Rabbi Tovia Singer's Evidence and Conclusion will Surprise You." Youtube.com. 21 Feb. 2015. Web. 1 Mar. 2015.

"Sirach." Wikipedia.org. 25 Oct. 2014. Web. 30 Oct. 2014.

Smith, George. *Assyrian Discoveries: An Account of Explorations and Discoveries on the Site of Nineveh, During 1873 and 1874*. London: Sampson Low, Marston, Low and Searle, 1875.

Smith, George. *Site of Nineveh*. New York: Scribner, Armstrong & Co., 1876.

Smith, Homer. *Man and His Gods*. Boston: Little, Brown & Co., 1952.

Smith, Mark S. *The Early History of God: Yahweh and the Other Deities in Ancient Israel (Biblical Resource Series)*, 2nd ed. Grand Rapids, MI/Cambridge, U.K.: William B. Eerdmans Publishing Company, 2002.

Smith, Mark S. *The Origins of Biblical Monotheism: Israel's Polytheistic Background and the Ugaritic Texts*. New York: Oxford University Press, 2001.

Solar Mythology and the Jesus Story: A Primer on Astrotheology. Solarmythology.com. 8 Dec. 2013. Web. 18 June 2014.

Spence, James Lewis. *Ancient Egyptian Myths and Legends*. New York: Dover, 1990.

Spong, John Shelby, Bishop. *The Birth of Jesus*. Progressivechristianity.org. 2014.

Stanford, Dale. Facebook.com. 21 Aug. 2014. Web. 21 Aug. 2014.

Stark, Thom. "The Most Heiser: Yahweh and Elyon in Psalm 82 and Deuteronomy 32." *Religion at the Margins: Postcards and Postscripts from the Periphery of Faith*. Religionatthemargins.com. 16 July 2011. Web. 12 May 2015.

Stedman, Ray C. "Woman and the Serpent." *Authentic Christianity*. Raystedman.org. 4 Mar. 1990. Web. 26 Feb. 2015.

Stein, Henry Binkley. *The Axe Was God*. Health Research Books, 1996.

Stenger, Victor, PhD. "How to Debate a Christian Apologist." Huffingtonpost.com. 28 Feb. 2014. Updated 30 Apr 2014. Web. 18 Mar. 2015.

Stern, M., ed. and tr. *Greek and Latin Authors on Jesus and Judaism*, 3 vols. Jerusalem, 1974-1984, II:480.

Stone, Merlin. *When God was a Woman*. New York: Dorset Press, 1990.

Strusiewicz, Cezary Jan. "6 Famous Symbols That Don't Mean What You Think." Cracked.com. 2 July 2012. Web. 27 Jan. 2015.

Sullivan, Meghan. "Dionysus—Just the God of Wine?" winetrailtraveler.com. 2006-2014. Web. 11 July 2014.

Supernatural. Created by Eric Kripke. 2005-present. TV show.

Tacitus, Publius. *Annals*. Book XV, Sec. 44. C. 109 CE.

Tarico, Valerie. "5 reasons to suspect that Jesus never existed." Salon.com. 1 Sept. 2014. Web. 1 Mar. 2015.

Tarico, Valerie. "Here are 9 'facts' you know for sure about Jesus that are probably wrong." Rawstory.com. 30 June 2015. Web. 2 July 2015.

Tarico, Valerie. "In Defense of Cherry Picking the Bible." Exchristian.net. 9 July 2015. Web. 10 July 2015.

Tarico, Valerie. "10 reasons Christian heaven would actually be hell." Rawstory.com. 31 Jan. 2015. Web. 31 Jan. 2015.

Tarico, Valerie. "These are the 12 worst ideas religion has unleashed on the world." Rawstory.com. 24 Jan. 2015. Web. 31 Jan. 2015.

"Tat Tvam Asi's 'Evidence' - Page 1." Kingdavid8.com. 2012. Web. 2 Jan. 2015 <http://www.kingdavid8.com/_full_article.php?id=63746a72-ca29-11e1-a119-842b2b162e97>.

Taylor, Robert, AB. *The Diegesus*. Whitefish, MT: Kessinger Publishing, 1992; facsimile of 1829 ed.

Taylor, Robert, PhD. *The Diegesus; Being a Discovery of the Origin, Evidences, and Early History of Christianity, Never Yet Before or Elsewhere So Fully and Faithfully Set Forth*. London: W. Dugdale, 1845.

Tertullian. *Ad Nationes*, I, Chapter XII. Tr. Q. Howe. Tertullian.org. 2007. Web. 25 Aug. 2014 <http://www.tertullian.org/articles/howe_adnationes1.htm>.

Tertullian, *Against Marcion*, Book 1, Chapter 13.

Tertullian. *Against the Valentinians*, I.4.

Tertullian. *The Prescription Against Heretics*, Chapter XL. Tr. and ed. S. L. Greenslade. *Early Latin Theology, Library of Christian Classics V* (1956). Tertullian.org. 11 May 2001. Web. 18 June 2014.

Testerman, Jason. "The Condensed Version of the Explanation Letter." *Why I am no Longer a Christian*. 18 Jan. 2014. Web. 17 Jan. 2015.

"Third Epistle to the Corinthians." Wikipedia.org. 16 Sept. 2013. Web. 20 Nov. 2014.

Tilghman, Joshua. "The Conclusion of Jesus, the Sun, and the Zodiac." *The Spirit of the Scripture.com: Uncovering the Hidden Meanings of the Bible!* Spiritofthescripture.com. 12 Sept. 2012. Web. 27 June 2014.

Tilghman, Joshua. "Horus and Jesus: Is There a Link Between the Two?" *The Spirit of the Scripture.com: Uncovering the Hidden Meanings of the Bible!*" Spiritofthescripture.com. 1 Jan. 2013. Web. 27 June 2014.

Tilghman, Joshua. "Jesus, the Zodiac, and Higher Consciousness." T*he Spirit of the Scripture.com: Uncovering the Hidden Meanings of the Bible!* Spiritofthescripture.com. 8 Sept. 2012. Web. 27 June 2014.

Tilghman, Joshua. "What Do the New and Old Testaments Really Mean?" *The Spirit of the Scripture.com: Uncovering the Hidden Meanings of the Bible!*" Spiritofthescripture.com. 21 Dec. 2014. Web. 22 Dec. 2014.

Tindal, Matthew. *Christianity as Old as the Creation: or, The Gospel, a Republication of the Religion of Nature*. London, 1732.

Tod, James. *Annals and Antiquities of Rajasthan*, or *The Central and Western Rajput States of India*, Vol. 2.

Tolle, Eckhart. *A New Earth: Awakening to Your Life's Purpose*. New York: Penguin Group, 2005.

Tomlinson, Sally. *Demons, Druids and Brigands on Irish High Crosses*. Ann Arbor, MI: ProQuest, 2007.

Tranquillus, G. Suetonius. *Lives of the First Caesars*. Reprint 1796. New York: AMS Press, 1970.

"True Origin of Christian 'FISH' Symbol Might Outrage, Shock Jesus Worshippers." Godlessgeeks.com. N.d. Web. 27 Jan. 2015.

Turner-Schott, Carmen, MSW, LISW. "The Shining Star of Bethlehem: Signs in the Sky." *About Astrology*. Astrology.about.com. N.d. Web. 19 June 2014.

Undercover Agnostic. "Joy Unspeakable (part three) Theology 101." 29 Dec. 2014. Exchristian.net. Web. 7 Jan. 2015.

Undercover Agnostic. "Joy Unspeakable (part four) The Miracle of 'No'." Exchristian.net. 6 Jan. 2015. Web. 7 Jan. 2015.

Underlings. "God Is Evil: Biblical Evidence Part 1." Youtube.com. 6 Aug. 2010. Web. 21 Jan. 2015.

Van den Dungen, Wim. "Great Hymn to the Aten." Maat.sofiatopia.org. 2005-2015. Web. 31 Jan. 2015.

Vati Leaks. "Why the Vatican purchased Encyclopedia Britannica." Vatileaks.com. 6 July 2011. Web. 11 Apr. 2015.

Vigliotti, Marco. "From preacher to atheist; how the former Rev. Bob Ripley lost his faith." *The Sarnia Journal*. 22 Oct. 2014. Web. 23 Oct. 2014.

Viklund, Roger. "The Jesus Parallels." *The Jesus That Never Was*. 2007. Web. 10 Nov. 2014 <http://www.jesusgranskad.se/jesus_parallels.htm>.

Vischer, Eberhard. *Die Offenbarung Johannis: Eine Judisch Apokalypse in Christlicher Bearbeitung Mit einem Nachwort v. A. Harnack*. Leipsic: J.C. Hinrichs'sche, 1886.

Von Bunsen, Ernst. *The Angel-Messiah of Buddhists, Essenes, and Christians*. London: Longmans, Green, and Company, 1880.

Von Bunsen, Ernst. *The keys of Saint Peter or The house of Rechab: connected with the history of symbolism and idolatry*. London: Longmans, Green, and Co., 1807.

Vos, R. L. *The Apis Embalming Ritual*. Leuven: Peeters Publishers, 1993.

Wagner, Belle M., and Thomas H. Burgoyne. *The Light of Egypt; or the science of the soul and the stars—* Volume 2. Denver, CO: Astro Philosophical Pub. Co., 1903. "Chapter IV: Astro-Theology." Kindle ed.

Walker, Barbara G. *Man Made God*. Seattle, WA: Stellar House Publishing, 2010.

Walker, Barbara G. *The Woman's Dictionary of Symbols and Sacred Objects*. San Francisco: HarperOne, 1988.

Walker, Barbara G. *The Woman's Encyclopedia of Myths and Secrets*. New York: HarperCollins, HarperSanFrancisco, 1983.

Walker, Jim. "Did a historical Jesus exist?" Nobeliefs.com. 12 June 1997. Ed. 22 Apr. 2011. Web. 2 Mar. 2015.

Walker, Jim. "Thomas Jefferson on Christianity & Religion." Nobeliefs.com. N.d. Web. 7 July 2015.

Walton, John H., PhD. *The Lost World of Genesis One: Ancient Cosmology and the Origins Debate*, Kindle ed. Downers Grove, IL: InterVarsity Press, 2010.

Watts, Alan, MA. "Jesus: His Religion or the Religion About Him?" Lecture transcribed by Scott Lahteine, 2004. *Phenomenology . . . with Thinkyhead*. Thinkyhead.blogspot.com. 16 Aug. 2012. Web. 3 Sept. 2014.

Wauchope, Bruce, PhD. "What Is the Good News Part 1?" Vimeo.com. N.d. Web. 29 Mar. 2014 <http://vimeo.com/34601629>.

Weaver, Sandra. "Precession of the Equinoxes Determines Astrological Ages and Mayan Great Ages." *Spiritual Growth Prophecies: Empowering Ways to Find Peace and Growth in a World of Chaos*. 2012-spiritual-growth-prophecies.com. 2008-2014. Web. 21 Dec. 2014.

Weigall, Arthur. *The Paganism in Our Christianity*. London: Hutchinson & Co., 1928; New York: G. P. Putnam's, 1928, and The Book Tree, 2008.

Weinstock, Stefan. "A New Greek Calendar and Festivals of the Sun." *The Journal of Roman Studies*, Vol. 38, Parts 1 & 2, 1948.

Westcott, Brooke Foss, MA. *The General Survey of the History of the Canon of the New Testament During the First Four Centuries*. Cambridge: MacMillan & Co., 1855.

Wheless, Joseph. *Forgery in Christianity*. New York: Cosimo, 2007.

Wheless, Joseph. *Forgery in Christianity: A Documented Record of the Foundations of the Christian Religion*, 1930; quoted by Gibbon, *History*, Chapter 37; Lardner, IV, 91.

"When was the Bible written?" *Biblica: Transforming lives through God's Word*. Biblica.com. 26 Dec. 2013. Web. 6 Apr. 2014.

White, Gavin. *Babylonian Star-lore*. London: Solaria Publications, 2008.

Wilken, Robert Louis. *The Myth of Christian Beginnings, History's Impact on Belief*, "Chapter III: The Bishop's Maiden: History Without History." Garden City, NY: Doubleday & Company, Inc., 1971.

Wilkinson, Richard H. *The Complete Gods and Goddesses of Ancient Egypt*. London/New York: Thames & Hudson, 2003.

Wilson, Aasha. "Are Church Steeples Pagan? YES! They Symbolize the Male Sex Organ." *Yah's Elect Network: Bringing People Out of the Dark and Into the Light of the Way of Yahushuwa!* Godselectpeople.ning.com. 30 Oct. 2012. Web. 8 Jan. 2015.

Winston, Edward L. "Skeptic Project." Conspiracies.skeptic.com. 29 Nov. 2007. Web. 13 June 2015.

Wood, Stella. "Winter Solstice—Sun on the Southern Cross." June 2008. PDF. 19 June 2014.

Wright, Robert. *The Evolution of God*. New York: Little, Brown and Company, 2009.

"Yaho/Yah/Iao/Yahweh/Jehovah." Jesus-messiah.com. N.d. Web. 12 Nov. 2014.

"Yalad." Strong's H3205. Blueletterbible.org. 2015. Web. 8 Nov. 2014.

"Yam." Strong's H3220. Blueletterbible.org. 2015. Web. 12 May 2015.

Yarker, John. *The Arcane Schools*. Triad Press, 2006.

Zorach, Rebecca. *Blood, Milk, Ink, God: Abundance and Excess in the French Renaissance*. Chicago: University of Chicago Press, 2005.

ABOUT THE AUTHOR

Tina Rae Collins is an internationally known, award-winning author who has published fifteen previous books, including a novel, four juvenile novels, a fable, two poetry books, a religious book for women and one for children, a collection of religious articles, a doctrinal book about the end times (*The Gathering in the Last Days*), a biography of her son Aaron (*Aaron Collins Did That*), her master's thesis (*Snow White: The Story of Eve's Redemption*), and her doctoral dissertation (*We Are Emmanuel: How Man Became God*). Her seventeenth book, coming soon, is *Yahweh on Trial*. She received a bachelor's degree in English from Pikeville College and a master's degree in Theology and PhD in Biblical Studies from Northwestern Theological Seminary. She resides in Lexington, Kentucky, and her greatest personal blessing is spending time with and enjoying her family.

aaroncollins.org
mykentuckybooks.com
moonmeanderings.wordpress.com
tinacollins@gmail.com

Made in the USA
Lexington, KY
02 August 2015